Mongolian Sound Worlds

Mongolian Sound Worlds

Edited by
JENNIFER C. POST, SUNMIN YOON,
AND CHARLOTTE D'EVELYN

UNIVERSITY OF ILLINOIS PRESS
Urbana, Chicago, and Springfield

Library of Congress Cataloging-in-Publication Data
Names: Post, Jennifer C, editor. | Yoon, Sunmin,
    editor. | D'Evelyn, Charlotte, editor.
Title: Mongolian sound worlds / edited by Jennifer
    C Post, Sunmin Yoon, and Charlotte D'Evelyn.
Description: Urbana: University of Illinois Press, 2022.
    | Includes bibliographical references and index.
Identifiers: LCCN 2021042966 (print) | LCCN
    2021042967 (ebook) | ISBN 9780252044373
    (hardback) | ISBN 9780252086441 (paperback) |
    ISBN 9780252053368 (ebook)
Subjects: LCSH: Music—Social aspects—Mongolia.
    | Music—Social aspects—China—Inner
    Mongolia. | Music—Mongolia—History and
    criticism. | Music—China—Inner Mongolia—
    History and criticism. | Mongols—Music—
    History and criticism.
Classification: LCC ML3917.M66 M66 2022 (print) |
    LCC ML3917.M66 (ebook) | DDC 780.9517—dc23
LC record available at https://lccn.loc.gov/2021042966
LC ebook record available at https://lccn.loc.gov/2021042967

Contents

Acknowledgments

This work would not have been possible without the contributions of the many Mongolian and Inner Mongolian musicians and musical instrument makers we have collaborated with over the years. We are indebted also to their families who opened their homes and included us in their daily life activities. We also acknowledge the scholars and teachers we have worked with in Mongolia and China, in North America, Europe, Australia, and other locations. Many people have generously shared their knowledge and we are ever grateful for all their support.

Each of us owes a debt of gratitude to home institutional and granting organizations that made the research for this volume possible. We offer a special thanks to the American Center for Mongolian Studies (ACMS) and Skidmore College for financial contributions toward the costs associated with bringing this volume to press.

Acknowledgments

Transliteration, Naming, and Place Names

Transliteration

The transliteration of Mongolian words follows the Tibetan and Himalayan Library Mongolian-Cyrillic Transliteration system (THL system) with a few exceptions: в, е, ё, ь, ы, ъ, and ю are romanized to v, ye, yö, y, ʼʼ, and yu, respectively. While this system is consistently used here, there are a few words that elicit varying opinions due to their popular use. For example, we use *khöömii*, although *khöömei* is also widely used in Mongolia, Inner Mongolia, and other regions where throat singing is practiced. We also use *Gov'*, a place name often written as *Gobi*. Similarly, names of ethnic groups used in scholarly and popular literature spelled in various ways follow the THL system. For example, we use Buriad (for Buryat), Tuva (for Tyva), and Oirad (for Oirat). Readers may note that we make exceptions to the system and adopt earlier transliterated names of toponyms and individuals. Mongolian terms and place names in Inner Mongolia (Chapter 2) follow a modified THL system with conventions adopted by the author. Kazakh terms (Interlude, Chapters 1 and 7) follow a slightly modified BGN/PCGN transliteration system; и and у are Romanized to i and u, respectively. Chinese terms (Chapter 2) follow the *Hanyu pinyin* system.

Names

When writing Mongolian names, the convention in Mongolia is for the family name (*ovog ner*) to precede the given name. A family name may be written in full or as a single initial. For example, in the case of Erdenetsetseg, whose father is called Münkherdene, Mongolians may use the full name as Mönkherdengiin Erdenetsetseg (using the genitive form of the patronymic), or M. Erdenetsetseg.

Mongolian Kazakhs also use the Mongolian system, although increasingly they follow the system in which a father's name follows the given name. This is especially apparent in Kazakh scholarship. With this complication, Mongolian names in the bibliography follow the Mongolian convention: the given name is presented first followed by family name (so Erdenetsetseg, M. or Erdenetsetseg, Mönkherdene), and Kazakh names are presented with family name followed by given name (as in Ulugpan, Beket).

Administrative Divisions in Mongolia: Aimag and Sum

We follow the convention of using Mongolian terms for province and district in Mongolia. The term *aimag* was used as early as the seventeenth century for social and administrative units and then adopted for provincial units in the early twentieth century. The term *sum*, used for smaller administrative units (often translated simply as *district*) can similarly be traced to seventeenth century use for a social division, but began to be used for administrative divisions within each aimag by the early twentieth century.

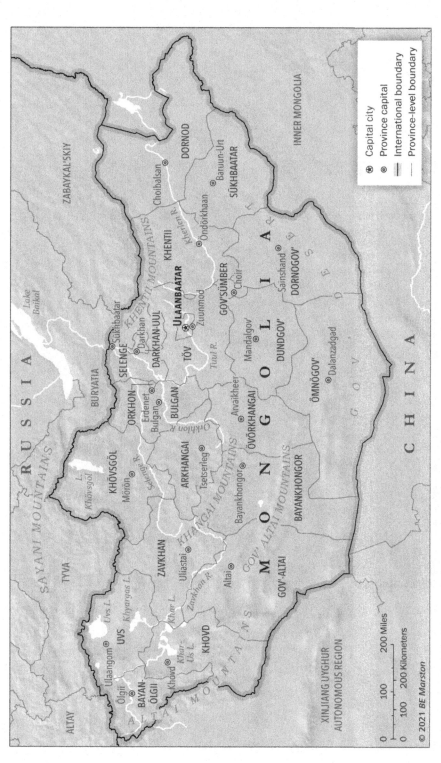

MAP 1. Mongolia. Map designed by Brooke Marston (used with permission).

MAP 2. Inner Mongolia. Map designed by Brooke Marston (used with permission).

Companion Website

Readers of *Mongolian Sound Worlds* are invited to visit the book's companion website. See: *mongoliansoundworlds.org*.

The site is populated with links to web-based video sources, supplementary images and color versions of some of the photographs in the volume, selected audio and video clips, and other data that will help interested readers learn more about the musical practices discussed in the volume.

We view the *Mongolian Sound Worlds* website as an information source that not only supports the articles in the volume but provides additional information on Mongolian music and musical events, organizations, and projects that may be of interest to the reader. As new research emerges we will direct users to additional web sources, news stories, podcasts, audio and video recordings, and provide citations for some of the latest literature on Mongolian sound worlds.

Mongolian Sound Worlds

Mongolian Sound Worlds

Opening Snapshots

SUNMIN YOON

Mongolia is a sounding land, its history rooted in pre-revolutionary times (before 1921) and shaped during the Soviet-inspired socialist period (1921–1990). Today it resonates with the effects of its rapidly changing contemporary society. Mongols, along with other ethnic groups, find themselves surrounded by sound in their daily lives as a part of their nomadic lifeways in rural regions and in urban centers such as Mongolia's capital Ulaanbaatar or the capital of Inner Mongolia, Hohhot (Höhhot, Khökhkhot). The physical territory of the Mongols once stretched over great distances under the Mongol Empire but is now situated within modern geographical borders and administrative and political divisions. Their cultures have moved across these boundaries, and they have also been preserved, diversified, shared, and assimilated with neighboring Turkic peoples and nations. In the western part of the Mongolian territories, close contact with Kazakhs, Tuvans, and other Oirad ethnic groups on the border between Bayan-Ölgii and the Xinjiang Uyghur Autonomous Region of China has produced unique and distinctive cultural forms. On the other hand, the people at the far eastern and northern borders of Mongolia, such as the Buriad[1] and Kalmyk, have merged their customs more generally with Mongolia's cultural landscape, and the stories of survival and adaptation that have characterized the cultural diversity of Inner Mongolia add further dimensions to this complex picture. Regardless of how all these micro-cultural features have been historically processed, one thing remains clear in their myriad cultural practices and identities: Mongolians have lived their lives in constant dialogue with musicking and sounding.

Mongolian in this volume is rather broadly defined. Mongolness and Mongolian culture are not simply built upon a monolithic and homogenous unity, but they have rather been strengthened through a constant process of exchange and mixing among neighboring cultures. On a single trip in Uvs aimag (province), I saw how Mongol singers who are pursuing professional work in nearby Khovd aimag also "commuted" to work in China's Xinjiang Uyghur Autonomous Region. The collapse of the Soviet Union and its impact on Soviet Central Asia has complicated the Mongolian Kazakhs' recent migration and counter-migration, and this has affected their cultural practices as well as their expressions of identity. Taking into consideration these dynamic exchanges, and the fluidity of national and cultural boundaries, the term *Mongol* here indicates the ethnically Mongol peoples of Mongolia and Inner Mongolia, while *Mongolian* indicates all people living in Mongolia and Inner Mongolia, including the Mongolian Kazakhs and the Mongolian Tuvans who hold citizenship in the country of Mongolia.

During the socialist period in Mongolia, and over the course of sinicization in the Inner Mongolian Autonomous Region of China, Mongolian traditional nomadic culture and widely varying musical practices became ideologized and remade according to more formulaic music-making processes. Despite these changes, they survived, both implicitly and explicitly, as part of a new twentieth-century cultural identity. As more Western musical genres were imported, traditional musical practices came to be seen as more professional and less connected to nomadic pastoralism, and in this way they became the basis of the current traditional music scene. Mongolian culture in the twenty-first century is thus being built upon two powerful frameworks of the past: the nomadic traditions maintained for centuries in rural regions, and the modernized remnants left behind by the twentieth century's political transitions in both Mongolia and China. This has left Mongolians with the task of creating a much more complex amalgam of different forms of musicking through unique sonic elements, fluid genres, social and spatial performativity, and sounding objects. Some music-making processes have stayed in tune with the powerful ideologies of communism and socialism, while others are still tied tightly to their deep past. At the same time, they look toward a future, impacted by modernity and the global world.

With all these dynamics in mind, *Mongolian Sound Worlds* embraces the complex predicament of early twenty-first century Mongolian sonic cultures, understood through the unique perspectives, positioning, and approaches offered by all the contributors to its chapters and interludes. The aim is to share information on a broad range of genres and musical landscapes in present-day Mongolian culture, from vocal traditions such as throat-singing (*khöömii*), long-song (*urtyn duu*), other folk song genres (*zokhiolyn duu, bogino duu*), and epic practices (*tuul'*), instruments such as *tovshuur, dombyra*, and *morin khuur*, combined fusion band culture (*khamtlag*), and urban popular music. The thematic framework likewise ranges from remote rural herders' nomadic music-making and instrument-building to the politics of ethnic boundaries and heritage-making, ideological influence, nationalism, and global circulation.

Each contributor to this volume carries stories from geographically different locations, engages with distinct communities as well as musical materials, and captures unique musical moments. Whether studying in Inner Mongolia, the western, central, or southern regions of Mongolia, one place through which most researchers pass on their journey is Ulaanbaatar, the country's capital. While visitors may imagine that their first sight in Mongolia will be a seemingly endless steppe in the countryside, and their first sound the unique styles of Mongolian folk music, a bustling city filled with traffic and people is in fact what visitors first encounter. Ulaanbaatar encapsulates historical and contemporary, local and global, disappearing and emerging musical forms, styles, and social scenes along with a vibrant mix of hybrid musical forms, as well as an established Western classical musical scene.

So it is in Ulaanbaatar that I start, drawing from my own experience in the city. In a series of three musical snapshots, I explain how these urban music scenes reveal Mongolia's complex musical history, from Mongolian Western art music scenes to the traditional and folk musical landscapes in order also to shed light on some of the musical practices that are mentioned throughout the text. I first show how one of the most respected classically trained composers in contemporary Mongolia reflects in his works not only the European values of his training but the traditional values of Mongolia's embodied nomadic life learned in his homeland. I then share the historical journey of Mongolia's staged performance, traced from the country's first opera and the continuing legacy of its opera singers on the world stage in the decades since. Finally, I discuss Mongolia's constantly changing musical culture seen in the vibrant fluidity of Ulaanbaatar's cityscapes experienced by visitors attending the performances of the national folk ensemble in the state theater.[2]

The Traditional Voice of a Modern Composer: B. Sharav

The death, on July 15, 2019, of one of Mongolia's most popular and beloved composers saddened the whole country. The documentaries, appreciations, and biographical articles that were published hastily in the media all recalled his contributions to Mongolia's musical landscape. Weeks before his death, he had been recognized, along with another composer, N. Jantsannorov, as one of Mongolia's central cultural figures, with the State award of "Hero of Labor" (*khödölmöriin baatar*). Born in 1952 in Khentii, a province northeast of Ulaanbaatar, Sharav grew up in a nomadic family and trained in European art music as a pianist and composer in the Soviet Union during the late 1970s and early 1980s. His most famous piece, *Sersen Tal* (Awakened steppe), composed in 1984, is one of the most frequently performed compositions at national events, such as the opening ceremony of the State Naadam, Mongolia's annual summer festival. In his obituary, his friend, the poet, G. Mend-Ooyo, wrote:

> B. Sharav was an artist who herded the calves and lambs all across the steppe in his bare feet, he sang the *gingoo* at the horse races, he grew tired from nomadic travel, he was a child of the countryside, a nomad who became a hero of the livestock markets. The hidden gifts which nature bestowed upon him were encouraged by the melodies of the *urtyn duu* and of the *morin khuur*, he was nourished by the best of western musical education, and became an artist famous in the modern world, and at the root of this was his Mongolian homeland and nomadic culture. (July 17, 2019, *Öglöögiin Sonin*).

A particularly valuable insight from Mend-Ooyo's obituary is Sharav's countryside childhood, a common enough feature of Mongolian lives, but one with particular resonance among the generation of Mongolian musicians and composers with European classical training. While these artists received a Soviet-style music education in Ulaanbaatar under the Soviet music teachers who had been sent to Mongolia, or by government-supported study-abroad programs to the Soviet Union or elsewhere in the Eastern Bloc, their musical expressions are closely reflective of the pastoralism they experienced in their youth. A good portion of Sharav's compositions, for example, incorporate folk tunes, particularly in his works written between the 1980s and the early 2000s. He used examples from folk songs such as "Zambuu tiviin naran" (The sun over the world) in his symphonies and cantatas, while his extensive piano repertoire adapts folk songs such as "Tümen ekh" (The best of the many) and "Önchiin tsagaan botgo" (Orphaned white camel), as well as lullabies (*buuvei*), ethnic Oirad folk songs such as "Torguud nutag" (Torguud homeland), and the song "Gooj Nanaa," which is often performed as the melody in *khöömii* (throat singing). Sharav also composed new pieces based specifically on folk literature such as *ülger* and *domog*, and even when he did not incorporate Mongolian traditional musical idioms directly into his scores, he infused their performance with stories and narrative devices.

Mongols and Turkic-speaking people living in Mongolian territories are well-known for living mainly as nomadic pastoralists, a lifestyle upon which their traditional customs are built and which is also shaped by their ecological environments. Mongolians' values are, then, deeply connected to their nomadic lifeways and understanding of their local natural resources (see Chapter 1 in this volume). For this reason, it is common in contemporary Mongolia to find people who reveal a vast range of traditional pastoral local knowledge and experience, not only among herders and musical practitioners in the countryside, but also among professional urban artists, writers, and musicians, with their memories and their embodied worldviews. It is surprising how often pastoral backgrounds are illustrated in the artistic work of some of the contemporary composers, no matter what genres or artistic products they create. Sharav's collaboration with Yo-Yo Ma on the latter's album *The Silk Road: A Musical Caravan* (2002) is a symphonic piece based upon an *urtyn duu* (long-song), "Kherlengiin bar'ya" (The banks of the Kherlen river), whose lyrics begin:

The banks of the Kherlen is my elder brother's homeland.
Do you see a bluish mist there?
The river called Kherlen is my beloved.
Where in Khentii is the source of the river?[3]

The River Kherlen flows from Khentii aimag across to the far east of Dornod aimag, and into the Hulunbuir (Khölönbuir) region of Inner Mongolia. Sometimes it seems to be hidden, but then it reappears as it journeys eastward. Two professional long-song singers, Ch. Sharkhüükhen (1939-) and G. Khongorzol (1974-), who had been employed as musicians in their respective hometowns in Khentii, often presented this song as the focal point of their repertoire. The younger singer, G. Khongorzol, played in Sharav's piece *Kherlengiin bar'ya* and, while the shared connection between composer and singer to their homeland (*nutag*) of Khentii might be happenstance, it represents a recurring practice in Mongolian music overall, reflecting and connecting performers (or composers with other collaborating artists) with their roots (*yazguur*), the places where they spent their childhoods, and which they think of as home.

These concepts of origin (*yazguur*) and tradition (*ulamjlal*) have been of critical interest among Mongols, particularly in the changing urban space of contemporary Mongolia. The negotiation between traditional values and newly introduced musical languages has sometimes been conflicted, but there remain places in which they can be presented, whether for nationalistic reasons or due to ideological reinvention. However, it is certainly true that this musical expression of Mongolia's pastoral and nomadic connection is essential, regardless of time, place, or who is participating, whether human or nonhuman. On Mongolia's endless steppe, in the desert (*gov'*) where one finds only low shrubs, stiffened in the sun, and in the forested and mountainous regions, Mongolians' herding lives and related traditions (*ulamjlalt zanshil*) offer a way of surviving using the ecological resources available, but also a way of finding comfort in and showing gratitude for what is given. Pastoralists ritualize these lifeways with sound and music in seasonal activities, not only for humans but also for nonhuman actors, such as coaxing a camel to nurse, milking cows and horses, branding horses, or raising their *ger* tents. For example, the coaxing ceremony is performed when a mother camel gives birth to a calf of a color different from her own. The song heard in this ceremony is not only about the camel, but it speaks also to a particular relationship: the strong bond between mother and child. When Sharav recalls this coaxing practice in a piano composition, *Önchiin tsagaan botgo* (Orphaned white camel calf), not only does he use the melody of the *urtyn duu* of the same name, but he also incorporates into his music his lived experience of such livestock practices from his childhood in a nomadic family. In modern musical compositions, even when composers do not directly reference such folk musical idioms, there still remains an awareness of environmental contexts. Therefore, it appears to be an indispensable part of becoming a musician or composer in Mongolia, even if the genre is Western art music, to be aware of traditional musical practice and to embody the environmental settings in which legends are born.

As was the case with Sharav and other composers in Mongolia, modern Mongolian composers in China have also written music according to the Western art music idiom, building bridges between the experiences of their native musical culture and their training in the language of Western art music. The a cappella choral piece "Naiman sharga" (Eight chestnut horses) composed in 1998, which has been performed frequently by choirs around the world, is a good example of this phenomenon in its relationship to the Inner Mongolian musical landscape. The work's composer, Se. Enkhbayar (b. 1956), was a herder when young, and a long-song singer; he was also a member of a traveling troupe during the Cultural Revolution. However, his formal education in Western art music came in Ulaanbaatar at the Mongolian State University of Culture and Arts (*Soyol Urlagiin Ikh Surguul'*) (Lin 2018). His longing for and sensibility toward the pastoral landscape is presented through his harmonized European choral music. In this way, the mixture of two different sources—the traditional and the contemporary—mirrors Inner Mongolia's process of modernization as it emerged from the external influence of twentieth-century musical culture. For Mongolia as much as for Inner Mongolia, the absorption of Western art music into the Mongol musical world between the 1920s and 1990s was more ideological; yet such a process made it possible for Mongolia to establish an array of new genres, such as composed songs (*zokhiolyn duu*), film music (*kinoni khögjim*) (Rees 2018), and opera (*duur'*). These genres continue to thrive, even after the waning of ideological power, and with the syncretic aspects borrowed from Mongolia's traditional and nomadic background periodically gaining strength.

Mongolia's First Opera and Its Continuing Legacy

In July 2015, a few days before Naadam, I went to Sükhbaatar Square, a large public gathering space that acts as Ulaanbaatar's center. At the center of the square there is a statue of the revolutionary hero Sükhbaatar, mounted on a horse, and another nearby of Chinggis Khan, at the entrance to the Mongolian parliament building to his north. An outdoor opera stage had been set up on

FIGURE 0.1. Temporary outdoor theatre for the opera *Uchirtai Gurvan Tolgoi* in Sükhbaatar Square, Ulaanbaatar. Photo by S. Yoon.

the southern side of the square. I arrived just before 10:00 p.m. on this characteristically cool summer night and found my assigned seat, mindful that there would be a large audience, since this was the first time the opera *Uchirtai gurvan tolgoi* (Three fateful hills) had been performed in the square (see figure 0.1).

The opera site was located at a dynamic performance hub, directly between Mongolia's two most vibrant theaters, the National Academic Drama Theatre (*Ulsyn dramyn erdmiin teatr*) and the State Opera and Ballet Academic Theater (*Ulsyn duur' büjgiin erdmiin teatr*).[4] The National Academic Drama Theatre is a venue for regular performances by the State Folk Ensemble, as well as for other music and theater genres (including pop music), while the State Opera and Ballet Academic Theatre is the main venue for performances of opera and Western art music. The National Academic Drama Theater was built in the 1940s, but the theater's history started with an earlier building, nicknamed *Nogoon Bömbögöör* (The green dome), that burned down during the 1930s, before the other theaters were built around the center.

The opera, *Uchirtai Gurvan Tolgoi* (1934), was originally a play by D. Natsagdorj (1906–1937), one of the founders of modern Mongolian literature. It was performed not as a composed opera, but with narrative dialogues set to folk tunes (*ayalguud jüjig*). However, in 1944, B. Damdinsüren composed an opera loosely based on the play, although the orchestration was arranged by the Soviet composer, folklorist, and music pedagogue Boris F. Smirnov (1912–1971).[5] Damdinsüren (1919–1992), along with L. Mördorj (1919–1996) and M. Dugarjav (1893–1946), was one of the most important representatives of Mongolia's Western art music during the second quarter of the twentieth century. Damdinsüren and Mördorj received their training in the Soviet Union, and while Damdinsüren is known for Mongolia's first opera, *Uchirtai Gurvan Tolgoi*, Mördorj composed the first Mongolian symphony, *Minii Ikh Ornoo* (My great country), as his graduation piece from the Tchaikovsky Conservatory in 1956 (B. Bold and Ch. Bold 2011). The composer of the Mongolian Internationale, M. Dugarjav, had not directly been influenced by Soviet musical training but, as the first state-sanctioned composer, he was active in composing revolutionary songs (ibid.). Moreover, all three composers, at various times, played a role in the composing and reworking of Mongolia's national anthem.

B. Damdinsüren's musical transformation of *Uchirtai Gurvan Tolgoi* from musical play into opera brought a change in the perception of actors, from being stage actors who could sing to opera singers.[6] The opera's principal characters, Yünden and his lover Nasalmaa, are portrayed as members of the poor working class (*ard*). In the first performance in 1944, Yünden was played by A. Tserendendev (1912–1986) and Nasalmaa by L. Tsogzolmaa (b. 1924-). Since then, to perform in *Uchirtai Gurvan Tolgoi* has become an honor for a male or female actor, and since 2009, Mongolia has held a competition to cast the leading roles. In the performance I saw in 2015, Yünden was played by Ariunbaatar Ganbaatar, who had won first prize in the male-vocalist category in both the XV International Tchaikovsky Competition and the European Grand Prix in 2014. As has happened with Ganbaatar, a few of Mongolia's leading opera singers have recently become national treasures after winning awards in prestigious international competitions outside Mongolia, and their fame and fanbase have spread across social media.

Like Ganbaatar, another opera singer, A. Enkhbat, has won numerous international competitions including the Tchaikovsky Competition (2011); B. Bayarsaikhan has also become famous for his operatic performances in Mongolia and abroad. The strength that Mongolia's Western art musicians have developed in the vocal genres is particularly noteworthy. In my conversations with several Mongolian musicians about this—whether traditional musicians or Western art musicians—they frequently expressed how these opera singers' powerful vocality has developed through their traditional nomadic lifestyles and diets. Many Mongolians have mentioned to me that traditional long-song singers or other folk song singers could sing Western opera, but not the other way around.

When *The Guardian* journalist Kate Mollesen (2018) interviewed the Mongolian musicologist K. Bayandelger about why Mongolians make talented opera singers, Bayandelger explained that it comes from how their "physical stature" embodies their "landscape, food, clean air, even historical narratives." When Western-style theater began in Mongolia, there was not so much distinction between folk music and opera. Actors were called *jüjigchin* (with no gender distinction), but this term referred not only to actors, but also to musicians, acrobats, and singers of revolutionary songs, as well as to folk song (including long-song) singers. This holistic and familiar quality of artistic identity seems to be one reason why the theatrical genres of opera, plays, and film have been so popular since the early period.

My experience that night watching the opera in the square, with the densely packed crowd, and with an audience watching on TV, was a simple example of how much the classical pieces composed under Soviet influence continue to be performed and appreciated in post-socialist Mongolia. The audience's interest in opera was not based solely on the musical styles, the performance, and staging, but also on the work's nostalgia and historical significance as a piece of Soviet-influenced art. Moreover, as I watched the story unfold, I noticed how many folk customs and traditional elements were also used to convey the narrative even though the plot itself was, both implicitly and explicitly, "revolutionary."

Fluidity and Movement: Ulaanbaatar—July 2019

The National Academic State Ensemble has established itself as an important venue for professional folk music performances in Ulaanbaatar, with an in-house folk ensemble consisting of professional musicians selected through national competitions. Since its creation under State sponsorship during the socialist era, it has continued until today as Mongolia's primary folk music performance ensemble. While other venues for folk performance have lost ground, disappeared, or been revived, the National Academic State Ensemble—housed in a theater across from the National Library—has been a staple of the capital's entertainment scene since I first arrived in Mongolia in 2006. During the summer months it is one of the most popular tourist destinations in the city. Recently, however, the building—like others such as the National History Museum that was built, and subsequently thrived, with State funding during the socialist era—has been threatened with demolition due to old age, as taller, more modern buildings come to dominate Ulaanbaatar's skyline.

I have attended one of these evening performances in the theater almost every year I have visited Mongolia, just to see if there have been any changes to the program or the singers. The first year I went, 2006, I saw a program full of traditional musics, mainly central Khalkh long-songs, one or two short-songs from western ethnic groups commonly performed in Ulaanbaatar, *khöömii*, and *morin khuur* (horsehead fiddle)—including the State Morin Khuur Ensemble playing orchestral pieces composed by Mongolian composers. Between 2011 and 2015, however, I noticed a surge in diverse regional styles of music and dance, although the changes were subtle, and with a few additional pieces in regional styles.

In July of 2019, however, attending a performance on the same day that B. Sharav died, I found a dramatic change in the program. The show started, as always, at 6:00 p.m., and the theater looked the same, with its characteristic Soviet style architecture and decorations, except in that year there was an exhibition of huge *tsam*[7] dance masks and costumes in the lobby. The concert still presented a long-song first in the program, but very briefly, and this was followed by a composition that featured *khöömii*. As the program continued, it focused more on regional songs and traditional dance styles as well as contortionists and pieces in symphonic styles played by the National Morin Khuur Ensemble, including B. Sharav's *Selenge Tal*. The most notable change was the inclusion of abstract dance and music based on traditional Mongolian music and dance that incorporated other aspects of world music and dance, implying possible connections between Mongolia's sound world and India and other Southeast Asian cultures. A Buddhist *tsam* dance had been added, and a dance that had been newly choreographed from the imagined lifeways of prerevolutionary nobles, quite different from the "nomadic/pastoral" images that had been frequently used in the past to describe the Mongols and Mongolians. This whole performance appeared to be searching for more traditional and religious elements beyond folk and nomadism, which had been lost during the peak of twentieth-century modernism. It seemed to suggest that Mongolia was no longer looking to the West—which in the early 1990s had meant either Russia or Europe—but to a greater breadth of world cultures. I felt that Mongolia might have been leaving Sharav's Western art music legacy behind, and that this quite different arrangement of the National Academic State Ensemble's concert program was pointing ahead to another, as yet uncertain, departure for Mongolia's sound worlds.

With the National State Ensemble changing its performance in this way, I have also noted that the streets of Ulaanbaatar outside of the theater are also increasingly filled with the movement of visitors, particularly at the peak of the season during the national Naadam in mid-July. They flock to tourist gift shops and visit noted sites such as Sükhbaatar Square and Gandan Monastery; some look for interesting art exhibitions or musical events such as the National Academic State Ensemble's performance. Some visitors seek adventure in the countryside, and some are travelers who stop by Ulaanbaatar on the way to Central Asia or Siberia on the Trans-Siberian Express. Tourists from Inner

Mongolia may also be searching for their "unchanged" homeland. When I travel to the countryside with Inner Mongolians, as we look out at the endless steppe with clear streams passing nearby they often say to me, "There is no open land like this in Inner Mongolia anymore. The Han Chinese have fenced off our land into enclosures [*khashaa*]." Some Inner Mongolians come to Ulaanbaatar to look for what they believe are "real Mongolian musical skills." T. Narantuya, a singer whom I met in 2009, had been the very last student of the great singer N. Norovbanzad and was then finishing up her doctoral study in Ulaanbaatar. Narantuya had been one among the early waves of Inner Mongolian singers who came to learn the techniques in Mongolia, considerably before the current stream of traffic between Mongolia and Inner Mongolia. Mongolians living and working overseas come back in the summer to accompany visitors—from the United States, Europe, India, S. Korea, and other locations—who are interested in Mongolia's cultural life, or to visit their families and relatives back home. Mongolians come back from China, too, including some musicians who travel to Inner Mongolia as music teachers. In 2018, I met with a singer who said she had been teaching at a school in Inner Mongolia, since they paid her well for her work, but that she would always come back to Ulaanbaatar. For such travelers, summer in Ulaanbaatar becomes a vibrant space until the end of August when the air grows chilly, and then when the city starts coming back to normal, the reflection of what this traffic of visitors has brought to Ulaanbaatar remains as a vestige of change.

The current shape of Ulaanbaatar and its culture is the result of a long-term process of historical transformation, yet it is not necessarily excluded from the rural lifeways of pastoral and nomadic Mongolians seen in the previous snapshots. How Mongolia now sees its own urban modernity, and how it regards itself in relation to outside influence, is essentially ambiguous, but Mongolians have always generally welcomed such changes without much resistance, in keeping with the adaptability that defines their nomadic instincts. Similarly, Mongolia's character as a sounding land does not exist within a single fixed environment; it has been created at different times and in different parts of the country. Just as nomadic cycles define the people's changing approaches to survival, as the ebb and flow of people through Ulaanbaatar and the influx of new cultures, so can all act as critical sources of Mongolia's sound worlds. And just like what remains of pastoralism in the work of Mongolia's modern composers of Western art music, so can the contemporary traditional music ensemble reflect the uncertain future of Mongolia's musical world, and the Soviet-developed musical phenomena, such as opera, still continue as a part of today's cultural experience. Mongolia's serendipitous discoveries in its music-making journey, and its searches for the future of its musical culture, will continue to absorb and transform an abundant flow of uncertain and unexpected influences.

The Structure of This Volume

This volume offers ten chapters and four interludes on a wide range of topics related to Mongolian sound worlds. Discussions about developing this collection began at the "Mongolian Sound Worlds" conference in 2017 at the Institute of East Asian Studies, University of California at Berkeley, attended by six of the authors in this volume. Our discussions at the event, and later in Mongolia, at conferences, and online helped the group identify the diverse practices maintained in contemporary rural and urban settings that would become this volume. Along the way we brought in additional authors who have contributed chapters and Interludes to offer a broader view of Mongolian musical practices. Each chapter's unique material and approach is drawn from field research in specific locations. We include what we have termed *Interludes* to bridge sections while also introducing new material from the point of view of local practitioners, each an artist with life experience as musician or musical instrument maker in Mongolia and Inner Mongolia.

Following this Introduction, *Part One: Landscapes and Soundscapes*, offers the first Interlude, a song about the steppe that Mongolian Kazakh herder Oktyabr shared with Jennifer Post. Oktyabr's lyrics reflect his abundant pastoral experience and knowledge of local resources. In Chapter One, Post introduces sound, music, pastoralism, and nature in Mongolia and Inner Mongolia, to address the significance of the land, sociality, spirituality, and sonic practices, and soundscapes. She also includes a case study on the sound and musical practices of Kazakh pastoralists who live in the far-western Mongolian province of Bayan-Ölgii.

Part Two: Ethnicity and Diversity includes an Interlude and three chapters. Interlude Two contains a life story that Tamir Hargana, from the Barga region of Inner Mongolia, shared with Charlotte D'Evelyn. Tamir's dynamic musical biography recounts his young life as a Mongolian musician in both his home country and the United States. In Chapter Two, D'Evelyn investigates ethnic politics and expressions of identity by Mongol peoples who live inside China's national boundary, focusing on two axes: the historical lens of the Mao era and the case study of Anda Union, an internationally successful Inner Mongolian folk ensemble supported by the Chinese government. Addressing ethnic politics and representation in Chapter Three, Sunmin Yoon uses ethnographic research on *urtyn duu* styles from various ethnic groups in the western provinces of Mongolia to challenge and rethink the concept of ethnicity and regionality. She argues that it has been politicized in part, not as an explicit political agenda, but as a process of Othering through singing techniques and musical discourses. In Chapter 4, Rebekah Plueckhahn provides a unique case study on music in a small Altai-Uriankhai settlement in western Mongolia. The author places herself among the people in the town to look at the role of gender and local musical knowledge, especially in the context of community dynamics.

Part Three: Material and Social History introduces musical instruments from different regions in performance and production—the Mongol *morin khuur*, the Altai Uriankhai *tovshuur*, and the Kazakh *dombyra*. In Interlude Three, the *morin khuur* maker, Bayarsaikhan Badamsüren, collaborated with Peter Marsh to offer his own musical life story, addressing through images and narrative the process of instrument-making and his thoughts about his musical experience. In Chapter 5, Peter Marsh and Charlotte D'Evelyn describe the historical narratives of the *morin khuur* tradition. They investigate the lives and contributions of three legendary fiddlers from both Mongolia and Inner Mongolia and discuss two contemporary fiddle players who have made further technical advances through their performance. In Chapter Six, Otgonbayar Chuluunbaatar introduces the characteristics, meaning, and performance practices of the plucked two-stringed *tovshuur*. Presenting the deep ties between the *tovshuur* and the Oriad ethnic group, the author illustrates how this instrument has expressed Oirad identity through its association with local epic traditions. In Chapter Seven, Jennifer Post unfolds ethnographic narratives of four Kazakh *dombyra* makers in two western provinces of Mongolia. She explores the social lives of the instrument reflected in its materials, tools, processes, practices, and changes over time. She also demonstrates that, while makers and musicians have connections outside of Bayan-Ölgii in Xinjiang in China and Kazakhstan, the region has been able to produce a unique Mongolian Kazakh *dombyra*.

Part Four: Heritage and Globalization considers Mongolian music-making at home and abroad, how music was mobilized, and some of the ways music is now returning to its source. To begin, in Interlude Four Andrew Colwell reconstructs a conversation about sound he had with Tserendavaa Dashdorj. Colwell's description of the land and their discussion of vocalizations reveal relationships between sound and music as well as pathways that the vocal arts have taken in Mongolia in recent years. In Chapter Eight, Johanni Curtet introduces the musical techniques of *khöömii*, and its important practitioners, illustrating how the transmission of this genre has shifted from a nomadic sonic practice to a heritage product. Using a case study of *khöömii* traditions in Chandman' sum (an administrative unit smaller than an aimag), Khovd aimag, Curtet explains the process of Soviet-influenced institutionalization and the current situation and policies of the district (sum)'s heritage center. In Chapter Nine, Andrew Colwell also draws from *khöömii* to consider tradition (*yazguur*), globalization (*dayaarshil*), internationalism, tourism, and concert culture as it relates to *khöömii* and ensembles (*khamtlag*), such as the German-based Mongolian music ensemble and Egschiglen within and beyond Mongolia. In the final chapter, Chapter Ten, Peter Marsh discusses Mongolia's most recent popular music sensation, the folk metal group The Hu. Using The Hu as his main prism, Marsh explores Mongolia's earlier popular music history, Mongolia's response to the global popular industry, and the syncretic sounds of the country's unique popular music.

Notes

1. Buriad can also be spelled Buryaad and Buryat.
2. See our companion website, www.mongoliansoundworlds.org, for additional information on the musical traditions included in this volume.
3. This version of the lyrics is found in Kh. Sampildendev and K. N. Yatskovskai (1984:223).
4. The official names of these two venues have changed over the course of the nation's political transitions.
5. In an interview with the poet and journalist B. Lkhagvasüren, the actress, L. Tsogzolmaa, who performed the lead female role in the first performance of this opera, said that Smirnov's precise involvement in the musical arrangement is debatable, and that the music, including the orchestration, was written entirely by B. Damdinsüren (*Mongol Tulgatny 100 Erkhem* 2015).
6. The opera's libretto, moreover, was adapted by the writer Ts. Damdinsüren (1907–1986) (Natsagdorj having died in 1937) from the original playscript to reflect the new ideology of Socialist Realism.
7. Ritual masked dance performed as part of Mongolian and Tibetan Buddhist ceremonies.

References

Bold, B., and Ch. Bold. 2011. *Cultural Figures of the Golden Age* [Soyol urlagagiin altan üyeiinkhen]. Ulaanbaatar: Sodpress.

Dashdavaa, Ch. 1987. "The Studies in the Development of the People's Arts, 1945–1960" [Ardyn uran büteeliin khögjiin assudald]. *Studia Historica, Studia Historica Instituti Historiae Academiae Scientiarum Reipublicae Populi Mongolici* 21:108–113. N.P.

Lin, Pei Chi. 2018. "A Performance Guide to Se. Enkhbayar's Choral Tone Poem Önchin Botgo (A lonely baby camel) for SATB soloists and SATB Chorus (with Divisions) Acapella." DMA diss., University of North Texas.

Mend-Ooyo, Gombojiin. 2019. "B.Sharavyn 'Nuuts Tovchoo'" (B.Sharav's secret history). *Öglöögiin Sonin* [17 07/17/ 2019].

Molleson, Kate. 2020. "How Mongolia Went Wild for Opera." *The Guardian*. 01/02/2018.

Mongol Tulgatny 100 Erkhen—L. Tsogzolmaa. 2015. YouTube video, 54:21, posted by Mongol Tulgatan, June 28, 2015, https://www.youtube.com/watch?v=VD5QhTYKUTA.

Natsagdorj, Sh. ed. 1981. *Cultural History of the Mongolian People's Republic* [BNMAU-yn Soyolyn Tüükh]. Ulaanbaatar: Ulsyn Hevleliin Gazar.

Sharav, Byambasuren. 2013. *Works for Piano I: Piece, Prelude Sonatina Composition of Folk Songs*. Ulaanbaatar: (n.p).

Yavuuhulan, B., ed. 1961. *Anthology of Mongolian Poetry* [Mongolyn shildeg yaruu nairag]. Ulaanbaatar: State Publishing House.

PART ONE

Landscapes and Soundscapes

Song about the Steppe

K. OKTYABR AND JENNIFER C. POST

In July 2007, I waited in the wide field below a ger nestled in a shallow hollow as Oktyabr carried a small notebook and his *dombyra* down to the steppe. The summer grazing site where his family was settled in Deluun sum, Bayan Ölgii aimag (province) is in the Altai Mountains along the Chinese border where Kazakh families have herded for generations. Located nearby is a small *arasan*[1] or mineral spring, where local residents value the "healing waters." Settling himself on the ground, Oktyabr opened his notebook and lay it on the ground in front of him. I could see that he had carefully written out the Kazakh verses of his songs. The musical form he assigned to the song he sang, *tolghau*, commemorates people and places, records local histories, and expresses emotional responses to place and to change. Such songs are valued in the countryside where they are often shared in social gatherings among Kazakh residents in this province.

In his song, Oktyabr refers to Zhalghyz aghash and to Mongolia as homeland (*tughan el*). The region in far western Mongolia where he was settled for the summer is valued for its nutritious grasses for livestock grazing in spring, summer, and autumn seasons. Some herders remain there throughout the winter, moving their animals and families to mud-clay winter homes that are tucked in depressions in the land that protect them from wind and cold. In his song, Oktyabr names his relatives and describes personal responses to place, indicating his long history in this location. He also names sites that have significance not only to his family but to the community of Kazakh herders who return to these lands each season. Many of the names he uses for sites are local Kazakh names shared by herders; they were established over time as Kazakhs settled in this region beginning in the mid-nineteenth century. As they name places they also claim them for Kazakhs. Many place names refer to landforms or natural sites,

FIGURE (INTERLUDE) 1.1. Oktyabr near his settlement at Zhalghyz aghash, Deluun sum, Bayan Ölgii aimag, 2007. Photo by J. C. Post.

such as a *dala* (field), *quyis* (hollow), *shoqy* (hill), *tau* (mountain), *say* (valley), and *dara* (ravine, gorge). Sites and their characteristics are also described in well-known place names. Zhalghyz aghash means "solitary tree," it is a location with few trees; Ayu dara is a place where bears (*ayu*) were often found historically; Qaskyr uya is a wolf's "nest"—they are animals that both fascinate and scare herders since they can ravage their sheep and goat herds during the night; and Burkit tau means eagle mountain—the landform is located on the way to Zhalghyz aghash and its silhouette reminds people of an eagle—and of the Kazakh's continuing heritage as eagle hunters. The song also references common herding practices in the region, including maintaining *mal*, their five kinds of livestock (sheep, goats, yaks, camels, and horses); keeping tethering places for animals (*zheli*); practicing *otar* during which a single or small group of herders takes a group of livestock to another location, such as an isolated pasture where grasses are rich in nutrition; and the valuing of medicinal resources, such as the *ular* (snowcock)—these mobile pastoralists use the meat of the bird to treat burns and heal stomach ailments.

ZHALGHYZ AGHASH ARASAN TOLGHAU	SONG ABOUT ZHALGHYZ AGHASH MINERAL SPRING[2]
Armysyng altyn besik, asqar belim	Greetings my golden motherland, my high plateau
Armysyng ayauly zhurt tughan elim	Greetings my dear people and my homeland
Öteyin el zherimdi tanystyryp	Let me introduce my place
Barsha zhurt qulaq turgey tughan elim	Everyone in my homeland, listen to me
Zhyr qylyp Zhalghyz aghash arasanyn	I created a *zhyr* about Zhalhyz aghash mineral spring
Du qylyp ortangyzgha ala keldim	And I offer it to you for your approval
Arnaghan arasangha syylyghym bul	This is my gift to my mineral spring
Tu qylyp ortangyzgha än sala keldim	The song I sing will be like a flag among you
Dombyra alyp ortangyzgha tolghanayyn	I'll take my dombyra and offer my thoughts to you
Zhasymnan öner qughan balang edim	I was your child chasing after art
Bürkit tau tulep ösip asqar shyngdy	Raised and then molted on high peaked Burkit tau
Qiyngha qanat qaghu arman etip	I stretched my wings to meet difficulties
Bastayyn Qarasumen Üyirtiden	Let me start with Qarasu and Üyirt
Zher eken shöbi shüygin örisi keng	The land has a wide pasture and fertile grasses
Qoy baqqan Qonshay atam sanglaq bop	My grandfather Qonshai was a noted herder who raised sheep here
Baylaghan asau qulyn zhelisimen	He tied his frisky colts, filling his *zheli*
Toghasbay Aqtas qora zherding säni	Toghas and Aqtas qora are gems of this land
Oredi Qara qaqta tülik maly	Five kinds of livestock graze in Qara qaq
Sholaq quys Keng quys Orta quys	Sholakh quys, Kheng quys, Orta quys
Zhäne bar Balta sappen Qara zhaly	We also have Balta sap and Qara zhal
Aqsaydyng gül boraghan zhan zhaghasy	Flowers blow on the edges of Aqsay
Kümistey Zharqyraghan taudan tasy	Stones from the mountain shine like silver
Ataqty Ülken buyra Shungyr qora	Ülken buyra and Shunkir qora are famous
Ezhelden meken bolghan Qaraqasy	Since olden days they were Qaraqas's place
Ömirding basy ghuzyr shyngyrau zhar	Life is like a high rocky cliff
Shyghugha qanat qaghyp bolacyng zar	That you rush about and flap your wings to climb
Uly atam baqyt qonghan Zhengsikbay	My great grandfather Zhengsikbai became rich here
Bul zherde sol kisining ziraty bar	His grave is in this place
Tögiler er zhigtting elge teri	*Zhigit* (boys) work hard for their people
Bul zherde ötti talay örenderi	Many passed through this place
Babalar bir aunasyn aruaghy	Let the spirit of our ancestors move us
Zharyqtyq torqa bolsyn zhatqan zheri	Let this place of rest be as soft as silk
Darasay, beles caymen Baruun sala	Darasay, Beles say and Baruun sala
Köldi dara, Zhurtqa äygili Ayu dara	Köldi dara and the well-known Ayu dara
Taldysay Zhalghyz aghash arasanym	Taldy sai and Zhalghyz aghash, my mineral spring
Usyndym bul zyrymdy saghan arnap	I offer this *zhyr* to you

Aynaldym qasietingnen arasanym	My beloved holy mineral spring
Keshegi umytylmas balashaghym	It is impossible to forget my childhood
Tolqyghan balalyqtyng zhas däureni	The playful times of childhood were exciting
Älide sol zhastyqqa talasamyn	Even now I try to reach for my youth
Degende Sary qabyrgha Dara sayym	My Sary Qabyrgha and Dara say
Köngilim bir tolghanady körgen sayyn	When I see you I am filled with emotion
Qayqayyp qasqa qummen shygha kelsem	As I come bending back from Qasqa qum
Aldymda sulap zhatyr Myktybayym	My Mykhtybai lies on its side in front of me
Zhanasqan Tölengitke Tary dara	Tary dara is joined with Tölengit
Ulary qoysha örgen Ayu dara	Ayu dara, your mountain grouse are grazing like sheep
Köktemey zherding keni ketip qaldy au	Yet it doesn't turn green and our resources are gone
Yapyrau ne bolasyng bara	Oh what will happen over time?
Tüye say basy töskey Qasqyr Uya	Tüye say at the top of Qasqyr uya is a sunny slope
Bolady Qara shaghyl tasty qiya	Qara shaghyl is a mountain pass with large rocks
Däm tartyp otarmenen munda keldim	This is where I came for *otar*
Zhyrlay ber aq qaghazgha qara siya	My black ink, write a *zhyr* on white paper
Qyrqyndap Örteng saygha men keleyin	Whenever I come to Örteng say
Kaptaldap Kök tuyyqty kenerleyin	I go along the edge to Kök tuiyq
Ushatyn ular qonyp Sary teriske	*Ular* land and fly from Sary teris
Ularyn qiqu salghan bir köreyin	Let me see your crying *ular* once more
Tölengit zhatangymen qiyp ötip	Passing through Tölengit gorge
Kök shoqy töbesine örmeleyin	I will climb over Kök shoqy hill
Qolyma qalam alyp zhazdym khatqa	Taking my pen and paper I write
Tängirim cözdi berdi tilmen zhaqqa	*Tängir* (God) has given words to my tongue
Basymen Sholaq quys zhygha kelsem	When I come out at the beginning of Sholaq quys
Dangyrap körinedi Äbzhäng taqta	I see Äbzhäng taqta in every direction
Engkeyip Fermgede kelip qaldym	I came downhill to Ferma
Aq qaghaz qolyma aldym	And took my white paper
Auyzyna Qyzyl esik zhetip kelip	Arriving at the mouth of Qyzyl esik
Aynalyp Töngirekke közim saldym	I turned and looked at Töngirek
Demeymin qara sözding dauylymyn	I do not have a "storm of prose"
Khalqymnyng arqaladym auyr zhügin	Yet I carry my people's heavy load
Qaratqan eldi auyzyma ölengmenen	I will draw my country's attention with my song
Ataqty Bodauqanyng bauyrymyn	I am the well-known Bodaukhan's brother

Notes

1. The language referenced in this section—including the song—is Kazakh, widely shared by the majority of Kazakh residents of Bayan Ölgii province.

2. Local residents Almagul Soltan and Janbolat Khurmarhan contributed to the translation of this song.

CHAPTER 1

Sound, Music, Pastoralism, and Nature in Mongolian Sound Worlds

JENNIFER C. POST

Images of Mongolia and Inner Mongolia often feature scenes of expansive grasslands with gers dotting the landscape and their animals grazing in unfenced fields. Some mobile pastoralists thrive in these locations and move seasonally across the steppes with their livestock, relying heavily on local resources. In recent years in Mongolia, though, there has been great movement of peoples from rural to urban locations that began most intensely at the end of the socialist period when state support for nature-based systems and lifeways was inadequate, infrastructure in rural and remote regions was poor, and herders felt the pull—and promise—of a market economy (Bruun and Narangoa 2006). In Inner Mongolia, the government has enacted comprehensive urban relocation projects as they repurpose large portions of the countryside for mining and industrial agriculture to suit the nation's economic needs, impacting the mobility and opportunity found in the Mongol pastoral way of life. As a result, Inner Mongolian urban populations are swelling, and in rural regions the growth of agricultural districts and land privatization have rendered pastoralists immobile (Rogers and Wang 2006).

The sound worlds of pastoral lands in both Mongolia and Inner Mongolia, even in the face of change, continue to provide ecological, economic, and spiritual support for residents. Despite diminishing numbers of rural residents, the long history of mobile pastoralism and its links to domestic animals, wildlife, grasslands, forests, and other resources, are embedded in the minds, values, sounds, and musics of many people, whether they live in rural or urban locations. Relationships to nature maintained in rural regions can be heard in herders' animal calls, melodies expressing the contours of a landscape, lyrics describing

FIGURE 1.1. Mongolian landscape, Bayankhongor aimag, 2012. Photo by S. Yoon.

the character of the steppe, timbres reflecting the sound qualities of natural resources, and other practices linking humans and nonhumans as well as animate and inanimate beings. References to place, practice, identity and heritage contribute to relationships between past and present lifeways and values, and shared concerns about sustainability and environmental responsibility contribute to interest in engagement and reengagement with nature through unique styles and forms of cultural production in each social group. The sonic practices that pastoralists maintain, often to benefit local human and ecological well-being, resonate in the lives of many non-pastoralists now living in urban or semi-urban settings, and this reinforces a shared nature-based Mongolian heritage.

How do pastoralists, with access to large tracts of rural land used to support livelihoods and lifeways, use sound and music to interact with and respond to nature and place? What shared social and spiritual values and beliefs are in place that support herders' sonic practices? What cultural impact do changes to climate and industrial growth, along with greater mobility, have on pastoralists and non-pastoralists in the countryside and city? This chapter explores sounds, soundscapes, and music and their connections to pastoralism and nature in Mongolia and Inner Mongolia, concluding with a case study from Bayan-Ölgii, the westernmost province in Mongolia. Addressing lands, lifeways, and sound worlds generally, the in-depth focus is on rural pastoral relationships to sound, soundscapes, and music, with more limited attention on urban scenes, a topic that will be taken up in later chapters in this volume in greater detail.[1]

The Lands and Lifeways

Mongolia and Inner Mongolia are located at the eastern end of the vast Eurasian steppe, a landmass known for its temperate grasslands that support a variety of plant and animal species. For centuries the steppes also played a role in sustaining mobile pastoral lifeways for residents representing different ethnic groups in various ecosystem settings. The grasslands, as well as forest and desert zones, offer habitats not only for humans and their domestic animals, but for various species of wildlife and plant life as well.

Mongolia

In Mongolia the lands and their ecosystems are diverse. The *alpine* systems in the Altai, Khangai, and Khentii Mountains maintain perpetual snow, glaciers, and a cold climate that are home to argali (wild mountain sheep), Siberian ibex, and snow leopards. The *mountain forest steppe* zone includes parts of the Altai and Khangai Mountains; the northern facing slopes are richly forested, while the southern slopes have distinct plant species for livestock grazing. The different habitats are home to rare animals and birds including Pallas's cat and black grouse. The cold and relatively humid *mountain taiga* of Khövsgöl and northern portions of the Khentii Mountains is rich in forests. Musk deer, elk, and lynx are found in this region. The expanding *arid steppe* zone in eastern and central Mongolia, comprising about twenty-five percent of Mongolia's land, is a flat plain that extends into the northwestern edge of the Khangai Mountains to Uvs aimag (province) where Mongolian gazelles are found. The *desert steppe* is also a habitat for unique species, including saiga antelope, and black-tailed gazelle. It is huge, spanning from the Great Lakes Depression in the western aimags, the Valley of Lakes between the Khangai and Altai Mountains in the central southern region, and the lowlands in the central and eastern regions. The *desert* in the south, with hills, shrubland, and sand dunes also hold rare animals and plants, such as the wild camel and Gov' bear (Batjargal et al. 1998). Twenty different ethnic groups maintain settlements in Mongolian lands. Among them, the Bayad, Dörvöd, Zakhchin, Ööld, Torguud, Myangad, and Altai Uriankhai peoples live in the western aimags and share land with the Turkic language speaking Kazakh and Tuvan residents. In the central north the Darkhad, Buriad, and Dukha people live in both Mongolia and south Siberia, and the Dariganga live in the east. The Khalkh people, the dominant population, are concentrated in the central, east, and southern regions (Sneath 2010).

Mongolian residents in the twenty-first century in rural and urban locations express relationships to nature and pastoralism as a way of life, a memory, or as imagined history. In recent years ongoing interest in nationalist values often linked to homeland (*nutag*) have reinforced these connections while new challenges have emerged that are affecting rural herders, urban markets, and the country's economy (Sneath 2010; Upton 2010).

Mongolia's recent history as a socialist country played a critical role in its urban and industrial growth. Soviet-inspired focus on collectivization and industrialization encouraged expanding industries and urban lifeways. Following the dissolution of old systems at the end of the socialist era in the early 1990s, relationships of Mongolian residents to urban and rural, industrial and pastoral ways underwent many changes (Sneath 2006). By the second decade of the twenty-first century, herders in many regions were experiencing the effects of the new market economy along with the impact of industrial development on the land they were stewarding. At the same time, climate change and its unpredictable weather patterns discouraged many pastoralists; they were unable to manage the extreme environmental and economic changes that were confronting them. The resulting exodus from the countryside caused exponential population increases not only in Ulaanbaatar (population 1.5 million), but even in provincial capital cities and other industrial cities such as Erdenet (population 100,000) and Darkhan (population 100,000). By 2018, sixty-two percent of the population of 3.1 million people in Mongolia were living in urban areas (MSIS 2019). Urban locations offer modern lifeways for some residents, but for too many, large cities such as Ulaanbaatar present extreme divisions between wealth and poverty for their residents.

Mining activities in Mongolia have also had significant effects on lifeways. The gold, copper, and coal mining industries—and others—promise economic benefits, although they have not always delivered. They provide instead a devastating impact on lifeways and culture in regions where businesses are located (Jackson 2015a; 2015b; Post 2020). The inevitably shrinking pastoral land is increasingly crisscrossed with new roads, upgraded and planned railway networks, and mines near rural and urban sites. Many of these projects have international contractors, and funding support for Mongolia includes substantial loans from international banks. The rail lines and roads in the north pass through the Erdenet copper mine, to coal and silver mines in the west of the country, and into Russia. In the South Gov' Desert, the huge Oyu Tolgoi gold-copper mine, along with Tavan Tolgoi coking coal mine and its nearby Ukhaa Khudag open coal mine are linked to China. These sites and many others throughout the country have had considerable impact on the health and well-being of local pastoral residents (Gunchinsuren et al. 2011; Pfeiffer et al. 2017).

FIGURE 1.2. Grassland in Hulunbuir, Inner Mongolia. Photo by Sodhuu Ormis Gunbilig (used with permission).

Inner Mongolia

Inner Mongolia is dominated by grasslands in its central region, desert in the east, and forests, forest steppes, grasslands, and wetlands in the northwest (see figure 1.2). In general, valued lands in Inner Mongolia have not been sufficiently protected from agriculture, mining, and livestock overgrazing causing considerable biodiversity loss (Ma et al. 2016; Xu and Wu 2016). The *temperate grasslands*, which comprise sixty-seven percent of the land, include *meadow steppe, steppe*, and *desert steppe* (Han et al. 2009). The Inner Mongolian Plateau holds vast temperate grasslands with lakes that sustained these pasturelands for livestock grazing for generations. In recent years, many lakes in the plateau have been shrinking and the grasslands are degrading. Near this region the Yin Mountains stretch across the north, and their sedimentary rock holds coal beds that are heavily mined. To the east, the Alashan Plateau ecoregion in both the Gov' (Gobi) desert in Mongolia and the westernmost desert of Inner Mongolia, bounded in both countries by mountain ranges, has generally arid conditions. Here many of the same wildlife found in Mongolia once thrived, but today in China they are gone. In the southwestern part of the ecoregion the Anxi Nature

Reserve offers the potential for conservation, but most wildlife there has also been decimated. There are plans to reintroduce the Saiga antelope although much of the Alashan Plateau region is now also being used for human population resettlement. A significant natural area, the Amur-Heilong ecoregion spans three countries: Russia, Mongolia, and China, and includes the Amur-Heilong River Basin that provides habitats for many species of fish and rare migratory water birds, such as the red-crowned crane and the hooded crane. Portions of the northern part of the North Da Xing'anling (Hinggan) Mountains that feed the Amur River are known for their coniferous forests that include evergreens, such as Manchurian or needle fir and Siberian spruce, and deciduous trees, such as Manchurian elm, Manchurian ash, and Mongolian oak. At the lowest elevations, the land becomes grassland (Simonov and Dahmer 2008). Mongol, Daur, Evenki, Nanai and Orochen peoples live in parts of Inner Mongolia, but heavy investment in mining and urbanization has impacted the residents' lifeways (ibid).

Mongol relationships to pastoralism and nature in Inner Mongolia have undergone extreme changes during the last century. Some of the biggest come from land use restructuring, expanding urbanization, and the growth of mining and other industries. The relationships Inner Mongolians have to the land varies by region, but state policy that impacts how land is managed mediates their experiences with pastoralism and nature, discounting or manipulating herders' knowledge and skills developed through local practice.[2] Lifeways for many have been altered by relocating residents or by changing the character of the land as it is repurposed. A key action that began to affect pastoralists in the 1970s was a grasslands contract policy in which the government divided the land and then monitored it to maintain focus on production, although the carrying capacity of land was often exceeded (Dickinson and Webber 2007). Addressing a Mongol dominant region such as Uxin Ju in the central western drylands, in the early 2000s, Hong Jiang (2005:643) suggested that grasslands in Mao and Post-Mao eras were treated "primarily as a political or economic instrument" thus "weakening ties between Mongolian identity and nomadic grazing." These changes have been responsible for a shift in Mongol identity from pastoralism "toward symbolic features of language and heritage" (ibid:651). Other land restructuring involved expanding agriculture into grasslands and development of privatization of once collectively managed grassland, discouragement of seasonal migration, and development of fencing strategies to indicate ownership and use of land by family. This, in conjunction with climate change, has led to widespread land degradation and the collapse of mobile grazing practices that play a critical role in maintaining biodiversity in Inner Mongolia (Li and Huntsinger 2011; Conte 2015).

Growing urbanization in Inner Mongolia offers commercial, industrial, political, and cultural opportunities that radiate from the capital city of Hohhot (population 3.1 million), an economic, political, and cultural center, to other cities such as the industrial and transport city of Baotou (population 2 million); the south central city of Ulaanchab (population 2.1 million), a transportation hub; the southeastern city of Chifeng (population 4.3 million), a commercial center; and the small northeastern city of Hulunbuir (population 250,000). While rapid urbanization plans during the last two decades were partially established to benefit rural residents economically, they have devastated the land ecologically in Inner Mongolia as well as other regions in China (Fang et al. 2015). The cities provide centers for new economic and social opportunities and at the same time cause Mongol language and culture loss largely because the Han Chinese are now dominant in the cities (Hohhot city is ninety percent Han).[3] As in Mongolia, grasslands are being repurposed for mining coal, natural gas and gold. The mining industries have played a role in displacement and loss of essential resources such as water, and have caused "deforestation, desertification, and dust storms" (Sanchez 2013). Socially and culturally, herders have experienced even greater marginalization due to the economic power the mining companies wield, the arrival of more Han Chinese into many regions, and additional aggressive land seizures from the Mongols (Baranovitch 2016).

Social Spaces

In Mongolia, rural family settlements continue to display historically established social divisions of labor and responsibility. The heart of many rural settlement spaces is the *ger* (see figures 1.1 and 1.3), the portable tent-like structure made of wood, felt, animal hair, and cotton that holds a household and reinforces social relationships both inside the structure and in the surrounding land (Humphrey 1974; Braae 2017). The ger is a home and social space for pastoralists, a symbol of belonging for rural and urban residents, and a "brand" for the nation (Krebs 2012). The way the ger is configured—its size, height, and how interior space is decorated and used in daily life—differs among Khalkh, Uriankhai, Kazakh, and Tuvan peoples in Mongolia, yet there are broad similarities that indicate common types of social relationships and responsibilities reflected in lifeways and cultural production. The customary actions that take place inside the *ger* come from a long history of the use of the yurt throughout the geographical region, from Central Asia to Mongolia, including Inner Mongolia, and they reflect similarities in pastoral lifeways, including different types of relationships with natural resources (Braae 2017).

While the portable ger itself has an identity and holds family practices and histories, the ger can also be considered just a segment of a larger social space, encompassing lifeways both inside and outside this moveable structure. Each seasonal site where the ger is set up becomes part of a family's social and acoustic living space that enables herders to maintain their multispecies lives. The herders coexist with the landscape to accommodate the social needs of animals, humans, plants, landforms, weather, and other entities. The acoustically porous walls of the ger allow sounds to travel in and out so families can hear their herds and potential threats, such as wolves. Similarly, what happens inside the ger can also be heard outside. The realm of the ger that extends beyond the structure forms a multispecies community made up of humans, their animals, and other resources they rely on (see Figure 1.3).[4] Natasha Fijn (2011:201) in her research in the Mongolian Khangai region says simply that "herd animals are seen as part of the extended family."

Stepping into a ger in the countryside, regardless of the ethnic group, there is an order to daily life practice that reinforces well-established gendered relationships among its residents and visitors (Benwell 2006). The different contributions women and men make to assure economic success in pastoral households, as they manage domestic animals and other resources, include customary practices that have been maintained for generations. In Mongolia especially, rural family settlements continue to display these historically established social divisions of labor and responsibility.

The prominent social and cultural roles that men play in families and herding communities is balanced by a powerful social role that women play in the realm of the ger. Men are said to be "in charge of the success or failure of the household to ensure their livelihood" (Agarin and Rudzīte 2018:169) as they manage decisions about the location of herding sites and when each move will take place; they dominate decisions about their domestic animals, travel more frequently to maintain relationships in neighborhoods and to gather supplies in a nearby sum center, and play leadership roles in their community. With the internal space in and around the ger as their base, rural women generally are entangled more fully with family responsibilities where they maintain relationships with and support for actors in this spatial realm, especially their spouses, children, relatives, visitors, and domestic animals.

The ger and the social roles it holds is today undergoing change that impacts family members in various ways. Since the end of socialism, the ongoing adjustments to local populations, available products, and access to conveniences have directly affected the inhabited space in and around the ger. More rural children are sent to school where they board for the winter, and as they grow many do not return to the settlements where they were raised, creating an absence in this space. The increasing use of electronics, from televisions to smartphones, has altered activities and soundscapes in the ger. Greater mobility also changes women's roles; for example, new economic opportunities that international organizations offer provide greater independence and more mobility for women. Despite all this, the ger and its social and cultural significance still remains a central component in the economic and ecological success of a rural herding family's existence and continues to be looked to as a significant Mongolian icon.

Values and Beliefs about Nature

To the Mongols the term "environmental protection" has the connotation of being governed by and to live in harmony with nature, respecting the soil and earth as one does their own mother, having compassion towards both the earth and its creatures, and to behave ethically when using ecological resources (Batbold 2015:10).

The long history of pastoralism and rural lifeways in the Eurasian steppe has reinforced connections between humans and their ecological environment and established active human nonhuman relationships in communities for many. The people, animals, plants, and landforms, as well as behaviors that sustain relationships among them, are part of networks in complex social-ecological systems that are linked to interactions of people and the natural world. Rural residents demonstrate that they value abundant grasslands and rare flora and fauna. Many people identify aspects of their heritage and/or family history with pastoralism, whether they live in the countryside or city. National themes in the post-socialist era in Mongolia have reinforced connections to nature by highlighting pastoralism as a nation-building tool used for "practicing Mongolianness" (Agarin and Rudzīte 2018).

Spiritual beliefs and ways of knowing have also helped shape values related to natural resources. In fact, many beliefs and practices promoted today linked to relationships with nature come from pre-socialist times; they are designed around reemergent, renewed, as well as invented beliefs identified with animism and Buddhism (Humphrey et al. 1993; Tseren 1996; Upton 2010; Sneath 2001:2014). Spiritual well-being—pathways to spiritual health expressed in different communities—is also often connected to nature. In fact, for Mongols, spiritual entities (*gazryn ezed*) are "land masters" "held responsible for the general conditions (rainfall, diseases, fertility etc.) upon which human and animal life depend" (Pedersen 2006:100).

> Such spirits were, and still are, propitiated in annual ceremonies held at ritual cairns made of stones and/or branches, called *oboo*. These ceremonies reflect the notion that humans do not hold land as they do other mundane possessions, but enter into relations with the spiritual powers of the locality to ensure favourable conditions. The spirits associated with a given *oboo* and locality have different preferences with respect to offerings (Sneath 2001:45).

Pastoralists in other ethnic groups in Mongolia also maintain older values, beliefs, and practices that help them connect with the land, engage socially with human nonhuman entities, and monitor and maintain some control over human and ecological well-being. For example, Altai Uriankhai epic song (*tuul'*) is a "repository of spiritual knowledge" combining shamanism and Buddhist ideas and expressing relationships of the Altai Uriankhai peoples with their geographic place and its embodied spirits (Plueckhahn 2013:200). The Kazakhs in Mongolia, who are Muslim, reference ancestors (*babalar*) and spirits (*aruaq*) that are embodied in specific sites. For all pastoralists, their relationships to place and sense of responsibility "are predicated upon the creation and ongoing maintenance of reciprocal relationships of care for the land, the ancestors and their descendents" (Dubuisson and Genina 2011:470). In Inner Mongolia, government policies during the twentieth century challenged spiritual values, not unlike Soviet-influenced socialist programs in Mongolia. Mongol religious beliefs and practices were considered unsophisticated and efforts were made to replace them with scientific thinking (Williams 2002). Today few Mongols in China have maintained spiritual and ecological knowledge, except in the most remote areas.

Sound Worlds

Sound worlds in both rural and urban Mongolia and Inner Mongolia show evidence of values and beliefs that support pastoralism and nature. Their soundscapes—ambient sound landscapes—are defined by knowledge built within their social worlds. In rural regions, sound-making and listening practices pragmatically and spiritually connect herders with the resources they need and value. Local sounds, songs, and melodies frequently reflect human lifeways and the particular configuration of wildlife, plant life, and landforms found locally (Post 2019). Sound is as fundamental to city life as it is to rural life, and city soundscapes help to establish a unique character that contributes to an urban sense of place. Music in urban settings can offer opportunities for residents to imagine or remember pastoral lifeways. The rural and urban sound worlds come together most directly in ritual activities: annual *naadam* celebratory events where "physical strength, precision and horsemanship are exhibited, and praised," *ovoo*, or sacred cairns, where offerings are made to spirits of the land, and travel to shrines such as mineral springs are all closely linked to pastoralism and nature (Lindskog 2016:21).

In rural regions, vocalizing is often tied to herding practices and interspecies communication. Herders listen to sounds of livestock, wildlife, trees, grasses, and people, and sounds of winds, rain, and thunder at different sites and times of day, the men more often in relation to grazing sites and women in and near the ger. They use what they hear to make decisions about safety and security, human and animal health and well-being, and seasonal movement (Pegg 2001; Levin and Süzükei 2006). Both women and men also vocalize to direct or control livestock while herding and to placate and communicate with their animals while milking (Fijn 2011; Yoon 2018a; Hutchins 2019). Documenting relationships between humans and domestic animals in the Khangai mountain region in central Mongolia, Fijn (2008) shows how herders communicate using sounds and body language. She identifies specific vocalizations for each domestic animal in her descriptive and visual information. "The herder communicates to the horse that is being ridden, mainly through body language, but the herder also vocalises to the goats, sheep, and, in a removed sense, to potential wolves to warn them away from the flock through yells and whistles: This is a complex system of multispecies communication" (2011:105). In the northern Altai-Sayan region, which includes parts of Mongolia and nearby south Siberia in Russia, scholars have documented sound customs of Turkic reindeer herders, the Dukha in Khövsgöl in Mongolia and in south Siberia among the Turkic Tozhu in Tuva and the Tofa in Irkutsk.[5] Charles Stépanoff (2012:296) suggests the Tozhu vocal cries to reindeer to get their attention, "are neither human nor reindeer language" but, as Natasha Fijn (2011) also notes, they use a unique language that humans adopt to communicate with their domestic animals. The Tofa, who are both herders and hunters, maintain similarly specialized sonic practices by "mimicking and stylizing the natural acoustic environment." David Harrison (2003:47) in his work with Turkic language and sound mimesis in Russia and Mongolia suggests, "These skills may confer an adaptive advantage by providing herders and hunter-gatherers a tool to manage wild animals, plants, and reindeer. Sound mimesis is manifested in hunting calls, animal-sound imitation, and more structured song and spoken forms."

The widely referenced practice of throat singing or *khöömii* is used throughout these regions to reference natural sounds, sometimes symbolically or metaphorically. Theodore Levin and Valentina Süzükei (2006:77) suggest that Tuvan throat singers' sounds that represent nature "are the sonic embodiments of landscapes, birds, and animals along with the spirits that inhabit them." When performed in rural western Mongolia, *khöömii* is said to mimic the sounds of winds whistling and rushing through local mountain crevices or water moving over rocks in brooks and streams (Pegg 1992). Johanni Curtet (2010:6) describes the practice not only as a way for pastoralists to mimic sounds, but also to "communicate with nature, as well to pass the time watching their herds or to enliven an evening in the *ger*." In its modern form, developed for the stage in Mongolia during the socialist period, *khöömii* can still play a role for some performers and audience members as a tool to draw and recall a landscape, thus *khöömii* lives as a musical form both inside and outside the pastoral environment (see Chapter 8 in this volume). In Inner Mongolia *khöömii* was imported from Mongolia during the 1990s through the efforts of Mongolian teachers (see Chapter 2 in this volume). Urban popular musicians also draw from Tuvan throat singing practices to enhance their style and mark their identity (D'Evelyn 2013; Wu 2019), and urban listeners in both countries enjoy not only the mimetic characteristics, but also the virtuosity that has been developed in recent years.

Pastoralist-musicians also create and perform compositions that reflect sounds and soundscapes in their daily lives. The music they perform may reference animals, birds, and weather with rhythms played on instruments to represent the gait of a horse or camel, sounds that reference the camel's cry or a bird's call, or melodies that draw a picture of a landscape in sound. The narrative instrumental form *tatlaga*, often played on the bowed Khalkh *morin khuur*, or the Oirad bowed *ikil* in western regions, tells stories and imitates sounds and movements using melody, rhythm, and timbre, and it is associated with the dance/gestural form *bie/biyelgee* (Levin and Süzükei 2006). Other narrative and lyrical forms and styles that link sound and sound quality with herding are performed on flutes in different regions of Mongolia and Inner Mongolia. End-blown flute players, such as Mongol and Oirad *tsuur*, Tuvan *shoor*, and Kazakh *sybyzghy* often produce a low vocal drone that acts as external amplifier for the sound, and side-blown flute *limbe* performers of eastern Mongols sometimes use circular breathing. Their compositions connect sound, sound quality, and performance with herding practices (Hamayon 1973; Pegg 2001; Chuluunbaatar 2013). Historically the flutes were made using local plants herders gathered near the fields where their animals grazed. Their music often includes timbrally rich sounds that—like the *morin khuur* and *ikil*—imitate animal sounds and tell stories about pastoral lifeways (Post forthcoming). Songs performed in rural settings may also describe shared grazing places or sites, identify spatial relationships to land and resources while herding, recount experiences with animals, and communicate values related to family, conservation, as well as spirituality (Post 2017, 2019).

The vocal form *urtyn duu* (long-song), while performed today in both rural and urban settings in Mongolia and Inner Mongolia, also maintains its roots in pastoral traditions (see Chapter 3 in this volume). It continues to be used in some regions, along with vocalization and other song forms, to communicate with livestock while milking and engaging in other activities (Yoon 2018b; Hutchins 2019). This song form and others, including *magtaal* (praise-song), may reference land and resources descriptively, as Carole Pegg (2001:179) identifies in a song she heard in Khovd aimag performed by an Oirad singer in a Myangad community. It describes the character of the land during the summer with references to rain, grasses, flowers, and the cuckoo, all valued resources in their daily and seasonal lives.[6] Other song forms, that Harrison (2004:208) refers to as domestication songs, are used by Tuvans in Bayan-Ölgii and Khovd aimags in western Mongolia (and in Tuva) to "make an animal calm down, stand still, feed a calf that is not its own, allow [it] to be milked, ridden, shorn, treated for sickness" and more.

The melodic contours used in some local songs can be linked to local topography (Yoon 2018a, 2019). Liliana Carrizo (2010:13) argues that the melodic contours of *urtyn duu* sung in Dundgov' aimag in Mongolia enable interaction between humans and *ezen*, the landscape deities. "Indeed, singing *urtiin duu* was an important aspect of human-*ezen* interaction, where individuals utilized mimesis to sonically interact with the spirits that reside in particular landscapes. In the case of *urtiin duu*, the melodic contours of songs are mimetic of environmental sounds and topographies unique to the landscapes of the *ezen* particular to a specific *nutag*, or geographical location."[7] Sunmin Yoon (2018b:94) suggests that *urtyn duu* practices in Mongolia function "as a critical, sensitive, and spiritual means to create relationships that regulate environmental balance in the singers' nomadic lives." She says further that songs provide a forum for humans and their animals to "connect with each other and contribute to the vitality of Mongolia's ecosystem." Conducting research in the western Alshaa (Alashan) region of Inner Mongolia, Oyuna Weina similarly found there is a spiritual dimension to *urtyn duu* in Inner Mongolia linked to relationships between the genre and the sky. The *urtyn duu* repertoire is seasonal, and "the start of the spring symbolizes the origin of *urtyn duu*, which the Alshaa people believe comes from the *tenger*, or sky" (2018:11).

Urban singers in both Mongolia and Inner Mongolia maintain relationships and develop new connections with rural values in *urtyn duu* training and performance. Yoon documents urban singers' growing interest in drawing from pastoral lifeways in rural locations for songs. Their experiences may be drawn from a childhood in the countryside and expressed in descriptive lyrics to create remembered places, emotions, and sensations for singers, and a virtual or imagined landscape for others with limited time in the countryside (Yoon 2019). Weina discusses expressions of nostalgia for nature and argues that artists invoke old practices, including elements linked to pastoralism, in order to maintain "consistent relationships with past traditions in the face of significant social change" (2018:5). Retaining these elements in *urtyn duu* performances acts to both "resurrect and reinterpret" original contexts for performance. She argues that "visual and zoological metaphors" related to lifestyle along with melodic and timbral characteristics in performance contribute to the expressions of longing and nostalgia in both rural and urban contexts. Inner Mongolian *urtyn duu*, Charlotte D'Evelyn (2018:33) notes, carries a "grassland sensibility, including the psychological and musical understanding of expansive, vast space" that is critical to the "proper performance" of long-song repertoire. She says, "When they study long song, Mongol youth who were raised in the city are often criticized for their inability to appropriately express the aesthetic of the grassland due to the fact that they grew up in crowded and fast-paced urban lifestyles" (ibid).

Musical performance can also capture both pastoralism and urban life values. Hybrid musical forms produced for both local and global markets give artists opportunities to perform identities and express national heritage, thus drawing from both the past and the present and the rural and urban worlds (Marsh 2006; Dovchin 2011; Marsh 2018). In urban settings people are separated physically from daily life in rural spaces and places; some of their songs show respect, and even entanglements with nature, and as Marsh (2006:134) says, include topics "such as love for one's parents, the beauty of the Mongolian landscape, or the wonders of the Mongolian horse." Thus, even while globalization contributes to the creation of new genres and styles, nationalist tropes that embrace pastoralism continue to emerge in musical forms. Examples include the ongoing promotion of music and musical instruments identified with pastoralism and nature, such as *khöömii*, the song form *urtyn duu*, and the instrument *morin khuur*.

Sound, Music, Pastoralism, and Nature in Bayan-Ölgii

Bayan-Ölgii aimag in western Mongolia offers local residents and visitors stunning views of mountains, grasslands, and forests in this region bordered by China and Russia. Most coveted are the Altai Mountains along the Chinese border and the lands and lakes in the Altai Tavan Bogd National Park (see figures 1.3 and 1.4).[8] Other valued sites include the Tsambagarav Uul National Park in the east shared with Khovd aimag and the transboundary Siilkhemiin Nuruu National Park (SNNP)[9] in the north along the Russian border, which offers alpine and mountain steppes, a prime habitat for argali sheep and snow leopards. Petroglyphs depicting wild and domestic animals in the Altai as well as Siilkhemiin, Tsambagarav, and other locations indicate that the lands have been used for pastoralism for thousands of years.[10]

The majority of the 105,000 Bayan-Ölgii residents who have lived in the region for generations are Kazakh, Tuvan, or Altai Uriankhai (see figure 1.4). Maintaining close ties to pastoralism, sixty-four percent of the provincial population lives in rural settings, in contrast to the Mongolian national rural population of thirty-two percent (MSIS 2018). This location is therefore particularly suited for discussing relationships between music, sound, pastoralism, and nature. Furthermore, the aimag is wholly in the Altai Sayan ecoregion, a conservation area located at the convergence of Mongolia, Russia, Kazakhstan, and China that is home for rare flora and fauna (Uluqpan and Knapp 2012). The Bayan-Ölgii herders' seasonal movement in support of their livestock takes some of them from desert steppe to grasslands to alpine forests. Maintaining herding practices linked through family values after 1991, the Kazakh, Tuvan, and Uriankhai pastoralists in the aimag use sounds, songs, and tunes to express relationships with the vulnerable resources that are all critical to their ecological and economic success and well-being.

FIGURE 1.3. Tuvan settlement at Tavan Bogd Mountains in western Mongolia, 2011. Photo by J. C. Post.

FIGURE 1.4. Kazakh summer settlements at Dala köl (Tal nuur in Mongolian) in Bayan-Ölgii aimag, 2018. Photo by J. C. Post.

Ölgii city is an expanding provincial capital, like so many other urban areas in Mongolia and Inner Mongolia, that has grown especially as herders come in from countryside locations where they have struggled with both economic difficulties and climate change. In the second decade of the twenty-first century, the city showed evidence of more wealth and greater poverty than it did just ten years before. While there is diversity, Altai Uriankhais, Dörvöds, Tuvans, and Kazakhs share pasturelands and urban spaces; the Kazakhs are the primary provincial residents. They dominate in the city as they do in the countryside. On Olgii city streets, Kazakh is the primary language heard, men wear embroidered Kazakh caps, women's heads are covered with colorful scarves, and it is not uncommon to see children carrying *dombyras* on their way to school or the local theater (where Kazakh music and instruments are also in the majority).[11]

The Kazakh residents, whose families have lived in the region at least since the nineteenth century, make up ninety percent of the provincial population. They began to move into western Mongolia primarily from the Altai region in western China beginning in the mid-nineteenth century. Some had been settled in China for generations after fleeing Russian imperial expansionism in Central Asia beginning in the seventeenth century (Soni 2003). Material indications of Kazakh long-term residence in the aimag are also seen in the countryside where not only current structures, but remnants of old winter homes made of stone, mud-clay, or wood dot the landscape. Other evidence is in the small local Muslim grave sites that generations of families that settled in each region have maintained. Even songs that were passed from previous generations reference the Bayan-Ölgii land over time. Rural residents also access urban soundscapes and musical traditions when they travel to Ölgii for supplies or to attend a *toi* (celebration). Radio, television, commercial recordings, and music shared at events in the sum centers and Ölgii city introduce new styles, but rural residents also continue to engage with older musical genres. They offer forums for sharing knowledge about their histories, the character of the land, and the resources they experience across wide expanses of land they use in their seasonal practices.

Sound Worlds in Bayan-Ölgii

Kazakh relationships to sounds and soundscapes in Bayan-Ölgii have developed in the context of local ecosystems and established social patterns. Social spaces in rural regions are defined by herders' sonic and other sensory experiences in families and residential communities (*auyl*) and in their daily lives in pasturelands and other natural sites. My discussions about sound with Kazakh herders in different locations in the aimag reveal that they draw on diverse forms of communication using sound as they care for their livestock (*mal*). They listen in different spatial settings not only to their horses, sheep, goats, yaks, and camels, but also to gauge the health of wildlife. Birds offer them signals and solace, insects are indicators of land health, and the sounds of water sources, grasses, and leaves of trees also provide knowledge about environmental health. Herders also influence animal behavior with sounds with vocalizations transmitted in families from generation to generation.

In the Altai Mountain region along the border with China where there is some forested land, Kazakh herders tell me they listen carefully where their animals are grazing for the sounds of specific kinds of winds, such as the *quyun zhel*, a fast-moving swirling wind dangerous to their livestock that may also be accompanied by a terrifying sound. The sound and wind signals them to collect their animals and seek protection in the forests. In contrast to this, the *samal zhel* is a soft wind and represents quieter sound, calmer animals, and a greater sense of well-being. Sounds of specific birds in the Tolbo sum region, where small lakes and protective rock outcroppings provide seasonal homes for the ruddy duck and the bar headed goose, offer herders acoustic reminders to prepare for their own seasonal moves (Post 2019). Many herders also refer to sounds of wildlife, such as ibex (*täueshki*), argali (*arqar*), and deer (*bughy*), that they value, yet are a rapidly disappearing part of their soundscape.

The Kazakh ger (*kiiz üy*) and the lands nearby are also interspecies social and sonic spaces in rural Bayan-Ölgii. Viewing a ger-dotted landscape from a distance one can immediately identify the Kazakh settlements: their gers are taller and often larger in diameter than those of Mongol and Tuvan peoples. Like other pastoralists in Mongolia, Kazakh indoor and outdoor spaces are carefully ordered according to the needs of both humans and animals, and herders' activities occur in accordance with traditionally maintained social roles, divided not only by age, but by gender. While men tend to engage with herding in grasslands and visiting away from their settlement during the daytime, and in the fields and at home provide care for the health of animals, women maintain relationships with the interior and more immediate space around the ger, interacting with family members, visitors, and domestic animals that are nearby. In this ger-centered context, sound is an outcome of the diverse activities supporting social obligations and interspecies relationships. I engaged with women producing, evaluating, and acting in relation to sound inside and outside the ger in settlements throughout the aimag. Day and night, the interior space includes their sounds of cooking, washing dishes, and making and maintaining a fire, which also engages women and children with gathering fuel in nearby resonant fields and forests and water in streams or a lake that is close by. The ger also includes the sounds of women caretaking children and the elderly along with very young animals, such as lambs and kids, that are provided shelter in the ger until a family is confident it will survive. At the same time, women listen for the arrival of family members and guests, for whom they are expected to

FIGURE 1.5. Kazakh women milking yaks in the early morning, Muzdy tau in Bayan-Ölgii aimag, 2013. Photo by J. C. Post.

prepare tea, and for warnings of trouble and need for action in connection with nearby livestock or changes in weather. Women are also responsible for milking (although men help to gather and tie up the animals); their yaks are milked typically once daily and sheep and goats once or twice daily. During their daily milking women engage, as men do in their own herding work, using sonically rich communication practices to call, direct, and calm the animals. Seasonally, in summer months, women milk horses every few hours, and typically men will provide a vocalization that calms the horses.

Some sonic relationships that Kazakh herders share with specific animals indicate spiritual connections and other relationships that provide a sense of well-being. Kazakhs in Bayan-Ölgii do not vocalize using *khöömii* (throat singing), popular in some other western Mongolian communities and developed as a performance genre throughout Mongolia and Inner Mongolia (see Chapter 9 in this volume), but they maintain beliefs about the timbral power of sound. Kazakh herders value the unique forms of communication they share with their animals. Altai Tügelbai, at his summer settlement (*zhaylau*) at Sary buyra near Dayan köl (Dayan nuur in Mongolian), described to me behaviors and sounds his horse makes before travel; they are signals to indicate whether horse and rider will be safe or may run into difficulty (Interview, June 3, 2014). According to Altai, relationships with some animals are also spiritual. He says animals provide an energy that allows herders to care for them. When Altai needs to sleep among his horses at night in a remote grazing area, their sounds and restlessness may keep him from sleeping but he never tires, and instead the animals' presence, both day and night, provides him energy. In Tolbo, Delüün, and Sagsai sums herders shared information on the calls of specific birds, such as the cuckoo (*kukuk*) and owl (*zhapalaq*), indicating that they are linked for them to both sense of place and to well-being.

Pastoralism and Nature in Mongolian Kazakh Music

Mongolian Kazakh musical forms and styles of music-making were greatly influenced by musical practices established during the socialist era. In this period, Russian musicians brought European forms to Ölgii city and Kazakh instruments were manufactured to specifications set by Russian makers, replacing styles that once favored locally available materials and skill sets (see Chapter 7 in this volume). The influences quickly reached the rural communities through cultural centers that were established in each sum, and some local musicians were drawn from the countryside to join the city theater.

Despite these changes, social gatherings of Kazakh herders in rural regions continue to contribute to maintaining older styles and ways of sharing music. Some of their forms (*terme, tolghau*) are linked historically to the improvised songs of the poet-singer (*aqyn*) and epic-singer (*zhyrau*). They also share social song forms that include *qara öleng* (literally black song, sometimes translated as "simple song") and *khalyq äni* ("people's song" or folk song) along with other forms, including *küi* (a narrative instrumental composition) and specific forms performed at weddings, funerals, and other life-cycle events (Kunanbaeva 2002).

In historical performances in Central Asia, Kazakh *terme* focused on "topical or ethical issues," while *tolghau* were "meditative poems" that were sung before the presentation of an epic poem (Reichl 1992:100). Originally connected to the *zhyrau*, the lyrical themes using a specific poetic structure were often improvised. The song forms are also identified with *aqyns*, or respected poet-singers, found throughout Central Asia who provided didactic and philosophical songs for a community. Yet as the revival of these historically valued forms in post-Soviet Kazakhstan took place through the media, they adopted new melodies and became more standardized (Kendirbaeva 1994). Songs produced in Kazakhstan and Kazakh China in the 1990s and the early 2000s were made widely available commercially on cassette, CD, VCD, and TV, and online in the new millennium. In rural Bayan-Ölgii, these genres developed somewhat differently as poetic forms not only of the *aqyn*, but as narrative songs of herder-musicians shared in small social gatherings. While songs had locally established characteristics, they were also influenced by performances available through Kazakhstani- and Chinese-produced media.[12] Some herders note down their songs in school notebooks to preserve them. In the twenty-first century they continue to be presented to rural residents who listen attentively for the local place names, settlement histories, commentary on lifeways, and expressions of herding values. Thus they engage active herders through song with references to events related to their daily lives in the natural world. The songs carry ecological knowledge built from their experience with the land and information shared from generation to generation. In an excerpt from a terme called "Tughan zher" (Homeland) written by his brother Qadan, Zharkyn Khuspan at his summer settlement (*zhaylau*) at Buzau köl (Tugal nuur in Mongolian) describes the land and seasonal moves they experience as herders (Interview, July 23, 2018). He names their winter settlement place (*qystau*) called Qysangbai, and references other landforms they value using descriptive language. Muzdy tau refers to an icy mountain, Shatang su to flowing water, Qonyr bel to a brown colored hill, and Qyzyl sai to a reddish-colored valley. He also sings about the *ular*, a snow-cock used medicinally by Kazakhs and other pastoralists in Mongolia, and the *sary ala qaz* or ruddy duck, which is valued for its sound that signals seasonal change for herders. Referencing herding and animals, locations that are used, and—most importantly—naming places helps the local herders reinforce their connection to place. When such songs are sung in a community, people listen carefully and recognize these places as locations they all share, and care for, as a community of pastoralists.[13]

Qysangbay qyrgha qonghan quz artym-ay	Qysangbai is the place I move to for the winter
Muzdy tau munarlanghan muzartym-ay	Muzdy tau is my foggy glacier
Bökterde böri ulyp ilbis zhortyp	Wolves howl and snow leopards run down there
Tepsengge zhayilady ular shulay	Ulars graze noisily in Tepseng
Kök qiya kökke örlegen zanggharym-ay	My Kök qiya scrapes the sky
Shatang su quldan aqqan anggharym-ay	Shatang su flows down the valley
Asylyp asau tolqyn Shegirtaygha	Its swelling waves at Shegirtay
Alghynyp algha umtylar zhardan qulay	Flow easily down the cliff
Malgha zhay zhylghaly say zhaylyghym-ay	My livestock at Zhylghaly valley are comfortable
Sayran köl saryala qaz aydynym-ay	Sairan köl is homeland for *saryalaqaz*
Saghyndym qozy zhayghan bala kündi	I miss my childhood, I used to graze lambs
Qaydasyng zamandastar tay qulynday?	Where are you, my peers who were like foals?
Anamnyng oyulaghan syrmaghynday	Like my mother's handmade rugs
Allaghyng gülge oranghan qyrdabynday	Like Allah's steppes covered with flowers
Alysqa arman quyl attanghanda	When I traveled far away to chase my dreams
Artyma qarayladym qimay-qimay	I looked back again and again with deep pain

shkende qozy aydaghan qongyr belim	My Qonyr bel, where I drove the lambs when we moved
zyl say kishkene köl mening zherim	Qyzyl sai Kishkene köl is my land
girgen tal boyyna aqyl ziyn	With intelligence and wisdom
giti er köngildi qyzy kerim	The zhigits are brave hearted and the girls are happy
tizem, üki tasim, zhotalarym	Ush tize, Uki tas, and my mountains
ymdy eske ap zhürsin dos adamym	Recognize my zhyr, my friends
tym bar äzheng sayda äkem qonghan	My zhurt is in Azhen sai where my father lived
-anam süyn ishken osy aranyng	My parents drank the water of this place

Qara öleng has been identified in Kazakhstan as a domestic unaccompanied song, sung by women, that use poetic and melodic formulas to provide opportunities for the singer to improvise lyrics and embellish melodies. Kunanbaeva (2016:182) describes the songs as enabling "dialogical interaction" in local gatherings. In rural Bayan-Ölgi, the *qara öleng* I experienced were sung by men with *dombyra* (two-string plucked lute) accompaniment at neighborhood gatherings using locally shared melodies. Visiting Aldanysh Untan from Sagsai sum, settled for the summer at his *zhaylau* at Muzdy tau, I asked him about place names used in social songs in these rural regions where pastoralists share stories about places they travel and value while herding and moving seasonally (Interview, July 8, 2018). To communicate about valued sites, he sang a *qara öleng* using Kazakh place names, which are descriptive of the geographic characteristics and embody local history. He sang about a flowing stream (*bulaq*) near their settlement site: "Taldi bulaq begins from Muzdy tau" (From there Taldi bulaq flows down). He references a place named by Uriankhai people (Modon khöshöö—a Mongolian wooden statue) and others shared by different groups such as Böken tau (Antelope mountain): "There are places called Modyn xöshöö and Böken / Where Dörvöd, Kazakh, and Uriankhai have lived;" and he discusses the character of the herding land and the isolated hill (Aral töbe) where he must take his sheep to graze: "Qorymdy, next to Muzdy tau is so rocky / I herd my sheep on the top of Aral töbe." His lyrics indicate his connections to place, landforms, Kazakh identity, and herding practices (including decisions about locations for herding). Aldanysh's song is largely descriptive, and as we traveled to each site I saw how his lyrics revealed the region's shared history and his knowledge about each place. He expressed support for grassland and livestock, revealed the essential role of water, and shared concern for the well-being of all.

Each settlement location for a herding family provides new forums for engagement with human nonhuman actors. Songs and tunes are used to express their relationships and to reinforce knowledge and communicate it to members of their communities. When herders leave their rural lifestyles due to ecological, social, or political challenges, their musical lives in urban locations are more fully engaged with national and international repertoires and their local songs (and sound practices) are often left behind (Post 2020). For those who have not lived in rural regions, but visit as actual or virtual tourists, the songs may be nostalgic and/or present imagined places. Songs remind listeners of the wealth of the land, as Altai Tügelbai sang in this family song (Interview, June 3, 2014).

Shopandar änge salar malyn zhayyp	Herders sing when grazing their animals
Myng qoyy qaltaghanda zher zhuzdi alyp	Thousands of animals are scattered all over the land
Ashysy suyda mol shöbi shüygin	Rich in water, the grass is moist
Oynaqtap asyp salar o tughan el	My homeland is where I am happy

Herders offer descriptive information and express emotional responses to the land and its resources, as Minäp Qazanbai did in the midst of a song about his travels to Zhasyl köl (Green Lake) near the Chinese border on horseback (Interview, June 17, 2007).

Tireldim bir burylyp Zhasyl kölge	I turned to go to Zhasyl köl
Ornaghan Zhasyl kölim asu belde	Zhasyl köl is on a hill at the border
Koyghanday qolmen zhasap zher şuluy	The land is as beautiful as things made by hand
Qazyna baylyq zhatyr osy zherde	This place is filled with treasures of the earth
Talsayda aghyp zhatyr muzdan bulaq	A spring flows from the Talsay glacier
Iilip zhayqalady tal men quraq	The willows bend beautifully
Eriksiz könilingdi sergitedi	My energy is refreshed
Quyylghan sarqyrama quzdan qulap	By a waterfall running down from the cliff

In Ölgii city, the local Music and Drama Theater, developed during the socialist era, has contributed to a unique Kazakh musical culture in the aimag. It was shaped in the twentieth century by cross-border relationships between Mongolian Kazakhs and musicians from the Kazakh Republic before 1991 (Yagi 2019). Musical repertoires, instruments, and practices were uniquely influenced by Russian-European music, evolving music of the Kazakh Republic, and local Mongolian Kazakh traditions. The small theater orchestra included musical instruments developed from the two-string plucked *dombyra* and two-string bowed *qobyz* to play both European and Kazakh repertoires. Both rural and urban performers were given opportunities to become professional musicians and these artists also began to teach in the local schools, offering opportunities for students to learn the russified Kazakh traditions on *dombyra* (Yagi 2018). This ongoing practice, emulating both the Soviet educational system and a new performance aesthetic from post-Soviet Kazakhstan, provides opportunities for students to develop skills on the *dombyra* through competition and in ensembles. With greater global influence, some young musicians in Bayan-Ölgii are now beginning to become involved in popular music, emulating both popular forms in Ulaanbaatar and in Kazakhstan. Musical interests in Ölgii in the twenty-first century also reflect their various life experiences. Some new city dwellers have recently arrived from the countryside; others have spent time for education or employment in Ulaanbaatar, Kazakhstan, or Turkey, while many are second or third general urban residents in Ölgii.

For pastoralists who spend much of their lives in rural regions in Bayan-Ölgii, sound production, listening, and music-making continue to play significant roles in their lives. Their songs and melodies are well integrated in local landscapes, and their melodies and lyrics also contribute to memories of nature for those living in urban or semi-urban areas as well as diaspora communities around the world. Local ecological knowledge embedded in sounds, melodies and song lyrics, and in other narrative information such as related discussions or stories that reference sounds, soundscapes, and places has helped to maintain the health of the land and the well-being of rural residents (Post 2017). Music that references these sounds and landscapes performed in urban contexts can also contribute to conservation of the land and lifeways when city residents use the memories, nostalgia, and values to support nature-based policies and actions rather than allowing industrial and technologically rich actions and sounds to dominate and erase their pastoral history.

Conclusion

Mongolian sound worlds have helped both rural and urban residents maintain connections to pastoralism and nature in the twenty-first century. The long history of mobile pastoralism and its links to domestic animals, wildlife, grasslands, forests, and other resources herders relied on for human and ecological health and well-being, are embedded in the minds, values, and musics of both rural and urban residents. They are well-represented in sounds they value and use and music they create and share. Changes from mid-twentieth to early-twenty-first centuries brought by social, political, ecological, and economic events have affected both urban and rural communities, generating loss of cultural production in some settings and the growth and development of new music that is filled with images of past practices.

The rural representations of nature, especially among pastoralists who continue to engage directly with the sources of valued sounds (their domestic animals, wildlife, winds, and water) and the entities in their songs and melodies (nature and social and spiritual relationships in herding contexts), have direct relationships to their daily lives in each seasonal location. When they abandon their lifeways because of devastating weather events, changes in the land brought by industry, or to "improve" their lives by moving to urban or semi-urban settings, the sounds and much of the music are left behind. Yet the ever-increasing mobility of rural and urban peoples in the twenty-first century may mediate some of these divisions. The actual and imagined movement back and forth between rural and urban worlds encourages the promotion of sounds, sound-scapes, and musical practices through media, helping all residents of these two Mongolian regions to continue to have access to nature and pastoral values.

Notes

1. See our companion website, www.mongoliansoundworlds.org, for additional information on the musical traditions included in this volume.

2. Williams (2002:10) argues that major restructuring of land use in the region is rooted in Confucian elitist attitudes toward mobile pastoralists and political efforts drawn from a Marx-Lenin-Mao philosophy to hamper "national growth, scientific rationalism, and economic development."

3. Fewer than twenty percent of the twenty-five million residents are Mongol (Bulag 2010; NBS 2018).

4. For discussions of coexistence with animals and other beings, see Haraway (2008) and Tsing (2015); and on relationships in pastoral settings, see Fijn (2008; 2011) and Petitt and Hovorka (2020).

5. This region is part of the Altai-Sayan ecoregion that not only stretches across Russia and Mongolia, and includes parts of Kazakhstan and China as well.

6. The song Pegg cites (2001:179–80) is "Suny Delger Sar—Abundant Month of Summer."

7. Other scholars who have documented and discussed relationships between melody and landscape include Pegg (2001), Legrain (2009), and Yoon (2018b).

8. Unless otherwise noted all non-English words referenced in this section are Kazakh.

9. In Russia, the range is called Sailugem.

10. Petroglyphs from the middle Holocene (c. 6200–3000 BCE) in this region show the growth of steppe vegetation and herding as an economic practice. The petroglyphs from the late Holocene (since c. 2000 BCE) indicate greater dependence on horses in the daily life of the nomadic peoples in this location (UNESCO 2011).

11. A few Uriankhai artists at the theater play *tovshuur* and *tsuur*. The *morin khuur* is also sometimes played in ensemble with Kazakh instruments, especially *dombyra*.

12. Kazakh Chinese CDs and VCDs were available in Xinjiang cities like Altay where Kazakhs traveled for trade, and they were then sold at the local market in Ölgii.

13. The author is grateful to Almalgul Soltan and Janbolat Khurmarhan for their contributions to the translations of songs in this section.

References

Agarin, Timofey, and Līga Rudzīte. 2018. "Making Modern Mongolians: Gender Roles and Everyday Nation-building in Contemporary Mongolia." In *Informal National-*

ism after Communism: The Everyday Construction of Post-socialist Identities, edited by A. Polese, O. Seliverstova, E. Pawlusz, and J. Morris, 164–183. London: IB Tauris.

Baranovitch, Nimrod. 2016. "Ecological Degradation and Endangered Ethnicities: China's Minority Environmental Discourses as Manifested in Popular Songs." *Journal of Asian Studies* 75(1):181–205.

Batbold, D., et al. 2015. "National Biodiversity Program 2015–2025." Ulaanbaatar: Ministry of Environment, Green Development and Tourism. https://www.cbd.int/doc/world/mn/mn-nbsap-v2-en.pdf.

Batjargal, Z., et al. 1998. "Biological Diversity in Mongolia (First National Report)." Ulaanbaatar: Ministry for Nature and Environment in Mongolia. https://www.cbd.int/doc/world/mn/mn-nr-01-en.pdf.

Benwell, Ann Fenger. 2006. "Facing Gender Challenges in Post-Socialist Mongolia." In *Mongols from Country to City: Floating Boundaries, Pastoralism and City Life in the Mongol Lands*, edited by Ole Bruun and Li Narangoa, 110–139. Copenhagen: NIAS Press.

Braae, Christel. 2017. *Among Herders of Inner Mongolia: The Haslund-Christensen Collection at the National Museum of Denmark*. Aarhus: Aarhus University Press.

Bruun, Ole, and Li Narangoa, eds. 2006. "A New Moment in Mongol History: The Rise of the Cosmopolitan City." In *Mongols from Country to City: Floating Boundaries, Pastoralism and City Life in the Mongol Lands*, edited by Ole Bruun and Li Narangoa, 1–20. Copenhagen: NIAS Press.

Bulag, Uradyn E. 2010. "Alter/Native Mongolian Identity: From Nationality to Ethnic Group." In *Chinese Society: Change, Conflict and Resistance*, edited by Elizabeth J. Perry and Mark Selden, 261–287. London: Routledge.

Carrizo, Liliana. 2010 "Urtyn Duu: Performing Musical Landscapes and the Mongolian Nation." Master's thesis, University of Illinois at Urbana-Champaign.

Chuluunbaatar, Otgonbayar. 2013. "The Cuur as Endangered Musical Instrument of the Urianxai Ethnic Group in the Mongolian Altai Mountains." In *Studia Instrumentorum Musicae Popularis* (New Series) 3, edited by Gisa Jähnichen, 97–110. Münster: MV-Wissenschaft Verlag.

Conte, Thomas J. 2015. "The Effects of China's Grassland Contract Policy on Mongolian Herders' Attitudes towards Grassland Management in Northeastern Inner Mongolia." *Journal of Political Ecology* 22:79–97.

Curtet, Johanni. 2010. *Dörvön Berkh—Four Shagai Bones: Masters of Mongolian Overtone Singing*. CD. PAN Records.

D'Evelyn, Charlotte D. 2013. "Music between Worlds: Mongol Music and Ethnicity in Inner Mongolia, China." PhD diss., University of Hawai'i.

———. 2018. "Grasping Intangible Heritage and Reimagining Inner Mongolia: Folk-Artist Albums and a New Logic for Musical Representation in China." *Journal of Folklore Research* 55(1):21–48.

Dickinson, Debbie, and Michael Webber. 2007. "Environmental Resettlement and Development on the Steppes of Inner Mongolia, PRC." *Journal of Development Studies* 43(3):537–561.

Dovchin, Sender. 2011. "Performing Identity through Language: The Local Practices of Urban Youth Populations in Post-Socialist Mongolia." *Inner Asia* 13(2):315–333.

Dubuisson, Eva-Marie, and Anna Genina. 2011. "Claiming an Ancestral Homeland: Kazakh Pilgrimage and Migration in Inner Asia." *Central Asian Survey* 30(3–4):469–485.

Fang, Chuanglin, Haitao Ma, and Jing Wang. 2015. "A Regional Categorization for 'New-Type Urbanization' in China." *PLoS ONE* 10(8). doi:10.1371/journal.pone.0134253.

Fijn, Natasha. 2008. *Khangai Herds: An Observational Film in Nine Parts.* khangaiherds.wordpress.com.

———. 2011. *Living with Herds: Human-Animal Coexistence in Mongolia.* Cambridge, UK: Cambridge University Press.

Gunchinsuren, B., Jeffrey H. Altschul, and John W. Olsen, eds. 2011. *Protecting the Past, Preserving the Present Report on Phase 1 Activities of the Oyu Tolgoi Cultural Heritage Program Design for Ömnögovi Aimag.* The Mongolian International Heritage Team for Oyu Tolgoi, Ulaanbaatar. https://www.ot.mn/oyu-tolgoi-report-on-phase-1-activities-of-the-cultural-heritage-programme.

Han, Xingguo, Keith Owens, X. Ben Wu, Jianguo Wu, and Jianhui Huang. 2009. "The Grasslands of Inner Mongolia: A Special Feature." *Rangeland Ecological Management* 62:303–304.

Harrison, K. David. 2003. "Language Endangerment among the Tofa." *Cultural Survival Quarterly* 27(1):53–55.

———. 2004. "South Siberian Sound Symbolism." In *Languages and Prehistory of Central Siberia*, edited by Edward J. Vajda, 199–214. Amsterdam: John Benjamins Publishing Company.

Hamayon, Roberte. 1973. *Chants mongols et bouriates.* CD notes. Paris: Collection Musée de LHomme.

Haraway, Donna Jeanne. 2008. *When Species Meet.* Minneapolis: University of Minnesota.

Humphrey, Caroline. 1974. "Inside a Mongolian Tent." *New Society* 30(630):273.

Humphrey, Caroline, Marina Mongush, and B. Telengid. 1993. "Attitudes to Nature in Mongolia and Tuva: A Preliminary Report." *Nomadic Peoples* 33:51–61.

Hutchins, Kip. 2019. "Like a Lullaby: Song as Herding Tool in Rural Mongolia." *Journal of Ethnobiology* 39(3):445–459.

Jackson, Sara L. 2015a. "Dusty Roads and Disconnections: Perceptions of Dust from Unpaved Mining Roads in Mongolia's South Gobi Province." *Geoforum* 66:94–105.

———. 2015b. "Imagining the Mineral Nation: Contested Nation-Building in Mongolia." *Nationalities Papers* 43(3):437–456.

Jiang, Hong. 2005. "Grassland Management and Views of Nature in China since 1949: Regional Policies and Local Changes in Uxin Ju, Inner Mongolia." *Geoforum* 36:641–653.

Kendirbaeva, Gulnar. 1994. "Folklore and Folklorism in Kazakhstan." *Asian Folklore Studies* 53(1):97–123.

Krebs, Melanie. 2012. "From a Real Home to a Nation's Brand: On Stationary and Traveling Yurts." *Ab Imperio* 2:403–428.

Kunanbaeva, Alma. 2002. "Kazakh Music." In *The Garland Encyclopedia of World Music: The Middle East*, edited by V. Danielson, S. Marcus, and D. Reynolds, 949–964. New York: Routledge.

———. 2016. "Singing Traditions of the Kazakhs." In *The Music of Central Asia*, edited by Theodore Levin, Saida Daukeyeva, and Elmira Köchümkulova. Bloomington: Indiana University Press.

Legrain, Laurent. 2009. "Confrontation on the River Ivd, or, How Does Music Act in Social Life?" *Inner Asia* 11:335–358.

Levin, Theodore, and Valentina Süzükei. 2006. *Where Rivers and Mountains Sing: Sound, Music, and Nomadism in Tuva and Beyond*. Bloomington: Indiana University Press.

Li, Wenjun, and Lynn Huntsinger. 2011. "China's Grassland Contract Policy and its Impacts on Herder Ability to Benefit in Inner Mongolia: Tragic Feedbacks." *Ecology and Society* 16(2). http://www.ecologyandsociety.org/vol16/iss2/art1/.

Lindskog, Benedikte. 2016. "Ritual Offerings to Ovoos among Nomadic Halh Herders of West-central Mongolia." *Études mongoles et sibériennes, centrasiatiques et tibétaines* 47:1–21.

Ma, Wenjing, Gang Feng, and Qing Zhang. 2016. "Status of Nature Reserves in Inner Mongolia, China." *Sustainability* 8(9):889. doi:10.3390/su8090889.

Marsh, Peter K. 2006. "Beyond the Soviet Houses of Culture: Rural Responses to Urban Cultural Policies in Contemporary Mongolia." In *Mongols from Country to City*, edited by O. Bruun and L. Narangoa, 290–304. Copenhagen: NIAS Press.

———. 2018. "Film, Video and Multimedia Reviews: *Mongolian Bling, Live from UB*." *Ethnomusicology* 62(1):157–162.

MSIS (Mongolian Statistical Information Service). 2019. National Statistical Office. Ulaanbaatar. http://1212.mn/.

NBS (National Bureau of Statistics). 2018. *China Statistical Yearbook*. National Bureau of Statistics of China. http://www.stats.gov.cn/tjsj/ndsj/2018/indexeh.htm.

Pedersen, Morten A. 2006. "Where Is the Centre? The Spatial Distribution of Power in Post-Socialist Rural Mongolia." In *Mongols from Country to City: Floating Boundaries, Pastoralism and City Life in the Mongol Lands*, edited by Ole Bruun, and Li Narangoa, 82–104. Copenhagen: NIAS Press.

Pegg, Carole. 1992. "Mongolian Conceptualizations of Overtone Singing (xöömii)." *British Journal of Ethnomusicology* 1(1):31–54.

———. 2001. *Mongolian Music, Dance, & Oral Narrative: Performing Diverse Identities*. Seattle: The University of Washington Press.

Petitt, Andrea, and Alice Hovorka. 2020. "Women and Cattle 'Becoming-With' in Botswana." *Humanimalia*. 12(1):145–166.

Pfeiffer, Michaela, Delgermaa Vanya, Colleen Davison, Oyunaa Lkhagvasuren, Lesley Johnston, and Craig R. Janes. 2017. "Harnessing Opportunities for Good Governance of Health Impacts of Mining Projects in Mongolia: Results of a Global Partnership." *Globalization and Health* 13(1). doi 10.1186/s12992-017-0261-5.

Plueckhahn, Rebekah. 2013. "Musical Sociality: The Significance of Musical Engagement among the Mongolian Altai Urianghai." PhD diss., Australian National University.

Post, Jennifer C. 2017. "Ecological Knowledge: Collaborative Management and Musical Production in Western Mongolia." In *Ethnomusicology: A Contemporary Reader Volume II*, edited by Jennifer C. Post, 161–179. New York: Routledge Press.

———. 2019. "Songs, Settings, Sociality: Human and Ecological Well-being in Western Mongolia." *Journal of Ethnobiology* 39(3):371–391.

———. 2020. "21st Century Trading Routes in Mongolia: Changing Pastoral Soundscapes and Lifeways." In *Silk Roads: From Local Realities to Global Narratives*, edited by Jeffrey D. Lerner and Yaohua Shi, 177–196. Oxford: Oxbow Books.

———. Forthcoming. "Making and Growing End-blown Flutes in the Mongolian Steppes." In *Instrumental Lives*, edited by Helen Rees.

Reichl, Karl. 1992. *Turkic Oral Epic Poetry: Traditions, Forms. Poetic Structure.* New York: Garland.

Rogers, Sarah, and Mark Wang. 2006. "Environmental Resettlement and Social Dis/Rearticulation in Inner Mongolia, China." *Population and Environment* 28(1):41–68.

Sanchez, Jamie N. 2013. "Cultural Colonialization: The Displacement of Mongolians in Inner Mongolia." SPECTRA 2 (2). http://doi.org/10.21061/spectra.v2i2.269.

Simonov, Eugene A., and Thomas D. Dahmer. 2008. *Amur-Heilong River Basin Reader.* Hong Kong: Ecosystems.

Sneath, David. 2001. "Notions of Rights over Land and the History of Mongolian Pastoralism." *Inner Asia* 3:41–59.

———. 2006. "The Rural and the Urban in Pastoral Mongolia." In *Mongols from Country to City: Floating Boundaries, Pastoralism and City Life in the Mongol Lands*, O. Bruun and L. Narangoa, eds., 140–161. Copenhagen: NIAS Press.

———. 2010. "Political Mobilization and the Construction of Collective Identity in Mongolia." *Central Asian Survey* 29(3):251–267.

———. 2014. "Nationalising Civilisational Resources: Sacred Mountains and Cosmo-political Ritual in Mongolia." *Asian Ethnicity* 15 (4):458–472.

Soni, Sharad K. 2003. "Kazakhs in Post-Socialist Mongolia." *Himalayan and Central Asian Studies* 7(2):100–115.

Stépanoff, Charles. 2012. "Human-animal 'Joint Commitment' in a Reindeer Herding System." *HAU: Journal of Ethnographic Theory* 2(2):287–312.

Tseren, P. B. 1996. "Traditional Pastoral Practice of the Oirat Mongols and their Relationship with the Environment." In *Culture and Environment in Inner Asia.* Vol. 2, edited by C. Humphrey and D. Sneath, 147–159. Cambridge: White Horse Press.

Tsing, Anna. 2015. *The Mushroom at the End of the World: On the Possibility of Life in Capitalist Ruins.* Princeton: Princeton University Press.

Uluqpan, Beket, and Hans D. Knapp. 2012. "Protection of the Natural and Cultural Heritage of the Mongolian Altai." *Erforschung biologischer Ressourcen der Mongolei* 12:335–352.

UNESCO. 2011. "Petroglyphic Complexes of the Mongolian Altai." *World Heritage List.* https://whc.unesco.org/en/list/1382/.

Upton, Caroline. 2010. "Living Off the Land: Nature and Nomadism in Mongolia." *Geoforum* 41:865–874.

Weina, Oyuna. 2018. "'You Can't Sing Urtyn Duu if You Don't Know How to Ride a Horse': Urtyn Duu in Alshaa, Inner Mongolia." *Asian Music* 49(2):4–33.

Williams, Dee Mack. 2002. *Beyond Great Walls: Environment, Identity, and Development on the Chinese Grasslands of Inner Mongolia.* Stanford: Stanford University Press.

Wu, Sarina. 2019. "To Share or Not to Share: Contested Heritage in Inner Mongolia, China—A Case of Overtone Singing (Khoomei)." *International Journal of Heritage Studies* 26(3):1–14.

Xu, GuangHua, and JianGuo Wu. 2016. "Social-ecological Transformations of Inner Mongolia: A Sustainability Perspective." *Ecological Processes* 5(1):23:1–11.

Yagi, Fuki. 2018. "The Theater Functioning as Music School: A Case Study of Modified Musical Instruments and the Orchestra of Kazakh Folk Musical Instruments in Bayan-Ölgii, Mongolia." In Japanese. *Sokendai Culture and Science Study* 14:109–126.

———. 2019. "Systematization of Kazakh Music in Mongolia: Activities of Theater and Radio Station during the Soviet Era." *Asian Ethnicity* 21(3):413–424.

Yoon, Sunmin. 2018a. "Echoes of Mongolia's Sensory Landscape in Shurankhai's 'Harmonized' Urtyn Duu." *Musicology Research* 4:121–144.

———. 2018b. "What's in the Song? *Urtyn duu* as Sonic 'Ritual' among Mongolian Herder-singers." *MUSICultures* 45(1–2):92–111.

———. 2019. "Mobilities, Experienced and Performed, in Mongolia's *Urtyn Duu* Tradition." *Asian Music* 50(1):47–77.

PART TWO

Ethnicity and Diversity

Musical Journeys in Inner Mongolia and Beyond

TAMIR HARGANA AND
CHARLOTTE D'EVELYN

The passage below is the product of an informal interview conversation between Tamir Hargana, an Inner Mongolian musician currently based in Chicago, Illinois, and Charlotte D'Evelyn. The text is not an exact transcript of the conversation, but it is a collaborative rendering of Tamir's musical life story. The Old Barga and New Barga Banners mentioned in this passage refer to the regional subdivisions that still exist in Inner Mongolia, historical relics of the administrative military divisions set up during the Manchu Qing Dynasty (1644–1911).

My name is Tamir Hargana and I am a member of the group of Mongols known as the Barga clan. I was born in 1991 in New Barga East Banner and spent most of my childhood in Old Barga Banner.[1]

My parents, Sugur Hargana (1960–present, raised in New Barga East Banner) and Erdengua Duulagchin (1965–present, raised in Old Barga Banner), began learning long-song from the age of thirteen or fourteen from a famous teacher by the name of Badmaa (1929–1999). Badmaa is one of the earliest great long-song teachers in Inner Mongolia and taught many prominent singers, including the famous married singers Buren Bayar (1960–2018) and Urnaa (~1960–present). My parents met in Badmaa's studio and eventually ended up getting married.

After they finished art school, my parents went back to their own villages and then eventually found positions together in his mother's home region of Old Barga Banner. I was already three or four years old at this point. I remember the time before we moved when we lived in my dad's village in New Barga East Banner, where my dad was employed at the local *ulaanmöchir*, a type of arts troupe in Inner Mongolia.[2] My parents were considered official government

FIGURE (INTERLUDE) 2.1. Tamir Hargana. Photo by Jim Wilkinson (used with permission).

workers and had secure employment for life, which included food and housing and a living salary. We stayed in the dormitory that was set up for the arts troupe performers that functioned as both a living and rehearsal space. Even though I was very young at the time, I remember hearing music coming at all times of the day from the second-floor dancing studio and the first-floor ensemble rehearsal room.

Today, my father is professor of long-song at Hulunbuir University, but is still a member of his old *ulaanmöchir*. He is well-known in Hulunbuir music circles for his work as a performer, teacher, and song collector. He personally transcribed and notated three thousand Barga long-songs, many of which he published in a collection. This work earned him recognition as an official inheritor of Barga long-songs in China. He also carries the title of "National Performer of the First Rank" (C: *guojia yiji yanyuan*).

My parents spent most of their time traveling with the *ulaanmöchir* out in remote grassland areas and only occasionally came back to visit me. My maternal grandmother was my primary caregiver at this time, so I had a lot of freedom to roam around in our local grassland with other neighboring kids. We rode horses a lot, practically every day. Once I made it to elementary school age, my parents realized that I could use some more attention and guidance, including musical education, so they tried to stay behind more often to look after my studies. After some limited success learning the electric keyboard from my dad, I decided I wanted to learn the horsehead fiddle.

When I first saw the horsehead fiddle, it immediately sparked my attention. I had already developed a closeness with horses and the instrument seemed to somehow magically channel the sound and spirit of a horse. That sound just hit me. I tried casually picking up the fiddle a few times and played around with it when I was young, but never learned formally until I was in late elementary school. Seeing my interest, my father sent me to take weekly lessons with his co-worker Daruu, a young fiddle player of the Daur ethnic group. It was not long before I gained enough musical skill to start performing publicly at local events and school shows.

For high school, I moved from my small banner town to the city center of Hailar, the capital of the Hulunbuir region in Inner Mongolia. One of the benefits of living in Hailar was continuing my music studies from a fiddle instructor at Hulunbuir Art Institute named Nachin. I started performing regularly throughout my high school years and began to think about music as a college major and career.

My teacher Nachin told me that I would need to move to Hohhot if I wanted to have a shot at getting into college. He introduced me to his own teacher, Erdenbökh, and encouraged me to attend his private horsehead fiddle boarding school in Hohhot, the capital city of Inner Mongolia. Over the phone, Erdenbökh warned my parents that this road would be rough and would require extreme discipline and many hours of daily practice. My parents, appreciating the seriousness of this program and satisfied that it would push me to work hard, signed me up immediately.

For my third year in high school, I moved all the way to Hohhot to attend Erdenbökh's fiddle school. This was a huge transition. Hailar had already seemed like a big city for me, so Hohhot (1,500 km away from Hailar) was on a whole different level. This was a completely new life for me and changed everything about my musical perspective. Erdenbökh challenged me to think carefully about my purpose and intention for music and made me realize that playing music is something that requires extreme discipline, but also artistry and internal enjoyment. I felt that everything I had done up to this point in my life was just a prelude to this moment.

Every year there are nearly five or six hundred horsehead fiddle students who audition for only a handful of spots at the top universities in Inner Mongolia. The prestigious Inner Mongolia Art College (IMAC, known at the time as Inner Mongolia University Art College) accepts only eight horsehead fiddle students each year. Inner Mongolia Normal University, which requires higher academic ability than IMAC, recruits ten or fewer students each year. The competition is intense and students from all ages and very high skill levels apply, including students who began training for college starting at age ten or professional performing artists who want to go back to school to get a college degree. Students like myself who only began their training in high school had no chance to get in.

It just so happened that the year I was applying for college was also the year that the Inner Mongolia Art College opened up a new major: the study of horsehead fiddle with a concentration in throat-singing (*khöömii*). This major was the result of a successful petition to the college, initiated by Erdenbökh in 2009 and signed by three hundred students. At this time, throat-singing was in an early state of revival in Inner Mongolia and there were only a few teachers from Mongolia living and teaching throat-singing in Hohhot. One of those teachers was Mendbayar, a young performer from Mongolia with a clear and powerful *isgeree khöömii* (whistle-style of throat-singing). Mendbayar was initially invited to Hohhot by Erdenbökh to join a seven-member musical group called Ayin Ensemble and later became the first full-time throat-singing teacher at the Inner Mongolia Art College. Many of us in Erdenbökh's studio began studying throat-singing with Mendbayar while continuing to improve our horsehead fiddle skills.

I was lucky enough to join the inaugural class of "horsehead fiddle and throat-singing" majors at Inner Mongolia Art College in the fall of 2010, through a combination of my horsehead fiddle ability and my new abilities with throat-singing. We were an experimental class for sure and had different mentors working with us during each of their four years in the program. We spent the first year under the tutelage of Mendbayar to learn *isgeree khöömii* (whistle throat-singing) and *shakhaa* (the tense vocal technique that is the foundation for *isgeree*). The second year, we studied with Nars, the leader of Anda Union, who formed us into an ensemble called Zamch Band and taught us to combine throat-singing together with traditional instruments. Anda Union was the earliest and most well-respected ensemble in Inner Mongolia to incorporate throat-singing with traditional folk songs and there were similar ensembles springing up all over the place at that time. Nars was the first teacher who introduced me to Tyvan throat-singing styles such as *ezengileer* (a style that sounds like horse trotting) and the Tyvan *doshpuluur* plucked lute (the three-stringed version of the Mongolian two-string *tovshuur*). I immediately fell in love with the bluesy sound of the *doshpuluur* and we all enthusiastically embraced Tyvan styles and sounds that year. During the third year of our studies, the college, recognizing the growing enthusiasm for Tyvan throat-singing, invited a Tyvan singer named Nachin to come teach at IMAC. Nachin is a specialist in *kargyraa* (the chest style of Tyvan throat-singing) and master of the *igil* (skin-faced, two-string fiddle from Tuva). He taught us a variety of Tyvan folk songs that year and introduced us to the meaning of these songs, both culturally and linguistically (since Tyvan is a foreign language for us). Our fourth year was spent studying with another professor from Mongolia, an expert in Altai styles of throat-singing, who taught us songs and styles from this region.

The summer before our graduation, a group of us participated in the 2013 International Throat-Singing Competition in Kyzyl, Tyva. This event was the first time that Inner Mongolians and Mongolians were invited to Tyva. We had a full delegation from Inner Mongolia, including students and members of the Inner Mongolia Song and Dance Theater (*Neimenggu Gewujuyuan*). Inner Mongolian performers took home many prizes that year, including the first prize for ensemble performance and first prize for *kargyraa*. For the all-around category (which included solo and ensemble singing, as well as technical and stylistic versatility), I received second place.

This competition was an important turning point for throat-singing in Inner Mongolia. Resources began pouring in from all directions. It was only a few years prior that not many people in China really knew much about throat-singing at all. It was relatively hard to find a throat-singing teacher in the early 2000s, but by the year 2013 there were many instructors teaching throat-singing and even many ways to study online. We started hearing a saying that if a tree fell on ten musicians in Inner Mongolia, nine out of ten would be horsehead fiddlers, eight of those fiddlers would be able to throat-sing, and seven would be named Nars.

Our inaugural class of throat-singing majors graduated in 2014, right at the peak of this energy for throat-singing in Inner Mongolia. That summer our performance together as Zamch Band gained first prize in the ensemble category at the annual International Throat-Singing Competition, held for the first time that year in China instead of Tyva. Managers from the Inner Mongolia Song and Dance Theater, a government-sponsored ensemble, approached us after our performance and essentially handed us lifetime employment contracts after our successful performance that day.

At this point, I saw two roads in front of me. One led to a reasonably comfortable life as a salaried government performer, developing my work with my classmates as part of Zamch Band. The other road—pursuing my studies in the United States—was more unknown, but somehow stood out to me as the right choice. In the summer of 2014, I quit my job at the Inner Mongolia Song and Dance Theater, packed my bags, and left for the United States. Everyone thought I was completely crazy.

I had already been to the United States twice during my college years and the experiences were unforgettable. My first trip was part of an ongoing exchange program that IMAC has with Leland and Gray High School in Vermont. The second trip was a delegation from Inner Mongolia that included a tour of the southern and western U.S. and an invited performance at a year-of-the-horse festival in the state of Kentucky. I had my first introduction to American jazz on these trips and even had an opportunity to play with a jazz ensemble. It was experiences like these, which broadened my musical knowledge and continued to open up my musical world, that made me determined to come back to the U.S. to continue my studies.

When I arrived back in Lexington, Kentucky, in the fall of 2014, I could barely speak a word of English. I could not even begin a college degree program before getting up to speed on my language skills, so I spent that whole first year learning English. During that year, I had some incredible musical experiences, including collaborating with bluegrass musicians and even joining a gig with a death metal band.

I gave a variety of performances and workshops at the University of Kentucky to introduce Mongolian music to American audiences and started thinking about what it takes to bridge cultural gaps and to appeal to audience tastes. Our official government-sponsored tours always filled the seats with audiences, but when I performed on my own it was hard to fill the seats. I also noticed that the audiences were intrigued, but not particularly moved by my music or interested to know more. Some thought my *isgeree khöömii* (whistle throat-singing) was a trick or sound effect instead of something with cultural or artistic value. In contrast, when I was collaborating with bluegrass musicians, listeners had an easier entry point to appreciate my throat-singing and horsehead fiddle playing. Since Kentucky audiences were familiar with Old-time American music, we could gradually throw in Mongolian sounds and draw them in that way.

While I was in Kentucky, I met Dr. Han Kuo-Han, the founder of the world music program at Northern Illinois University (NIU). Dr. Han encouraged me to apply to the Master's degree program in World Music Performance at NIU, where I could add new knowledge and skills and continue learning how to collaborate with musicians from different cultural backgrounds.

I enrolled at Northern Illinois University (NIU) in 2015 and received the MA in World Music Performance in 2017. These two years provided me even more opportunities for growth as a musician. I had a chance to participate in a variety of ensembles there, including the Chinese Ensemble, Gamelan Ensemble, and

Middle Eastern Ensemble. I even took a short trip to Bali, Indonesia through a university program to learn gamelan in a rural village. At NIU, a few of us came together to form a fusion ensemble called Northern Wind Trio, featuring handpan and jazz guitar together with my Mongolian and Tyvan music.

My time at NIU enabled me to make a smooth transition to living in Chicago after graduation. I began teaching throat-singing at the Old Town School of Folk Music and performing on occasion at the University of Chicago or for the Mongolian community in Chicago (which has one of the largest concentrations of Mongolian nationals in the U.S.). I have been able to keep up my musical career through lessons, local performances, invited workshops at university campuses across the United States, and annual events put on by Mongolian communities, such as the summer Naadam festival in Bloomington, Indiana, and the November Chinggis Khan Ceremony in Princeton, New Jersey.

One of the best musical experiences during my time in the United States was my short time as a member of the folk metal band Tengger Cavalry. This band was formed in Beijing in 2009 and moved to New York in 2013 under the leadership of Nature Ganganbaigal, a talented musician and singer with part-Mongol ancestry. My very first appearance with Tengger Cavalry was a sold-out performance at Carnegie Hall in September of 2018. After that we took a two-month tour all across the United States and Canada. Audiences went crazy about our music! I learned how to lose myself in the heavy metal sound—to totally forget about playing right or wrong notes and just focus on the energy exchange between the performers and the audience.

After our concerts, audience members and metalheads came up to me with enthusiastic comments and questions, wanting to know all about the *kargyraa* style (deep, chest style of Tyvan throat-singing that works so well in heavy metal) and asking me things like, "Hey, your music is so cool. Is it connected to war or shamanism?" I saw this as a great sign. They were genuinely intrigued about these sounds and wanted to know more about the history and culture. Bands like Tengger Cavalry and the Hu Band (a newly formed hard rock band from Mongolia that went viral on YouTube in 2018) have unexpectedly helped grow the world's interest in Mongolian music. Neither of these ensembles really intended to use Mongolian music in traditional ways, but the Mongolian instruments and throat-singing combined with hard rock and metal gave audiences something new, but also familiar at the same time.

Unfortunately, Nature passed away in 2019 so we are unsure about the next steps for Tengger Cavalry at this point. I will never forget my experience touring with the band, the musical experiences we shared, and friendships we made together in the American metal community.

I am amazed by the ways that the horsehead fiddle has shaped my life. As soon as I touched the fiddle it started taking me to bigger places. Each time I needed to advance I had to travel to a bigger and more central location—from the grassland countryside, to our local banner town, to the capital of Hulunbuir (Hailar), to the capital city of Inner Mongolia (Hohhot), and later to the United States (Kentucky and later Chicago). My music background continues to bring me new opportunities and to meet new people. I consider the horsehead fiddle like my ticket to the whole world and look forward to seeing where my music will bring me in the years to come.

Notes

1. These sub-regions of Hulunbuir are across from the Dornod aimag (province) of Mongolia, not far from the Russian border. The region is home to a number of ethnic groups, including Barga Mongols.

2. *Ulaanmöchir* (literally "red branch") refers to the traveling song and dance ensembles that were set up in Inner Mongolia during the communist period for the purpose of putting remote herders and village people in touch with government messages through the performing arts. Some of these herders did not realize that their lands were under control of the People's Republic of China, so one purpose of the troupes was to "educate" the herders about the new China and the new society that was being built. The *ulaanmöchir* continued as a song and dance institution in Inner Mongolia even after the Mao period, although the tone of the performances has become less political.

CHAPTER 2

Music and Ethnic Identity in Inner Mongolia

CHARLOTTE D'EVELYN

Until the year 2002, my mental map of China did not include Inner Mongolia. That year as an exchange student in Shanghai, I gained my first exposure to Chinese music and the two-string fiddle (*erhu*), but also serendipitously had my first encounters with Mongolian culture and music. My roommate, who happened to be from the country of Mongolia, held late-night drinking and singing parties with her Mongolian friends. Far from being a nuisance, these parties and their music stimulated my interest in Mongolia, and our conversations introduced me to the existence of an Inner Mongolia Autonomous Region within China, separate from Mongolia. These experiences from 2002 led me to my current ethnomusicological career and to the fieldwork visits to Inner Mongolia and Mongolia that inform the subject of this chapter.

Awareness of Inner Mongolia still remains limited largely due to the difficulties of reconciling Inner Mongolia's position vis a vis Mongolia and its illegibility using the logic of borders and nation-states.[1] This chapter sheds light on this lesser-known southern half of the Mongolian steppe, focusing on the unique music and ethnic landscape that sets contemporary Inner Mongolia apart from Mongolia. The musical ecosystems that I encountered in urban Inner Mongolia and urban Mongolia, though interconnected, differ in profound ways. Despite an increasing closeness in institutional ties and connections between musicians in Hohhot and Ulaanbaatar (the respective capitals and centers of musical activity in Inner Mongolia and Mongolia, respectively), music in these two regions is categorized, conceptualized, and regulated in vastly different ways that influence ideas about music, if not musical sounds themselves. While Mongolia and Inner Mongolia share many treasured musical practices, particularly *urtyn duu* (long-song) and the *morin khuur* (horsehead fiddle), there are a range of local, sub-regional genres and practices that are unique to each of these greater

FIGURE 2.1. Hohhot-based ensemble, Anda Union (used with permission).

regions. Below I discuss some of the conceptual and political frameworks that structure musical practice in Inner Mongolia and introduce a small selection of music styles unique to this region.

This chapter is organized around the following topics: 1) regional diversity, 2) political-artistic movements since the Mao era, and 3) a case study on the neo-traditional ensemble, Anda Union. My work draws from previous studies of music in Inner Mongolia in the English language (Pegg 1989, 2001; Baranovitch 2003, 2009; Henochowicz 2008, 2011; Stokes 2013; Weina 2018) and landmark studies in the Chinese language (Ulanji 1998; Khogjilt 2006; Botolt 2015), as well as six field visits to the region since 2009. I rely on over a decade of data gained through formal interviews, observations, one-on-one music lessons, listening sessions, rehearsals, concert attendance, and ongoing social media communications with hundreds of musicians and local scholars. I recognize my status as a cultural outsider and am indebted to the many, many people who have trusted me with their stories, without which this chapter would not be possible.[2]

Inner Mongolia and the Conundrum of Ethnic Diversity

The Inner Mongolia Autonomous Region (IMAR) is the third largest territorial region of the People's Republic of China (PRC) and home to six million registered ethnic Mongols. Established in 1947, two years prior to the founding of the PRC, Inner Mongolia owes its name to divisions that began during the Qing Dynasty (1644–1911)—between "Inner Mongolia" (*Neimenggu* in Chinese, *Övör Mongol* in Mongolian) and "Outer Mongolia" (*Waimenggu* in Chinese, *Ar Mongol* in Mongolian). These territorial divisions are largely based on geographic separation between regions north and south of the Gov' Desert. Due to its looser administrative ties to the Qing Dynasty, "Outer Mongolia" (henceforth Mongolia) was able to declare its independence after the fall of the dynasty in 1911, whereas Inner Mongolia became a site of contested sovereignty for thirty-five years (Atwood 2002; Bulag 2010) and ultimately became incorporated as an autonomous region of the PRC (Bulag 2002, 2006).

Before the era of nation states, a variety of Turko-Mongolic ethnic groups migrated across the expansive region to the north and northwest of the central Chinese plain. While these groups shared commonalities in lifestyle (mobile pastoralism) and spiritual practices (animism, shamanism, and later Buddhism), they exhibited—and today still exhibit—a great deal of regional diversity in linguistic dialect, clothing, diet, and of course, musical practices. Contemporary borders, fixed provincial boundaries, and nationally recognized ethnicity categories do little to represent premodern communal identities of these mobile groups.

By the mid-1950s, Mongolians in China became recognized as a single "minority nationality" (*xiaoshu minzu*) under the new fifty-six nationalities system (Mullaney 2010). Far from homogenous, most of these Mongolians (*mengguzu*) distinguish themselves from one another based on a wide number of *yastan* (literally "bone group," *buluo* in Chinese) sub-ethnic or Mongol clan group affiliations, such as Barga, Üzemchin, Chakhar, or Torguud. Other more remote Mongolic groups, such as the Oirad who live in parts of the Xinjiang Uyghur Autonomous Region and the Buriad who straddle areas of northeastern Hulunbuir through Mongolia to southern Siberia, have linguistic and historical reasons for claiming their own *minzu* category, but were still categorized as "Mongolians" by Chinese ethnologists and culture workers during the 1950s.[3] Ironically, despite all government efforts to represent Mongols as a homogenous ethnic minority group subordinate to the Han Chinese, Mongols across Inner Mongolia, Xinjiang, and other neighboring regions often emphasize more differences between one another than similarities.

In Inner Mongolia, sub-ethnic identities are sometimes, but not always linked to districts and place names. Under the Qing Dynasty, many of *yastan* labels became attached to administrative, territorial divisions associated with the military banner system (Crossley 2006; Elliott 2001), a system that still lingers in many of the banner regions (*khoshuu* in Mongolian; *qi* in Chinese) in Inner Mongolia, such as today's Khorchin (*Ke'erqin*) Banners, Barga (*Ba'erhu*) Banners, and Üzemchin (*Wuzhumuqin*) Banners. Inner Mongols continue to identify themselves according to these region-based clan names, even when they have been dislocated from their home regions due to migration or urban resettlement. Those I met in the music community reinforce a set of features that distinguish regional music, cuisine, habits, and personality traits connected to these sub-ethnic clan groups. My first experience doing research in Inner Mongolia left me overwhelmed with the task of sorting out what musicians meant when they referred with precision and insistence to the representative musical features and genres of each recognized region, such as the regional styles of long-song (*urtyn duu*) from Shilingol, Hulunbuir, and Alashan; narrative songs (*ülger, kholboo*) uniquely varied among the Khorchin, Ar Khorchin, and Ordos regions; and the varied names given to box fiddles across the western (*ikil*), central (*khiil khuur* and *morin khuur*), and eastern (*choor*) regions of Xinjiang and Inner Mongolia. This localized sense of ethnic and sub-ethnic difference retains a vocabulary of features, hierarchies, and even stereotypes with which most Mongols in China are distinctly aware. For instance, the Khorchin and Ar Khorchin Mongols from the Jirim region of Inner Mongolia are numerically populous and have tended to hold positions of power, but have been subject to ridicule and marginalization in certain settings due to their thick dialect (Borchigud 1996, Bulag 2003). These northeastern Mongols were some of the first to transition to sedentary agriculture, to adopt Chinese and Manchu loanwords, and to adopt Chinese influences into their culture, cuisine, and music.

Further complicating this picture of regional diversity in Inner Mongolia, individuals' Mongol identities may be inflected according to urban or rural upbringings, whether and to what degree they speak the Mongolian language, whether or not they attended Mongolian language primary schools (*minzu xuexiao* in Chinese), and their overall level of assimilation into Chinese culture (*hanhua*, Sinicization). My friends and collaborators in Inner Mongolia define this last point in a variety of ways, including mannerisms as seemingly subtle as "speaking too loud in restaurants" (a sign of adopting Chinese habits).

The linguistic and dialectical diversity of these Mongols in China challenges the noticeably more stable notion of "Mongol-ness" that exists in the nation of Mongolia. For Mongolian nationals, "being Mongol" generally is associated with traits of the Khalkha majority ethnic group (Bulag 1998) and at its worst, is defined in opposition to anything associated with Chineseness (being Mongol means being "not Chinese") (Billé 2015). Bulag (1998) writes about the Soviet-era, Khalkh-oriented nationalism that consciously excluded the non-Khalkh Inner Mongols due to their presumed assimilation into Chinese culture.

Mongols in China have the complex challenge of negotiating their own cultural and linguistic hybridity, their dislocation from mobile pastoralism due to rapid urbanization and forced "ecological resettlement" (Zhang 2012), and increasing challenges related to language maintenance (Atwood 2020, Bilik 1998, Bulag 2003). They are challenged by a decades-long separation and isolation from the nation of Mongolia (particularly during the years of 1956 to 1990 from the beginning of the Sino-Soviet split until the year of Mongolia's democratic revolution), in addition to their status as a diverse group of sub-ethnic Mongol clans, diverse in aspects of linguistic dialect, cultural customs, and both traditional and contemporary musical practices (styles, genres, and instruments). My work investigating the variegated experiences of ethnic inclusion and exclusion in Inner Mongolia points to the inherent instability of ethnic identity, varied as it is in different contexts, within a variety of relationships, and from insider and outsider perspectives. Mongol ethnic identity, like its music, is diverse and contested; Mongols speak and sing in diverse voices, manifested in dialectical differences and in musical styles.

Insider understandings of what it means to be Mongol in China are as diverse as the people themselves. Outsider-oriented representations of Inner Mongols predominate in the Chinese media, however, offering Han Chinese viewers very little sense of nuance, complexity, diversity, or internal dissent in how Mongols choose to express themselves on the stage. National recognition and valuation of local diversity in Inner Mongolia has appeared only within the past decade through the lens of national heritage projects. The next section offers a brief summary of the changing politics of representation that Mongols have experienced in China from the Mao period until today, which contrasts homogenizing efforts of state policy with the diversity of identities just described.

Minorities on Stage from the Mao Era to Today

During the Mao Zedong era (1949–1976), music in China was used as a tool to instill national unity and to instill socialist values among the masses, a project that drew inspiration and guidance from Mao's famous Yan'an Talks on Literature and Art (McDougall 1980; Schein 2000; Rees 2000; Baranovitch 2003). Researchers were sent to distant locations across China to collect, rearrange, translate, and disseminate regional folk songs, including songs from China's ethnic minorities (Wong 1984, Mackerras 1995). Newly arranged songs and compositions were performed in elaborate, large-scale concerts of ethnic song and dance (called *huibao yanchu* in Chinese) for important occasions and as entertainment for local work units. In Inner Mongolia, troupes called *Ulaanmöchir* in Mongolian (red branch) even traveled to distant grassland locations to perform for local herders and to continue collecting folk music for future arrangements.

In the 1950s, select Mongol musicians who had enough musical background and ability in the Chinese language were admitted into newly opened, state-run conservatories in China. These included Central Conservatory (established in 1949 in Zhangjiakou, the capital of Inner Mongolia at the time, and later moved to Beijing) and the Inner Mongolia Art Academy (originally established in

1951 in Zhangjiakou and moved to Hohhot in 1957). In the process of adapting minority folk songs, Han and Mongol composers were encouraged to enhance the mass nature of the songs, to apply party ideologies, and moreover to distill a set of iconic musical "ethnic qualities" (*minzu tese, minzu fengge*) that could be used as a vocabulary for future compositions.

The optimism of the 1950s, including celebration of minority diversity, gave way during the political campaigns and turmoil of the Great Leap Forward era (1958–1960) and the Cultural Revolution (1966–1976). From the 1960s until the death of Mao, Chinese policies toward minorities emphasized national conformity and punished expressions of minority culture as signs of ethnic separatism (*minzu fenlie*). Songs during this period were composed in homophonic mass-song style, which existed prior to 1958 (e.g., "Song of Mongol-Han Unity" of 1948), but now dominated the musical landscape and reflected the propagandistic political campaigns of the 1960s and 1970s (e.g., "Building an Iron and Steel City on the Grassland" of 1958 and "Herders Sing of the Communist Party" composed in 1972).

At the death of Mao in 1976 and the conclusion of the Cultural Revolution, China entered a new phase in its history. In the 1980s Deng Xiaoping opened China to the world after many years of closed-door policies, and economic liberalization took the place of staunch political ideologies. Since the 1980s, Mandarin-language songs by Mongol and Han composers have continued to appear in state song-and-dance troupe performances, but also in media and commercial settings, the most notable of which is tourism. In the 1980s, the IMAR government reinvigorated programs to promote Mongol arts, largely as a way to make up for the devastations of the Cultural Revolution (see Jankowiak 1988, 1993; Baranovitch 2001). The Inner Mongolia Party Committee at this time declared its decree to "Build a Great Region of Nationality Culture" (*jianshe minzu wenhua daqu*), which became the basis for a general policy for the promotion and marketing of Inner Mongolian performing arts through tourism. The basis for such an arts policy seems to come at a time when many of China's interior regions, those largely inhabited by minority peoples, facing a paucity of support from the central government, needed to market their ethnic culture in order to survive in Deng-era China (Oakes 2000, Hillman 2003).

Large segments of the Han Chinese population, particularly those in modernized urban areas along the coast, felt and continue to feel strong fascination with the minority "other." Organized trips to minority villages, including grassland *ger* (yurt) camps in Inner Mongolia, offer opportunities for Han Chinese tourists to temporarily escape the alienation of modern life and to experience a window into an imagined past (Gladney 1994). Chinese national and local governments promote tourism among minority cultures of the northwest and southwest as a way to stage orthodox representations of these cultures, while appealing to the fantasies of the Han masses at the same time. Thomas Mullaney (2010:125) writes that the fifty-six *minzu* paradigm, used as a logic for state unity since 1949, became a new logic for tourism and commodification of minorities in the 1980s.

Nimrod Baranovitch refers to a broad category of state-sponsored "minority pop" that rose in popularity as a commodity for Han Chinese and includes state-sponsored Mandarin-language songs from a range of minority groups in China.[4] Mongol grassland songs (*caoyuan gequ*), which emerged in the 1980s and are still being composed by the hundreds every year, closely resemble the Mandarin-language ballads composed during the Mao era. Songs maintain *minzu fengge* (ethnic flavors) features such as arching melodies and vocal ornaments and contain the now-established grassland features of synthesized accompaniment and, typically, a smooth vocal timbre with vibrato.

For most young musicians in urban Inner Mongolia today, the grassland song industry is simply one part of a bigger musical ecosystem, one that tends to be vastly more saturated in government funding and regulation than in Mongolia. Musicians in Inner Mongolia have access to a wide variety of musical career paths, most notably in state-sponsored arts troupes, restaurants, and ger camps, but also in the recording industry and as music teachers. As most musical careers are supported in some way by government funds, the industry grows at a greater rate than it would through market forces in ways that does support Mongols who seek to be performing artists. During my summer fieldwork, I found it easy to spend my time attending two to four musical events per day, including both free-admission concerts and week-long festivals that culminate in stadium-packed concerts. Aside from many active and independent underground music scenes in Inner Mongolia, the packaged and glamorous musical experiences that I encountered on the ground level in Inner Mongolia—with their vibrant colors, flashing stage lights, masters of ceremony, and choruses of dancers, not to mention government officials in the front rows—might best be described by the Chinese term *daguimo* (large-scale or "over-the-top").

Institutional Trends and Cultural Heritage

Music in Inner Mongolia clearly witnessed profound impacts from Mao-era political and post-Mao market forces, leading to the loss, change, and abandonment of many pre–PRC-era, grassland-based musical practices and sensibilities. Although many musicians and institutional forces are concerned with musical loss and preservation today, the idea that the past has something valuable and worth preserving did not always exist as a dominant paradigm in Inner Mongolian music institutions. During the late 1980s and 1990s, a handful of Mongol musicians worked diligently to develop and "improve" Mongol music, which they saw as unprofessional, out of tune, and backward. Musical professionalization and "stagification" (*wutaihua*) operated in a world of hierarchical musical value in which Mongol music needed to be improved in order to rise to the level of European classical performance (D'Evelyn 2018). Whereas instruments in the pre-PRC period varied widely in construction, tuning, sound quality, and playing technique according to regional and personal preferences, modern instruments were altered in order to achieve standardized intonation, systematized teaching methods, sufficient volume and tuning stability to hold up in a concert hall, and a body of technically difficult compositions to demonstrate stage virtuosity (see Chapter 5 in this volume). Large-scale compositions continued to be written for Mongolian instruments in the 1980s and '90s that called for extended techniques and expressive emotionalism rarely seen in traditional Mongol musical practices. Those surviving professional musicians and singers who had their origins in the Mao-era propaganda troupes became respected as teachers in music academies and universities and developed their own systematic and structured teaching methods, fostering a new generation of instrumentalists and vocalists, among which include the members of Anda Union ensemble discussed later in this chapter.

These attitudes toward concert music and professionalism shifted dramatically in the mid-2000s, making way for a renaissance of interest in local folk song styles and a slightly more rustic, roots-oriented aesthetic. My first visits to Inner Mongolia in 2009 coincided with the beginning of this crucial turning point, just as the roots music movement was beginning to take off in Hohhot. Even as I observed entrenched ideas about musical hierarchy that sought to professionalize Mongol music and elevate it to standards they believed were set by European concert music, I also saw many young people and institutional forces starting to embrace a counter trend toward folk revival and conscious rejection of Westernization and Sinification (D'Evelyn 2018). This revival came in response to a variety of converging forces, including the passing away of great folk masters, such as the great Shilingol singer Lhajav (Hazhabu), but perhaps due to even more systemic changes as a result of China's increasing involvement with national and international systems of Intangible Cultural Heritage (ICH).

In the early 2000s, the United Nations Educational, Scientific and Cultural Organization (UNESCO) launched a series of programs aimed at nominating and helping to safeguard oral and intangible cultural heritage. The final lists that emerged, the "List of the Intangible Cultural Heritage in Need of Urgent Safeguarding" and the "Representative List of the ICH of Humanity," were designed both as a way to combat the disappearance of cultural forms due to globalization and modernization and as a way to provide geographical balance and opportunities for nations currently excluded from the UNESCO World Heritage Sites list (Aikawa-Faure 2010). As of early 2020, China has forty inscriptions (seven of those are included on the list of items in need of urgent safeguarding), twelve backlogged nominations, and two ongoing nominations. Of the forty inscriptions on China's Representative List, thirteen are cultural heritage practices from minority groups in China (such as the Mongols, Uyghurs, Tibetans, Kyrgyz, Dong, and Qiang). Several other items on the list, including Hua'er folk songs and traditional paper cutting, are practiced by both Han and minority groups, putting that number potentially even higher. Although minorities comprise only about eight percent of China's population, their overrepresentation in national displays of Chinese culture (including more than thirty percent of China's UNESCO inscriptions) follows a pattern in which government forces collect and codify minority cultures and determine orthodox systems for how and when they can be staged (Gorfinkel 2016).

Helen Rees (2016) documents the rapid change from modernization-driven, conservatory and tourist-style adaptation of folk songs in China in the 1990s to a frenzy of activity surrounding what are known as "original ecology folk songs" (*yuanshengtai minge*) and other "original ecology" (*yuanshengtai*) cultural products. A bizarre and confusing term when translated to English, "original ecology" is intended to evoke a sense of primordial connection to an uninterrupted past. Yuanshengtai is often used to refer to any product, place, or practice that is uncontaminated from outside influences, though the term has mostly been associated with Chinese minority groups and their performing arts practices.

The *yuanshengtai* movement has had a profound impact on the musical lives and conceptualization of musical value in Inner Mongolia, including in the arenas of national and local institutions, the arenas of media and entertainment, and down to the level of individual musicians and independent ensembles. The movement is filled with contradiction and hypocrisy (Wong 2019); it continues to trivialize and misrepresent minority cultures as rooted in the past and has fueled China's zeal for ICH applications to UNESCO, but it has also offered perhaps unexpected benefits to musicians in the process. It is now accepted practice that Mongols and other ethnic groups in China sing folk songs on television and on the conservatory stage in their local languages and with local flavors, rather than singing composed, harmonized, and midi-accompanied folk songs in Mandarin. It has provided institutional funding for the documentation and study of disappearing or neglected musical styles that were formerly seen as backward. The *yuanshengtai* phenomenon has encouraged and celebrated ethnic and linguistic diversity in regions like Inner Mongolia rather than emphasizing homogenous and simplistic minority ethnic styles (*minzu fengge*). It has, furthermore, launched the career of a group of young musicians named Anda Union who have traveled the world and who proclaim themselves as the "voice of Inner Mongolia."

Anda Union

In 2006, Anda Union became involved and benefited directly in the *yuan-shengtai* movement when they participated and won third place in the National Young Singer's Competition, a popular television program that featured a *yuan-shengtai* category for the first time in 2006 (Yang 2009). Although the members of Anda Union were all trained in music academies and conservatories, they ironically became the leading voices in developing a staged *yuanshengtai* Mongolian sound—a sound that supposedly represented "pure," original, and untainted music from the grasslands. The last section of this chapter tracks the career, contributions, and musical repertoire of this influential group.

Anda Union is by no means alone in the global Mongol music scene. The Hu Band from Mongolia, an ethno-rock group that went viral on YouTube in 2018, has become a household name and is bringing Mongolian sounds into living rooms across the world (through Spotify, YouTube, and vinyl records). Although much less viral than The Hu, Anda Union has been touring abroad for over a decade and has dazzled thousands of audience members in North America and Europe. Their performances have been described as "rousing masterclass in folk revivalism" by the Guardian (2018) and they have received recognition from *Songlines* for their albums *Wind Horse* (2011) and *Homeland* (2016), which won the "Top of the World" (2011) and "Asia & Pacific" (2017) awards, respectively. Other internationally recognized Mongol ensembles from China include the folk-rock ensemble Hanggai, the eclectic fusion ensemble Haya, the heavy metal group Nine Treasures, and the folk band Ikh Tsetsn, all four of which are based in Beijing.

Anda Union, the earliest neo-traditional ensemble of its kind in Inner Mongolia, profoundly impacted the urban music scene. Cities like Hohhot, Baotou, Tongliao City, and Hailar have seen a sharp rise in Anda Union "look-alike" ensembles in the last decade, a musical path that enables young people to make a living after graduation and to reconnect with their roots at the same time. Interestingly, the ensemble style inherited and developed by Anda Union offers musicians both a sense of creative agency and a pathway to conform with the current state-sanctioned *yuanshengtai* orthodoxy. In a climate where musicians often have to determine how to remain artistically sincere while still receiving opportunities for state funding and television air time, a neo-traditional or Anda-style *yuanshengtai* ensemble seems to be the pathway to satisfy all of these concerns at once.

Anda Union received sponsorship from state-run institutions from the very moment of their founding. The original members of Anda Union graduated as horsehead fiddle (*morin khuur*) majors and proceeded directly into careers at the Inner Mongolia Song and Dance Theater, supporting themselves on the side with evening work at restaurants entertaining Han Chinese tourists. In 2003, the Inner Mongolia Song and Dance Theater invited the Mongolian teacher Odsüren Baatar to take up a residency with the troupe in order to teach throat singing (*khöömii*) to the state artists. Odsüren had visited Inner Mongolia briefly around the year 1993 to teach *khöömii*, which at that time was almost entirely unknown except among a few individuals who found access to cassette tape recordings from newly opened Mongolia.

During his residency in the early 2000s, Odsüren taught numerous students in Hohhot (both within the troupe and privately on the side), but recognized potential in the group of recent Inner Mongolia Art College graduates. In 2003, he gathered the ten original members into an ensemble arrangement molded after Transmongolia, a neo-traditional ensemble (*khamtlag*) from Mongolia (Hadan Baatar personal communication, July 20, 2009). The members of Anda Union represent a wide array of sub-ethnic groups and homelands within the 1.2 million square kilometers that encompass the land mass of Inner Mongolia. Signifying their unique friendship across the lines of clan identity, the ten-member band adopted the name Anda Union (*anda* means "blood siblings"). Not long after, they began performing arrangements of standard Mongolian folk songs, using a catchy combination of *isgeree khöömii* (whistle-style *khöömii* for singing untexted syllables) and *shakhaa* (constricted throat technique for singing texted syllables), along with smooth, harmonically rich textures of *morin khuur* (horsehead fiddle), *tovshuur* (two-string plucked lute), and percussion accompaniment. The first Inner Mongolian *khamtlag* (ensemble, *zuhe* in Chinese) was born.

After their work with Odsüren, the Anda musicians became keenly attracted to the sound of neo-traditional Tuvan ensembles such as Huun Huur Tu, Chirgilchin, and Yat-Kha, and the troupe subsequently invited the singer Aldar from Chirgilchin to Hohhot for a residency. They appreciated the relaxed, natural sound of the Tuvan throat-singing styles (*khoomei, sygyt, kargyraa*, and others; see Beahrs 2019) compared to the professionalized sound of Mongolian *isgeree khöömii*. They began to adopt arrangements, styles, instruments (such as the Tuvan *igil* fiddle, *doshpuluur* plucked lute, and skin-faced drum), and singing techniques from the Tuvan ensembles, adjusting to the "world music" aesthetic fashioned by Huun Huur Tu in collaboration with Ted Levin in the 1990s (Levin and Süzükei 2006; Beahrs 2014). The Tuvan formula adopted by Anda Union adapts solo and duet folk practice in a variety of ways—including contrasts between fast and slow, verse-interlude arrangements with texted and un-texted throat-singing, limited harmonic movement, and the addition of blue notes and syncopated rhythms—intended to please global audiences through short, packaged stage arrangements.

When I interviewed several Anda members for the first time in 2009, they were painfully aware of the derivative and imitative nature of their work during the early years of their performance career and had begun the process of searching for their own sound. With some help and encouragement from their new British managers, Tim Pearce and his wife Sophie Lascelles, the band realized that they could keep the same ensemble sound but localize their music as their own and as uniquely Inner Mongol by creating arranged adaptations of folk songs they grew up with in their respective grassland homes—hometowns they had left decades prior. Tim and Sophie were captivated by the group's performance in 2006 at an international expo in Shanghai and proposed that they film a documentary of the group and include footage of the ensemble members' lives in the city contrasted with footage shot of each of the members revisiting their hometowns. The resulting documentary, *Anda Union: From the Steppes to the City* (2011), produced by Eye 4 Films, was filmed over the course of thirty-three days in 2009 and across a distance of over 10,000 kilometers (and as the credits amusingly mention, involved the slaughter of thirty-seven sheep to feed the crew over the production time period).

The film depicts the musical and cultural diversity represented by each of Anda Union's members and captures the complexities of the urban-rural divide in Inner Mongolia. It shows the challenges of negotiating a life in the city of Hohhot, the population of which is more than eighty-seven percent Han Chinese, and the seamlessness with which these city dwellers are able to reconnect with their families on trips back to their grassland homelands. Through an observational mode and an absence of narration, the film conveys Anda Union's desires to keep the sounds of their grassland past alive even as they adapt those sounds to the needs of global, urban audiences.

In the section that follows, I offer a brief musical "users' guide" to several pieces in Anda Union's repertoire, including musical selections introduced in the documentary film and selections from their discography. The musical examples below[5] offer a useful entry point into understanding regional diversity in Inner Mongolia and the tensions that exist between local, pan-ethnic, and transnational Mongol identities.

"Sumaro" and "Derlcha"

These two pieces from Anda Union's repertoire, which appear on their album *Wind Horse* (2011), emerged out of the fieldwork experiences the ensemble members conducted during the filming of their documentary, *Anda Union: From the Steppes to the City* (2011). The film traces their visits to their grassland and village homes, including several regions of northeast Inner Mongolia. At one point in the film, Nars, the ensemble leader, visits his hometown of Ar Khorchin in Chifeng (formerly Ju'uda) and sits side-by-side with his father while he transcribes the lyrics to the song "Sumaro." The strophic song, about two

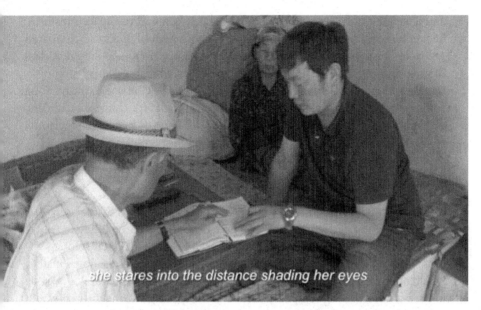
she stares into the distance shading her eyes

FIGURE 2.2. Nars and his father transcribe the tune "Sumaro" during Anda Union's visit to Ar Khorchin, Nars's hometown. Screenshot from the film *Anda Union: From the Steppes to the City* (2011).

lovers joyfully reunited after a period of separation, features a bouncy metrical rhythm, minor pentatonic scale, and balanced, arching phrases typical of narrative songs (known in Chinese as "eastern folk songs" *dongbei minge*) from this region. "Sumaro" appears repeatedly throughout the film as the musicians work on it on their journeys and arrive at a final stage arrangement at the end of the film. This stage arrangement uses a blend of traditional elements from the original song, as well as creative additions using the horsehead fiddle and insertion of various throat singing styles.

As mentioned earlier, the southern regions of Inner Mongolia bordering Chinese territories—such as Ju'uda and Jirem (formerly known as "leagues" or *chuulgan* under the Qing system and now retitled as Chifeng and Tongliao Municipalities)—were some of the earliest regions of Inner Mongolia to transition from herding economies to semi-pastoral, semi-agricultural ways of life. This transition profoundly impacted musical forms. These impacts are beginning to be seen as not wholly negative, but as a process that involved both loss and gain. Ju'uda and Jirem developed music cultures that demonstrate evidence of rich cross-fertilization between Mongol, Manchu, and northern Han Chinese culture. Borderland Mongols began to face a changing sense of time and space as their region became organized into smaller, sedentary agricultural units. With the decrease in pastoralism, long-songs (a genre intimately connected with the steppe and a feeling of expansiveness) became the first genre of music to transform, becoming considerably less elongated with shorter vowel melismas compared with long-song in remote pastoral regions like Hulunbuir and Shilingol. A class of musicians emerged who specialized in self-accompanied story-singing— merging Mongol-style melodies with stories from the Chinese narrative song (*shuochang*) repertoire (Botolt 2007). These itinerant bards (known as fiddlers, or *khuurch* in Mongolian) mastered hours and hours of narrative repertoire, received in many cases through training in Buddhist temples (ibid).

One *khuurch* from Inner Mongolia still living today is the master storyteller Jalasen. Midway through the Anda Union documentary, Nars and Urgen visit Jalasen for an interview and to hear him play. They ask questions about the social and historical context for the song "Derlcha," a song form that Jalasen used to perform. An arrangement of this song has become a cornerstone of Anda's concert repertoire. In the documentary, Jalasen explains to Anda Union members Nars and Urgen how the piece "Derlcha" (meaning conversational match) would often be used alongside wrestling competitions through a dialogue-style or back-and-forth song competition. Each of the ten neighboring districts would nominate one singer as a representative, a competition resembling a Mongolian epic rap battle. Singers were paired off and required to come up with creative and witty lyrics on the spot in response to their competitor's sung couplet. The loser would be the one who couldn't keep up or respond in time, while the winner would compete against the rest of the singers until there was no one left, finally receiving a prize as well as the right to throw insults at the losing singers. Jalasen's sparsely accompanied, text-oriented rendition of "Derlcha," using a skin-faced box fiddle (*choor*) and four-stringed tube fiddle (*sihu* in Chinese, *dörvön chikhtei khuur* in Mongolian) differs from the version of the song that Anda performs on stage with its mix of arranged throat singing styles, harmonies, sectional form, and dramatic shifts between fast and slow. However, Nars and Urgen reassure master Jalasen that they maintain the dialogic nature of the song and sing five whole verses.

Anda's performance of "Derlcha" opens with a dramatic chant in parallel fourths sung with heavy *shakhaa* (constricted throat singing technique) and exaggerated rolling "r" sounds in their delivery of the Mongolian text. This section is followed by a horsehead fiddle ostinato and the first presentation of the folk song melody by Urgen. He sings with flavorful nasal timbre, yodel-like vocalizations, and ornaments typical of Khorchin and Ar Khorchin songs of Jirem and Ju'uda. Following this first presentation, the folk song melody gets passed among the band members with each rendering it with a different *khöömii* technique, including various forms of *shakhaa*, *kargyraa*, and even an *ezingeleer* interlude by Nars. This demonstrates a conscious process of musical hybridization, as they transform the eastern-region Inner Mongolian folk song with a variety of western-region throat singing styles and an inventive musical form.

"Jangar" and "Holy Mountain"

Two pieces in Anda Union's repertoire are informed by instrumental and vocal music of Oirad Mongols of China's Xinjiang Uyghur Autonomous Region. Scholars (Siriguleng 2009; Botolt pers. comm. July 29, 2009) recognize the music of these regions—including Xinjiang's Bortala and Altay Prefectures—as the western section of three important divisions of Mongol music in China; the other two are the music of the central and northeast regions. Learning and performing Mongol music from Xinjiang ironically makes Anda Union a fitting representative of the "voice of Inner Mongolia," due to its role in the musical consciousness of Inner Mongolian musicians and scholars. Their arrangement of the Jangar epic song genre and use of instruments from this distant region serve to further amplify the ensemble's regionally diverse repertoire, while also performing a complex understanding of sub-ethnic Mongol identities in China.

"Jangar," Anda's rousing piece, opens their album *Homeland* and is a lively rendering of the traditional Oirad epic song tradition of the western Mongol regions. Considered a masterwork of folk literature, the Jangar epic is performed by singer-storytellers called *janggarch* (singers of Janggar) and involves a story about the hero Jangar Khan and his battles against great opponents and monsters. Anda Union's version of this song starts with a gentle solo *tovshuur* ostinato, punctuated by the jingle of percussive bells, followed by the entry of an energetic set of *morin khuur* and a shout of "Shog!" The group then holds several long *kargyraa* and *khöömii* drone notes before launching into their first verse, one with an upbeat chorus of voices and texted *kargyraa*.

Nars (pers. comm. December 17, 2020) described Anda Union's early exposure to Xinjiang Mongol music in the early 2000s while they were working in the Inner Mongolia Song and Dance Theater. Just as Odsüren had come in to teach Mongolian *khöömii* to members of the ensemble, a teacher named Yerkesh was brought from Xinjiang to Hohhot at that time to teach *tovshuur* and other styles of music from his hometown in the Bortala Mongolian Autonomous Prefecture near the Kazakhstan border. In addition to learning from Yerkesh, the group also learns by close listening to recordings, a form of learning that gave the member Chinggel his first access to performance on the *tsuur* (an end-blown flute known as *modyn tsuur* in Inner Mongolia).

Chinggel's solo composition for *tsuur* called "Holy Mountain," appears on their album *Wind Horse* (2011). An Ongud Mongol from the grasslands of eastern Inner Mongolia, Chinggel grew up in the city for most of his life. His *tsuur* playing and deep *kargyraa khöömii* style draws more from his individual interest in music from the distant Altai mountains than it connects to his own ethnic background. *Tsuur* and other related instruments (the Tuvan *shoor* and Kazakh *sybyzgy*) are played by Oirad, Tuvan, and Kazakh communities in the greater Altai-Sayan mountain regions (see Chapter Four in this volume). The *tsuur* was largely unknown in Inner Mongolia until a respected Mongol professor, Mergejikh (Moerjifu; 1931–present), traveled to Altay Prefecture in Xinjiang in the 1980s and discovered evidence of both *tsuur* playing and a multiphonic vocal practice known in the region as *khooloin tsuur* (literally "throat flute"), similar to *khöömii*. He documented his findings in a 1986 essay, which eventually generated interest among scholars and musicians in Hohhot (Mergejikh 1986). When Chinggel began playing the *tsuur* there were very few teachers or practitioners to learn from in Hohhot; today, many ensembles feature a player of this instrument.

Chinggel's piece "Holy Mountain," consists of several unmetered sections, each of which involves predetermined ornamental motives, and substantial flexibility in phrasing and embellishment. The unmoving *khöömii*-like drone note emitting from the performer's vocal cavity sets up a rich foundation for the layered overtone partials and fluttering sounds of the flute. These sounds set up a drone-overtone sound structure (Süzükei 2021) that evoke the timbral richness of the Altai mountain region, over two thousand kilometers away from Hohhot.

"Buriat"

Like Chinggel, Tsetsegmaa contributes to Anda Union's musical sub-ethnic diversity, but also reveals the complexities of Mongols' distribution and classification in and across the borders of China. Tsetsegmaa is part Buriad,[6] a group whose homeland territories are dotted across China, Russia, and Mongolia. Tsetsegmaa grew up in Hulunbuir Banner, the far northeast region of Inner Mongolia on the border with Russia. Reflective of its borderland position, Hulunbuir is the most diverse region of Inner Mongolia and is home to Mongols (including several sub-ethnic groups), Russians, and three smaller recognized groups—the Evenk, the Daur, and the Oronchon—that have links to Siberia, but share many cultural similarities with the Mongols. Although Buriad people have their own language, customs, and historical identity, the Chinese communists who led the efforts to classify minority nationalities in Hulunbuir somehow did not see fit to recognize the Buriads as a separate ethnic group.[7]

Tsetsegmaa's song "Buriat" and her rendition of the widely popular Buriad song "Altargana" are heartfelt evocations of longing for homeland felt by women who move away from their homeland after marriage. Such sentiments of longing for homeland are now felt by many urban Buriads and Mongols due to their displacement and dislocation from their roots in the grasslands. Tsetsegmaa's powerful vocal sound projects Buriad flavor in its rich and dense, even grainy, timbre and in the stylized trills and ornaments distinguishable from vocal ornaments typical in Mongol folk songs. Tsetsegmaa has received great honors in China and abroad for her vocal talents, having won prizes at many song competitions in China and having also been featured on the international album, *Between the Sky and Prairie*, of Grammy-award-winning artist Daniel Ho. Her inclusion as a member of Anda Union fills in the map of Inner Mongolia, offering vocal musical flavor from the far northeast of the region, while also contributing to the complex conundrum of what it means to be Mongol in China. Tsetsegmaa, a professionally trained, half-Mongol, half-Buriad, Chinese passport-holder and singer of local songs from her home region of Hulunbuir on the border near Mongolia and Russian Siberia, does not fall easily into one clean ethnicity or nationality. The longing and raw emotional color she expresses in her music might therefore be lost upon audiences who are unaware of the challenges she faces as a minority ethnicity (Buriad) among an already marginalized minority nationality (Mongols) in China.

"Drinking Song"

Anda Union's "Drinking Song" ("Jiu Ge" in Chinese), the closing track on Anda Union's award-winning album *Homeland*, is a ubiquitous and often performed song in Inner Mongolia. The tune itself is a cheerful, bouncy melody with a medium melodic range and an anhemitonic (major-sounding) pentatonic scale. In their arrangement of this song, Anda Union brings their audiences into the grasslands with an atmospheric, unmetered section of long tones performed by Chinggel on the *tsuur*, Urgen on the *morin khuur*, Chinggel on the *ikh khuur* (bass horsehead fiddle), and Nars on the *igil*. These long tones are punctuated by sounds of the *aman khuur* (jaw harp) played by Saikhannakhaa and improvised licks by Uni on the *tovshuur* and then built into a denser texture when Chinggel switches from *tsuur* to layering in Tuvan *kargyraa* (chest-style throat singing). Uni gradually sets up a rhythmic pattern on the *tovshuur* and the other Urgen joins with a gentle rhythmic foundation on the large Tuvan skin-faced drum. The fiddles start the melody and then the group joins with the texted verses, alternating between regular-voiced and *shakhaa* (constricted throat singing technique) and varying among pairings, solos, and full group singing. The lyrics include toasts to a nobleman or honored guest and shouts of "hey!" when glasses of alcohol might be raised. The title, "Drinking Song," refers to a whole genre of songs, most of which come from the Ordos southwest desert region of Inner Mongolia bordering China's Gansu, Ningxia, and Shaanxi provinces.

Anda Union's longtime percussionist and drum maker, Baatar (replaced by the other Urgen at this performance), hails from the Ordos region of Inner Mongolia and is featured prominently in the *Anda Union* documentary film, including footage shot in his drum workshop.

The close linkage between Mongolians and drinking culture appears to be a relatively recent phenomenon (Williams 1998:15), but it has become a salient marker of Mongolness in China today. Traditionally, fermented mare's milk (*airag*) was shared for only the most important celebrations and used as an offering to bless a new *ger* or to welcome guests into one's home. Although a complete discussion of the codes and meanings of Mongolian drinking culture in China is beyond the scope of this chapter, it is significant that both Han Chinese and Mongols in China today consider Mongols to be among the best drinkers of all fifty-six ethnic groups. This phenomenon both reinforces a particular (and gendered) stereotype and simultaneously offers Mongols a valuable symbolic resource to exert their ethnic separateness. The stereotypical linkage of drinking with Mongol culture means that tourists who visit Inner Mongolia expect to be served alcohol (usually *baijiu*, distilled rice liquor of typically forty to fifty percent alcohol) and to be entertained with songs and a drinking ceremony upon arrival in the grasslands. Many of the earliest tourist camps were located in the grasslands of the Ordos region, directly outside the city centers of Hohhot and Baotou, and Mongol and Han managers of these tourist camps developed a greeting ritual using local tunes so that tourists coming off the bus could each be greeted with song, a small bowl of alcohol, and a *khadag* (colored ceremonial cloth). Ordos folk songs tend to be rhythmically bouncy and melodically lively, with a wide vocal range and nasal vocal timbre. Proximity to the Chinese borderland meant that Ordos Mongols mixed and mingled with Han Chinese immigrants from the Shaanbei region of Shaanxi, resulting in a fascinating site of musical exchange that can be observed in both Mongol and Han Chinese vocal and instrumental music across this region (Gibbs 2018).

Such associations with Ordos style, tourism, and the drinking Mongol stereotype make the meaning of this song much more loaded than immediately meets the eye and ear. This particular drinking song is often sung by all-male groups and sometimes in a highly performative way, with members raising invisible glasses of alcohol in emulation of an all-night drinking party. Anda Union's rendition of this song, however, is much softer and gentler. The inclusion of Saikhannakhaa's female voice and the tender, mellow voices of the male group members (in addition to their smaller body builds) changes the usual macho masculinity aesthetic that many groups such as the folk-rock group Hanggai exude in this song. Without knowing the lyrics to this song, it would be difficult to catch that this is a song about drinking at all. For Anda Union, this musical selection offers the group a way to represent both the Ordos desert region, hometown of the drummer Bater, and also—due to the song's ubiquitousness—Inner Mongolia itself.

SONG OF ARKHI

Inside the bottle,
the pure arkhi is level.
When it's with you nobles,
the pure arkhi is crazy.
In your cups, it's good, and
in your actions, it's good, this carousing.

Inside your thoughts,
the arkhi is warm.
When it's with you all,
the pure arkhi is crazy.[8]

Conclusion

Anda Union's career has spanned, and has been fundamental in leading, a decade of dramatic cultural and musical transitions in Inner Mongolia. Anda Union remains an active part of Inner Mongolia's musical life and represents Inner Mongolia abroad on tours to the United States. In 2016 the Inner Mongolia Art College, the premier institute for the study of Mongol music in China, opened an "Anda Major" (*andaban*) for students to study under the tutelage of the band leaders so that they could form their own groups specializing in the Anda Union style. This successful style and musical formula, combining local folk songs with Mongolian *khöömii* and Tuvan *khöömei* styles, will continue to permeate the music scene in Inner Mongolia for some time to come. Although members have come and gone since the 2010s, the core members of the ensemble continue to perform, teach, arrange, and promote the local music of China's Mongols—including Khorchin, Ar Khorchin, Ordos, Buriad, and Oirad sub-ethnic groups.

Anda Union realizes its identity as the "voice of Inner Mongolia," perhaps not just through repertoire and the members' own diverse sub-ethnic backgrounds, but also through a conscious process of musical selection, fieldwork collection, and arrangement. Nars and other members of Anda Union have become performer-ethnographers; they are conscientiously researching their musical past, creatively adapting it to the present, while reckoning their ethnic and musical diversity and their "Inner Mongolness" in the process. Music provides a symbolic resource that codes these layers of meanings and contradictions in a catchy, locally and internationally appealing package. Meanings about sub-ethnic identity, regional diversity, and transnational borrowing must certainly be lost on most Chinese and foreign audiences—those who are unaware of the dynamics of *yastan* identity or the politics of *khöömii* as heritage in Inner Mongolia.

This chapter unpacks only a few of the many ways that Mongols make and experience music in China. Mongol sensibilities in Inner Mongolia exhibit a variety of gradations—between rural and urban; pastoral and semi-pastoral; east, west, northeast, and central; assimilated and unassimilated; unified and regionally unique. The members of Anda Union, like many musicians in Inner Mongolia today, are uniquely and creatively working to revive and reinterpret Mongolian music in China, to make it relevant to young audiences around the world, while also navigating Chinese heritage policy and ethnic orthodoxy in the process. Music thus continues to enable musicians to work out what it means to be an Inner Mongol in the twenty-first century and how to exhibit Inner Mongolian diversity on the national and international stage.

Notes

1. The complexities of Inner Mongolia's history and ethnic politics recently entered mainstream global conversations in September 2020 when Mongol parents and school teachers were marching on the streets on Inner Mongolia to protest changes to the region's language education policy (see Atwood 2020).

2. See our companion website, www.mongoliansoundworlds.org, for additional information on the musical traditions included in this volume.

3. At least four other official Chinese minority groups speak Mongolic languages, but were classified as separate ethnic groups, notably the Daur (*dawa'erzu*), Ewenke (*ewenkezu*), Oronchon (*elunchun*), and Monguor (*tuzu*).

4. See Baranovitch 2003, 2007, and 2009. See also Upton 1996, 2002 for a discussion of minority pop in Tibet and Harris 2000, 2005a, and 2005b for treatment of Uyghur pop.

5. The songs included here are widely accessible on YouTube, Spotify, Apple Music, and other streaming services using the Romanized spellings given.

6. The term "Buriad" can be Romanized in a variety of ways, including "Buriat" as it is spelled here by Anda Union.

7. See Mullaney 2010 and Kaup 2000 for more on the idiosyncrasies of the minority classification project.

8. Translated by Sunmin Yoon and Simon Wickhamsmith.

Bibliography

Aikawa-Faure, Noriko. 2010. "From the Proclamation of Masterpieces to the Convention for the Safeguarding of Intangible Cultural Heritage." In *Heritage and Globalisation*, edited by Sophia Labadi and Colin Long, 13–43. New York: Routledge.

Atwood, Christopher P. 2020. "Bilingual Education in Inner Mongolia: An Explainer."

Made in China Journal, August 30. https://madeinchinajournal.com/2020/08/30/bilingual-education-in-inner-mongolia-an-explainer/.

——. 2002. *Young Mongols and Vigilantes in Inner Mongolia's Interregnum Decades, 1911–1931.* Boston: Brill.

——. 2001. "Between Alterity: New Voices of Minority People in China." *Modern China* 27 (3): 359—401.

Baranovitch, Nimrod. 2003. *China's New Voices: Popular Music, Ethnicity, Gender, and Politics, 1978–1997.* Berkeley: University of California Press.

——. 2007. "From Resistance to Adaptation: Uyghur Popular Music and Changing Attitudes among Uyghur Youth." *China Journal* 58:59–82.

——. 2009. "Compliance, Autonomy, and Resistance of a 'State Artist.'" In *Lives in Chinese Music*, edited by Helen Rees, 173–212. Urbana: University of Illinois Press.

Beahrs, Robert. 2014. "Post-Soviet Tuvan Throat-Singing (*Xöömei*) and the Circulation of Nomadic Sensibility." PhD diss., University of California, Berkeley.

——. 2019. "Tuning a Throat Song in Inner Asia: On the Nature of Vocal Gifts with People's *Xöömeizhi* of the Tyva Republic Valeriy Mongush (b. 1953)." In *The Oxford Handbook of Voice Studies*, edited by Nina Sun Eidsheim and Katherine Meizel. Oxford Online.

Bilik, Naran. 1998. "Language Education, Intellectuals, and Symbolic Representation: Being an Urban Mongolian in a New Configuration of Social Evolution." In *Nationalism and Ethnoregional Identities in China*, edited by William Safran, 47–57. Portland, OR: Frank Cass.

Billé, Franck. 2015. *Sinophobia: Anxiety, Violence, and the Making of Mongolian Identity.* Honolulu: University of Hawai'i Press.

Borchigud, Wurlig. 1996. "Transgressing Ethnic and National Boundaries: Contemporary 'Inner Mongolian' Identities in China." In *Negotiating Ethnicities in China and Taiwan*, edited by Melissa J. Brown, 160–182. Berkeley: Institute of East Asian Studies, University of California.

Botolt [Yang Yucheng].2007. *Khuurch: Narrative Artists of the Khorchin Region Tradition and Their Music [Hu'erqi: Ke'erqin Difang Chuantong Zhong de Shuochang Yiren Jiqi Yinyue].* Shanghai: Shanghai Conservatory Press.

——. 2015. *Mengguzu Chuantong Yinyue Gailun [Introduction to Mongolian Traditional Music].* Hohhot, China: Inner Mongolia University Press.

Bulag, Uradyn Erden. 1998. *Nationalism and Hybridity in Mongolia.* New York: Oxford University Press.

——. 2002. *The Mongols at China's Edge: History and the Politics of National Unity.* World Social Change. Lanham, MD: Rowman & Littlefield Publishers.

——. 2003. "Mongolian Ethnicity and Linguistic Anxiety in China." *American Anthropologist* 105:753–63.

——. 2006. "Municipalization and Ethnopolitics in Inner Mongolia." In *Mongols From Country to City: Floating Boundaries, Pastoralism, and City Life in the Mongol Lands*, edited by Ole Bruun, and Li Narangoa, 56–81. Copenhagen: Nordic Institute of Asian Studies Press.

Crossley, Pamela. 2006. "Making Mongols." In *Empire at the Margins: Culture, Ethnicity, and Frontier in Early Modern China*, edited by Pamela Kyle Crossley, Helen F. Siu, and Donald S. Sutton, 58–82. Berkeley, CA: University of California Press.

D'Evelyn, Charlotte. 2018. "Grasping Intangible Heritage and Reimagining Inner Mongolia: Folk-Artist Albums and a New Logic for Musical Representation in China." *Journal of Asian Folklore* 55(1):21–48.

Elliot, Mark C. 2001. *The Manchu Way: The Eight Banners and Ethnic Identity in Late Imperial China*. Stanford: Stanford University Press.

Gibbs, Levi S. 2018. *Song King: Connecting People, Places, and Past in Contemporary China*. Honolulu: University of Hawai'i Press.

Gladney, Dru C. 1994. "Representing Nationality in China: Refiguring Majority/Minority Identities." *Journal of Asian Studies* 53(1):92–123.

Gorfinkel, Lauren. 2016. "From Transformation to Preservation: Music and Multi-Ethnic Unity on Television in China." In *Music as Intangible Cultural Heritage: Policy, Ideology, and Practice in the Preservation of East Asian Traditions*, edited by Keith Howard, 99–112. New York: Routledge.

Harris, Rachel. 2000. "From Shamanic Ritual to Karaoke: The (Trans)Migrations of a Chinese Folksong." *CHIME Journal* 14–15:48–60.

———. 2005a. "Wang Luobin: Folk Song King of the Northwest or Song Thief? Copyright, Representation, and Chinese Folk Songs." *Modern China* 31(3):381–408.

———. 2005b. "Reggae on the Silk Road: The Globalization of Uyghur Pop." *China Quarterly* 183:627–643.

Henochowicz, Anne. 2008. "Blue Heaven, Parched Land: Mongolian Folksong and the Chinese State." *Graduate Journal of Asia-Pacific Studies* 6(1):37–50.

———. 2011. "'For the Land of All Mongols': Gada Meiren the Bandit, Hero, and Proto-Revolutionary." *Journal of Wenzhou University: Social Sciences* 24(2):44–50.

Hillman, Ben. 2003. "Paradise under Construction: Minorities, Myths and Modernity in Northwest Yunnan." *Asian Ethnicity* 14(2):175–88.

Jankowiak, William R. 1988. "The Last Hurrah? Political Protest in Inner Mongolia." *The Australian Journal of Chinese Affairs*, no. 19/20: 269—88.

———. 1993. *Sex, Death, and Hierarchy in a Chinese City*. New York: Columbia University Press.

Kaup, Katherine. 2000. *Creating the Zhuang: Ethnic Politics in China*. Boulder, CO: Lynne Rienner Publishers.

Khogjilt [Hugejiletu]. 2006. *Mengguzu Yinyueshi* [History of music of the Mongol nationality]. Shenyang: Liaoning Minzu Chubanshe.

Levin, Theodore Craig, and Valentina Süzükei. 2006. *Where Rivers and Mountains Sing: Sound, Music, and Nomadism in Tuva and Beyond*. Bloomington: Indiana University Press.

Mackerras, Colin. 1995. *China's Minority Cultures: Identities and Integration since 1912*. New York: St. Martin's Press.

McDougall, Bonnie S. 1980. *Mao Zedong's "Talks at the Yan'an Conference on Literature and Art": A Translation of the 1943 Text with Commentary*. Ann Arbor: Center for Chinese Studies; University of Michigan.

Mergejikh 1986. "Searching for the Traces of the Hujia: A Second Investigation of Mongolian Music." *Music Art* 1986(1):1–11.

Mullaney, Thomas. 2010. *Coming to Terms with the Nation: Ethnic Classification in Modern China.* Berkeley: University of California Press.

Oakes, Tim. 2000. "China's Provincial Identities: Reviving Regionalism and Reinventing 'Chineseness.'" *Journal of Asian Studies* 59(3):667–692.

Pegg, Carole A. 1989. "Tradition, Change and Symbolism of Mongol Music in Ordos and Xilingol, Inner Mongolia." *Journal of the Anglo-Mongolian Society* 7(1–2):64–72.

———. 2001. *Mongolian Music, Dance, & Oral Narrative: Performing Diverse Identities.* Seattle: University of Washington Press.

Rees, Helen. 2000. *Echoes of History: Naxi Music in Modern China.* New York: Oxford University Press.

———. 2016. "Environmental Crisis, Culture Loss, and a New Musical Aesthetic: China's Original Ecology Folksongs in Theory and Practice." *Ethnomusicology* 60(1):53–88.

Schein, Louisa. 2000. *Minority Rules: The Miao and the Feminine in China's Cultural Politics.* Body, Commodity, Text. Durham, NC: Duke University Press.

Siriguleng. 2009. "Bianqian Zhong de Matouqin—Neimenggu Diqu Matouqin Chuangcheng Yu Bianqian [In the changing of morinhuur—Research on the transmission and change of morinhuur in Inner Mongolia]." Inner Mongolia Normal University.

Stokes, Thalea. 2013. "Across the Red Steppe: Exploring Mongolian Music in China and Exporting It from Within." Master's thesis, Western Michigan University.

Süzükei, Valentina. 2021. "*Khöömei*—Ambassador to the World." *Asian Music* 52(2).

Ulanji. 1998. *Mengguzu Yinyueshi* [A musical history of the Mongol nationality]. Hohhot: Neimenggu Renmin Chubanshe.

Upton, Janet L. 1996. "Home on the Grasslands? Tradition, Modernity and the Negotiation of Identity by Tibetan Intellectuals in the PRC." In *Negotiating Ethnicities in China and Taiwan*, edited by Melissa J. Brown, 98–124. Berkeley: Institute of East Asian Studies, University of California.

———. 2002. "The Poetics and Politics of *Sister Drum*: 'Tibetan' Music in the Global Cultural Marketplace." In *Global Goes Local: Popular Culture in Asia*, edited by Tim Craig and Richard King. Vancouver: University of British Columbia Press.

Weina, Oyuna. 2018. "'You Can't Sing *Urtyn Duu* if You Don't Know How to Ride a Horse': *Urtyn Duu* in Alshaa, Inner Mongolia." *Asian Music* 49(2):4–33.

Williams, Dee Mack. 1998. "Alcohol Indulgence in a Mongolian Community of China." *Bulletin of Concerned Asian Scholars* 30(1):13–22.

———. 2002. *Beyond Great Walls: Environment, Identity, and Development on the Chinese Grasslands of Inner Mongolia.* Stanford, CA: Stanford University Press.

Wong, Chuen-Fung. 2019. "'Original Ecology' Style of China's Minority Performing Arts: Examples from Uyghur Music." In *Chinese Shock of the Anthropocene: Image, Music and Text in the Age of Climate Change*, edited by Kwai-Cheung Lo and Jessica Yeung, 202–223. London: Palgrave MacMillan.

Wong, Isabel. 1984. "*Geming Gequ*: Songs for the Education of the Masses." In *Popular Chinese Literature and Performing Arts in the People's Republic of China*, edited by Bonnie S. McDougall, 112–143. Berkeley: University of California Press.

Yang, Man. 2009. "The Yuanshengtai Movement: Remaking of Chinese Ethnic Minority Identity." Master's thesis, University of Hawai'i at Manoa.

Zhang, Qian. 2012. "The Dilemma of Conserving Rangeland by Means of Development: Exploring Ecological Resettlement in a Pastoral Township of Inner Mongolia." *Nomadic Peoples* 16(1):88–115.

CHAPTER 3

The Politics of Regional and Ethnic Identities in Contemporary Mongolian *Urtyn Duu*

SUNMIN YOON

Singers of *urtyn duu*, a genre whose name is often translated as long-song, have tended to focus, both in their teaching and learning, on the songs' elongated and ornamented phrases. *Urtyn duu* is a widespread and frequently-practiced traditional vocal genre, closely associated with Mongolia's traditional nomadic culture, and has always been considered by Mongolians as one of their most important traditions. As I traveled from the far eastern border all the way to the western regions, close to Bayan-Ölgii aimag (province), I observed that local variations are significant characteristics of the *urtyn duu* genre, while certain traditional customs, technical ideas, and terms around it are commonly shared by singers throughout Mongolia.

At the earlier stage of my field research, I noted that singers were constantly using the terms *aizam, besreg, baruun,* and *züün* in their conversations. I learned over time the ideas and knowledge Mongolian singers embedded in the concepts, and the historical background behind their discourses and terminology. *Aizam* and *besreg* indicate certain categories of Mongolian *urtyn duu*. *Aizam* is considered among singers as the most respected category due to the advanced vocal techniques it requires and, among linguists and folklorists, due to the philosophical and spiritual content it expresses. In contrast, *besreg* is musically simpler and less demanding in terms of musical technique, and is thematically closer to everyday life. Whenever I asked singers (especially rural herder singers) to sing certain *aizam* songs,[1] they would say that they would not attempt to sing them because the songs are too difficult, but that they would happily sing *besreg* songs for me. Thus, in conversations with singers, *aizam* usually implied "difficult" songs that "skillful and professional" *urtyn duu* singers would sing, while *besreg* songs indicated a repertoire of songs that any singer could sing. At times, then, their discourse about *aizam* songs made me feel that this constituted a respected and superior area in the realm of singers.

The Mongolian word *baruun* indicates the right side, which is also the western direction in Mongolia, while *züün* indicates the left side, and thus the eastern direction.[2] I learned that *baruun ayalguu* (west-melody) often indicates songs from the culture of the Oirad, who have settled mostly in the western aimags. In contrast, *züün ayalguu* (east-melody) indicates songs from the majority ethnic Khalkh culture and from other ethnic cultures, which are mainly found in the central and eastern aimags, although songs from certain Khalkh styles are also distinguished from other eastern ethnic groups such as Dariganga and Üzemchin.

In developing conversations with singers and getting used to these terms as time passed in the field, I started to get a sense of an invisible division between the eastern and western cultures, between the "privileged singers" and "less-privileged singers," which created a sense of Othering and belonging within this *urtyn duu* tradition. The Othering in this case, as Edward Said (1978) showed in *Orientalism*, seemed relational, but with one apparently more dominant than the other; here, the Other is imagined. A great number of singers who mainly practice the "east-melody" would tell me in our interviews that the western regions do not have *aizam urtyn duu* or even *urtyn duu*. *Urtyn duu*, as a genre, is characterized—or reinforced—by long and elongated ornamental techniques, but *aizam duu*, even with its more elongated ornaments, could certainly be seen as not "existing" in the western region where singing practices emphasize the elongation far less. In my earlier fieldwork, when I worked primarily with singers in the eastern regions, I somehow inherited this as common knowledge and practice about *urtyn duu* among singers, and for a long time did not reconsider it, until I made two extensive trips to the western aimags and Khövsgöl aimag in 2013 and 2015.

This chapter presents the various regional (local) and ethnic styles of *urtyn duu* in the western region of Mongolia, particularly focusing on the different singing techniques and song repertories in order to offer a reevaluation of the discursive fields of current *urtyn duu* singers. In this way, I explore how the meaning of ethnicity and regionality has been represented and interpreted, not only in the *urtyn duu* tradition, but also as it reflects Mongolia's culture as a whole. I start with a brief introduction to the current heightened interest in ethnic diversity in contemporary Mongolia and continue by exploring the historical backdrop of the formation of ethnic boundaries, which ultimately defined the basis of the division between east and west. This is followed by a discussion of the politicization of ethnicity during the socialist period. I then illustrate the currently accepted taxonomy of the *urtyn duu* tradition and its related musical techniques in historical and social terms, which play a significant role in the construction of singers' views of what constitutes a skillful singer and a non-skillful one, accepted and not accepted, us and them. Finally, I share stories and observations from my ethnographic journeys to the western regions in 2013 and 2015 during which I had opportunities to learn about the various styles and practices of *urtyn duu* existing in this region, as well as how their ways of life are reflected in their geographical environment.

My findings from these journeys challenge the view, which I sensed in the central and eastern regions (including Ulaanbaatar), of the impact of ethnic authority upon certain singing techniques or certain *urtyn duu* categories. I suggest instead that the infusion of power dynamics in singers' understanding is a socially constructed one derived from the historical settlement of these ethnic groups and from ideological and political interference. In fact, however, the dissimilar musical techniques and repertoire unique to the local Mongolian singers are more of a culturally relative response to their geographical and environmental access and needs over time. My discovery process offers a challenge to long established beliefs that could not have been based on concrete knowledge, but on social practices that have been historicized, politicized, and Othered, especially when they have been orally transmitted.

The Rise of Ethnic and Regional Debates in Post-Socialist Modern Mongolia

Most of my time in Mongolia since 2006 has confirmed the country's gradual transition as a post-Socialist democratic nation. This drive for new nation-building has led to a reevaluation of racial purity and ethnic diversity. While the well-known Mongolian writer O. Dasbalbar (1957–1999) reinforced the unification of Mongols through the historical symbol of Chinggis Khan (Myadar and Deshaw Rae 2014:567), their coming together as one nation in remembering this figurehead has evoked among Mongolians a sense of the ethnic diversity that existed during the Chinggisid period. In 2016, an album called *Khamag Mongol* (*Every Mongol*) by one of Mongolia's well-known country folk-pop singers, S. Javkhlan, offered a reflection of the ethnic diversity, which was then in the ascendant. Javkhlan, who was also famous for his activist work against government corruption, had won his seat in the Parliament in 2015, in part through his great popularity among Mongolia's citizens due to the emphasis in his music on the importance of national identity. His album's subtitle, "*Gal duudsan mongol ayalguu*" (Mongol melody summoned by fire), reflects the pre-modern traditional Mongolian image in which three stones support the brazier (*tulga*) in the nomadic ger, emphasizing the importance of community, and of unity through diversity. In the music video for the album's title song Javkhlan presents the neighboring ethnic groups—one from Inner Mongolia, and Kalmyk, Buriad, Tuvan from Russian regions—wearing their own traditional ethnic clothing and symbolically sitting around a brazier. We see from this that the search for diverse ethnicity under the umbrella term of Mongol seems to be a part of Mongolia's nationalistic ideology in recent years.

Perhaps parallel to the phenomenon described above, it seemed that Mongols might imagine that having ethnic diversity, beyond the ethnic identity of Khalkh, was in part a turning away from what remained of Soviet influence. The majority of Mongols believe that the emphasis on Khalkh ethnic identity is the result of "Soviet modernism" (Sneath 2010:260), and that the rejection of this modernism through the revival of Mongolia's traditional cultural roots would provide the necessary fresh start for a new Mongolia. Orhon Myadar and James Deshaw Rae (2014:563) point out that bringing back an iconic figure from the thirteenth century is a rather unique move in the sociohistorical landscape of post-Soviet countries in Central Asia, where personality cults have tended to center around contemporary political leaders. Mongolia, though, has traveled to the distant past to represent the nation, and the distant past is where more diverse ethnic groups exist.[3]

In addition to discussions around ethnicity, the close connection to regional particularity and to their cultural identity are also unique aspects of Mongolia's ethnic cultural presentation. David Sneath (2010:260) points out that "many Mongolians do not think of their 'ethnic' designation as particularly important whereas most are very conscious of their locality identities." In my fieldwork, I have consistently observed that singers often mention both their name and ethnic group when asked, but mainly they describe the topography of the places where they were born, and ecological markers that distinguish those places—the dunes, steppes, or valleys, which are part of the "root" (*ündes*) from which they come. This seemed to be dependent upon the extent to which ethnic identity might have been replaced by local identity, as certain ethnic groups have come to reside in certain locations.

The concept of ethnicity in contemporary and post-socialist Mongolia can be emotionally complex, intertwined as it is with ideology and both ethnic and local identity. Anthropologist Zbigniew Szmyt (2012) explains that the complexity of ethnic cultures and discourses is not limited only to ethnic groups within the boundary of the Mongolian nation-state, but also to those which lie beyond. He addresses the discursive scope of "Mongol/Mongolness" among a variety of ethnic groups such as Mongolian-speaking groups living in the People's Republic of China and the Russian Federation, or the Buriad, Kazakh, and Tuvan diaspora living in Mongolia. They feel a strong sense of national identity as Mongolian citizens yet also struggle to locate clearly their ethnic and national identities in relation to the Mongolian state and to other nation states in which their members live.

The formation of ethnic settlement has thus been constantly fluid, reshaped, and reconsidered in relation to local contexts and the process of history. In this way, most of the ideas about ethnicity and regionalism observed in the late twentieth and early twenty-first centuries provide a helpful framework through which to understand the premodern period of Mongolia's ethnic founding.

Khalkh as Mongol and Oriad as Other?

Historical discussions regarding the divisive formation of ethnic/regional cultures in Mongol territory date back to the time of the Qing dynasty (1691–1911), when Mongolia's present-day territory consisted of four main states (*aimag*), different from the current twenty-one administrative provinces (also called aimag). Those four states were, from west to east, Zasagt Khan, Sain Noyon Khan, Tüsheet Khan, and Tsetsen Khan, and there were two additional frontier regions—Tannu Uriankhai in the north, including the Khövsgöl region,[4] and Khovd in the far west—that were also a part of the Züüngar State (1636–1755), which includes part of the current Xinjiang Uyghur Autonomous Region of China (see figure 3.1).

While the Uriankhai and Khovd frontiers, as well as part of the western region of Zasagt Khan aimag, were mainly dominated by the Oirads and their culture, the Khalkh and Chakar, who make up the majority of the people and culture of contemporary central and eastern Mongolia and part of Inner Mongolia, were mainly located in the three eastern aimag—Sain Noyon Khan, Tüsheet Khan, and Tsetsen Khan. According to Pamela Crossley (2006:64) "The Oyirods [Oirads] did not call themselves 'Mongols' but rather 'Four Oyirods' (*dörbön oyirad*), but 'Mongols' (*monggoli*) was their term for the eastern alliance under the Chakar Khaghans." The Oirads who settled in the western region, as opposed to the groups in the east of Mongolia, were a combination of diverse ethnic groups, such as the Altai Uriankhai, Darkhad, Myangad, Bayad, Zakhchin, and Dörvöd, whom I also encountered during my own fieldwork in Khövsgöl, Uvs, and Khovd aimags. Some of the ethnic groups, such as Buriad and Kalmyk, which are currently distributed more in the northeastern region of Mongolia, were also considered as a part of the Oirad in the earlier period; now they are distinguished from both the Oirad and Khalkh ethnic groups.

Based on this historical development of ethnic and administrative formation in the early period, Mongolians largely distinguish their cultures as Oirad and non-Oirad culture, or as Khalkh and non-Khalkh, or even as Khalkh and Oirad. They mention Khalkh and Oirad as, respectively, eastern and western cultures

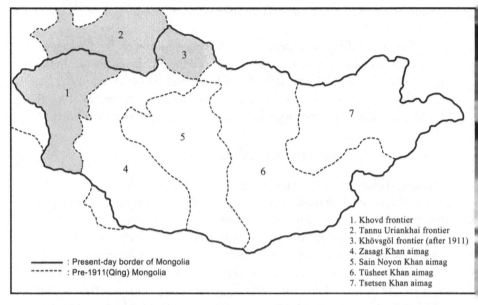

FIGURE. 3.1. Mongolia's administrative aimags and frontiers in 1911. Map drawn by Youngjin Yoon.

and people: the eastern as Khalkh and other groups in the eastern aimags such as Dariganga and Üzemchin, Barga, and the western as the Oirad groups I mentioned earlier. Within this major division between Oirad and Khalkh cultures, I often observed that people placed different emphases on different musical genres as well. For example, genres such as epic (*tuul'*) (see Chapters 4 and 6 in this volume), dance forms such as *biyelgee*, *khöömii* (see Chapters 8 and 9 in this volume), flute (*tsuur*), and string instruments such as *tovshuur* (see Chapter 6 in this volume) are often mentioned as traditions strong among the Oirads in the west, while song genres were much more dominant in the eastern regions. My colleague, A. Alimaa, who often travels with me to the countryside, once told me that greater numbers of longer *urtyn duu* had once existed in the west, but that they had now mainly disappeared. In contrast, some genres such as epic, which are still performed in the west, had once also existed throughout the eastern region, but they have been less historically preserved and are now disappearing (personal communication 2015). The current situation regarding these musical genres, then, in terms of what has changed and what still remains, could have arisen in part due to the music-cultural changes during the socialist era when Soviet folklorists penetrated Mongolian culture, creating a different dynamic of traditional culture.

Several scholars, including Christopher Kaplonski (1998), Uradyn Bulag (1998), and Carole Pegg (2001) have examined how Mongolia's premodern concept of ethnicity was reinforced and transformed under the influence of the Soviet Union between 1921 and 1990. During this time, the diverse ethnicities that had appeared in Mongolia's premodern history were suppressed, with the notion of uniting all the country as a single ethnic group, the "Khalkh." Although the Khalkh was the largest ethnic group, before the revolution, as Kaplonski (38) claims, the Mongols did not recognize themselves as a single collective nation state. Yet Mongolia formed the sense of itself as the MPR nation state by prioritizing the Khalkh people and Khalkh culture as a response to national policy, and by a process that artificially omitted any notion of ethnic sub-categories (Bulag 1998). Bulag refers to this process as *ugsaatny tseverlegee* (ethnic cleansing),[5] which indicates the suppression of ethnic diversity (1998:36).

> To be a Halh [Khalkh] means one is a proper citizen, a real Mongol, and to
> be Buryat means to be peripheral. In Dadal, the majority of children of Halh
> and Buryat [Buriad] unions have chosen to be Halh. Particularly interesting is
> one family: the parents are both Buryat, and they have six children, of whom
> two born before 1977 are registered as Buryat, while the four younger ones
> are Halh. The pressure to become Halh became stronger from the late 1970s.

Thus, Khalkh is viewed as "the Mongol of Mongols," which produced the idea that "Khalkh equals Mongol," which in turn led to Khalkh being considered the definition of a genuine Mongol (Bulag 1998:37). According to Bulag, this phenomenon was based on the perspective of Soviet ethnologists, which was expected to be strictly evolutionary: small ethnic groups (*yastan* or sub-ethnic groups) merged with a bigger group (*ündesten* or nation),[6] and people who were considered "backward" were to be improved by their assimilation into more "progressive nationalities," in this case, the Khalkh.

This evolutionary concept discussed by Bulag runs parallel to Pegg's discussions in the context of the performing art music scene in Mongolia (2001:256). Pegg explains that most traditional art musics were "neutralized" and "stabilized" under socialism, centralizing the standardized song and dance forms according to the Soviet-inspired policies and "development." In this process, ethnic minority musical cultures were discouraged, and merging with Khalkh styles was encouraged. In contrast, B. Tsetsentsolmon (2015:127) suggests a slightly different approach to the Soviet impact, based on what might be called "Soviet cosmology." This concept implies a much broader application of Soviet ideology than the idea of "current Party policy." She claims that "Soviet cosmology," therefore, allowed for Mongols to generate their own musical cultures, permitting them the space to celebrate their own "national tradition" even if it was in an edited and censored form. Tsetsentsolmon's statements allow us to understand how distinctive characteristics of ethnicity might have survived in the oral performance traditions even during the period of Soviet influence. I found Tsetsentsolmon's view confirmed in my interviews with older singers, especially in the case of *urtyn duu*; the *urtyn duu* tradition as a whole, including ethnic *urtyn duu*, was not encouraged on stage, yet remained alive during the period of Soviet influence.

Singing Techniques, Taxonomy, and Their Relations to Issues of Ethnicity

The historical basis of the cultural distinction between east and west relates to singers' discussions about *baruun ayalguu* (west-melody) and *züün ayalguu* (east-melody) which I learned in the field. However, I also experienced the subtle awareness and concretization of boundaries between "us and them" among singers, through particular songs, singing techniques, and certain technical *urtyn duu* terms. In our conversations, Khalkh *urtyn duu* singers from eastern regions generally seemed reluctant to describe the songs from the western regions as *urtyn duu*, because the western melodies were not especially elongated compared to the way of singing in the central and eastern regions. Instead, they were expressed through the short and segmented phrases of *urtyn duu*, which are understood as not being particularly difficult since they require a shorter breath. Some Khalkh singers accept the existence of *urtyn duu* among the Oirad but claim that these are not *aizam urtyn duu*, but only *besreg urtyn duu*. Even *urtyn duu* singers in the western region also hesitated to call their own songs "*urtyn duu*." Instead, the singers would refer to relatively elongated songs from the western regions simply as songs (*duu*), as opposed to *urtyn duu*, adding the ethnic group's name—for example, Darkhad *duu* and Buriad *duu*. When I told the singers from western ethnic groups that their songs sounded like *urtyn duu* to me, particularly when I noticed interesting techniques of elongation, they would say, "Well, it could be *besreg urtyn duu*." In an interview with a singer named B. Darimaa, who is ethnically Darkhad, she also described these songs as "Darkhad *duu*" and said they were not *urtyn duu* because they were not elongated, and they did not present relatively difficult techniques, such as *tsokhilt* (*tsokhilgo*: glottal vibrato) and *shurankhai* (a falsetto-like technique). She added that these would only appear in *urtyn duu*, or *aizam urtyn duu*, which are the most respected forms among the taxonomy of *urtyn duu*.

Kh. Sampildendev and Kh. Yatskovskai in their book *Mongol Ardyn Urtyn duu* (*Mongolian Long-song*) illustrate that the development of *urtyn duu*'s classification reflects a long historical discourse among Mongolians themselves, providing evidence from the Russian folklorist B. Ya. Vladimirtsov, who observed Mongolian folk songs during the 1920s. Sampildendev and Yatskovskai explain that, first of all, Mongols had their own ways of grouping and distinguishing the variety of forms of *urtyn duu*, particularly depending upon their different content, from religious themes to local heroes, from animals and landscape to emotions, and using terms such as *aizam* (or *aidam*), *shashtir* (religious), and *jargaa* (celebration) (Kh. Sampildendev and Kh. Yatskovskai 1984:4).

In addition to the recognition by Mongols themselves of the different lyrical meanings, early Soviet researchers such as B. Ya. Vladimirtsov, C. A. Kondratsev, K. H. Yatskovskai, and D. Maisar seem to have observed different musical styles in different regions, and among different ethnic groups. Like these earlier Soviet scholars, I was also able to learn a variety of different songs and singing styles in different regions and observe the ways *urtyn duu* are classified from singers themselves, from contemporary local scholars, and even from lay Mongolians who were interested in the genre. The classification I learned in the field consisted of *aizam urtyn duu*, *jiriin urtyn duu* (or *sumun urtyn duu*), and *besreg urtyn duu*. Later I found that most recent scholars also followed this taxonomy (Sampildendev and Yatskovskai 1984; Pegg 2001; Rinchensambuu 2011; Alimaa 2012), although Pegg used the term *tügeemel* (general) *urtyn duu* instead of *jiriin urtyn duu* (or *sumun urtyn duu*).

Aizam urtyn duu (extended long-song), or *aizam duu* (extended song), is the most elongated and ornamented (*chimeglelt*) style of *urtyn duu* and is often regarded as the most technically challenging style among singers. It requires longer and fuller breathing with specific improvisational vocal techniques in the articulation of lyrics. *Jiriin urtyn duu* or *suman urtyn duu* can be translated as "ordinary/common long-song" or "local long-song," in which the word *jir* ("regular, normal") implies the medium length of long-song and the word *sum* refers to an administrative unit of Mongolia's countryside (smaller than an aimag) and implies "local." The final category is *besreg urtyn duu*, which translates as "simplified long-song," and is understood among singers as technically the easiest of the three since the musical phrases are shorter and require less ornamentation and shorter breath. These three categories of long-song were clearly identified among singers I met as the expression of different musical characteristics and different degrees of vocal technique and performance practice, and this has led to the hierarchical notion that singers who can sing *aizam urtyn duu* were the most technically advanced singers. These singers are inevitably Khalkh, since this taxonomy evolved principally around the Khalkh *urtyn duu* styles and repertories that are common in the central and eastern regions of Mongolia.

Furthermore, singers in the eastern and central regions, and later in the western region, often explained to me that certain techniques could be employed as discrete markers in the classification of *urtyn duu*. Among the most critical vocal features, two distinctive techniques stand out: *shurankhai* and *tsokhilt* (*tsokhilgo*). The first, *shurankhai*, is similar to falsetto in Western art music and often appears—mainly once but sometimes twice—at the highest note of the song's melody. This technique is always found in *aizam urtyn duu* and also occasionally in some *jiriin urtyn duu*, but it is never found in *besreg urtyn duu*. Having this challenging technique in a song, as well as the fact that singers can manage this technique only on a full breath, raising their thin head voice to the highest point of a song's melodic range, is an indication of a song's difficulty and also how accomplished the singer could be within the community of singers.

The second technique, *tsokhilt*, is a strong laryngeal trill. When discussing improvisatory ornaments (*chimeglel*), *urtyn duu* singers mention several different kinds. These include a short appoggiatura (*nugalaa*) and a soft trill (*bönjignökh*), which are both very common. Some trills sound like a simple vibrato, and some sound like a mimicry of sheep's bleating and range in length from the very short, stretching across a few notes, to the very long, lasting for several seconds. As one of the family of ornaments (*chimeglel*), *tsokhilt* involves a strong, elongated, vibrato produced by a forceful movement of air striking the larynx. I have observed that singers often consider *tsokhilt* a more advanced technique than other elongated ornaments such as *nugalaa* or *bönjignökh*, and a singer who mastered *tsokhilt* and included it in one of the lengthened song forms such as *aizam duu* or *jiriin duu* was likewise considered to be more technically skilled. For this reason, it seemed, it was through the existence and presentation of techniques such as *shurankhai* and *tsokhilt* that singers seemed able to identify different levels of songs or technical ability among singers.

The classification of Mongolian *urtyn duu* might at first seem like a simplistic folkloric or musicological discussion. However, I often saw that this taxonomy focused on particular singing techniques and that singers also expressed their pride or humility or even artistic authority with regard to these techniques. This led me to rethink the meaning of the discursive field of categorization and musical techniques, and furthermore the connections with ethnic politics among Mongolians. What does it mean to talk here about "advanced" and "skillful," how do we determine the long-song's aesthetic values, and who gets to decide these questions?

A Journey to the Western Aimags

After a great deal of time with singers mainly in the eastern and central regions and in Ulaanbaatar, I decided to visit the west to explore these traditions further. Since the journey to the western region, about 1400 km (about 850 miles) from Ulaanbaatar, requires long-distance travel of many days and a large budget, I had to wait a long time to make the trip. Instead of staying with one singer for an extended period, I decided to move around to search for as

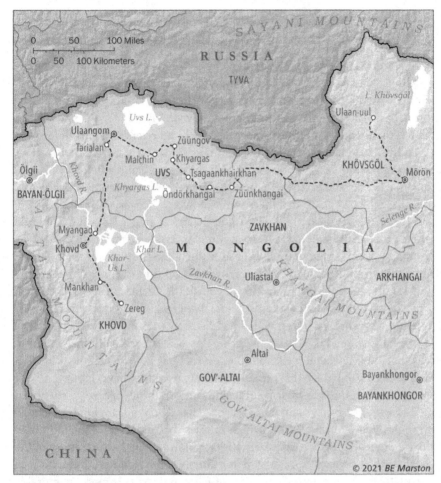

FIGURE 3.2. Travel route to the western aimags in 2013 and 2015. Map designed by Brooke Marston (used with permission).

many different singing styles as I could find among different ethnic groups and in different aimags and sums. This mobile ethnographic fieldwork (Yoon 2019) has been useful for comparing many different ethnic and regional styles of *urtyn duu*. It has also made it possible for me to observe their singing within their daily lives and further to experience the ecological environment in which singers live. In this way, my long journey introduced me to different landscapes of Mongolia (see Chapter 1 in this volume)—mountains, small and large lakes, taiga, and bare ridges—especially as I moved toward the western regions and away from the central and eastern landscape.

Through the Taiga to Khövsgöl Aimag: Darkhad and Khoitgid Singers

In December 2013, accompanied by my colleague and collaborator, linguist A. Alimaa, and by a driver, Mönkhbayar, who had also traveled with me previously through other regions, I headed north from Ulaanbaatar and passed through Erdenet, Mongolia's third largest city, on my way for the first time to Khövsgöl aimag. In the freezing winter cold, the rivers which we often encountered were frozen solid. The mountain ridges were covered with snow, their bright white ridges contrasting with the blue-green conifers in this taiga region. After several hours, we reached Mörön, the aimag center (*aimgiin töv*) of Khövsgöl. I had heard that there were Khotgoid and Buriad singers in town, and that there was also a well-respected theatrical singer from the Khotgoid ethnic group. Although it was not common for the singers from diverse ethnic groups to work as state theater singers in the aimag's cultural center, female Khotgoid singer, R. Lkhamjav (b. 1947) was at that time the only singer among non-Khalkh singers bearing the title of *gav'yat* (lit. talented; a state-sanctioned singer during the socialist and post-socialist eras). She performed regularly in the theater and had also traveled to Ulaanbaatar to make a recording with Mongolian National Broadcasting during the socialist era. In our meeting in an old Soviet-style elementary school classroom, I had no expectation as to what kind of songs and voice this rather elderly singer might have. However, once she started singing, her high volume and fiery, high-pitched voice surprised me. As with Lkhamjav's singing, I learned that Khotgoid singing is extended through the use of undulation, which mimics the landscape of the mountain ridges. Their singing is particularly strong (*khüchtei*), making great use of the vocal cords (see Yoon 2015 for video example). The frequent undulation in the relatively short-phrased melodies of Khotgoid songs is more memorable for listeners, and the unique melodies of some of these songs are already well known in Ulaanbaatar in the form of arranged country pop music.

Each time I traveled through Khövsgöl aimag, I could not help noticing the landscape that unfolded in front of me, in contrast to the open steppe of the central Khangai region and the endless open grassland of the east. I saw steep ridges surrounding the path along which I was moving, and while I was remembering R. Lkhamjav singing "Deltei tsenkher" (Light grey horse with a mane). Her strong undulating voice, and the short melodies of the song echoed in my head as I passed up and over the mountain pass (see figure 3.3).

Leaving Mörön behind, I traveled to northwest Khövsgöl, close to the Russain border, to visit a small rural district, Ulaan-uul sum. Although I had heard the characteristics of Darkhad singing from B. Darimaa, whom I had met in Ulaanbaatar in 2009, I was hoping to hear some Darkhad singers performing

FIGURE 3.3. Winter mountain pass in Khövsgöl 2013. Photo by S. Yoon.

in their local geographic environment. According to historian Christopher Atwood (2004:132), "the origin of the Darkhad appears to be mixed Mongolian
and Tuvan," and "the Darkhad dialect today is quite close to Khalkha [Khalkh]
but contains forms that indicate it was originally a Kalmyk-Oirat [Oirad] type
dialect later subject to very strong Khalkha influence." I quickly noticed their
subtle accent when I met with a male Darkhad singer called N. Tsogbadrakh
(b.1961). Hoping to listen to some Darkhad *urtyn duu*, I sat with Tsogbadrakh.
He first sang mainly short-songs (*bogino duu*).[7] When I asked if he could sing
long-songs, Tsogbadrakh said that *urtyn duu* style songs had been practiced
in the old days, but they had mostly disappeared. It seemed that, during the
socialist era, the short-song had become much more popular in the theater.
Short-songs with unique styles and tunes from the western region especially,
including Khövsgöl, were more frequently promoted and performed in concert
settings. This process seemed to reinforce the gradual extinction of elongated
Darkhad *urtyn duu*.

Both Darkhad singers—B. Darimaa, whom I had met in Ulaanbaatar before this trip, and Tsogbadrakh—were not explicitly singing in the *urtyn duu*

style, and it also seemed to me that they were reluctant to try to sing using the particular techniques of elongation. However, the CD of her own songs that Darimaa gave me contained an *urtyn duu* style of singing. These *urtyn duu*-style songs, however, felt similar to Khalkh *urtyn duu*, except that their closing phrases often dropped or jumped abruptly to a particular pitch. Even at the end of the short-songs, I observed that Darkhad singers often include a performative exclamation of the syllable *khoi*, on which the pitch usually descends. Instead of *urtyn duu*, Tsogbadrakh sang for me the short-song style of repartee songs, *khar'ltsaa duu*, that were often performed by singers sitting together in parallel rows. I later learned from other ethnic singers that the western region kept more diverse and communal performance styles, rather than keeping to a strong solo tradition. Later, I discovered that Tsogbadrakh was making regular visits to older singers in order to learn those songs that seemed to have remained as *urtyn duu*. Unfortunately, we could not visit these older singers together due to the heavy snow and bitterly cold days during my stay.[8] Planning to return to Ulaan-uul sum in the future, and due to the cold winter weather, I headed back to Ulaanbaatar, spending more time in the south as I did so, passing through Arkhangai and Övörkhangai aimags where I heard mainly Khalkh singers.[9]

Eljigen Khalkh Singers in Eastern Uvs Aimag

I was back on the road again in the summer of 2015, going further into the western regions, again accompanied by A. Alimaa and Mönkhbayar. Following the route we had taken to Khövsgöl in 2013, we set off directly toward Zavkhan aimag, and from there to Uvs aimag. With the excitement of a second trip to the western region, we had only brief meetings with some Khalkh singers in the Khövsgöl aimag and in the northern part of Zavkhan aimag. Thus, after about four days of driving from Ulaanbaatar, we arrived at the eastern border of Uvs aimag. When we stopped in a district called Züünkhangai sum, the landscape and the pass around the sum had briefly become less mountainous and more like the central Khangai region, with more open steppe, just as the name Züünkhangai might indicate (eastern Khangai; the neighboring sum to the west was called Öndörkhangai, or "high Khangai"). The singers I met here were Eljigen Khalkh people.[10]

According to what I had learned in the field, the Eljigen Khalkh was originally a Khalkh group living in the eastern region, but they had relocated to the western region along with other ethnic groups. For that reason, perhaps, Eljigen Khalkh singing exhibits similar features to the singing style of the Khalkh, whose homeland is in the eastern regions. I found that their principal songs consist of the same repertory as that among the Khalkh, but their vocal styles bore notable Oirad influences, such as singing in shorter phrases just like the simpler versions of the Khalkh songs. Eljigen Khalkh singing, therefore, does not employ the *shurankhai* or the more elongated and complicated ornamentations, although it does exhibit similar ornamentation techniques, such as *bönjignökh* and occasional *tsokhilt*. One of the female singers, A. Tsagaankhüü (b. 1950) from Züünkhangai sum, illustrated all the Khalkh styles mentioned earlier in her singing, but she employed greater volume and a broader vocal timbre, which is relatively common among other non-Khalkh singers in the western regions. I noted another example of this when she sang a song called "Zes guai" (Mr. Zes), incorporating the style of the Khotgoid ethnic group into the Khalkh style of singing, which places greater emphasis on a strong undulating melodic contour. Another male Eljigen Khalkh herder-singer, J. Nyamjav (b. 1974), sang with rich emotion a local *urtyn duu* and showed a vocal skill that many male Khalkh singers employed, with forceful trilling, striking the larynx using chest voice/breathing (*tseejnii tsokhilt*), particularly where the melodic line became more even. This technique is often found in *aizam duu*, particularly in the central Khangai region and the Gov' region of Khalkh. The mixture of central Khalkh style, augmented by techniques common to the western regions, made the Eljigen Khalkh style unique among other western ethnic groups. It also reflected the historical process by which they had moved away from their homeland in central Mongolia and, like their songs, had found a new home. The musical characteristics clearly represented their original homeland and their historical movement as part of the Khalkh ethnic group, living through their interactions with other ethnic groups in the western regions.

Similarly, the far eastern side of Uvs aimag, where the three districts of Züünkhangai sum, Öndörkhangai sum, and Tsagaankhairkhan sum are located, and where I encountered Eljigen Khalkh people, revealed a far more steppe-like landscape, rather than mountainous taiga. I was thinking that, perhaps when the Eljigen Khalkh people settled, they needed to be in similar surroundings, just like their songs had found a way into the new landscape. As I left these regions, I reached locations even further to the north, districts called Khyargas sum, Züüngov' sum, and Malchin sum. These regions were less grassy, more barren, and quite close to the Tuvan frontier. Here I encountered the Bayad people.

Bayad and Khoton Singers in Central Uvs Aimag

Interestingly, there are a lot of relatively young Bayad male singers[11] in the central regions of Uvs aimag, particularly in Ethnic group. Züüngov' and Malchin sum, which are much closer—perhaps within 50 km—to Mongolia's northern border with Russia, and where one of the country's biggest lakes, Uvs nuur, is located. As we drove into the region, the natural surroundings became more barren, and even more open in comparison to the southern part of Uvs aimag where the Eljigen Khalkh people were living.

In Khyargas sum, the Bayad singers I met were aged between forty and eighty years old. They sang with rather refined voices, each phrase short, but moving through a pattern of set intervals using sliding tones. However, Bayad singing also exhibits small ornaments, such as *bönjignökh* and *nugalaa*, and similar characteristics in its melodic contour to those found in Eljigen Khalkh singing. Despite seeing the slightly different landscapes of Khyargas sum from the southeastern part of Uvs aimag where the Eljigen Khalkh had settled, I recognized how the relative closeness of the neighboring settlements of Bayad and Eljigen people resulted in their influencing one another and producing similar styles.

About thirty kilometers south of Ulaangom, the aimag center of Uvs, and about 100 kilometers from Khyargas sum, I had another interesting encounter with a Khoton singer near Tarialan sum. The Khoton people in Uvs originate mainly from the Türkic Khoton, and they are predominantly Muslim. Although I had a hard time understanding other singers' language in western regions, I found it nearly impossible to understand the different intonation and vocabulary of the Khoton singers, having learned much of my Mongolian in Ulaanbaatar. I was constantly asking my colleague Alimaa, who had grown up in Ulaan-baatar, about vocabulary and what they were talking about, and she admitted that she, too, did not understand some of the words. I found that the Khoton songs are also short but repetitive, much closer to the singing styles of Dörvöd and Zakhchin (described in the following sections), but they are distinct from the particular stylistic characteristics of songs among the Bayad and Eljigen Khalkh, and Khotgoid, which employ longer phrases than the Dörvöd and Zakhchin singing styles. The verses of Khoton, Dörvod, and Zakhchin songs, having shorter musical phrases, are repeated numerous times, so the length of songs is extended not by elongated vowels in one verse but by repeated verses. I once heard that western *urt duu* (that is, *urtyn duu*) was so called, not because of the elongated verses, but because each verse is repeated so much, and this offered a good example.

Coming out of the second Khoton singer's ger, I saw the mountain in the distance, but was thinking that I had never seen such high mountains from a distance in other regions of Mongolia. With that vast mountain behind him like a screen, the singer pointed in the opposite direction, toward Gov'-Altai in response to Mönkhbayar's question about the direction of Khovd aimag, and so we departed in the direction indicated.

Dörvöd and Myangad Singers in Northern Khovd Aimag

The landscape again opened up as I traveled south from Uvs, with greener trees, more winding mountain ridges, and small rivers and lakes. With all the rain in the summer of 2015, I observed the herders taking their cattle across a river, a process that lasted about four hours. In this area, I saw people from different ethnic groups living together. I met Dörvöd singers here, but also Myangad singers. It was at Myangad sum, Khovd aimag, that I met a male Dörvöd singer, L. Törtogtokh (b. 1962). In our interview, Törtogtokh explained that despite the fact that people from different ethnic groups now tend to live together in certain regions, people in earlier times (*khuuchin üyed*) really didn't distinguish between their own and others' cultures but tried to blend them together to live harmoniously. When it comes to the musical styles, people were clearly aware of the different singing characteristics among neighboring ethnic groups and while they sometimes kept their unique characteristics, they also mixed them together.

According to the Mongolian scholar Ganbold (2012), the Dörvöd ethnic group is historically Uigaryn Mongol (Mongols living in the Xinjiang Uyghur Autonomous Region of China) and its people are distinguished from the Muslim Khotons by their adherence to Tibetan Buddhism. The Dörvöd are famous for their rich performing culture, including game songs and several other genres of song, and they make up one of the largest populations among western ethnic groups. The vocality of the Dörvöd, I observed, includes a plaintive sound and a lot of sliding tones. M. Dorjdagva (2016) describes Dörvöd singing as being "like a wolf howling" and identifies this as the region in which *urtyn duu* was first practiced. This Dorjdagva's description of the sound was generally applicable to the voices of some Khoton singers I met, which also can be characterized by extended sliding tones and by a highly pressed voice. Songs usually begin with an accented shout, using a relatively strong, loud voice, and singers emphasize the end of a phrase when they finish a song.

Pegg (2001:47) mentioned that Dörvöd singing is more ornamented than that of the Bayad, according to her interviewee, Jargaland Ireedüi, but my observation in the field, comparing three male and female Dörvöd singers in this southern Uvs aimag with seven Bayad male singers I met in northern Uvs aimag, provided some different perspectives. The important differences between Dörvöd and Bayad singers do not depend upon which group uses more ornamentation but their melodic contour and timbral quality. The melodies of Bayad songs are smoother and exhibit a softer timbre, with much smaller interval slides and gentler trills. In contrast, the Dörvöd songs include more abrupt and larger movement in their melodic contours. They discussed these techniques using Mongolian terms such as *khadgalakh* (small intervallic upward slides), *gulsakh* (small intervallic downward slides), and *örgölgt* (some upward emphasis).[12] This indicates that these techniques were consciously practiced and transmitted among the singers.

After my visit to the Dörvöd Törtogtokh in Myangad sum, I learned that Törtogtokh's mother was living in Khovd city, Khovd aimag, south of Myangad sum, and we decided to go visit her, taking Törtogtokh with us. As we journeyed south together, we were informed that Törtogtokh knew a good Myangad singer on the edge of Myangad sum. When we visited the singer's house, no one was home and the next door neighbor said that she had gone to Ulaanbaatar to see her children. Thinking that I would not be able to see her on this trip, we set out for Khovd city. Driving away from the Myangad sum, we saw a Russian-style bus coming in the distance, and Törtogtokh shouted with joy, confident that the singer was on the bus. With such serendipity, soon enough, I was sitting in her house. This female singer, G. Chuluunbat (b. 1944), used the term *besreg duu* in describing where Myangad songs might be musically located in the realm of *urtyn duu*. Similar to those of the Eljigen Khalkh and Bayad songs, the musical styles she sang also were decorated with trills such as *bönjignökh*, *nugalaa*, and *tsokhilt*. She sang a few very specific regional songs, such as "Sukhaityn chin' argal'" (Wild sheep among the tamarisk) and "Shild n' orson tsas" (Snowfall on the ridges), which I had never heard anywhere else. She sang another song, "Zunyn delger sar" (In high summer), and explained that this is used as a feast song (*nairyn duu*), which in context means that it is more formal and extended than the two previous songs. In the Khalkh tradition, feast songs were usually either *aizam urtyn duu* or *jiriin urtyn duu*, yet Chuluunbat specifically categorized it as *besreg urtyn duu*, implying this is typical to feast songs in the region. The melodic line was similar to the Khalkh melodic contour and more elongated than that of other ethnic songs.

One Mongolian long-song researcher, M. Dorjdagva (2016:33), mentioned that someone listening to Myangad *urtyn duu* might confuse it with western Khalkh *urtyn duu*, because Myangad *urtyn duu* can be mixed with Eljigen Khalkh. It also can be mixed with other ethnic songs in the Oriad style, which are stronger in the western regions; this process, though, has been all but forgotten. As Dorjdagva notes, I could clearly hear that Chuluunbaatar's singing was indeed quite close technically to the Eljigen Khalkh, yet also affected by the Oirad style. Also, my experience of meeting a Myangad singer and a Dörvöd singer in the same sum, and noticing that the Dörvöd singing style was similar to that of Khoton singing, helped me confirm the comments of the Dörvöd singer, Törtogtokh, about the song "Öndör khökhii" (High and dark). This song refers to the nearby mountain, Altain Khökhii, to which all three ethnic groups—Myangad, Dörvöd, and Khoton—have access, and the song is also shared by all three (Yoon 2019:52–54). And the singing practices from different ethnic groups who are living close by are uniquely captured in their own ways but have also developed over time certain shared features.

Through Khovd City to Southern Khovd Aimag: Zakhchin Singers

During our stay in Khovd city, a big competition of epic (*tuul'*) singers was going on in the city theater, where I met epic singers who played *tovshuur* (see Chapter 6 in this volume) and dancers. I also met an Uriankhai singer who had also come for the epic competition. This young male Uriankhai singer, E. Galbadrakh (b. 1992), came from Mönkhkhairkhan sum, which was some way from the route we were taking, which meant that we could not visit him at his home. He mentioned a recent drive among Uriankhai singers to revive *urtyn duu*, particularly in his home region. He sang a unique Uriankhai *urtyn duu* with a great number of sliding tones, a feature also found in the songs of the Zakhchin people whom I would meet on the next leg of my trip. They lived in Mankhan sum and Zereg sum, both in the far south of Khovd aimag and close to the Gov'-Altai aimag. The young Uriankhai singer Galbadrakh's hometown, Mönkhkharikhan sum, was even closer to the Altai Mountains and further to the southwest.

According to Atwood (2004:617), most Zakhchin (lit. "borderlanders") were historically guards brought from other regions to protect the regional boundaries as part of their military duties, and they have become a cultural-ethnic group formed through the fulfillment of duty and by being in a certain place at a certain time. They are not formed from ethnic groups that are culturally and biologically related. They were stationed along the borders shared with other ethnic groups in the Altai, such as Torguud, Ööld, and Dörvöd (Ganbold 2012). This demonstrates another good example of how Mongolian ethnicity is closely related to regional divisions in early history. The Zakhchin possess a strong repertoire of short-songs (*bogino duu*) with satirical content, which I heard very frequently, but I was also lucky to hear some of the Zakhchin *urtyn duu* in Zereg sum. They were melodic and heavily ornamented, yet similar in style to those sung among the Dörvöd, exhibiting sliding tones (*gulsakh*) and emphatic rise (*örgölt*). There were some songs that also existed only among the Zakhchin singers, such as "Khan uulyn oroi" (The peak of Khan uul), "Tsagaany tsookhor" (White-speckled [horse]), and "Altan aaruulyn amt" (The golden taste of aaruul [dried curd]).

As we drove away from Zereg sum, I noticed a more desert-like landscape—more open, but more brown than green (that is, more rocky, figure 3.3), with the mountainous ridges and the distant topography becoming generally far less undulating. I started finding fewer and fewer non-Khalkh singers as I moved back to Bayankhongor aimag, and I realized that my "western" journey to learn about the distinctive western *urtyn duu* singing styles, their diverse ethnic cultures, and their response to their natural environment was coming to an end.

Discussion and Conclusion

I traveled for just over a month through the western aimags and met with singers from a diverse pool of younger and older, female and male singers from different ethnic groups. Throughout my conversations with diverse ethnic singers, I made a point of asking them to sing only *urtyn duu*, or at least songs that have been understood as "*urtyn duu*" by their community, and it became clear to me that this genre exists in the western region in various ways as part of different ethnic cultures. It was also clear that the emphasis of vocal styles of *urtyn duu* in the western aimags is different from that of the Khalkh styles in the central and eastern regions. The songs in the western regions were lengthened by the repeating of verses, whereas those in the eastern regions are lengthened through the elongated words in the lyrics. Among ethnic groups themselves in the west—the Khotgoid and Darkhad (Khövsgöl aimag), Eljigen Khalkh, Bayad and Khoton (Uvs aimag), and Myangad, Dörvöd, Zakhchin, and Uriankhai (Khovd aimag)—there were also significant differences in intonation and dialects, as much in their speech as in their singing. The songs of the Zakhchin, Dörvöd, and Khotgoid people were characterized by peaks and troughs in their melodic lines, articulated through sliding tones, whereas the songs of the Myangad, Bayad, and Eljigen Khalkh were less undulating but expressed greater melodic phrasing.

The ornaments (*chimeglel*) frequently found in eastern melodies (*züün ayalguu*), such as soft trills (*bönjignökh*) and short appoggiaturas (*nugalaa*), also appeared frequently in various contexts of the west-melody (*baruun ayalguu*). Some techniques such as *tsokhilt* (a strong laryngeal trill) and *shurankhai* (the high falsetto technique), which are considered important in east-melody (*züün ayalguu*) due to their frequent inclusion in extended (*aizam*) songs, appeared only rarely. Regardless of these unique differences in the emphasis of the vocal techniques and performance styles between the eastern and western melodies, a majority of singers, not only in the central and eastern aimags but also in the western aimags, place more importance on certain vocal techniques such as extended strong laryngeal trills (*tsokhilt*) and high falsetto techniques (*shurankhai*). The west-melody, which lacked those techniques, thus came to be viewed as less authoritative in this cultural hierarchy. Yet sliding tones, a greater volume coming from a fuller breath, and undulating melodic contours, just like the landscape through which I had journeyed, are also, I learned, techniques just as difficult to master as those of Khalkh *urtyn duu* in the central and eastern regions.

Thinking particularly about the northern high mountain range of Khövsgöl aimag and the singing of R. Lkhamjav, who had expressed an undulating and reverberant acoustic in the melodic movement of her singing, I later recalled a casual conversation with the Mongolian musicologist Kh. Erkhembayar, who was from Khovd aimag. He had mentioned that the phrases of western *urtyn duu* are short because the western songs are not focused on elongation, reflecting the landscape of the steppe, but more likely respond to the undulating mountains, which create more echoes (*tsuurai*). He felt that those echoes would be the core essence and beauty of the western songs. When I stand outside on the open steppe of the central Khangai region further to the east, the sound of my own voice and my auditory senses are both traveling straight into the air and, seemingly without end, blend together with the occasional sounds that emerge from the livestock in the distance. In the west, on the ridges of the mountains, with sharp trees on the taiga shooting up into the sky, I had a different sense when I listened to my speaking voice: it was more resonant (See figure 3.4). Through my own acoustic experiences of landscape, and after observing various singers, I have come to the conclusion that the difference between the west-melodies (*züün ayalguu*) and the east-melodies (*baruun ayalguu*) of *urtyn duu* is the result of where and in what kind of geographical environment the singing has been nurtured and developed, along with the relative historical formation and local knowledge of the ethnic cultures among the Oriad and Khalkh.

Nevertheless, the discourse surrounding the "genuine" form of *urtyn duu* has generated more than simply the essential relationship between music-making and the natural surroundings, which has resulted in a shift in the focal balance of the musical aesthetic. Singers throughout Mongolia often identify the more "advanced" or more "challenging" singing techniques, and these have tended to be centered around the *urtyn duu* heard among the Khalkh in the central and eastern regions. This would seem to be a result of how Soviet influence promoted a centralized Mongolian musical culture through professionalism centered around Ulaanbaatar during the early twentieth century, as we learned from Bulag (1998) and Pegg (2001) earlier in this chapter. This process was strengthened through a particular focus on encouraging singers' virtuosic mechanical or technical complexity and mastery rather than their understanding of the organic relations sustained by the local performance style and customs or by the meaning behind the songs. In this way, the traditional and local value and philosophy became downplayed in the light of Soviet ideology.

This approach by which the tradition of *urtyn duu* became centralized might have gained greater traction through the evolutionary concept that emerged along with the idea of professionalism during the socialist era. This profes-

FIGURE 3.4. Leaving Uvs aimag, on the way to Khovd aimag. 2015. Photo by S. Yoon.

sionalism has resulted in a vertical classification of singers and has created the concept of what is to be preferred, making a boundary between those who belong and those who do not belong, along with the feeling of being selected and not selected, and perhaps after all those who are privileged and not privileged. It is true that *aizam duu* requires musically more defined techniques than *jiriin urtyn duu* or *besreg urtyn duu* within the Khalkh tradition. However, in the more traditional performance context of *urtyn duu*, such as feasts (*nair*), *aizam duu* were selected to be performed and respected not only for their musical style but also for how their lyrical meaning reflected traditional values. The ethnic songs from the western regions, though, lacking the extended singing techniques typically used in *aizam urtyn duu*, were also incorporated into a variety of feast-style contexts, regardless of the technical level of the songs, but in the same way reflecting the social and cultural value from the singers' own ethnic groups.

Placed alongside what I discovered on my journey to the west, my conversations with two Khövsgöl singers, a Darkhad singer, B. Darimaa in 2009, and a Khalkh herder singer, B. Javzandolgor in 2013, offer further insights into the ethnic and regional dynamics in the singing tradition during the socialist and post-socialist eras. Darimaa, who travels back and forth between Ulaanbaatar and her hometown, observed that local ethnic songs, such as those among the Darkhad people, were not considered suitable for performance in Ulaanbaatar, since the musical elements of those local songs were associated with the local environment and local cultures and could not be understood and contextualized on the Ulaanbaatar stage. Also, instead of stating that it had been State policy that had suppressed their ethnic customs in response to the rise of Ulaanbaatar culture, as Bulag illustrated earlier (1998), Darimaa pointed out that, with the central Khalkh becoming more dominant in the traditional musical scene during the socialist period, ethnic singers in fact did not appear to have felt proud about presenting their ethnic customs. Javzandolgor, indeed, who is Khalkh but whose entire life was rooted in the local Khövsgöl aimag as a herder, preferred to sing the version of the song rendered by professional singers in Ulaanbaatar, even though she had kept the local version, which she had learned from her mother.

My conversations with these singers leave me with two important points. First, it is clear that Mongolia's ethnic communities and local populations have developed their vocal arts and expressive cultures in close relation to their ecological environment. This shaped their local and ethnic customs along with their local languages, so that it might have been more suitable for these ethnic styles of songs to have been performed and understood in their birthplaces, which required that they remain in their locale. The second important point from these conversations confirms that there was certainly a centralization of culture in Ulaanbaatar during the socialist period; this was not only due to Party policy and political activities, however, but had perhaps been exercised to a greater extent by the musical practitioners themselves as well as by the participating audience. This reinforced their own discrete notion separating the privileged group from the Others. The ethnic and regional dynamics provided in this case a readily available leverage.

Returning in this context to Said's notion of "orientalism," introduced at the beginning of this chapter, the Other, in the case of *urtyn duu*—the singing and singers of the west-melodies—is imagined by dint of its ethnic and cultural distance, rather than by the actual differences in the singing and performance. The lack of *aizam duu*, and of particular techniques such as *shurankhai* or *tsokhilt*, in the Oirad traditions, became a way to create distance, and thereby the means to imagine at once a distinction between us and them, and an increased sense of belonging/displacement. The singing techniques of *shurankhai* and *tsokhilt* became, in this case, merely cultural assets that have been used to empower or disempower. Once such skills acquire value, the singers who can use those techniques gain an advantage, and the songs marked by such techniques achieve a greater importance, thus fashioning a power relationship that exists more in the singers' *minds* than anywhere else.

As Mongolia stepped into the post-socialist era after 1990, a new cultural trajectory was instigated, and ethnic diversity faced a new situation, which is still ongoing. One could argue that the Mongols' attitude toward their ethnic cultures has been shifting since 1990, as the country has developed its democracy through a series of political changes. These cultural shifts have sometimes been contradictory and sometimes complementary. While Mongols are now in a constant search for their united identity as "Mongol," and use their diverse ethnic identity to strengthen their holistic identity, as shown in Javklan's album *Khamag Mongol*, I see this notion of ethnic cultures as once again becoming imagined through a process of politicization, creating different and nuanced "us and them" binaries, although now they are focused on new nation-building. By the same token, the ephemeral and fluid nature of Mongolia's oral tradition has made it more accessible in the politicized and ideologized processes. Singers now use *urtyn duu* in order to emphasize the nostalgic idea that *urtyn duu* has been a continuing and constant feature of Mongol culture since the Hünnü era and to promote in particular their own unique ethnic *urtyn duu*. More Mongol scholars are drawing from the work of local ethnic singers, and the western (Oirad) culture as a whole is being more actively discussed. And now these ethnic and cultural issues are again being mentioned in relation to the current predicament of Mongol identity. In this way, the *urtyn duu* tradition—and perhaps orally transmitted traditions in Mongolia—is continuously shifting and being negotiated through a constant process of cultural transition. Nevertheless, the fact that Mongolia has a rich ethnic diversity, and that each ethnic group retains its own distinctive voice, is central to their oral tradition, no matter how this tradition might be represented, and it is through this process of establishing who precisely they are that Mongolians recognize themselves.

Notes

1. Mongolian singers often use the term "*aizam duu*" (extended song) instead of "*aizam urtyn duu*" (extended long-song) since *aizam* is already a well-known category of long-song. This also applies to *besreg* and other category names as well. Thus, *besreg urtyn duu* (simplified long-song) are often called "*besreg duu*" (simplified song).

2. The direction of east and west in the Mongolian worldview is determined by the fact that Mongolians conceive of the south as being in front of them, and the north as being behind them. Therefore, Mongolians use the word *baruun* for the right-hand side and the west, and *züün* for both the left-hand side and the east.

3. The Buriad ethnic group occupies part of the Russian Federation and the northeastern part of Mongolia, while ethnic groups such as the Dariganga and Üzemchin are found in the southeast. Darkhad and Khotgoid, and some Uriankhai, are found in Khövsgöl aimag, slightly to the northwest of Ulaanbaatar, while ethnic groups such as Eljigen (Eljigin) Khalkh, Myangad, Dörvöd, Khoton, Zakhchin, and

other Uriankhai are further scattered throughout Uvs aimag, Khovd aimag, and northern Gob'-Altai aimag in the western region.

4. The current Khövsgöl aimag was originally a part of Tannu Uriankhai Frontier, and later remained in Mongolia when the rest of Tannu Uriankhai Frontier became part of the Russian Federation in 1911. For this reason, some Mongolian maps illustrating these regions under the Qing dynasty mostly show two Frontiers: Tannu Uriankhai and Khovd.

5. Bulag (1998) translates this term as "ethnic process" in his work.

6. Although Mongolian scholars tend to use two terms, *ugsaatan* and *yastan*, interchangeably for the English word "ethnicity," they have slightly different connotations. Atwood (2004) translates *yastan* as "sub-ethnic group," and *övög* (lit. clan) also as a "tribe" among different ethnic groups, while *ündesten* (lit. "having a root") implies the "nation." Bulag (1998) references those terms from Russian translations and claims that the word *yastan* was a direct translation from the Russian *narodnost'*, which refers to ethnic groups and was commonly used in Mongolia during the socialist era. However, the word *ugsaatan* was later used to describe the small ethnic minorities, or *yastan*, and *ugsaatan* has now become the more common word for an ethnic group.

7. *Bogino duu* (short-song) is another Mongolian folk song genre that is often discussed in contrast to *urtyn duu* because its metric and strophic styles of singing contrast dramatically with the characteristics of the long-song.

8. His practice of *urtyn duu* with an older singer was later recorded in a documentary by an independent Mongolian filmmaker and distributed with the title "Singer from Taiga" (2013, A Zoljargal and Son Film).

9. During the rest of the trip, I was able to meet singers who sang and explained religious long-songs (*shashtir duu, gür duu*), which were mentioned in the earlier part of this chapter.

10. This term is also frequently spelled "Eljigin."

11. In this region, I had a chance to sit down with about ten singers at the same time in the theater of the cultural center. Thus, the information here comes not from one singer alone: it was gathered from the interactions of a group. For this reason, I do not provide the individual singers' names in this section.

12. These Mongolian terms are the words that my interviewee singers used, but my impression was that they were not widely used, either by these particular singers or by local singers.

Bibliography

Alimaa, A. 2012. *Urtyn duuny töröl züil, tarkhalt, kuvilbaryn ontslog* (Special features in the taxonomy, distribution and variations of long-song). Ulaanbaatar: Academy of Science.

Atwood, Christopher. P. 2004. *Encyclopedia of Mongolia and the Mongol Empire*. New York: Facts on File.

Bulag, Uradyn E. 1998. *Nationalism and Hybridity in Mongolia*. Oxford: Clarendon Press.

Crossley, Pamela Kyle. 2006. "Making Mongols." In *Empire at the Margins: Culture,*

Ethnicity and Frontier in Early Modern China, edited by Pamela K. Crossley, Helen F Siu and Donald S Sutton, 58–82. Berkeley: University of California Press.

Dorjdagva, Myagmarsürengiin. 2016. *Oirad Mongolchuudyn urtyn uuu: Zan Yil, Övlögchid* [Oirad Mongol's long-song]. Ulaanbaatar: Suvarga Buyan Publishing.

Ganbold, Möngönkhüügiin. 2012. *Oirad Mongolchuudyn baigali kamgaalakh ulamjlal* [Oirad Mongol's tradition of protecting nature]. Ulaanbaatar: N.P.

Kaplonski, Christopher. 1998. "Creating National Identity in Socialist Mongolia." *Central Asia Survey* 17(1):35–49.

Myadar, Orhon, and James Deshaw Rae. 2014. "Territorializing National Identity in Post-Socialist Mongolia: Purity, Authenticity, and Chinggis Khan." *Eurasian Geography and Economics* 55(5):560–577.

Pegg, Carole. 2001. *Mongolian Music, Dance and Oral Narrative: Performing Diverse Identities*. Seattle: University of Washington Press.

Rinchensambuu, G. 2011. *Mongol Ardyn urtyn duuny tuurvil züi goo saikhan* [The beauty of Mongolian long-song]. Ulaanbaatar: N.P.

Said, Edward. 1978. *Orientalism*. New York, NY: Pantheon Books.

Sampildendev, K. H. and K.N. Yatskovskai. 1984. *Mongol ardyn urtyn duu* [Mongolian long-song]. Ulaanbaatar: State Publishing House.

Sneath, David. 2010. "Political Mobilization and the Construction of Collective Identity in Mongolia." *Central Asian Survey* 29(3):251–267.

Szmyt, Zbigniew. 2012. "The History of Nation and Ethnicity in Mongolia." *Sensue Historiae* 8(3):11–28.

Tsetsentsolmon, Baatarnarany. 2015. "Music in Cultural Construction: Nationalisation, Popularisation, and Commercialisation of Mongolian Music." *Inner Asia* 17:118–140.

Yoon, Sunmin. 2015. "Survival of the Fittest: The Urtyn duu Tradition in Changing Mongolia." *Smithsonian Folkways Magazine*. https://folkways.si.edu/magazine-summer-2015-survival-of-the-fittest-the-urtyn-duu-tradition-in-changing-mongolia/article/smithsonian.

———. 2019. "Mobilities, Experienced and Performed, in Mongolia's Urtyn Duu Tradition." *Asian Music* 50(1):47–77.

CHAPTER 4

Gendered Musicality in the Altai Mountains

REBEKAH PLUECKHAHN

In a remote rural district (sum) fringed by rolling hills within the Altai Mountains in western Mongolia, a concert was held on a cold, clear, icy evening in February in the early 2010s. The concert, held in the sum cultural center on this crystal-clear evening in winter, just over a week before *Tsagaan Sar*—or the Lunar New Year—featured the sum's cultural center workers. Each of the *Soyolyn Töviin Khamt Olon* or cultural center employees, from well-known musicians to the center staff, all took part in the event. Renowned singers from the sum and their family members were invited to perform. All were given the opportunity to perform the genre they knew best, with some singing and others reading poetry they had written. This concert became a place of veneration, where musical and moral personhood was recognized and celebrated. Musical and moral personhood, and its gendered dimensions were made manifest through performance.

This chapter explores the gendered aspects of performance and musical practice in a rural district (sum) in Mongolia. People who live in this particular sum are predominantly Altai Uriankhai people. It is renown as a place where spiritually significant musical genres are practiced—typically by men who inherit the rights to do so through patrilineal lines. It is also a place where people love to sing—on long jeep journeys, at ceremonial occasions such as weddings and hair-cutting ceremonies, or on the concert stage. The preferred way of singing is doing so with a loud projected voice, holding a lilting melody clearly and confidently, as others join in singing along with the first singer or an audience claps along to a concert performance. Drawing from approximately fifteen months' ethnographic fieldwork conducted between 2009 and 2012, this chapter explores the ways in which wider social life, familial roles and ensuing expected cultivations of moral personhood form an integral part of musical practice. Doing so reveals how forms of musical sociality are highly gendered.

Women's musical practices, performances and forms of musical sociality in-nately combine musical knowledge with familial roles and moral personhood. While within the sum there is the presence of spiritually significant genres prac-ticed by men, women's musical practice, discourse and sociality constitute sig-nificant ways in which musical and moral personhood are cultivated and musical knowledge transmitted. Through exploring sum concert performance, classifica-tions of musical ability in ceremonial music performances as well as the transmis-sion of heroic epics (*tuul'*), this chapter highlights the gendered dimensions of Mongolian musical practice. The wider social synthesis made between musical and moral personhood is not something exclusively experienced by women, but men too are understood and morally assessed through their actions. Skills in musical performance provide one of many ways in which moral personhood can be constituted among those living in the district. Looking at musical sociality through a gendered lens opens up a wide understanding of the constitution of moral personhood and musical practice in Mongolia more generally.

Venerating a Musical Exemplar

At the sum concert, Saraa,[1] an older woman in her '60s, entered the stage dressed in a fine *deel* (traditional long coat) and hat. She took the microphone in preparation to sing and waited for the person presiding over the concert to introduce her. He presented her as an "*öndör eej bolson*," or "someone who has become an esteemed mother." Saraa sang with a loud projecting voice, deftly leading the musicians who modified their accompaniment to follow her. Her song titled, "Alsaas domog duu" (A song of a legend from far away), had a lilt-ing melody that filled the expansive cultural center. The audience responded enthusiastically to her commanding stage presence, at one point applauding her mid-song. Toward the end of her performance, a group of women from the audience ascended the stage to offer Saraa gifts of money and chocolates. Typically reserved for the conclusion of a concert as a sign of respect for visiting performers, several women on this occasion walked up to the stage immediately after Saraa's performance even though many performers had yet to ascend the stage.[2] The people gifting the money were younger women, and the gifts formed an exchange with the singer who had just gifted the audience with her song.[3] While it is not necessary or common for every performer to receive a gift, on this day the gifts given by the young women formed an expression of respect toward Saraa and an opportunity for the givers to receive auspiciousness as well.

The concert performance illustrates one of the many ways in which gendered musical roles become apparent through performance. In this discussion, I take a wide perspective on what constitutes musical practice, drawing from the work of Anthony Seeger who writes that "music is an emotion that accompanies the production of, the appreciation of, and the participation in a performance. Music is also ... the sounds themselves after they are produced. Yet it is intention as well as realization; it is emotion and value as well as structure and form" (Seeger, 2004[1987]:xiv). Musical engagement among the Altai Uriankhai is far more than simply the physical act of playing and performing music. Musical practice includes audience members' participation in performance and the discussions and evaluations that occur about musical performance and music's significance. It includes research and documentation residents conduct with older family members; it is listening to and discussing concerts on television, and talking about musical life during the socialist period. Musical practice is performing on concert stages and singing songs in ceremonial celebrations (*nair*) held to celebrate weddings or children's first hair-cutting ceremonies. Each of these form integral parts of musical social life in this area and Mongolia more generally.

Definitions of what constitutes a "musician" (*khögjimchin*) and a "good singer" (*sain duuchin*) form important conceptual frames through which musical practice takes place in this area. Such definitions are implicated in the cultivation of officialdom—what is considered "official" musical knowledge and who should impart it, both within the sum and to visitors. Interwoven throughout this are complex ways in which musical practice is highly gendered. By gendered, I am not solely referring to the presence of musical genres typically performed by men and women. Instead, a gendered analytical lens reveals the roles of women's musical sociality within the cultivation of locally official musical knowledge and ways that performative practice is encouraged. Women are often conduits of knowledge. They also are recognized and esteemed for musical *practice* rather than necessarily being viewed as carriers of spiritually esteemed genres such as epics (*tuul'*). While epics are practiced by men, the ongoing practice of these and other spiritually significant genres and performative contexts such as weddings are highly dependent on women's knowledge and social acumen. Women's wider social roles are firmly entrenched and interconnected with their musical roles. The recognition given to Saraa at the concert was an acknowledgment not only of her performance, but her role as a mother, as a *performer* and all the generative possibilities that such performative ability can bring. These wider forms of musical practice are pivotal ways in which people define themselves—both personally in relation to each other but also how they situate themselves within wider Mongolia.

Altai Uriankhai Musical Practice

The Altai Uriankhai are considered to be a branch of the Uriankhai, a group of Turkic origin connected to a broad area that includes current-day Tuva in Russia (formerly the area of Tannu Uriankhai) (Baabar, 1999:145–147), parts of

Bayan-Ölgii and Khovd aimags (provinces) in western Mongolia, and northern Xinjiang in China. People often referred to themselves as a *yastan* (literally meaning bone-group), referring to a type of sub-ethnic delineation defined during the socialist period (Bulag 1998). In contemporary Mongolia, the Altai Uriankhai are considered part of the Oirad group of Mongols of western Mongolia, an area that encompasses the aimags of Bayan-Ölgii, Khovd, Uvs, and Zavkhan (see Chapters 3 and 6 in this volume). This region is home to more than fifteen different *yastan* groups. The western Mongolian region is often characterized by many Mongolians I spoke to as a place of many older "traditional" (*ulamjlalt*) cultural practices. Since the end of socialism in 1990, there has been an ongoing discovery and articulation by artists, scholars, and lay people (to name a few) of the importance of Mongolian culture and its historical origins (Humphrey, 1992a; Kaplonski, 2004). Certain Altai Uriankhai musical genres are now included in national cultural heritage programs and classifications. Their cultural and musical practices—some of which reference animist spiritual realms in the surrounding landscape—are regarded as linking Mongolia to an ancient past.

Musical practice forms a part of the way contemporary Altai Uriankhai identity can be performatively brought into being. The Altai Uriankhai in western Mongolia are essentially a Mongolian people. They practice the same kind of herding transhumance practiced across Mongolia. Many sum residents speak an Altai Uriankhai dialect of Mongolian. Since the socialist period, many younger Altai Uriankhai people speak Khalkh Mongolian, the Mongolian spoken in Ulaanbaatar, in official discourse, and throughout most of Mongolia. Altai Uriankhai historical narratives form part of wider Mongolian narratives of movement and group or clan formation.[4] Delineations of what practices are considered typically Altai Uriankhai are extremely important among the Altai Uriankhai themselves. It was partly through performative action that a form of difference was created. For example, people were quick to tell me how a certain food they were preparing, clothing they were wearing, or term they were using was distinctly Altai Uriankhai. A significant indicator of Altai Uriankhai–ness was the performance of Altai Uriankhai music.

Doing ethnographic research on musical engagement resulted in me becoming well acquainted with people's love of singing. Whether at a wedding, a child's first hair-cutting ceremony, a small reunion of friends, or a journey by jeep along a winding mountain road, people would not hesitate to break out in song. A song was usually initiated by a single person in a clear, strong, and projected voice, after which others would follow their lead until most people were singing together in a boisterous chorus of voices. During ceremonial contexts singers would select songs that are *ikh uchirtai* or songs with 'great meaning' or significance. Singers chose songs that had meaningful lyrics that evoked a love for one's mother, father, and/or homeland, drawing from a selection of well-known Altai Uriankhai short-songs (*bogino duu*) and long-songs (*urtyn duu*). They also consisted of *Mongolyn ündestnii duu* (national songs), a repertoire well known throughout Mongolia. The musical genres that are passed according to a custodial tradition of family inheritance include the inherited rights between males of particular familial lineages to perform heroic epics or *tuul'* (Pegg 2000). This genre allows people to cultivate understanding of and spiritual relationships with the mountainous environment and land masters (*gazryn ezen*) that live in the surrounding landscape. The lyrics of epics are rich in both shamanic and Buddhist content and often recount a shamanic creation story in which a hero (*baatar*) travels through a spiritually imbued, malleable geography.[5] The practice of such spiritually powerful musical genres were restricted and bowdlerized by successive Mongolian socialist governments during the socialist period (Pegg 2001; Marsh 2009). In the post-socialist context, when restrictions on spiritual, animist ritual practices were lifted, the practice of these spiritually powerful musical genres forms a continual process of rediscovery, rearticulation and discussion. This discussion occurs both among Altai Uriankhai as well as in the media and government cultural heritage programs.

Becoming Female: Gender and Fluidity through the Lens of Musical Practice

Framing musical practice through a gendered lens reveals diverse, integral musical roles. This analytical lens widens our focus away from a focus on inherited genres and the types of officially recognized discourses of knowledge that surround them (Buyandelger 2013:169), to encapsulate and reveal other kinds of diverse social activities that form a fundamental part of musical practice. I argue that musical practice forms a space in which women take on social roles and thus enact forms of femaleness. Taking such a focus allows the consideration of several key themes in the anthropological literature on gender in Mongolia. As I will argue, musical practice forms not only a space in which roles become enacted and forms of femaleness are constituted. Musical practice also becomes a space in which the fluidity of women's roles is apparent and becomes utilized. Women's presence as both insiders and outsiders within a husband's familial group forms an integral part of the perpetuation of musical practice and knowledge.

Such a discussion engages several interrelated phenomena including age, kinship roles, and gendered hierarchies, each of which can underlie family life in Mongolia. As noted by Caroline Humphrey (1993), Rebecca Empson (2011:177) and Manduhai Buyandelger (2013:185), femaleness in Mongolia forms a set of characteristics and virtues that are obtained and cultivated over the course of one's life. This unfolds over several significant life stages including girlhood, the young wife (or more specifically, daughter-in-law), and her emergence as a mother-in-law with her own descendants (Humphrey 1993). Marriage patterns typically (but not always) consist of patterns of virilocal residence. In rural areas, wives often move to live in their husband's district or in their husband's *khot ail* (encampments).

The experience of new brides (*shine ber*) forms one of gradual and unfolding separation and integration as they physically and emotionally move away from their natal household to live with and rear children alongside their husband's kin (Empson 2011:176–177). The bittersweet emotions that form part of these unfolding processes of separation and containment form the basis of some long-songs (*urtyn duu*) sung at Altai Uriankhai weddings (Plueckhahn 2014). A newly arrived daughter-in-law is often under a lot of pressure from her mother-in-law to conform and contribute in particular ways while maintaining a demure and deferential manner (Humphrey 1993:84). This can form a context that includes considerable challenges. A daughter-in-law may focus on the rearing of their own children in order to simultaneously improve their status among their husband's family, while at the same time, establish a separate household from their in-laws (Empson 2011:175–176). Humphrey discusses how women experience a culmination of these two blended ideological aims when they become mothers-in-law themselves, overseeing the work of their own daughters-in-law and thus occupying an elevated position in the hierarchy of female roles (Humphrey 1992b). The lived experience of these unfolding processes and the milestones of motherhood and marriage that they involve become part of a larger expectation of "gender proficiency" that women are expected to cultivate (Buyandelger 2013:185). Here, motherhood and marriage are viewed as being "equally important for completing a woman as a moral being" (Ibid:186).

Musical practice forms an action that allows one to cultivate the transition through these often expected, significant life roles. However, rather than be a way in which existing sociocultural expectations are merely reinforced, musical performance is a way in which the fluidity of roles can be not only negotiated, but indeed cultivated at different points to emphasize one's subjective position as a person of esteem and status in her or his own right. Gender is a relational phenomenon, and one's relational position changes over the course of a lifetime (Doubleday 2008:6). In the transition between different states of femaleness over the course of one's life there emerges a fundamental contradiction: as a daughter-in-law supports and makes a home for her husband's kin and grows his patrilineal line, she herself is in the process of transition, creating and cultivating her own children and household. What emerges is the mother-in-law, who is simultaneously now an established person of esteem within her husband's familial household and extended relatives, yet at the same time has her own authority and esteem as an "esteemed mother"—something that is applauded and venerated, as seen in the opening description of Saraa's concert performance. I now turn to explore a series of musical practices undertaken by married women, revealing how they negotiate changing gendered expectations through musical practice during this life stage.

In order to explore this, I examine the way in which gendered relationships become manifest through the activity of musical performance and wider musical practices. In performance choice and actions during performance people both adhere to and negotiate what is "expected." As noted by Sally Moore (cited in Turner 1986:78), "established rules, customs and symbolic frameworks" contain elements of ambiguity. Performance can be a space where different kinds of relations become manifest through actions that reveal nuance and ambiguity surrounding established expectations. Performance reveals interrelatedness between people and shared concepts of social obligations and connectedness. The existence of these interrelated factors means that in performance there are references to several factors occurring at once (Moore 1987:730).

Officialdom and Age: Authorities of Knowledge

When I first arrived in the sum, the first people I was directed to were considered authoritative wellsprings of musical knowledge and of culturally specific Altai Uriankhai customs (*zan zanshil*). This included men and women (but often men), usually elder people who were considered respected heads of families. I met with esteemed men and women alike to discuss musical practices and found these discussions to often reveal gendered authorities of knowledge. Men often appeared as "mediators of certain types of knowledge" (Empson 2011:35), where they frequently, publicly detailed significant and important historical facts and the general knowledge of particular musical genres. While women and men both had extensive musical knowledges, this type of exegesis formed part of the cultivation of authoritative musical knowledge.

When I took up other offers to meet with women with a long history of performance practice, their status as a mother and grandmother were features that were also viewed with high esteem. Early in my research I was encouraged one morning, with very little warning, to go with my friend to visit the local singer Pujee in a herding encampment some considerable drive away from the sum center. At the time, Pujee was in her fifties and known for being a good singer who had performed in regional theaters in the early 1970s. Upon arriving at her *ger*, I was, at first, planning a social visit in order to hear some collective singing, if it occurred. However, it quickly became clear that people present expected me to record Pujee. Pujee soon left the *ger* to get changed into a good *deel*. Upon her return she chose to sing the song "Khoyor nutgiin erkh" (The power of two homelands), a well-known Altai Uriankhai song. She sang it along with two of her daughters and then encouraged her granddaughter to sing another well-known folk song. Once they finished singing, I played back the recording to everyone; all family members present exclaimed and laughed when hearing the recording.

This recording session formed a musical encounter that, while more formalized, was nonetheless a familiar and accepted form of musical sociality within the sum. Such exchanges highlighted performers as esteemed musical exemplars. In Pujee's performance, these distinctions of esteem, and forms of hierarchy or difference, were not fixed, but were fluid and variable. This could be seen in how the focus often was shifted beyond the "main" singer, often by the singers themselves. Pujee chose to sing her first song with her daughters and then encouraged her granddaughter to follow with a solo song. This formed a way that Pujee not only allowed herself to be recognized, but also brought attention to the growing musical abilities of her own familial line. Such Altai Uriankhai specific song knowledge and the ability to sing these songs well, including to an outside researcher, are part of a wider form of preferred social action, of being a good person. Singing formed part of "ideas to do with the right way of doing things" (Empson 2011:95) or a preferred social aesthetic. Such cultivation of preferred social aesthetic was also deeply implicated with Pujee's role as an esteemed mother. As her inclusion of her grandchildren demonstrated, Pujee's cultivation of her own musical personhood was bound up in her status as a grandmother, her role in musical transmission between generations, and her role as a nurturer of future singers. Through performance, one's selfhood as an individual and as a relation were not mutually exclusive but were mutually reinforced through practice.

This focus on performance as a demonstration of women's musical knowledge was a common theme throughout this research. Such performances formed a fundamental exercising of familial relations that extended into ceremonial singing, where domestic practices associated with households, and often with women (Empson 2011:37), were not separate from the ways in which forms of musical knowledge were defined and practiced in the sum. Indeed, in this current context, previous socialist era definitions of a removed "cultural" "official" practice on a concert stage, and the role of domestic household tasks and constitutions of personhood were blurred.

Musical Practice and an Emphasis on Actions: Musicians and Good Singers

In discussions of musical ability, distinctions were often made between musicians (khögjimchin), people who were well known for performing in concerts; and people with great voices who performed well in ceremonial occasions and are known as good singers (*sain duuchid*). Singers who have long and ongoing associations with cultural centers and have won medals for concert performances are generally considered "musicians" (*khögjimchin*). Singers well known for singing within the sum in ceremonial contexts were described as "knowing many songs" and described as good singers or *sain duuchin*, but overall they were not called musicians. Such singing formed a fundamental part of ceremonial events such as weddings and hair cutting ceremonies, where people initiated songs that other attendees joined in and followed. Being a good initiator of songs and singing well at such ceremonial events within the sum earned particular people the status of someone who was a *sain duuchin*. When finding out about the extensive musical abilities of a familial group, I exclaimed to one of the extended family members that they are indeed a very musical family. This person replied to me, "they are not musicians, they are herders," "*ted nar khögjimchid bish, malchid baina.*" Upon speaking to several people who I knew were known for singing well in *nairs* (ceremonial occasions including weddings and children's hair-cutting ceremonies), some told me that they themselves were not musicians and that I should talk to someone more knowledgeable about musical genres. However, during ceremonies these same people would often sing extremely well.

Emphasis was sometimes placed on musical action and ability over knowledge about music. Older female singers who took the lead at important family life-cycle ceremonies, such as hair-cutting ceremonies for their grandchildren, often skillfully initiated the beginning of songs by starting a song with a loud projected, clear voice. In this instance, the ability to sing the melody in the right way forms part of the "right way of doing things." It created the required musical and also social aesthetic in a ceremonial context and formed a ceremonial way of "knowing" songs. Singing at a grandchild's *nair* formed a way in which a grandmother, for instance, contributed, through performative, musical action, to the "social birth" cultivated through a grandchild's hair-cutting ceremony (Empson 2011:174).

The ability and willingness to contribute songs in domestic, informal or ceremonial situations such as *nair* was a favored quality and one that correlates with a person's overall character. The preferred form of musical, social behavior included the combined actions of preferred hosting behavior, joking, sharing of food and drink in a stylized way, and the initiation of a known melody in a projected clear vocal tone. Just as a person's willingness to contribute well to one's networks earned someone the title *sain khün*, or good person, contributing to their social networks by contributing well to inclusive, preferred musical sociality resulted in the term *sain duuchin*, or good singer, a holistic term very much evocative of the same qualities imbued in the term *sain khün*, or good person. Calling someone a good singer was an encompassing and great compliment that conjured up the image of someone who was often willing to participate and contribute to one's networks in a positive way.[6] While there are many other ways good moral character can be constituted, and the fact that musical abilities vary and not everyone is able to be a good singer, singing well in ceremonial contexts was for some a way in which such moral character can be cultivated.

In this way, categorizations of musical prowess formed part of a larger moral categorization of both men and women. Musical engagement and demonstration of good musical skill and musicality formed a powerful act that equated a melody and performance behavior with the innate character and goodness of that person. The women I met who were well known as "good singers" were also often esteemed mothers and grandmothers within extended familial networks. This conflation of moral and musical personhood formed an innate co-constitution of musicality, willingness to contribute through performance, and preferred female personhood. As seen in the opening description of Saraa's concert performance and the gifting of money that she received as a result, this ability was holistically celebrated and acknowledged in public ways.

Mediation: Women and the Fostering of Musical Knowledge

Esteemed women's musical roles in this sum were not only limited to musical performance, but also extend to the cultivation of musical activity within musical lineages. This example of gendered musical practice extends into the spiritually significant genres inherited and performed by men, such as the practice of epics or *tuul'*. This musical practice consists of the cultivation of musical activity that forms part of the role as parent and nurturer of the next generation of epic performers.

As Humphrey (1993:86) notes, older mothers in Mongolia, who have successfully cultivated their own households, are often expected to undertake the role of mediator between "senior men of the lineage and the incoming junior wives." Such a mediatory role reflects first the skill that women need to cultivate over the course of their lives as married women in negotiating the twofold role of supporting their husband's family while growing and raising their own. Second, this mediatory role is ongoing, as women negotiate unfolding, fluctuating forms of insider/outsider status at different subjective vantage points within their familial group (Empson 2011:177). The following musical role I will now describe does not necessarily reflect a mediation between a husband's familial group and a woman's own household, but it does reflect another kind of mediatory role that women undertake in relation to spiritually significant musical genres practiced by men. Their accumulated life experience of gradual incorporation and negotiation of different familial branches make them particularly adept at these musical mediatory roles.

Altai Uriankhai epics are challenging to learn and perform. Young men of epic lineages (*tuul'chyn udam*) are gradually taught epics by an elder epic custodian, or *tuul'ch,* into adulthood. The lyrics of epics begin with "an account of the origin of the earth and the creation of people" (Pegg 1995:93). This creation story describes the formation of the shamanic separation between three *sansar,* or realms: the sky, the ground and the underworld. Epic texts are rich in poetic devices including, "vowel harmony, formal parallelism and line-initial alliteration" (Pegg 2001:51).[7] Although knowledge of epic texts is paramount, it is the ability to perform them with specific musical techniques that denotes someone who has mastered Altai Uriankhai epic knowledge and performance. As Reichl writes, what constitutes knowledge of epics can be described in fundamentally musical terms, "as part of the living performance of epic, music is no mere ornament but an essential element of the communicative event" (Reichl 2000:26).

An epic custodian's (*tuul'ch*) identity and status is inextricably bound up in his skillful epic performance practice and knowledge, a practice that implicates his wider family. Bolor, the wife of an epic custodian, had considerable knowledge of who performed musically within the sum—whether they are known as "musicians" or "good singers"—and the familial networks they moved within. She and her husband encouraged their four children to develop their ability to perform in multiple musical genres. Due to the complexity of epics and the important custodial role of epic lineages, members of the wider familial networks of an epic lineage also play a large part in wider epic performance *practice*. Bolor herself was deeply invested in the understanding of and research on Altai Uriankhai epics. During visits with her and her husband to discuss epics and wider musical practice, our discussions would be wide ranging—from descriptions of the history of epic practice to different familial groups that practice epics and wider spiritual understandings of the surrounding landscapes (see Chapter 6 in this volume).[8] As we continued discussions, Bolor would point out and correct me on different facts on family genealogy and intricate cultural terms and definitions.

Historically, I was to learn, women have taken on roles in the transmission of contextual, orally transmitted knowledge about epics and their cultural referents. Pegg in 1995 wrote that, "women rarely performed epics and when they did so it was only in intimate gatherings. But often they knew them because of the frequency with which they had heard them, and they sometimes assisted in the learning process" (Pegg 1995:90). This familial knowledge has sometimes formed a fundamental part of continuations of epic custodianship and knowledge transmission at moments where there are no suitable male heirs. One woman, a relative to Bolor's husband, is included as a significant person in the same epic lineage. This woman's father was a renowned epic patriarch who did not have any sons. Instead, she learned epics from her father and was known as a good singer herself. Subsequently, while it was said she did not perform, she assisted her sons in their successful memorization of particular epics, forming an integral link in the custodianship and transmission of epics of this particular lineage in the sum.

Throughout my research in this sum, women and wider family members of the epic lineage played an important part in the transmission and understanding of the wider social networks of epic performance practice and musical knowledge exchange. Bolor held important knowledge of who practiced what and how, and how they related to wider musical lineages. She often kept abreast of performance opportunities for her family. She not only was able to do so as the long-term wife of an epic custodian, but she is the mother of their son, a young future *tuul'ch*-in-training. Thus, her cultivation of musical activity within the lineage formed part of her role as parent and nurturer of the next generation of epic performers. However, rather than simply reinforce the roles as daughter-in-law and wife, or solely form part of one's role as a nurturer of the next generation, musical practice became a way to cultivate and negotiate the fluidity between both. Such an ability to cultivate and encourage performance formed a fundamental part of ongoing epic practice.

Conclusion

Women's musical practices, performances, and forms of musical sociality innately combined musical knowledge and ability with familial roles and moral personhood. They constituted significant ways in which musical and moral personhood were cultivated and musical knowledge transmitted. This synthesis between musical and moral personhood was not something exclusively experienced by women; but men also were understood and morally assessed through their actions—actions which implicated their musical lives as well. However, taking the musical lives of women as a perspectival lens opens up a wide understanding of the constitution of moral personhood and musical practice in Mongolia.

This myriad form of musical practice underpins and perpetuates forms of authority from the bottom-up, making it difficult to make clear distinctions between official and unofficial musical practice. While the cultivation of particular Altai Uriankhai musical genres are significant in their exclusive inherited rights to practice and their significant spiritual associations, family members of these lineages also performed other non-spiritual songs on stage. Their family members recited poetry and initiated songs known as national Mongolian folk songs at weddings. Taking women's performance practice as an analytical entry point reveals the multifaceted nature of contemporary performance practice in

Mongolia—in ways that enrich our understandings of "culturally significant" forms of practice (Buyandelger 2013:154).

This chapter explores musical practice through three themes: age and kin delineated roles of women; an emphasis on musical action; and women's roles as mediators and cultivators of future musical practice. One overarching phenomenon that emerges throughout these three themes is that musical practice forms an important part in negotiating the fluidity of different roles that women need to take over the course of their lives—in particular, the way that women as wives and mothers both support their husband's kin and, at the same time, raise and nurture their own households. This gendered focus takes into account that while there may be genres predominantly practiced by men, many other people are involved in contributing to their musical practice and its significance (Doubleday 2008:7). Musical esteem, for men as well as women, is interlinked with their wider social roles and forms part of the constitution of the "right way of doing things" and the cultivation of good moral character. Such cultivation is inextricably linked to one's age and gender delineated roles within the household or family. The social knowledge of women forms an inextricable part of the perpetuation and practice of musical sociality and the ceremonial and musical life in Mongolia.

Notes

1. Pseudonyms are used throughout this chapter.

2. The amount of money each woman gave, roughly 100–1000 *tögrög*, was enough to show respect for the performer but not so much that it would provoke jealousy. Jealousy can engender misfortune for those to whom it is directed (Empson 2011).

3. As Jagchid and Hyer (1979:160) note, a failure to return a "gift" in rural Mongolia is "inauspicious for all involved."

4. Because of this, some scholars are reluctant to call the Altai Uriankhai a distinct ethnic group. Atwood (2004:9) writes: "The term *Uriangkhai* in modern Mongolia denotes a vaguely defined *yastan* (subethnic group) in western Mongolia. The Altai Uriangkhai form a coherent group within this . . . subethnic group" (see Chapter 3 in this volume).

5. See Pedersen (2011) for further description of Mongolian shamanic ontologies and the interrelationships between shamanism and Buddhism in Mongolia.

6. Portisch (2010:S73) also discusses the links made between Kazakh women's embroidery and the evaluation of the embroiderer's character.

7. Much of this veneration of the literary qualities of epics can also be seen in recent scholarship through the documentation of complete epic song texts (c.f. Katuu 2001, 2010; Tsoloo and Mönhtsetseg 2008).

8. In Chapter 6 of this volume Chuluunbaatar provides further details on the cosmological significance of epic performance, text, and the accompanying instrument.

References

Atwood, Christopher P. 2004. *Encyclopedia of Mongolia and the Mongol Empire.* New York: Facts on File.

Baabar, Bat-Èrdènin. 1999. *History of Mongolia.* Cambridge, UK: The White Horse Press.

Bulag, Uradyn Erden. 1998. *Nationalism and Hybridity in Mongolia.* Oxford, UK: Clarendon Press.

Buyandelger, Manduhai. 2013. *Tragic Spirits: Shamanism, Memory and Gender in Contemporary Mongolia.* Chicago: Chicago University Press.

Doubleday, Veronica. 2008. "Sounds of Power: An Overview of Musical Instruments and Gender." *Ethnomusicology Forum* 17(1):3–39.

Empson, Rebecca. 2011. *Harnessing Fortune: Personhood, Memory and Place in Mongolia.* Oxford; NY: Oxford University Press.

Humphrey, Caroline. 1992a. "The Moral Authority of the Past in Post-Socialist Mongolia." *Religion, State and Society* 20(3, 4):375–389.

———. 1992b. "Women and Ideology in Hierarchical Societies in East Asia." In *Persons and Powers of Women in Diverse Cultures*, edited by S. Ardener, 173–192. NY: Oxford, Berg.

———. 1993. "Women, Taboo and the Suppression of Attention." In *Defining Females—The Nature of Women in Society*, edited by S. Ardener, 73–92. NY: Oxford: Berg.

Jagchid, Sechin, and Paul Hyer. 1979. *Mongolia's Culture and Society.* Boulder, Colorado; Folkestone, UK: Westview Press and Dawson.

Kaplonski, Christopher. 2004. *Truth, History and Politics in Mongolia.* London, NY: Routledge.

Katuu, Balchigiïn. 2001. *Altain urainghain tuul'* (Altai Uriankhai epic song), Khovd Aimgiin Zasag Dargyn Tamgyn Gazary (Office of the Governor of Khovd Province), Ulaanbaatar, Mongolia.

———. 2010. *Nert tuul'ch S. Choisürengiin tuul's* (The epics of distinguished epic song singer Choisüren), Mongol Ulsyn Shinjleh Uhaany Akademiin, Khel Zohiolyn Khüreelen. (Mongolian Academy of Sciences, Institute of Language and Literature), Ulaanbaatar, Mongolia.

Marsh, Peter K. 2009. *The Horse-Head Fiddle and the Cosmopolitan Reimagination of Tradition in Mongolia.* NY: Routledge.

Moore, Sally Falk. 1987. "Explaining the Present: Theoretical Dilemmas in Processual Ethnography." *American Ethnologist* 14(4):727–736.

Pedersen, Morten Axel. 2011. *Not Quite Shamans: Spirit Worlds and Political Lives in Northern Mongolia.* Ithaca, NY: Cornell University Press.

Pegg, Carole. 1995. "Ritual, Religion and Magic in West Mongolian (Oirad) Heroic Epic Performance." *British Journal of Ethnomusicology* 4:77–99.

———. 2000. "The Power of Performance: West Mongolian Heroic Epics." In *The Oral Epic: Performance and Music*, edited by K. Reichl, 171–190. Berlin: VWB—Verlag für Wissenschaft und Bildung.

———. 2001. *Mongolian Music, Dance and Oral Narrative.* Seattle: University of Washington Press.

Plueckhahn, Rebekah. 2014. "Fortune, Emotion and Poetics: The Intersubjective Experience of Mongolian Musical Sociality." *Asia Pacific Journal of Anthropology*, 15(2):123–140.

Portisch, Anna. O. 2010. "The Craft of Skillful Learning: Kazakh Women's Everyday Craft Practices in Western Mongolia." *Journal of the Royal Anthropological Institute* 16(1): 62–79.

Reichl, Karl. 2000. "Introduction: The Music and Performance of Oral Epics." In *The Oral Epic: Performance and Music*, edited by K. Reichl, 1–40. Berlin: VWB—Verlag für Wissenschaft und Bildung.

Seeger, Anthony. 1987. *Why Suya Sing: A Musical Anthropology of an Amazonian Peoples*, Cambridge: Cambridge University Press.

Tsoloo, J. and Mönhtsetseg, A. 2008. *Uriankhain öv soyol* (Uriankhai cultural heritage). Documenta Oiratica Collecta, Oirad Sudlalyn Chuulgan VI, (Oirad studies forum VI) Mongol Ulsyn Shinjleh Uhaany Akademiin, Khel Zohiolyn Khüreelen. (Mongolian Academy of Sciences, Institute of Language and Literature), Ulaanbaatar, Mongolia.

Turner, Victor. 1986. *The Anthropology of Performance*. New York: PAJ Publications.

PART THREE

Material and Social History

Consistency, Patience, and Perseverance

Maintaining the Fiddle-Making Tradition

BAYARSAIKHAN BADAMSÜREN
AND PETER K. MARSH

While there are many workshops and factories in Mongolia today constructing horsehead fiddles (*morin khuur*) for domestic and international markets, only a handful of them construct professional quality or "master" fiddles. Since opening his first instrument-making studio in 1999, Bayarsaikhan Badamsüren has established a reputation as one of the best master fiddle makers in Mongolia.

FIGURE (INTERLUDE) 3.1. Carved horse heads in B. Bayarsaikhan's workshop, 2008. Photo by J. C. Post.

FIGURE (INTERLUDE) 3.2. B. Bayarsaikhan at work in his workshop, 2008.
Photo by J. C. Post.

I was born on July 15th, 1975. In 1992, after working a few years in a furniture making factory, I realized I wanted to switch to making horsehead fiddles. I loved everything about the instrument—its sound, shape and symbolism. My first teacher was the master fiddle maker Dorj Jugder. He taught me the craft of fiddle making, showing me not only how to make a good fiddle but also helping me to understand how deeply rooted this instrument is in our cultural heritage.

I opened my first instrument making workshop in 1999 with my two brothers. It was named Zeebad,[1] but I changed this in 2009 to Pegasus, the winged horse in Greek mythology.

In my opinion, making a good instrument requires consistency, patience, and perseverance. It can take up to two months to complete the many steps in making a master fiddle.

I begin by crafting the horse's head and neck and the front and back of the soundbox. I then join the pieces together, color and varnish the instrument, and then attach the strings. The final steps are tuning and the final setting up.

I feel truly happy when I am constructing the horsehead fiddle, and I especially love to carve the horse's head. Each head is different. I try to express the character of each horse I'm carving, and I often think about countryside horses, especially racehorses, which are powerful and brave.

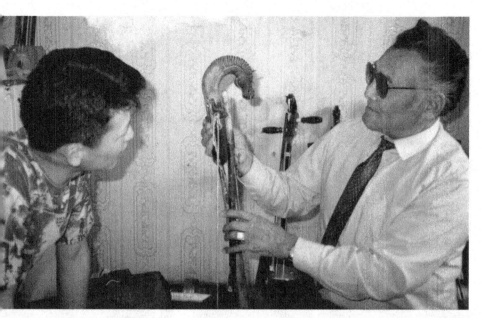

FIGURE (INTERLUDE) 3.3. B. Bayarsaikhan with his fiddle teacher Dorj Jugder in 1996. Photo by P. K. Marsh.

FIGURE (INTERLUDE) 3.4. B. Bayarsaikhan with his brothers in their first instrument-making workshop in 2000 (used with permission).

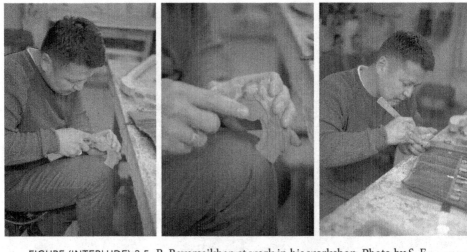

FIGURE (INTERLUDE) 3.5. B. Bayarsaikhan at work in his workshop. Photo by S. E. Morel (used with permission).

FIGURE (INTERLUDE) 3.6. B. Bayarsaikhan at work in his workshop. Photo by S. E. Morel (used with permission).

The horsehead fiddle is the national pride of the Mongol people. Because of this, I really do not like to change the traditional form of the instrument or the traditional style of making it. But the tradition is changing, in part because musicians who order my instruments want something unique or different.

I try to mix the traditional and modern styles of fiddle making. In the early 2000s, I studied for several weeks with a famous violin maker in the United

FIGURE (INTERLUDE) 3.7. B. Bayarsaikhan with a master fiddle he constructed (used with permission).

Kingdom. He taught me the art of creating a violin by hand and I have incorporated many of these ideas into how I make the horsehead fiddle.

To me, it's very important that my fiddles have the pure Mongolian sound. I want my fiddles to be both powerful and easy to play.

We must protect the horsehead fiddle's unique Mongolian characteristics. The sound and melody of this instrument is not only heard by the ears of each listener, it also has a special effect upon their heart, too. The art of crafting horsehead fiddles is part of the invaluable heritage of the Mongolian people that has been passed down through the generations to the present. It is our responsibility as Mongolians to keep intact the foundation of this precious tradition.

Notes

1. A *zeebad* is a zoomorphic creature rooted in Hindu legend and closely connected with Tibetan Buddhism. The *zeebad* is often paired with a horse's head on the crown of the horsehead fiddle.

CHAPTER 5

The Horsehead Fiddle

A Biographical History

PETER K. MARSH AND
CHARLOTTE D'EVELYN

The horsehead fiddle or *morin khuur*, a two-stringed bowed lute crowned with a carved horse's head, has become one of the most visible symbols of Mongolian national identity in the twenty-first century. In the socialist period (1921–1990), the fiddle became a mainstay in performances of folk and folklorized music in Mongolia and Inner Mongolia, a province of China. From the mid-1990s on, it was increasingly used by musicians in a variety of popular music genres, including rock, "ethno-punk," and hip-hop. The phenomenal recent success of the heavy metal rock band The Hu, which has swapped electric guitars for stylized horsehead fiddles, has exposed many people to the instrument throughout Europe, North America, and Australia via the internet, social media, and concert and festival venues. This has raised the visibility of the instrument to a level that it has never achieved. In 2019, the Mongolian government awarded The Hu the Order of Chinggis Khaan, a prestigious state prize that recognizes the work of Mongolians who promote the values of the nation. In the award ceremony at the State Palace in Ulaanbaatar, the President recognized the group for "promoting the name of Mongolia to the world and glorifying the nation on the international arena" (Baljmaa 2019).

We find, however, that in the first three decades of the twentieth century the horsehead fiddle occupied a very different place in Mongolian society. This was a period of social, political, and economic upheaval. Mongols in the People's Republic of Mongolia worked to lay the foundations for a new socialist nation in collaboration with the Soviet Union, following the 1921 People's Revolution, while those in Inner Mongolia found themselves in the middle of a larger battle between the Chinese government and Japanese Imperial forces. Soviet Marxists deemed the Mongols' traditional pastoral nomadic ways of life to be at the feudalist stage of historical development, which must make way for more progressive stages, such as socialism. Mongols in both regions struggled in this period with the idea that long-held aspects of their traditional culture and customs had almost overnight become "backward" or "old." Some chose to embrace these revolutionary ideologies, others did not.

When the Danish explorer and ethnographer Henning Haslund-Christensen (hereafter Haslund) visited the *banner* (i.e., regional subdivision) of Khorchin, in the Hinggan region of Inner Mongolia, he found a community turned upside down—one in which Inner Mongolian youths, allied with the Japanese, were in positions of authority:

> On my arrival . . . in 1936 the Khorchin Mongols and other East Mongols in the Hsingan area had attained the status of an autonomous state under Japanese control and authority. There were many signs indicating that the East Mongols were now marching towards a brighter future, for one of the Japanese interests in Mongolia was to re-create wealthy nomad communities that could deliver wool, hides and other raw materials of which the industry of the home-country stood in such pressing need. The ideals that had now been adopted by the formerly so dispirited Mongol youth had, however, their roots outside the frontiers of their country, and had nothing in common with the traditions of their fathers (Haslund 1971:26).

Haslund was particularly intent on finding and recording the singers and musicians of the time before the arrival of the Japanese. When he asked these Mongol youths where these "fathers" were to be found, he was told that they "had long since fled to remote valleys where they were now endeavoring to spend the rest of their lives in conformity with the traditions of the past," and that those who chose not to flee, "were incarcerated in the prison of the town for having been too deeply rooted in the past to be able to understand the message of the new era" (28).

It was in one of these prisons that Haslund met the elderly fiddle player or *khuurch* named Sangrup ("The All-Knowing"), who had been employed as a court musician for the Khorchin prince Otai. Haslund arranged the release of Sangrup and spent several weeks traveling with him throughout the region, searching for and recording the music of other elderly musicians and singers of the "old" era. For Haslund, Sangrup represented one of the few remaining links to an earlier age of music-making that he feared was then, in the 1930s, being suppressed out of existence. Similar stories of suppression in Mongolia exist, as well. Mongolian musicologist J. Enebish says that he heard stories about Russian and Mongolian soldiers seizing fiddles from nomadic herders' *gers* and burning them along with their Buddhist *sūtras*. The ruling Party, he says, was "intent on destroying all parts of the old order, including anything of great value within it"

(Enebish interview, Ulaanbaatar, October 1998). Anthropologist Carole Pegg writes about some musicians in western Mongolia who hid their traditional instruments in the mountains and others who "were reduced to living in holes in the ground" because of political persecution (Pegg 1995:78).

This suppression of, or perhaps ambivalence toward, the Mongol fiddle in this period of revolution in the 1920s and 1930s is a far cry from the embrace, even worship, of the instrument we can see today, nearly a century later. Marxist ideas of progress and "cultural uplift" came to dominate the ideological space in both Mongolia and Inner Mongolia in the socialist period, but the traditions of "old" Mongolia never went away, as Haslund had feared might happen. Instead, successive generations of Mongol youths from the 1930s on have adapted elements of the old and new, the traditional and the modern, to continually reimagine the shape, sound, and importance of the fiddle within Mongolian society. The Hu's use of the horsehead fiddle and *tovshuur* to play heavy metal rock music is just the latest example of this.

In this chapter, we tell a version of this story of generational reimagination by focusing on the work of Mongols, from both Mongolia and Inner Mongolia, who have shaped—or are shaping—the horsehead fiddle traditions of the twentieth and twenty-first centuries. We begin with the fiddler Sangrup, who, as seen through Haslund's interpretations, provides us with a window into the pre-Revolutionary world of the Mongol musician. We then consider the fiddlers G. Jamiyan from Mongolia and Sangdureng and Chi. Bulag of Inner Mongolia, all three of whom played important institutional roles in shaping the fiddle traditions of the twentieth century, and we end by examining the contributions of several young Mongols who, we argue, represent contemporary trends in the development of the horsehead fiddle and of Mongolian music in general. With such a historical scope, we can only provide a snapshot of this larger historical narrative; many stories will necessarily be left untold. Yet those included here will highlight the important role that insightful, imaginative, and assertive individuals can play in shaping a musical tradition.[1]

The Life of a Pre-Revolutionary Fiddler

The People's Revolution occurred in Mongolia in 1921, but the process of uprooting and overturning the social, religious, and political institutions that had shaped Mongolian life for centuries up to then took years to bring about. The suppression brought to bear upon this so-called old order in both Mongolia and Inner Mongolia in the 1920s and 1930s was intense, and at times brutal, given the depth to which this order was rooted in Mongolian society. The important elements of pre-Revolutionary society—including the pastoral nomadic ways of life, the strong influence of Buddhism and shamanism, and a hereditary political structure that favored descendants of Chinggis Khan—have roots that extend to the Mongol Empire, if not earlier.

Haslund, who lived among the Mongols at various points in the 1920s and 1930s, gives us his understanding of how music and song were entwined with all aspects of life in pre-Revolutionary Mongolia. His reflections on what he heard when visiting nomadic herders conveys the close connections that existed between the Mongolian nomads and their natural and spiritual environment:

> For myself, Mongol music and the moods that are evoked by the old folk-songs are a great personal pleasure, by which I have often been entranced, and which has always been able to banish the feeling of emptiness that a European may experience during a prolonged stay among a foreign people in a remote country. These songs have helped me to an understanding of the aesthetic values in the often bleak landscapes of their origin. It was the singing milk-maids and the melancholy tones of the caravan-folk in the dead stillness of the desert that gave me an insight into the deepest thoughts of the people, and on the evenings when I have sat at the warming tent-fire while the soughing wind from the steppe evoked the very atmosphere of what had been sung, it was the songs and epics of the old men that helped me to glimpse the contours of the mighty pictures that make up the great and richly changing history of the nomads (Haslund 1971:23).

Haslund's focus on Sangrup provides us with a glimpse of how pre-Revolutionary fiddlers learned their art. Sangrup's talents as a fiddler and epic singer were recognized and nurtured while he was still young. At a certain age, his skills were tested by an older epic singer or *tuulch*, which included asking him "to imitate the clear gurglings of streams, the gentle soughing of the wind in the rushes of the river-bank and the mystic echoes of eternity issuing from the invisible interior of the conch [shell]" (29). When the *tuulch* felt assured of Sangrup's abilities, he began to teach him the texts and melodies of the "old songs," including those that sing "the praises of high gods, proud heroes and famous horses" (30). He was taught what songs were appropriate for which contexts, as well as the "mysteries of acoustics," which was achieved "by studying the sound effects that the wind could coax from the hollow interiors of human and animal skulls." He also learned how to construct by hand two string instruments, the four-stringed *khuuchir* and the two-stringed fiddle.

Sangrup eventually became the favorite musician and singer of Khorchin Prince Otai, with whom he traveled to Peking (Beijing) during the last decades of the Qing dynasty and performed for its "proud princes and romantic princesses" in the Forbidden City (Haslund 31). When he returned to his homeland, he was in demand by the common people who wanted him to perform in their *gers*. "No festival was in those times regarded as complete by the Khorchin tribe," says Haslund, "unless Sangrup Khurchi was present" (ibid).

FIGURE 5.1. Sangrup *khuurch* performing on a *khiil khuur.*
Photo by Henning Haslund-Christensen. National Museum of
Denmark (used with permission).

During the battles between the Mongols and Chinese that accompanied the
end of Qing dynastic rule, from 1911 to 1913, Sangrup lost everything that he
owned, including his instruments. He constructed a new fiddle (see figure 5.1)
and then set about "consoling and inspiriting the survivors with the mighty
songs of the past" (ibid). But as the older generations passed on, the Mongolian
youths responded to the promises offered by the Japanese. Haslund tells us
that the youth "had become tired of listening to the songs and epics glorifying
the past, and [they] turned their faces resolutely away from the dispirited old

men to join their voices enthusiastically in the new marching songs, that were full of golden promises about the splendid future they themselves would build up" (29). Sangrup spent the years after the civil war in relative obscurity, often being "abused by the younger members of his tribe" for not joining with "the singers and expounders of the new songs" of the Mongol people. His loyalty to the old songs of his tribe finally landed him in prison, where he sat until Haslund found him.

Haslund's story of Sangrup provides us with an example of how the turmoil that accompanied the coming of the Revolutionary period disrupted deeply rooted musical traditions. Not all talented artists were suppressed in this period in the way Sangrup was. Luvsan *khuurch* and Jigmed *khuurch* were two famous Mongolian singer-musicians who chose to reinvent themselves musically in ways suitable to the new regime, and so continued their careers into the new period (Marsh 2009:45). But it would be the next generation of Mongolian musicians that would shape the new musical cultures in Mongolia and Inner Mongolia.

The Life of a Revolutionary Fiddler

Following World War II, the Mongolian People's Revolutionary Party (MPRP) increasingly turned its attention to bringing about a "cultural revolution" (*soyoliin khövsgöl*) among the Mongolian people, which it envisioned would return them to the path of national development and the eventual attainment of Communism. The introduction of a book for young cultural workers published by the Party puts it this way:

> Raising the level of cultural and intellectual knowledge of the workers will not only help direct the work at improving Communist education and raising the workers' aesthetics and knowledge, but it will also renew their knowledge of theory and politics, enrich their forms of work, and strengthen the growth of the material base of socialist culture (Chuluunbat 1972:12).

For the MPRP, the institutionalization of culture and the arts was as vital to the development of the nation as was expanding the economy and reforming the political structure. The Party opened cultural centers (*soyolyn tövüüd*) in communities and towns throughout the country. Overseen by Party officials, they mostly served to disseminate news and Party information, but they also became locations for educational and cultural activities like the teaching of literacy and hygiene, theater productions, film screenings, and concert performances (Natsagdorj 1981:260). Aside from introducing rural communities to new forms of entertainment, these centers provided Party officials opportunities to spread propaganda, keep an eye on local community activities, and identify young artists who showed potential.

Such artists were then often sent to new music schools in Ulaanbaatar. The Fine Arts School (*Uran saikhany surguul'*) opened in 1930 and then was expanded into the Music & Dance College (*Khögjim büjgiin dund surguul'*) in 1958. By the 1960s, it became the largest and most important institution for the training of the national cadre, many of whom would, in turn, be sent back to work in the schools and cultural centers in the countryside (Tsendorj 1983:30; Enebish 1982:30).

Fiddler G. Jamiyan was one of these young students who made the journey from the countryside to the city. Born into a herding family in Bulgan *sum* (the smallest level of land-based division), in the northern Mongolian aimag of Dornod, Jamiyan learned to play the horsehead fiddle from his father and performed with him throughout his youth in their family *ger*, at community festivals, and in the local cultural center. His family moved to Ulaanbaatar in 1937 and the same year, at age 18, Jamiyan entered the Fine Arts School as a horsehead fiddle player. By the following year he had secured a position in the Central Theater in Ulaanbaatar, performing with many other talented folk musicians, and he quickly established a reputation for his fiddle technique and sound (Batchuluun 2017:31). In his school, overseen by Mongolian and Russian teachers, Jamiyan learned to read musical notation for the first time, studied Western music theory and composition, and began to play Western classical music on the horsehead fiddle. He also began to study the violoncello, which he played in the fledgling orchestra in the Central Theater. Jamiyan described how the paucity of professional players in this period required musicians to play on both "folk" (*ardyn*) and "classical" (*songodog*) musical instruments. On some days, he said, he performed on the horsehead fiddle and on others, the violoncello (G. Jamiyan interview, October 1999).

By the mid- to late-1950s, the increased attention to professionalism within the new musical culture accelerated the assimilation of European classical performing traditions, a process often undertaken by the artists themselves rather than from Party directives. Jamiyan had developed techniques for playing the horsehead fiddle that incorporated performance techniques from the violoncello, including ways of holding the horsehead fiddle and its bow, of fingering the notes on the strings, and of moving the bow over the strings. In 1958, with the opening of the Music & Dance College, Jamiyan became the leading teacher of the horsehead fiddle and violoncello in Mongolia.

His ideas about playing and teaching methodologies contributed to the modernization of the horsehead fiddle and its tradition. He adopted the Western pedagogical practices of insisting his students learn to read musical notation, master abstract exercises such as playing arpeggio and scalar exercises, and understand a composition's "musical grammar," such as its pitch, rhythm, and timbre. Jamiyan also demanded that his students play with clear and precise tuning (he had a piano in his office that he would use in his lessons to check students' intonation). He also encouraged instrument makers to replace the traditional sheepskin face (soundboard) of the horsehead fiddle with a wooden one, making it more closely resemble a violoncello in sound and shape. Such instruments also allowed the instrument to better project its sound in larger rooms and halls and to stay in tune when performing in countries with different climates.

Jamiyan's efforts to meld Mongolian and Western musical elements dramatically changed the look, sound, and performance practice of the horsehead fiddle and helped to standardize the ways in which it was taught. His many students went on to become teachers, performers, and cultural administrators, thus spreading and institutionalizing his ideas and artistic standards across the country. By the 1970s, the horsehead fiddle, once only associated with the traditional ways of nomadic herders, had become reimagined as an instrument associated with the rising cultural aspirations of Mongolians increasingly interconnected with the wider world.

Fiddle Revolutionaries in Inner Mongolia

Inner Mongolia, China, has followed a musical trajectory and orientation that is at once similar and also vastly different from Mongolia. This section highlights these similarities and differences through the life and work of Sangdureng (1926–1967) and Chi Bulag (b. 1944). In many ways, the contributions of these two Inner Mongolian fiddlers parallel the work of Jamiyan in Mongolia, but the instruments and compositional output that resulted from their work are strikingly different. The wood-faced horsehead fiddle developed by Chi Bulag (see figure 5.2) is smaller and thinner than Jamiyan's instrument. Its strings are also placed closer together and its bow is modeled closer to a Tourte violin or cello bow. The sound of Bulag's fiddle is also perceptively brighter, tighter, and more nasal than the deeper, lower, and more subdued sound of its Mongolian counterpart. The section that follows briefly explores the circumstances that led Chi Bulag to modernize the horsehead fiddle and some of the aesthetic and practical reasons for his choices.

Chi Bulag visited Mongolia in 1988 as part of the first cultural delegation to Mongolia from Inner Mongolia since the beginning of the Sino-Soviet split (1956). Much had happened during the thirty-odd year gap in contact to make these Mongols feel like strangers to one another. Life in the Mongolian People's Republic had been shaped by the nation's close relationship with the U.S.S.R. and its adoption of Soviet-style socialism. In Inner Mongolia, in contrast, life had been shaped by the region's integration into the Chinese Socialist system, the Mongolians' new status as a minority nationality (*shaoshu minzu*), and the ordeals experienced during the Mao Zedong era. Chi Bulag's slim, high-pitched

FIGURE 5.2. Horsehead fiddle performer, composer, and
innovator, Chi Bulag (used with permission).

horsehead fiddle and his technically virtuosic ensemble performances were seen
as aural and visual evidence of just how separate the two regions had become.
His performance in Ulaanbaatar inspired strong reactions from the Mongolian
audiences (see Marsh 2009) and demonstrated just how little exchange had
taken place during the years of isolation between the two regions. Some of the
most acute changes to the instrument happened during this period, resulting
in the emergence of two very distinct horsehead fiddle traditions.

By 1988, in both Mongolia and Inner Mongolia, the urban horsehead fiddle
had transitioned from a skin-faced instrument played by herders in their *gers*
to a wood-faced instrument played by professionals on concert stages. During
the preceding decades, the aims of instrument makers were similar on both
sides of the border: to standardize the instrument's construction, tuning, and

technique; to increase its sound volume for larger performance spaces; and to achieve a steady and reliable tone quality that could hold up under a variety of climatic conditions. Both regions were influenced by ideologies that identified European concert music as the highest level of musical achievement. European instruments such as the violin and violoncello became standards by which local instruments were judged. However, the ways in which the Mongolians and Inner Mongolians approached instrument modernization diverged due to different political contexts, availability of materials, advice of foreign luthiers, and individual preferences, as well as the overall differences in attitudes toward modernity, tradition, and ethnic nationalism.

Separated from Mongolia by the vast Gobi Desert, Inner Mongolia had already developed unique regional musical cultures prior to the administrative separation of the two during the Qing Dynasty (1644–1911). In fact, there is quite limited written evidence of instruments bearing the name "horse fiddle" or "horsehead fiddle" (Mongolian: *morin khuur*; Chinese: *matouqin*) in Inner Mongolia prior to the 1950s. Mongol music scholars Ulanji (1998), Khogjilt (2006), and Siriguleng (2009) discuss the prominence of the *sihu* (or *dörvön chikhtei khuur*, a skin-faced cylindrical spike fiddle with a suspended bow) in the eastern and southern regions of Inner Mongolia, *choor* (a skin-faced box-shaped spike fiddle) in the eastern Khorchin region, and *igil* (skin-faced ladle fiddle) in the far western regions (including in Xinjiang). These local scholars emphasize historical and structural differences between tube-shaped spike fiddles (resembling the Chinese *erhu* and related to the Song Dynasty *xiqin*) and box fiddles (resembling the *morin khuur* and related to the ancient *shanagan khuur*, a ladle fiddle). They suggest that the earliest forms of the *morin khuur* in Inner Mongolia may have been called *khikhil khuur* or *khiil khuur* and had different types of headstocks, including likenesses of animals (horses, swans, wolves, and others), supernatural beings, or no decorations at all.

Musicians in Inner Mongolia, as in Mongolia, undertook efforts in the mid-twentieth century to develop a standardized (rather than regionally divergent) musical representation of the Mongol people. The earliest fiddle performers to be recruited onto public concert stages included folk artists who had backgrounds as herders or Buddhist lamas, such as the celebrated early-twentieth-century box-fiddlers Balgan (1913–1966) and Serashi (1887–1968) (as well as several other well-known *sihu* fiddlers). These performers used skin-faced fiddles of varied names (*morin khuur*, *khuur*, and *choor*; sometimes interchangeably), materials, box sizes, and neck lengths. These differences in construction represented not only divergent regional communities and conventions, but also available materials and preferences of individual folk musicians who often built their own instruments. Instrument tuning, generally in perfect fourths or fifths, varied depending on string tension and preference.[2]

The musician and composer Sangdureng (1926–1967), a student of both Balgan and Serashi, is recognized today for catalyzing a new and modern fiddle tradition, a project that Chi Bulag (b. 1944), his student, completed in the 1980s. A Mongol from eastern Inner Mongolia, Sangdureng became conductor of the Inner Mongolia Song and Dance Ensemble in the 1950s, and in this capacity worked to more effectively stage and program Mongol music and musical instruments in state-sponsored performances.

According to Inner Mongol scholar Ulanji, Sangdureng was present when a musical delegation from Mongolia performed in Inner Mongolia in 1953 (Ulanji interview, Hohot, 2010). Not only was Sangdureng impressed by the performances, which consisted of several of Jamiyan's new compositions for fiddle, he was also inspired by the fingering technique that he saw—the Mongolian method of placing the knuckles of the index and middle finger on the side of the string instead of fingering on the pads of the fingers from the top. He was, furthermore, likely to have observed details about the newly modernized, louder, and more stage-worthy fiddle models from Mongolia and to have seen the potential of the horsehead fiddle—with the horse positioned at the headstock—as a viable musical icon to represent the Mongol people in local, national, and international performing venues.

Sandgureng experimented with a variety of fiddle models in the 1960s and worked with Han Chinese instrument maker Zhang Chunhua to develop snakeskin and wood-faced models as well as an orchestra consisting of horsehead fiddles of different sizes. The two received support for their work by the local Inner Mongolian government, which promoted "improvement" of Mongol performing arts as evidence of positive government intervention in the region. Sangdureng went on to compose and publish solo repertoire for the instrument and to develop the first notated horsehead fiddle teaching method in Inner Mongolia. Unfortunately, Sangdureng's innovative work was cut short in 1967 when he was killed in the purges that occurred during the Cultural Revolution in Inner Mongolia.

Despite his early passing, Sangdureng's fiddle experiments, and perhaps even his choice of the horsehead fiddle as an instrument worthy of modernization, profoundly influenced future generations of fiddlers in Inner Mongolia. His attention to the horsehead fiddle set the instrument on a path of professionalization and modernization that continued after the Mao era ended in 1976. Were it not for Sangdureng's exposure to Jamiyan's horsehead fiddle in Mongolia, he may have never developed an interest in this instrument over other popular fiddle forms in Inner Mongolia such as the *choor* or the *sihu*. Through the combined and government-supported efforts of Sangdureng and Zhang Chunhua, the horsehead fiddle became a primary locus of musical attention in Inner Mongolia and emerged as an instrument with the capacity for displays of virtuosity and a new repertoire of solo compositions.

Chi Bulag followed closely in his mentor Sangdureng's footsteps and continued to experiment with the design and sound of the horsehead fiddle. He worked
together with Zhang Chunhua and another Mongol instrument maker, Duan
Tingjun (b. 1949), in the early 1980s until they arrived at a model that would
project well, achieve a clean and precise tone, and hold steady intonation on
the concert stage. The skin-faced horsehead fiddle, though rich in timbre, could
not adequately accomplish any of these musical requirements. Bulag's work of
transforming this skin-faced instrument into a viable wood-faced horsehead
fiddle was by no means linear (D'Evelyn 2014), but he eventually arrived at a
viable model that became the standard for instrument construction in Inner
Mongolia from the late 1990s to the early 2000s.

As mentioned above, the Bulag model of the horsehead fiddle sounds remarkably different from the fiddle modernized in Mongolia. His instrument
is tuned higher (G-C instead of F-B-flat) and sounds much tighter and more
nasal than the lower and mellower sounding Mongolian counterpart. A reason
for the timbral differences between the two instruments might be explained by
Chi Bulag's fascination with Niccolò Paganini, the nineteenth-century Italian
composer famous for his virtuosic violin music. In our conversations, Bulag
explained how he consciously crafted the body of his instrument to be small,
narrow with strings positioned close together in order to facilitate rapid, virtuosic playing techniques akin to those found in Paganini's solo violin music. In
contrast, the standard instrument model made in Mongolia has a significantly
wider and thicker body and has strings that are both farther apart from one
another and positioned higher off the fingerboard than Chi Bulag's model.

Ironically, although Bulag is considered a national and ethnic hero in China,
most fiddlers today import their instruments from Mongolia or use instruments
made by local makers in the Mongolian national style (tuned F-B-flat and positioned with wider spacing between the strings). Horsehead fiddle students
in Inner Mongolia develop fiddle bi-musicality and are often equally versed in
repertoire from both sides of the border as well as the fingering and technical
requirements of both fiddle models.

Chi Bulag's most important and lasting legacy might very well be his composition "Galloping Horses" (Chinese: *Wanma Benteng*). Among all the works
that form the backbone of the Inner Mongolian fiddle repertoire, this one has
endured as the most beloved and timeless. It successfully merges the traditional
tatlaga style of double-stop playing—a style that evokes the rhythms of a horse's
gait—with virtuosic and extended fingering and bowing techniques. The piece
has a rousing energy that functions well at the end of a concert, inspiring audiences to clap along, and its interchangeable eight-bar sectional form provides
ample room for performers to add their own creative additions. It has been
covered by every prominent ensemble in Inner Mongolia regardless of genre,

from horsehead fiddle orchestras to ethno-rock bands. "Galloping Horses" is one of the only Inner Mongolian contributions to the canon of horsehead fiddle repertoire in Mongolia and is still performed regularly on television and stage performances in Ulaanbaatar. Although Chi Bulag has composed dozens of pieces and songs, "Galloping Horses" is his most loved, signature piece that he has brought around the globe, including during his first official visit to Mongolia in 1988, in a performance at the Musikverein (Golden Hall) of Vienna in 2005, and in a world-record public performance by one thousand horsehead fiddlers during the lead-up to the 2008 Beijing Olympics.

Chi Bulag's accomplishments have attracted many young and mostly male musicians in Inner Mongolia, many of whom now view horsehead fiddle as a viable career choice. Prior to 1990, only a handful of fiddlers were active, including Na Huhe, Qian Baila, and Chen Bayar. But the students they taught helped to generate a resurgence of interest in the horsehead fiddle tradition. Many families from smaller cities and towns in the region sent their children to take lessons or enroll in horsehead fiddle boarding schools under the tutelage of these teachers with the hope that their children might succeed as musicians and ultimately find careers in a government-sponsored arts ensemble. Before long, there were far more aspiring and talented horsehead fiddlers than openings available at the top Chinese universities with fiddle programs. Horsehead fiddle students from Inner Mongolia began applying to arts universities in Mongolia, where they now form a critical mass of the horsehead fiddle majors.

The predominance of male horsehead fiddlers and relative absence of female fiddlers resembles a pattern we have seen in education and professional music-making in Mongolia and Inner Mongolia since the early decades of the twentieth century. This pattern is one that appears to be deeply rooted within Mongolian culture. According to Carole Pegg (2001, 2002), the most valued musical forms in Mongol society, including the horsehead fiddle tradition, were traditionally maintained by men. The association of men and their horses is found in many parts of Mongol society (see figure 5.3). In the division of labor in nomadic en-campments, it is customary for men and boys to look after horses, while women and girls look after the sheep, goats, and other animals (Fijn 2011:59, 84–85). Numerous legends and epic tales tell the stories of Mongol men who, with the help of their wise and powerful horses, overcome and defeat their enemies.

The connection of men with the horsehead fiddle is just as persistent in his-torical narratives. Musicologist J. Enebish connects the fiddle with horses and men, writing:

> A horse-head fiddle is also considered to be a good fortune to one's horse or herd of horses. Therefore, there is a custom where the male horse herder, after putting his horses out to pasture in the evening, will come to his *ger* and make music with his horse-head fiddle (Enebish 1991:77, n. 2).

FIGURE 5.3. A Chakar Mongol performs for his horse on a *khiil khuur*. Photo by Henning Haslund-Christensen. National Museum of Denmark (used with permission).

Musicologist D. Nansalmaa emphasizes this connection of the fiddle with males in her description of where fiddles are traditionally placed within a nomadic *ger*.

> In the highly structured sphere of the Mongol ger, the *khoimor* is also the part of the home where the eldest or most senior males of the ail would sit, further suggesting the traditional association of the fiddle, like the horse, with the male gender. In addition, the fiddle was also customarily positioned to face towards the fireplace (*golomt*), which is located in the very center of the ger, and never to the "east" (*züün tal*), which is the "women's side" of the *ger* (Nansalmaa 1987:350).

Such narratives may suggest that women were, historically speaking, not allowed to play the instrument. But our research finds, on the contrary, that women in rural society have actively participated in learning, teaching, and performing on fiddles alongside men, and continue to do so today. Marsh documents numerous sources that describe how all members of rural households, regardless of gender or even age, were expected to participate in musical performances in the pre-Revolutionary period (2009:30–32). In his fieldwork in rural Mongolia in the 1990s and 2000s, he encountered many families in which women played fiddles in their homes and at social gatherings. Pegg (2001:69) reported on how some women faced the challenge of performing the horsehead fiddle without holding the instrument between their legs, a posture considered unsightly and perhaps even overtly sexual. Based on her research in Inner Mongolia, D'Evelyn has found that women of an older generation rarely chose to play the fiddle, but that those who did typically played it in a seated position on the floor to avoid the open-leg posture. D'Evelyn did encounter stories about older women or grandmothers who played with open legs in a chair, suggesting a lack of consensus among Mongol communities with regard to the appropriateness of the sitting posture.[3] Indeed, local stigmas varied with regard to the appropriateness of the fiddle posture. But there does not seem to be an overt taboo that restricted women's involvement with the horsehead fiddle as there was in the past for throat-singing (see Chapter 8 this volume; Pegg 1992); nor was fiddle playing as exclusively male-dominated as the genre of epic singing (*tuul'*). Yet, we do recognize that very few women were encouraged to become local fiddle specialists who would be sought out to play for public gatherings or to pursue careers as professional fiddle players.

It is curious, but perhaps not unsurprising, that in contemporary Mongolia and Inner Mongolia, in a period in which practically no limits exist on who can or cannot participate in fiddle playing, there is still a great gender imbalance. For instance, the first two professional female horsehead fiddle players in Mongolia, Uyanga Baasansuren and Uugantuyaa Jantsannorov, only graduated from the Music & Dance College and began their careers in 1997. Most horsehead fiddle players in the Mongolian State Morin Khuur Ensemble, the premiere fiddle ensemble in the nation, continue to be male. The ensemble's female performers typically perform on instruments associated in Mongolia with their gender, including the violoncello and *yatga* (zither). In Inner Mongolia, there are a small number of prominent women horsehead fiddlers who have achieved success in a musical world dominated by men. Perhaps most notable among them is Saikhannakhaa, a member of the world-famous ensemble Anda Union. Another notable performer and rising star in the fiddle scene in Inner Mongolia is the performer Sorgog, a soloist and member of the all-female throat-singing band, Mongolia Ensemble (see figure 5.4).

A New Generation of Fiddlers

We end our chapter by exploring the lives of two musicians whose career trajectory has taken them to the West, where they have introduced the sounds of the horsehead fiddle to new audiences and offered local members of the Mongol diaspora a means to connect to their roots. Tamir Hargana (b. 1991, see Hargana Interlude in this volume) is part of this new generation of fiddlers from Inner Mongolia who specialize in both the horsehead fiddle and *khöömii* (throat-

FIGURE 5.4. Horsehead fiddle performer, Sorgog (used with permission).

singing). Describing himself as "a grassland boy" in his childhood, Tamir now lives and works in Chicago, Illinois, and is the first professional musician from Inner Mongolia to make a career teaching and performing folk and folkloric Mongolian music in the United States.

Through numerous public performances and workshops, Tamir has introduced audiences across the United States to the Mongolian and Inner Mongolian traditions of the horsehead fiddle and the Mongol and Tuvan forms of throat-singing, often accompanying himself on the *tovshuur, doshpuluur,* or *igil*

FIGURE 5.5. Horsehead fiddle performer and teacher, G. Urtnasan (used with permission).

(lutes). He is eager to experiment with new musical styles and has collaborated with musicians across a range of genres, most famously being the Mongol fusion metal band Tengger Cavalry. Tamir regularly performs for Mongolian-American communities and has presented his work and performed at several major academic conferences. He is part of a small but growing rank of Mongol scholar-performers who research, write, and transmit knowledge about Mongolian music in the English language.

Like Tamir, Urtnasan Gantulga (see figure 5.5) is another young fiddle player and teacher who is bringing important innovations to the contemporary horsehead fiddle tradition. Urtaa was raised in rural Töv aimag, outside of Ulaanbaatar, by his grandfather, who was a horse trainer and a folk song singer. When he was eleven years old, his grandfather began to teach him to play the horsehead fiddle. Six years later Urtaa enrolled in the Music & Dance College in Ulaanbaatar, the same school at which Jamiyan taught. There he studied first with master teacher Yo. Batbayar and then with Ts. Batchuluun, one of Jamiyan's most successful pupils. Batchuluun quickly recognized Urtaa's talent and, in his first year at the school, placed him in the State Horsehead Fiddle Ensemble. Urtaa praises Batchuluun as a great teacher: "He showed us how artists should be and how we should live. I think he never said 'that's perfect' after I performed something for him. He usually said, 'that's close,' which meant that he wanted us to understand that there was always room to be better and learn more" (G. Urtnasan interview, Seattle, February 2020).

In 2006, Urtaa emigrated to the United States. "I was young," he said, "and wanted to improve myself and learn a foreign culture. But also, I wanted to become a horsehead fiddle expert in the United States." Making a living as a horsehead fiddle player proved to be difficult, but he did find many people who were eager to learn to play it. The problem was, he lived in Seattle, in the state of Washington, and many of his potential students lived hundreds or even thousands of miles away. So, he innovated by creating online instruction videos and teaching students with online lessons. "At that time, some people said that teaching the fiddle online would be impossible, that it would never work. But some others said, 'Why not?'" Urtaa has trained many students around the nation from his home and has a popular YouTube channel with his video lessons and recordings of his performances and those of his students. Urtaa was selected to perform B. Sharav's Concerto for Horsehead Fiddle and Orchestra at the Pan Asian Music Festival at Stanford University in 2011, which marked the first time a horsehead fiddle concerto had been performed in the United States. "My main goal," Urtaa says, "is to keep teaching horsehead fiddle and to expand its presence around the United States. My teacher, Ts. Batchuluun, told me that my work here could help Mongolians to create an International horsehead fiddle ensemble, one that draws together people from around the world."

Young artists like Urtaa and Tamir are helping to extend the horsehead fiddle tradition far beyond the borders of Mongolia and Inner Mongolia. They have each found ways to adapt to the rigors of surviving as a Mongolian performing artist outside of their respective homelands and to the challenges of translating traditional Mongolian music to non-Mongolian audiences.

As should be clear by now, the horsehead fiddle traditions are not frozen in time. As recently as the early decades of the twentieth century, fiddles varied considerably in appearance and sound, only coalescing in the past six or seven decades into the modernized and standardized forms we see on concert stages and music videos today. Mongolians around the world have continued to adapt the instrument and its traditions to a variety of regional, cultural, political, and ideological needs.

In an interesting reversal, recent interest in musical roots and origins in Mongolia and Inner Mongolia (Mongolian: *yazguur*; Chinese: *yuanshengtai*) has led some musicians to look backward in time, focusing less energy on virtuosic displays of modernity and giving more attention to the revival and restoration of styles and instruments that were previously rejected as backward. The ability to play with amplification, as well as developments in instrument construction, have made skin-faced instruments effective for use on the concert stage in ways that were not possible in earlier decades. The horsehead fiddle is also finding new expression through the music of contemporary fusion ensembles such as The Hu, whose instruments are designed with an ethno-punk flavor and played with amplified distortion for the purpose of a heavy metal aesthetic (see Chapter 10 in this volume). One can only speculate about the ways the horsehead fiddle will continue to change as it travels the globe in the next century.

Notes

1. See our companion website, www.mongoliansoundworlds.org, for additional information on the musical traditions included in this volume.

2. Sound recordings of Balagan and Serashi reveal that the lowest string was generally pitched around an E, one note lower than the lowest string on the modern Mongolian horsehead fiddle.

3. One Inner Mongolian fiddle innovator, Darma, formulated a way for the horsehead fiddle to be played in a standing position (with a belt that supports the instrument at the waist) and used this innovation to establish an all-female, standing horsehead fiddle ensemble that he saw as a strategy to overcome any stigmas from the past about the sitting posture.

Bibliography

Baljmaa, T. 2019. "The Hu Awarded Order of Chinggis Khaan, Supreme State Prize in Mongolia," *Montsame*, November 27. https://montsame.mn/en/read/208232.

Batchuluun, Ts. 2017. *Khogjmiin dursang* [Musical memories]. Ulaanbaatar: Soëmbo.

Chuluunbat, Ts. 1972. *Sain duryn uran saikhanchdad tuslamj* [Help for amateur artists]. Ulaanbaatar: State Publishing House.

D'Evelyn, Charlotte. 2014. "Driving Change, Sparking Debate: Chi Bulag and the *Morin Huur* in Inner Mongolia, China." *Yearbook for Traditional Music* 46:89–113.

Enebish, Jambaliin. 1982. "Mongolyn khögjim" [Mongolian music]. *Soyol* 1:28–32.

———. 1991. "Morin khuur" [The horse-head fiddle]. In *Khögjmiin ulamjlal shinechleliin asuudald* [Problems of the renewal of the study of music], 77–85. Ulaanbaatar: State Publishing House.

Fijn, Natasha. 2011. *Living with Herds: Human-Animal Coexistence in Mongolia*. Cambridge: Cambridge University Press.

Haslund-Christensen, Henning 1971 [1943]. "On the Trail of Ancient Mongol Tunes." *The Music of the Mongols, Part I: Eastern Mongolia*, 13–38. New York: Da Capo Press.

Khogjilt [Hugejiletu]. 2006. *Mengguzu Yinyueshi* [History of music of the Mongol nationality]. Shenyang: Liaoning Minzu Chubanshe.

Marsh, Peter K. 2009. *The Horse-Head Fiddle and the Cosmopolitan Reimagination of Tradition in Mongolia*. New York: Routledge.

Nansalmaa, D. 1987. "Ardyn khögjim" [Folk music]. In *Khalkha ugsaatny z 0i (XIX–XX zuuny zaag üye)* [Ethnography of the Khalkha, 19th–20th century], Vol. I, edited by S. Badamkhatan, 334–357. Ulaanbaatar: State Publishing House.

Natsagdorj, Sh. 1981. *BNMAU-yn Soyolyn Tüükh (1921–1940)* [Cultural history of the MPR (1921–1940)], Vol. I. Ulaanbaatar: State Publishing House.

Pegg, Caroline. 1992. "Mongolian Conceptualizations of Overtone Singing." *British Journal of Ethnomusicology* 1:31–55.

————. 1995. "Ritual, Religion and Magic in West Mongolian (Oirad) Heroic Epic Performance." *British Journal of Ethnomusicology* 4:77–99.

————. 2001. *Mongolian Music, Dance, & Oral Narrative: Performing Diverse Identities.* Seattle: University of Washington Press.

————. 2002. "Mongol Music." In *The Garland Encyclopedia of World Music. Volume 7: China, Japan, and Korea.*, edited by Robert C. Provine, Yosihiko Tokumaru, and Lawrence Witzleben, 1003–1020. New York: Routledge.

Siriguleng. 2009. "Bianqian Zhong de Matouqin—Neimenggu Diqu Matouqin Chuangcheng Yu Bianqian" [In the changing of morinhuur—Research on the transmission and change of morinhuur in Inner Mongolia]. Master's thesis, Inner Mongolia Normal University.

Tsendorj, G. 1983. *BNMAU-yn mergejliin khögjmiin khamtlaguud üüsej khögjsön n'* [The origin and development of the Mongolian People's Republic's professional music ensembles]. Ulaanbaatar: State Publishing House.

Ulanji. 1998. *Mengguzu Yinyueshi* [A musical history of the Mongol nationality]. Hohhot: Neimenggu Renmin Chubanshe.

CHAPTER 6

The *Tovshuur* and Oirad Identity in Mongolia's Western Provinces

OTGONBAYAR CHULUUNBAATAR

The Oirads (Oirats) have a long history in Mongolia, Kalmykia in the Russian Federation, and in Xinjiang and Qinghai Regions in northwestern China. Ethnically homogeneous and linguistically linked to Mongols, they are diverse peoples who immigrated to the Altai mountain regions in western Mongolia at early but different times. Oirad peoples settled today in Khovd, Uvs, and Bayan-Ölgii aimags (provinces) include the Torguud, Zakhchin, Khoshuud, Dörvöd, Ööld, Altai Uriankhai, Myangad, and Bayad (Ochir 2006; Chuluunbaatar 2010). In contemporary Mongolia, Oirads share some traditions with Mongols, but they also maintain their own customs. This is especially apparent in their musical performances and their musical instruments.

One iconic instrument of the Oirad people is the *tovshuur*, a two-string fretless, long-necked lute. The instrument has been modernized and used in contemporary urban music, but an old form of the *tovshuur* continues to be played by the Oirads and occasionally by Khalkh Mongols also living in the Altai Mountains. The instrument has not received the scholarly attention that other instruments have received, yet it plays an important role in Oirad communities.[1] Its social role is tied especially to its position as an accompanying instrument for epic (*tuul'*) traditions. Beyond this, the *tovshuur* is entangled with performance, repertoires, beliefs, and values of peoples, some of whom have maintained pastoral practices into the twenty-first century, even while others have embraced new economic and technological opportunities. In this contribution, based on both scholarly research and personal experience, I position the *tovshuur* as an important instrument worthy of focused attention, not only for its role as an accompanying instrument for epic song, but as an instrument emblematic of Oirad ethnic identity.[2]

The word *tovshuur* stems from the Mongolian verb *tovshikh*, which means "to pluck." Early historical evidence of the instrument is seldom found in written documents. The lack of such information can be explained by ways of life that did not support written records. From the time after the defeat of the Oirads by the Manchu in 1757–1759, political conflicts further contributed to the scarcity of local documents (Gongor 2006). The effect of this is confirmed by the Oirad dictionaries compiled by Krueger (1978–1984), mainly using words from earlier Oirad texts, in which the term "tovshuur" cannot be found. The *tovshuur* is also rarely mentioned in earlier sources by non-Mongolian authors.[3] One possible reason may be due to its role primarily as an accompanying instrument for epics, resulting in the production of relatively few instruments. The instrument is referenced in very few early travel reports in Kalmykia (Pallas 1776). It is conceivable that when the Oirads immigrated to Kalmykia at the beginning of the seventeenth century, the *tovshuur* was abandoned in favor of the *balalaika* and *dombyra*, also referenced as accompanying instruments for epic singing by scholars such as the Russian Mongolist Vladimirtsov (1923).

Constructing the *Tovshuur*

The traditional *tovshuur* in western Mongolia are built almost exclusively by epic singers who use the instrument to accompany their performances. The structure and style can hold special significance for a musician. Knowledge about its construction is passed orally and thus there are differences in the ways they are built, such as the shape of the soundbox (*tsar*), the headstock (*tolgoi*), as well as certain ornamental forms. The materials used to make the instrument depend on various criteria. These include above all the tradition of the musician, the experiences and oral transmission of a teacher, and the environment of the settlement area, but also other aspects that are often ignored. For example, Enkhbalsan and Batmunkh, musicians I encountered during my field research, draw from their expertise as a carpenter (Enkhbalsan) and son of a carpenter (Batmunkh), respectively, as they carve their own *tovshuur* from local resources (see figures 6.1 and 6.2), including the soundboard (*tsarny nüür*).

In most cases, makers construct the *tovshuur* soundbox, neck (*ish*), and headstock from a single piece of wood. Occasionally, the *tovshuur* is built with a separate neck (see figure 6.2). The shape of the soundbox is designed individually according to a maker's or musician's wishes; soundboxes can be oval, trapezoidal, hexagonal, octagonal or, rarely, round (called cup *tovshuur—aagan tovshuur*). Many of these forms are rounded toward the body of the musician, and when they are, such instruments are also called *shanagan tovshuur* (ladle *tovshuur*) (Badraa 2017). Shapes of soundboxes are designed differently not only due to ethnic differences (groups, clans), as other scholars have stated (Pegg 2001; Chao 2001), there are other factors to consider when assessing differences, including musicians' contact with instruments in other regions, available wood species, as well as the skills of the respective instrument maker.

The soundboard of the *tovshuur* body is made of skin, often goat skin, or occasionally of wood of the larch (*shines, khar mod*) or pine (*nars*) tree.[4] The processing of goat skin by makers involves drying after blowing up the skin with air immediately after the animal has been skinned. Next the skin is softened by wetting it and when pliable it is pulled over the body of the instrument and fastened laterally, generally, with glue and nails. Makers say that for a good sound the skin needs to be thin.[5] Very rarely, a small number of tiny superficial holes are punched into the skin of the soundbox in the shape of geometrical forms.[6]

Depending on the maker, the tuning pegs (*khöglöch chikh*) are mounted on the instrument either laterally (see figure 6.2) or on the rear (see figure 6.1). They are called "ears" (*chikh*) by the locals, one of several anthropomorphic designations of instrument parts used. The instrument headstock is individually designed, but there are several common forms. The headstock can be of the same solid wood as the neck or be hollowed out in the center (see figure 6.4). The latter variant makes it easier to mount the tuning pegs from the side and thus achieve better string tension. Often the hollowing out is done by the musician. Sometimes the area of the whole neck between the soundbox and headstock is decorated with carvings. On the lower narrow side of the instrument there is a short extension (*dood bekhelgee*)—often made of wood or a nail—to which the strings (*chavkhdas*) are attached.

Most *tovshuur* players in Mongolia today use strings made of nylon. Performers report that they prefer the sound quality obtained with strings made of goat intestines or the hair of a stallion's tail.[7] In general, strings made from natural materials, due to their texture, sound pleasant and soft, whereas strings from industrial materials present a stark, intense, and harsh sound. Nomads hear the human strength and warmth along with the vitality expressed by the natural materials' sound. When made of hair, the lower string should have an odd number of hairs, while the upper string an even number (Badraa 2017). For performance, the strings are tuned a fourth apart. The thinner lower string is tuned upward by a tuning peg, while the thicker upper string is tuned downward. This can be explained with the significance "heaven" has for local residents (Jukovskaya 2011).

The length of the *tovshuur* is often adapted to the needs of each musician. I received a *tovshuur* as a gift from the musician and instrument maker Batmunkh (see figure 6.5); it is much shorter and the soundbox is also narrower than other instruments. This same construction can also be seen in a picture from 1981, which shows Batmunkh's sister with a similarly short and narrow *tovshuur*. This is significant because *tovshuur*-playing women are extremely rare because women rarely practice epic singing. From my own experience, there is an existing opinion in society that this style of music could lead to health problems for

FIGURE 6.1. T. Enkhbalsan, Zakhchin epic singer, 2006. *Tovshuur* made by the singer from wood and painted; tuning pegs rear-mounted (note the *khadag)*. Photo by Otgonbayar Chuluunbaatar.

FIGURE 6.2. B. Batmunkh, Zakhchin epic singer, 2016. *Tovshuur* made by the singer. Photo by Otgonbayar Chuluunbaatar.

FIGURE 6.3. Bold, Altai Uriankhai epic singer, 2012. Artistically executed decor e.g. dragon's head as well as wooden milk spoon, oval body (note used lighter as lower bridge as well as different *khadags*). Photo by Otgonbayar Chuluunbaatar.

FIGURE 6.4. Grandson of Dügersüren, Altai Uriankhai epic singer, 2010. Note the cavity for better fixing of tuning pegs. Photo by Otgonbayar Chuluunbaatar.

FIGURE. 6.5. Tovshuur for women, produced by B. Batmunkh, 2016. Note the shape as well as smallness of the sound body, and the lucky symbol of the fish. Photo by Otgonbayar Chuluunbaatar.

women. However, it is sometimes the close female relatives of epic singers who, according to reports, pass on the knowledge to their descendants (see Chapter 4 in this volume).

The *tovshuur* is plucked by means of percussive movements or strummed with the thumb, the index, or middle finger. This instrumental technique during playing called *tsokhilt* (hitting) is used for specific musical themes such as epics with warlike content or to imitate animal or nature sounds. As an exception, I have witnessed a special *biy* dance that is performed with the *tsokhilt* when playing the *tovshuur*. However, this dance melody is now rare and can be assigned to the Jangar epic (Chuluunbaatar 2016). The Torguud ethnic group also has only a single dance song, called *savardakh* (to skewer with the dungfork), that is accompanied with the *tovshuur* (Badraa 2017).

Iconic Meaning of Individual Instrument Parts

The *tovshuur* often exhibits symbolic elements. Such ornamental elements found on the headstock and neck originate mostly from Tibetan Buddhism (fire symbol, the wheel of the Dharma, the eternal knot, lotus flower, fish (see figure 6.5), moon and sun) or they are taken from mythology, such as a carved dragon head (see figure 6.3) or the Soyombo symbol (Bulag 1998). Some *tovshuur* decorations also have lucky symbols (see figure 6.3), such as the wooden milk spoon *tsatslyn khalbaga* (Ganbold 2014; Hudgins 2014) used by Mongolian nomads. The same is used for the daily sacrifice of the first milked milk to the spirits of heaven. This spoon usually has nine (in the form of three times three) even depressions. This number, a symbol of the nine treasures, signifies auspiciousness for Mongolians (Jukovskaya 2011). Quite exceptionally, I have seen this form also as the lower connecting part of the soundbox.

An animal headstock on the *tovshuur* can have symbolic and spiritual significance. I have seen *tovshuur* with the ibex as a headstock (*yangir tovshuur*) acting as a motif. Such an instrument was once used by the epic singer Enkhbalsan as a symbol of happiness with reference to a corresponding myth involving this animal (Dulam 1987).[8] It is possible, however, that local geographical conditions also play a role here, since ibexes can be found in the immediate mountain environment of the singer.

A swan's head on the headstock of *tovshuur* is rarely found in Oirad settlements. The swan, though, does have a long history in Oirad mythology as an animal motif in epics that conveys a specific magical power. The concept of the swan virgin is also said to be of totemic significance in various regions (Poppe 1981). In accordance with the text of the early Oirad epic Jangar, a female yellow-headed swan, hatches her eggs and also produces the melody of an Oirad musical instrument with its own voice, namely the end-blown flute *tsuur* (Jangar 2000; Chuluunbaatar 2013). The swan also has significance in Mongolian shamanism where it is used as an *ongod* symbol (Pürev 1999) in theriomorphic representations.[9] The swan also appears in ritual songs such as the *dallaga* ritual (Chabros 1992), which can be performed for various occasions (Rintchen 1959). The swan headstock on the *tovshuur*, though, was first created in workshops in Ulaanbaatar where it has become quite popular and is sometimes also bought by tourists. The soundboard on these manufactured instruments also occasionally displays painted swans.

Sometimes, local people refer to the *tovshuur* according to its form or symbolic ornamental elements attached. Examples are *böörönkhii tovshuur* (round *tovshuur*), *khun tovshuur* (swan *tovshuur*), *yangir tovshuur* (ibex *tovshuur*), or *chandman' tovshuur* (gem *tovshuur*) (Badraa 2017). Furthermore, it should be noted that individual Oirad ethnic groups sometimes use their own designations.

The *Tovshuur*'s Social Relationships

The *tovshuur*, as performed as an accompanying instrument by an epic singer (*tuul'ch*), is above all an expression of the Oirad social and cultural system and a marker of Oirad identity. Epic singing with *tovshuur* accompaniment symbolizes the local community's ideal world. The epic singers communicate by means of acoustic patterns, attaining variants of spiritual forms of existence via a trance state in which they perform (see figure 6.2). The artists are regarded as ambassadors who overcome and eliminate detrimental events with their epic songs. The epic text presented is regarded as something extraordinary, the contents of which—together with the accompanying sounds—local participants listen to reverently. The epic performer is thus regarded as a mediator between earthly society and a transcendent world (Khabunova and Kornusova 2005). Therefore, the sight of a *tovshuur* in the rural settlement area awakens a special connection between the Oirad people and their emotional world. Furthermore, a continuous ontological connection between humans and nature is thus shown; this relationship is rooted in the reproduction of ecologically significant elements as well as in folklore (Grebennikova 2012; Post 2019).

Epic singers are invited to perform for different kinds of occasions. Today a musician is treated as a guest of honor during his stay, and relatives, neighbors, and special guests come from nearby areas to listen to his performances. With his music, the epic singer both appeases and mollifies the local spirits of nature. Epic song performances are traditionally of eminent importance for the rural populations who rely on the natural world, including communion with the master nature spirits of the land, for survival (see Chapters 1 and 9 in this volume). The following list offers a sampling of ceremonial events, each of which may involve an epic singer and are performed to satisfy local nature spirits (*baigaliin ongoduud*): commencement of the winter season, New Year's festival (*tsagaan sar*), family celebrations, yurt processions, requests for rainfall, success in a hunt or war, requests for healing from human and animal diseases, and support from various misfortunes such as childlessness. (Ganbold 2012).

In the sung form of the epic of the Oirads, the required melody and the *tovshuur* accompaniment play essential roles. Oirad epic singers are intrinsically drawn to the *tovshuur* to accompany their singing. The sounds have a calming effect and help the musician reach the required trance-like state during performance. Above all, the creation of meditative sounds enables the singer to maintain the rhythm of the verses in order to achieve the state of mind needed to build up the epic chant. Relationships between epic singing and *tovshuur* sound and rhythm is also important for a successful performance. Vladimirtsov (1923) suggested that a musician encounters difficulties when singing epics without a *tovshuur*. About his experience with a western Mongolian Bayad (Bait) bard, he says,

> Many times the following scene ensued: a singer was dictating a heroic epic to me, knew it masterfully, dictated it excellently, and suddenly some circumstance, a minute mis-recollection and the thread of the tale was broken; then

the bard would take up his tobshuur and sing the last few lines just dictated to me, and at once the further passage would come to mind, and he again could continue to dictate the bylina [epic] for some hours, until a new similar mishap. For the Oirat singer the heroic epic is linked with accompaniment, with the tobshuur, in an unbreakable association; the accompaniment and the words of the epic for the Oirat singer are one and the same thing, one fused and unbreakable whole (Vladimirtsov and Krueger 1983–84:41).

When no musical instrument is available, Heissig (1979) suggests that rhythmic tapping with a riding whip or a baton (*tashuur*) may prove helpful.[10]

A person is often designated as the chosen inheritor of a *tovshuur* instrument even before the death of the musician. Sometimes epic singers find a worthy successor within members of their own family. In such a case, the student receives the musical instrument from the closest relative of the deceased during a ceremonial celebration. For this ceremony a new *khadag* (silk scarf for Buddhist rituals of auspiciousness) is attached to the neck of the instrument (see figure 6.1), to which another scarf is usually attached after the death of the previous owner. Other instruments may remain in the family of the deceased in the absence of a worthy successor until one has been found. The *tovshuur* is typically stored slightly elevated at a place of honor in the dwelling. In the yurt, this is opposite the entrance area directly behind where the elders sit. It is rare to find such valued family instruments in a museum.

Stories Involving the *Tovshuur*

Various musical instruments are mentioned in texts of epics and many other song categories. On the one hand, this shows how important instruments and their traditions are among the Oirad people, but it also shows how traditional ways of life are incorporated in epics. The *tovshuur* not only appears in various song forms, it also tells us stories of different ethnic groups (Tsoloo 1987). In a folk song of the Oirad Zakhchin ethnic group, which has the instrument name *tovshuur* as its title, the instrument becomes a symbol for the nomadic way of life.[11] It deals with material components such as larch and aspen wood, willow or horse tail strings, making the instrument, various horse colors, the cleansing ceremony of the instrument using incense (*arts*), and a reference to the strong significance of age (grey horse) among Mongolians (Chuluunbaatar and Hofer 2006).

Ulia-san ge-deg mo-doo-ro-o	With the artfully made *tovshuur*,
Ur-laj khii-sen tov-shuu-ra-am	Of larch wood,
Una-gan zeer-diin süü-lee-re-e	From the tail of a chestnut horse,
Khyal-ga-salj khii-sen tov-shuu-ra-am	The *tovshuur*'s strings are tight.

Khar-gai ge-deg mo-doo-ro-o	With the smoothed *tovshuur*,
Khar uul daj khii-sen tov-shuu-ra-am	Of aspen (*khargai*) wood,
Khaliu-khan chikh-tiin süü-lee-re-e	From the tail of a dun horse,
Khyal-ga-salj khii-sen tov-shuu-ra-am	The *tovshuur*'s strings are tight.

Ar-tsan ge-deg mo-doo-ro-o	With the *arts* (juniper incense),
Ariu-laj khii-sen tov-shuu-ra-am	Purified *tovshuur*,
Ag-sam zeer-diin süü-lee-re-e	From the tail (*süül*) of a wild chestnut horse,
Khyal-ga-salj khii-sen tov-shuu-ra-am	The *tovshuur*'s strings are tight.

Burg-san ge-deg mo-doo-ro-o	The crafted from a willow (*burgsan*),
Bu-daj khii-sen tov-shuu-ra-am	Colored *tovshuur*,
Buu-ral mori-ny süü-lee-re-e	From the tail of a gray-colored old horse,
Khyal-ga-salj khii-sen tov-shuu-ra-am	The *tovshuur*'s strings are tight.

Other songs with information about the *tovshuur* can also be found among other neighboring peoples. This includes the Republic of Altai and the Tuva Republic of the Russian Federation (Levin and Süzükei 2006; Pegg and Yamaeva 2012).

The *Tovshuur* in Contemporary Use

In western Mongolia the *tovshuur* maintained a consistent construction and musical use even during the period of Soviet influence when other instruments in Mongolia, such as the Khalkh *morin khuur*, were adapted for use in European-influenced orchestras (Tsetsentsolmon 2015). When the *morin khuur* achieved status in Mongolia as a national icon (see Chapter 5 in this volume), the *tovshuur* in the western regions remained an instrument used almost exclusively by epic singers. Other Oirad instruments, such as *ikil* and *tsuur*, also remained in their original forms. Adoption of the *tovshuur* for wider use was also hampered by the state's disregard for the Oirads, especially during the early days of the social-ist government (Bulag 1998). This can be linked also to Oirad rule during the Zungarian Empire (Namsrai 2015; Zlatkin 2015) in the seventeenth to eighteenth centuries. In this period, some of the traditional Mongolian musical forms were not included in the developing national guidelines and thus they were rarely performed. As an epic instrument the *tovshuur* represented an obsolete form ac-cording to the new lifestyle proclaimed under Soviet-influenced socialism. This development was compounded by the official revocation of numerous ethnic minorities' rights (Bulag 1998), which had a strong effect on the epic-singing Oirads.[12] These circumstances, along with the fact that the Oirad settlement areas were so distant from the ruling authorities, presumably contributed to the preservation of local epic singing and traditional forms of the *tovshuur* and other musical instruments.[13]

Political changes brought not only democracy to Mongolia in 1990, but also a capitalist market economy and, subsequently, the influences of globalization. At that time many ethnic groups and individuals still felt a desire to acknowledge and maintain older lifeways. In the case of the Oirads, this was also expressed through their traditional music. However, these aspirations were soon pushed aside by their economic needs and opportunities. Thus, a growing mobility, the introduction of transnational media, migration, and the increasing rural exodus of young people to the capital have affected the nomadic population throughout Mongolia, including the western region, during the last three decades. As Western influences in music and its genres began appearing in rural regions, notably with the introduction of mobile antennas throughout the country, there was a shift of interests, especially among young people. Today there seems little place for the *tovshuur* and its social life in modern Oirad society in western Mongolia. However, all these aspects were never a part of the idiosyncrasies of the *tovshuur*. In today's increasingly fast-moving society there is, relatively speaking, a lack of adequate access to other cultures and modern media. This is a clash of two extremes. On the one hand, there is the need for the quiet world of thought of an epic singer and, on the other hand, a lifestyle shaped by a capitalist market economy. Some Oirads believe the *tovshuur* has no place in popular music. Its sounds represent a nomadic way of life of the herders. The *tovshuur*, along with other traditional instruments, can be regarded as a vivid symbol of rural identity.

Conclusion

In the Altai Mountains, the Oirads have preserved numerous traditions that are distinct from those of other peoples living in Mongolia. Their expression of ethnic identity can be attributed, mainly, to their remote rural life in the Altai Mountains. The *tovshuur*, an instrument traditionally used to accompany epics, provides an unchanging connection between their identity and their way of life. For the singer, this instrument is an essential component in order to achieve a certain trance state, which helps the performer remember the lengthy texts. Thus, an Oirad epic is inextricably linked with the *tovshuur*, expressed by saying: "one without the other is like a fishing rod without the hook."[14] The musicians' interpretation is guided by an inner intuition for the natural landscape, whose spirits are to be appeased. Thus, the mere sight of such a musical instrument in the rural areas, creates a special bond between the Oirads and their emotional realm.

Throughout this region, the *tovshuur* is made by the musicians themselves. Knowledge of this musical instrument is passed on mainly within the family; it is therefore not widespread among the population and hardly documented in specialist literature. The *tovshuur* has specific unchanging characteristics and only in the ornamentation can it show certain individual preferences of the musicians; symbols that can be of traditional, spiritual, and religious nature.

During the socialist, Soviet-influenced, rule, the *tovshuur* was rendered useless for the then promoted concert music of Mongolia. Therefore, the instrument remained unaltered by the state. In recent times, the performance of traditional music in the Altai Mountains has become increasingly difficult owing to growing mobility and the introduction of transnational media. This is especially true for the epic and its accompanying instrument. Many years of personal experience clearly show that information provided by epic musicians about their music as well as their instruments depends on long-built trust, Oirad origin as well as, often, the musical expertise of the interviewers.

Notes

1. The *tovshuur* is rarely discussed in contemporary scholarly literature and, if at all, generally makes up only a few short paragraphs within any given text (Pegg 1995, 2001; Amgalan 2000; Tsedev 2009; Enebish 2012; Katuu 2013; Badraa 2017).

2. See our companion website, www.mongoliansoundworlds.org, for additional information on the musical traditions included in this volume.

3. The *tovshuur* is also mentioned in an earlier source of the Manchu Dynasty (Fu 1782) under the name *tuobushu'er*.

4. Sheepskin can also be used in principle. But the reason goat skin is used more often is that goat is slaughtered far more often and the skin is less valuable (excluding cashmere goat) than that of sheep. Pegg noted in 1995 that the Altai Uriankhai Avirmed used camel calf skin and that sheep and adult camel skins were also used in addition to goat (Pegg 1995:87). Usually, camel calves are not slaughtered. The skin of adult camels is used by nomads for products such as saddle bags, leather cords for yurts, and boots. According to Avirmed's younger son Baldandorj goat skin is softer and evenly finer, making it a better material for the purpose, and he rejects the notion of using camel skin (conversation with Baldandorj on January 17, 2020). Avirmed's older son Dorjpalam (1959–2011) in numerous conversations mentioned nothing contrary to this.

5. This is because the sound from an instrument with fine skin is a soundboard much smoother and softer to the human ear. This is especially audible when the instrument is played in a yurt.

6. Presumably, this procedure is used only on thicker skin because such openings would impair the stability of a thinner skin.

7. Owing to a widely held nature religion's belief, only tail hair from male horses of a specific age should be used.

8. The origin story that encouraged Enkhbalsan to use the ibex head is quoted in Pegg (1995) as well. Another similar story involving an epic singer, however,

with a maral deer instead of an ibex as prey, was told by the epic singer Avirmed, on December 9th, 1971, to the scientist Tsoloo (Tsoloo and Mönkhtsetseg 2008).

9. A corresponding representation of a carved swan fixed in a tree can be seen on a picture in Chuluunbaatar (2017, figure 6b).

10. Vladimirtsov (1923) reports that alcohol may be used, sparingly, as well.

11. This folk song that I have known since my childhood is sung in the Zakhchin micro-dialect in the Oirad dialect, which differs from the Khalkh Mongolian dialect.

12. This was especially the case during the reign of Kh. Choibalsan (1939–1952).

13. Relatively late—especially in the 1960s to 1980s—the Mongolian Academy of Sciences collected and recorded traditional folk music that also included a large number of epics (Sampildendev, Gerelmaa, and Gansukh 2004). Most of the recordings were made in urban buildings, primarily in Ulaanbaatar, and the performances thus did not reflect the traditional setting for epic singing.

14. Ene n′ Tuul′ch tovshuurgüi bol, zagasny degeegüi zagaschlakh gesentei adil tul neg n′ nögöögüigeer baikh bolomjgüi yum [literally: "because the epic singer without the *tovshuur* is like a fishing rod without the hook, so you can't have one without the other"].

References

Amgalan, Mishigdorjyn. 2000. *The Cultural Monuments of Western Mongolia.* Ulaanbaatar: Monsudar.

Badraa, Jamtsyn. 2017. *Ardyn urlag sudlal* [Folk art studies]. Ulaanbaatar: Mongolian National University.

Bulag, Uradyn E. 1998. *Nationalism and Hybridity in Mongolia.* Oxford: Clarendon Press.

Chabros, Krystyn. 1992. *Beckoning Fortune: A Study of the Mongol dalalya Ritual.* Asiatische Forschungen 114. Wiesbaden: Otto Harrassowitz.

Chao, Gejin. 2001. "The Oirat Epic Cycle of Jangar." *Oral Tradition* 16(2):402–435.

Chuluunbaatar, Otgonbayar. 2010. "The Cultural and Ethnic Identity of the Oirat Peoples." In *Along the Great Wall: Architecture and Identity in China and Mongolia*, edited by Erich Lehner, Alexandra Harrer, and Hildegard Sint, 165–172. Vienna: IVA-ICRA.

———. 2013. "The Cuur as Endangered Musical Instrument of the Urianxai Ethnic Group in the Mongolian Altai Mountains." In *Studia Instrumentorum Musicae Popularis III* (New Series), edited by Gisa Jähnichen, 97–110. Münster: MV-Wissenschaft Verlag.

———. 2016. "Jangar tuul′d khamaaragdaj bolokh Doldoi zeerd khemeekh bii" [A dance called Doldoi zeerd as a special feature of the Jangar epos]. *Bibliotheca Oiratica* LXIV:152–164. Ulaanbaatar: Tod nomyn gerel töv.

———. 2017. "Musical Instruments as Paraphernalia of the Shamans in Northern Mongolia." In *Studia Instrumentorum Musicae Popularis V* (New Series), edited by Gisa Jähnichen, 1–32. Münster: MV-Wissenschaft Verlag.

———. 2019. "Mongolia, Inner Mongolia, and Mongols." In *The SAGE International Encyclopedia of Music and Culture*, edited by Janet Sturman, 1468–1471. Thousand Oaks, CA: SAGE Publications.

Chuluunbaatar, Otgonbayar, and Wolfgang Hofer. 2006. *Zast Altai*. CD. Audio mastering by Elzbieta Mól, Studio S-3, Radio Kraków, Poland, produced by Otgonbayar Chuluunbaatar.

Dulam, Sendenžavyn, 1987. "Conte, chant et instruments de musique: Quelques légendes d'origine mongoles" [Stories, song and musical instruments: Some origin legends of the Mongols]. *Études Mongoles* 18:33–47.

Enebish, Jambalyn. 2012. *Mongolyn khögjim sudlalyn deej bichig* [Book of Mongolian music research]. Ulaanbaatar: Soyombo Printing.

Fu, Heng. 1782. *Qin ding huang yu Xiyu tu zhi* [(Imperially endorsed) illustrated treatise on the imperial western territories)]. Chap. 40.

Ganbold, Möngönkhüügiin. 2012. *Oirad Mongolchuudyn baigal´ khamgaalakh ulamjlal* [Oirad Mongol's tradition of protecting nature]. *Bibliotheca Oiratica* XXVIII. Ulaanbaatar: Tod nomyn gerel töv.

———. 2014. "The Milk-sprinkling Ceremony." In *Oirat People: Cultural Uniformity and Diversification*, edited by I. Lkhagvasuren, and Yuki Konagaya, 245–257. Senri Ethnological Studies, 86. Osaka: National Museum of Ethnology.

Gongor, D. 2006. "Khovdyn khuraangui tüükh" [Summary of the history of Khovd]. *Bibliotheca Oiratica* IV. Ulaanbaatar: Tod nomyn gerel töv.

Grebennikova, N.S. 2012. "Landscape Codes in the Culture of Gorny Altai." In *Scientific Bulletin of Gorno-Altaisk State University (Collection of Scientific Articles)*, edited by Danielle Forshay, 51–59. Gorno-Altaisk: GASU Press.

Heissig, Walther. 1979. *Die mongolischen Heldenepen—Struktur und Motive* [The Mongolian heroic epics—structure and motifs]. Opladen: Westdeutscher Verlag.

Hudgins, Sharon. 2014. "Tsatsal: The Symbolism and Significance of Mongolian Milk Spoons." In *Food & Material Culture*, edited by Mark McWilliams, 161–174. Totnes: Prospect Books.

Jangar [Epic]. 2000. [Translation from Kalmykian into Mongolian]. P. Khorloo, ed., Ulaanbaatar: Poligraf.

Jukovskaya, N. L. 2011. Nüüdelchin Mongolchuud [Nomadic Mongolians]. Ulaanbaatar: Soyombo Printing.

Katuu, Balchigiin. 2013. *Mongol tuurgatny tuul´chid* [Mongolian Epic Singers]. Ulaanbaatar: Mönkhiin üseg.

Khabunova, E. E., and B. E. Kornusova. 2005. "Folk Epic "Djangar" as a Source for Preservation and Development of Modern Spiritual and Material Culture of the Kalmyks." In *Languages Promotion and Planning in Europe and Russia*, edited by B. Kornusova, N. Bostchaeva, and T. Bogrdanova, 343–356. Elista, Republic of Kalmykia: Russian Federation.

Krueger, John R. 1978–1984. *Materials for an Oirat-Mongolian to English Citation Dictionary, I-III*. Bloomington, IN: Mongolia Society.

Levin, Theodore, and Valentina Süzükei. 2006. *Where Rivers and Mountains Sing: Sound, Music, and Nomadism in Tuva and Beyond*. Bloomington: Indiana University Press.

Namsrai, 2015. *Züüngar khaant ulsyn tüükh* [History of the Zungarian Kingdom]. *Bibliotheca Oiratica* XLIV. Ulaanbaatar: Tod nomyn gerel töv.

Ochir, A. 2006. "Ethnic Groups." In *History and Culture of the Mongols*, 136–151. Ulaan-baatar: International Institute for the Study of Nomadic Civilizations.

Pallas, Peter Simon. 1776. *Samlungen historischer Nachrichten über die Mongolischen Völkerschaften, Erster Theil* [Collections of historical information on the Mongolian peoples, first part]. St. Petersburg: Kayserliche Akademie der Wissenschaften.

Pegg, Carole. 1995. "Ritual, Religion and Magic in West Mongolian (Oirad) Heroic Epic Performance." *British Journal of Ethnomusicology* 4(1):77–99.

———. 2001. *Mongolian Music, Dance, and Oral Narrative: Performing Diverse Identities.* Seattle: University of Washington Press.

Pegg, Carole, and Elizaveta Yamaeva. 2012. "Sensing Place: Performance, Oral Tradition, and Improvisation in the Hidden Temples of Mountain Altai." *Oral Tradition* 27(2):291–318.

Poppe, Nikolaus. 1981. "Die Schwanenjungfrauen in der epischen Dichtung der Mongolen" [The swan virgins in the epic poetry of the Mongols] In *Fragen der mongolischen Heldendichtung*, Teil I, Asiatische Forschungen 72, edited by Walther Heissig, 101–108. Wiesbaden: Otto Harrassowitz.

Post, Jennifer C. 2019. "Songs, Settings, Sociality: Human and Ecological Well-being in Western Mongolia." *Journal of Ethnobiology* 39(3):371–391.

Pürev, Otgony. 1999. *Mongol böögiin shashin* [Mongolian shamanism]. Ulaanbaatar: Admon.

Rintchen, B. 1959. *Les Materiaux pour l'Étude du Chamanisme Mongol, I. Sources Litterai-res* [Materials for the study of Mongolian shamanism, I. Literary sources]. Asiatische Forschungen 3. Wiesbaden: Otto Harrassowitz.

Sampildendev, Kh., G. Gerelmaa, and G. Gansukh, eds. 2004. *Registration of Written Materials Kept by Collection of Mongolian Folklore and Local Dialects*, compiled by A. Alimaa et al. Ulaanbaatar: Institute of Language and Literature, Mongolian Academy of Sciences.

Tsedev, D. 2009. *Khögjmiin urlag sudlal* [Mongolian music research]. Ulaanbaatar: So-goo nuur.

Tsetsentsolmon, Baatarnarany. 2015. "Music in Cultural Construction: Nationalisation, Popularisation and Commercialisation of Mongolian Music." *Inner Asia* 17:118–140.

Tsoloo, J. 1987. *Arvan gurvan khülgiin duun* [The melody of the thirteen horses]. Ulaan-baatar: Ulsyn Khevleliin Gazar.

Tsoloo, J., and A. Mönkhtsetseg. 2008. *Uriankhain öv soyol* [The cultural heritage of the Uriankhai ethnic group]. Ulaanbaatar: Mongol Ulsyn Shinjlekh Ukhaany Akademi, Khelzokhiolyn khüreelen.

Vladimirtsov, Boris Ya. 1923. *Mongolo-Oiratskii geroicheskii epos* [Oirad-Mongolian heroic epic]. Petersburg: Gosudarstvennoye Izdat.

Vladimirtsov, Boris Ya., and John R. Krueger. 1983–1984. "The Oirat-Mongolian Heroic Epic." *Mongolian Studies* 8:5–58.

Zlatkin, I. Ya. 2015. *Züüngaryn khaant ulsyn tüükh* [History of the Zungarian Kingdom]. *Bibliotheca Oiratica* XLV. Ulaanbaatar: Tod nomyn gerel töv.

CHAPTER 7

Social Lives of the *Dombyra* and Its Makers in Western Mongolia

JENNIFER C. POST

During the first decade of the twenty-first century in the small city of Ölgii in western Mongolia, it was not uncommon for me to see a child walking to a school or toward the local theater carrying a long-necked lute without a case. Grasping the thin neck of the Mongolian Kazakh *dombyra* in one hand the child cradled the pear-shaped soundbox with the other, often holding the instrument face forward. I have noted over the years players carry the *dombyra* similarly in a procession at local village celebrations, as it is moved from one ger to another in the countryside, or when it is passed from singer to singer at a social gathering. The *dombyra* is also often displayed face forward on the wall in a living area of a permanent home or in a prominent place in a ger. Held or displayed this way, the Kazakh design applied to the *dombyra's* wooden soundboard is available for all to see. The design not only indicates Kazakh identity, it also often identifies the maker. When local Kazakh artisans began to produce the *dombyra* in the 1990s as participants in a new market economy, a soundboard design many displayed included the Bayan-Ölgii aimag (province) seal or emblem featuring an eagle (*qyran*),[1] the wooden crown (*shangyraq*) of the Kazakh ger, and the seal of Mongolia. Kazakhs are eagle hunters, the crown symbolizes family and home among ger dwellers throughout the region, and the local Kazakh residents are proud citizens of Mongolia. In recent years, instruments display other symbols and patterns tied to Kazakh identity; many makers create variations on historical patterns also found in textile art, and a few designs are more innovative. In my early years in the field watching children walking the streets with their *dombyra*, I worried about the vulnerability of the instrument to wind, rain, and sun, and the damage a drop or knock might bring about. Yet after years of visiting families, especially pastoralists in the countryside, I recognize that as a *dombyra* is passed among singers, moved to a new location, or left within easy reach of a very young child, it is not unusual for the instrument to be irreparably damaged. The active musical life of a Mongolian *dombyra* in a community is often quite short. The makers, then, for many years have focused on providing a constant supply of instruments for children, youth, teachers, families, countryside musicians, as well as tourists. At the end of the second decade of the twenty-first century in Ölgii, when a child transports a *dombyra* to school or the theater, they are more likely to carry the instrument in a case that was made in China or Kazakhstan. This change in behavior seems to mirror the development of *dombyra* making among independent artists since the end of the socialist era who have experienced changes in availability and use of materials, opportunities for innovation in their designs, stability of their products, and their social position as makers of the unique Mongolian Kazakh *dombyra*.

While musical instrument makers typically do not achieve the social recognition that performers receive, musicians are wholly dependent on makers' skills, including their knowledge about materials, construction practices, and sound production. Their efforts to maintain an instrument-making practice engages them socially with their communities and with the materials they use in their production. Instruments and the materials they are made of also have stories to tell (Qureshi 2000). They are products of history and innovation, they too hold information about the land, and their characteristics can help to define a community's identity. Instruments also provide evidence of a region's biological diversity and show the changes in the quality of and access to natural resources (Post 2019).

In settings such as Mongolia, where the primary materials used for musical instruments are natural resources, such as woods or skins, the life of an instrument begins with the growth of plant and animal matter used for its construction, and it continues to grow as makers work with the materials and fashion the instrument (Hallam and Ingold 2014). In many ways an instrument is never completed because once it leaves the hands of a maker it also grows as performers play or it is on display, and its life may even be punctuated by a return to a maker for repair and a new cycle of growth will occur when parts are replaced. Instrument makers, like other artists, engage with what Tim Ingold (2013:6) refers to as "the art of inquiry": how a craftsperson "thinks through making" and engages broadly not only with the materials themselves, but with processes and practices that make up bodies of knowledge about acoustic and artistic practices. Ingold (ibid.:7–8) says, "the art of inquiry moves forward in real time, along with the lives of those who are touched by it, and with the world to which both it and they belong." Similarly, the social lives of instruments and their makers that I experienced in Mongolia helped me grow through "correspondence" with their practice; Ingold describes this as "anthropology *with* art" rather than anthropology *about* or *of* art.

Recent musical instrument research explores how the social lives of musicians, makers, and instruments are entangled with materials. Kevin Dawe (2003:269) posits that instrument makers "inhabit a unique world formed out of the intersection of material, social, and cultural worlds." Eliot Bates (2012:364) suggests addressing the lives of instruments is an important step in understanding "relationships—between humans and objects, between humans and humans, and between objects and other objects."[2] Such frameworks are effective when instruments are not just objects, and makers are not simply "agents setting a variety of social practices in motion." Instead, our knowledge grows when we consider the breadth of possible relationships materials and makers express as they interact in forests and workshops, and the local knowledge instruments hold over time. Materials used for musical instruments, such as those made in western Mongolia, are often entangled with the characteristics of local lands and they hold evidence of the effects of weather events as they grow; yet today many are deeply impacted by climate change.

This chapter explores the social lives of the Mongolian Kazakh *dombyra* and its makers in two western Mongolian aimags, drawing especially from the experiences of four instrument makers who shared stories about entanglements with materials, tools, processes, practices, and change. I interviewed and developed friendships with the artists and members of their families and communities during visits to their homes and home-based workshops between 2005 and 2018. My information on the *dombyra* and makers in different social contexts highlights relationships between maker and materials; the significance of community knowledge; the impact of social, political, and ecological changes on music; and the entanglement of makers, materials, and the instruments they make.[3] The narrative information privileges local knowledge and the Mongolian-specific experiences of these makers, especially what I learned from them over time about the *dombyra* and its social life in their family and community settings. While Kazakh people in Mongolia have lately been linked more directly with Kazakhstan, exploring Mongolian Kazakh music and musical instrument practices demonstrates that theirs' is a unique musical culture linked more directly historically to Xinjiang, China, an ancestral place for many, and more recently to Mongolian lifeways and values.[4]

Kazakhs in Khovd and Bayan-Ölgii

The majority of the Kazakh citizens of Mongolia live in the western aimags of Khovd and Bayan-Ölgii.[5] Most Mongolian Kazakhs carry family histories of arrival from western China in the nineteenth and early twentieth centuries and often reference western China as an ancestral place in stories and songs (Finke 1999; Soni 2003; Post 2014). Today they consider Mongolia their homeland (*tughan zher*). Herders who move seasonally in support of their livestock, and city-dwellers in the provincial centers in Khovd and Ölgii (each with populations of about 30,000), as well as Kazakh residents who have moved to the capital city of Ulaanbaatar or its suburbs, continue to maintain cultural practices that reinforce their Kazakh identities.

Economic structures that developed in newly democratic and market-based Mongolia have impacted lifeways and cultural production as well. As Russians and Russian Kazakh elites brought new cultural expectations into the region during their Soviet era, they introduced musical ideas, contributing to an already unique cultural landscape. In the following decades, after the end of Soviet control, there was a swirl of movement of Mongolian Kazakhs migrating to Kazakhstan at the invitation of the government interested in the practices they maintained while Central Asia was experiencing russification and cultural loss. Their movement continued in the late 1990s and into the twenty-first century as many returned to their Mongolian homeland (Diener 2009; Barcus and Werner 2010; Finke 2013; Post 2014). Kazakhstani music scholars in this period began to visit Mongolia seeking information from Mongolian Kazakhs on what the residents of Kazakhstan believed to be their own history. A goal appears to be to construct a shared history of the peoples who have lived in two very different countries. In this period as well, the changing economy for Mongolian Kazakhs provided support for greater access to technologies, from solar panels and satellite dishes to cars and trucks, an impetus for even greater geographic and musical mobility. Increasing opportunities to travel to the capital city of Ulaanbaatar, as well as China, Kazakhstan, Turkey, and other locations have had a huge impact on Mongolian Kazakh musical culture, including their *dombyra*.

The Mongolian Kazakh *Dombyra* and Its Makers

The two-string, long-necked fretted lute *dombyra* is an iconic instrument of the Kazakh people. The instrument plays multiple roles in Mongolian Kazakh social life and in the lives of Kazakhs in Kazakhstan and other locations where they reside. In Mongolia, the *dombyra* accompanies songs of *aqyns* (poet-singers) and punctuates the social commentary of dueling *aitys* (improvisational sung poetry) singers. It is also played to accompany songs offered at a rural or urban *toi* (celebration), such as a wedding (*üilenu toi*) where it becomes a tool to ritually remove the bride's veil to reveal the bride's face (*betashar*) in the rural *ger* or more recently in local community halls. The *dombyra* is used to play *küi*, a solo narrative instrumental form; it is a principal instrument in the folkloric orchestra at the local theater in Ölgii city (established in 1959) and has also become an important ensemble instrument in local pop bands (Yagi 2019).[6] While some musicians and instruments in western Mongolia may be identified with a musical elite, the *dombyra* in Bayan-Ölgii and Khovd today is widely shared regardless of social class or community standing.

While Mongolian Kazakh social history has produced *dombyra* with unique characteristics, the instruments did not develop in isolation from Kazakhstan or Xinjiang, China. In Kazakhstan, wide variations in shapes and styles developed for the *dombyra* over time.[7] Scholars representing that country separate the *dombyra* in Kazakhstan into two primary geographically based structural styles: instruments from the western region that have a pear-shaped soundbox and a long thin neck, and the *dombyra* of eastern and southern regions with a spade-shaped (or sometimes triangular) soundbox and a shorter and wider neck (Kendirbaeva 1994; Kunanbaeva 2002).[8] Since many families now in Mongolia traveled several centuries ago from the region that is now eastern Kazakhstan to Chinese lands and then into western Mongolia, both spade- and triangular-shaped instruments were prevalent in Xinjiang and Mongolia in the nineteenth and early mid-twentieth centuries.

Oral evidence in Mongolia indicates that early makers were local residents, building techniques were learned in families, and production was focused in neighborhoods and relied on locally accessible materials. These circumstances offered opportunities for variations in style and quality. During the Soviet-influenced socialist period, "culture-building processes" impacted musical repertoires, styles, and instruments throughout Central Asia and Mongolia (Marsh 2009; Levin 2018). In this period, the western Kazakhstani pear-shaped *dombyra* with a long neck became a standard in the local theater, and it was adopted more widely then for *dombyra* making. Makers from the Soviet's Kazakh Republic, or trained by Kazakhs from the Republic in Mongolian workshops, provided a standardized, "improved" instrument for the Mongolian Kazakhs (Yagi 2018). These instruments also made their way from Ölgii to the countryside. Today Mongolian Kazakh makers build the *dombyra* according to standard dimensions and maintain a unified form based on the standardized *dombyra* of the twentieth century. While standardized in form and measurement, Mongolian Kazakhs express their unique identities as they make the instruments. Memories of older *dombyra* that local musicians and makers once made in different styles, predating the most aggressive improvement efforts, appear to be fading. Such instruments are preserved in museums but are seldom found in homes.[9]

In the post-socialist era, some *dombyra* makers in Mongolia who had been making instruments as artisans for the collectives in the socialist period continued their instrument making independently. At the same time, other woodworkers began to experiment with *dombyra* making as well, and together they began to provide these Mongolian-made instruments for local use.[10] The goal for many makers is economic; making a functional musical instrument for everyday use (for learning, taking part in social events, and gifting), and their standards provide a customer base for them. The makers establish home-based workshops; the spaces are typically carved out of a portion of a home; sometimes the space is as small as a closet. A few have developed separate workshops next to their homes. Their instrument making takes place in both a designated workshop space and in shared family spaces where family members may contribute to the process and a variety of visitors also come and go.

Contemporary Mongolian *dombyra* makers abide by standards for shape and size established in the twentieth century during the socialist period. They typically note the measurements as follows: the neck (*moiyn*) should be 48cm, the soundbox (*shanaq*) no larger than 40x23cm, and the headstock (*alaqan*) 10cm. In earlier times the soundbox was carved from a single piece of wood, but today it is made with ribs (typically seven) glued together to form a rounded back. The soundboard (*qaqlaq*) is made using three to five pieces of well-planed wood glued together.[11] The frets (*perneler;* singular: *perne*) (up to twenty-one) made of nylon are tied on the thin neck. The strings (*shekter*) are also made of nylon, typically fishing line from China, Russia, or Kazakhstan have replaced the locally made gut strings largely abandoned a generation ago. The woods used for all parts of the Mongolian *dombyra* are typically purchased at the local market. Siberian pine (*qaraghai*) and Siberian fir (*samyrsyn*), the most commonly used woods, are cut from the northern forests in north central Mongolia along the Russian border and brought to the Ölgii market by truck. Other local woods used include larch (*balqaraghai*), poplar (*terek*), and Siberian spruce (*shyrsha*).[12] A few makers seek other woods such as reclaimed wood from old furniture and buildings, old abandoned logs in a nearby forest, or wood from Xinjiang.[13]

When I traveled to western Mongolia in 2005 to learn about the *dombyra*, its construction, and musical repertoires, I established relationships with many makers that I have maintained over the years. The stories of four—Sultanbai, Daniyal, Säken, and Medixat—illustrate the breadth of knowledge and experience both maker and instrument convey in their social lives.[14] The instruments and the processes makers used for building tell tales of relationships with mentors and materials, and their stories are tied to rural and urban lifeways, resource access, historical events, and ecological and sociopolitical changes. I met with Sultanbai in Khovd sum and Daniyal in Ölgii city only in 2005, and I have followed the careers of Säken and Medixat (along with other makers) for over fifteen years.[15] Discussions with these artists not only provide evidence of the *dombyra*'s contributions to social lives and music over time in western Mongolia, but they demonstrate the entanglements of maker, materials, and a changing ecological, social, and cultural environment.

Sultanbai

In May 2005 at the home of a local family in Khovd *sum* in Khovd aimag, a small group of local residents shared information with me about the *dombyra* and its makers.[16] They began by telling me that no one in the village was making *dombyra* anymore. Leading the discussion, a local cultural official and *dombyra* player spoke nostalgically about the instrument and its different styles in twentieth-century Mongolia. Taking my notebook (see figure 7.1), he first sketched a *dombyra* with a spade-shaped soundbox, noting it had a flat back and seventeen to nineteen frets, and then he drew a *dombyra* with a pear-shaped soundbox that he said had up to twenty-one frets.[17] The latter is the style associated with the pear-shaped *dombyra* with ribs that became the standard instrument for Mongolian Kazakhs in the late twentieth century. Below these he sketched a second type of spade-shaped *dombyra* with fewer frets (up to nine) that he said was typically built at home and never manufactured for sale. Next to it he drew a *dombyra* with a triangular shaped soundbox and shorter neck also with up to nine frets, and next to that a similar short-necked instrument with a round soundbox. These instruments represent the range of *dombyra* models once common in Mongolia which still live in the memories of older residents. In Ölgii city it is possible to see examples of some of these instruments at the local museum.

Even though access to the *dombyra* in Khovd sum was limited, the residents I spoke with indicated their ongoing interest in the instrument and its music. At the local school, the music teacher reported that there were not enough instruments for the number of students interested in learning to play. They had just a handful of *dombyra,* which they repaired with tape when soundbox seams split. When no longer repairable, the teacher traveled to Ölgii city, the aimag center in nearby Bayan-Ölgii aimag, to purchase another for the school at the local market. The departure of local residents for Kazakhstan during the previous decade, including valued makers, and the deteriorating quality and availability of woods made it difficult for the community to maintain local support for the instrument's production.

Exploring the subject of *dombyra* makers and the status of woods and other materials with the residents, I learned from the teacher that instruments available in the community were generally in disrepair. He showed me one *dombyra* with a pear-shaped soundbox made by Bayan Murat, a former resident who moved to Kazakhstan in 1990, returned to Khovd a few years later, but then went back to Kazakhstan. He distinguished his *dombyra* with his own Kazakh design on the soundboard. Some local residents characterized his *dombyra* acoustically, referencing the sound as "thick" and "not very pleasing." They did not attribute this to Bayan Murat's skill but to his limited access to quality woods; he had access to only lumber grade wood for his instruments, they said, such as larch.

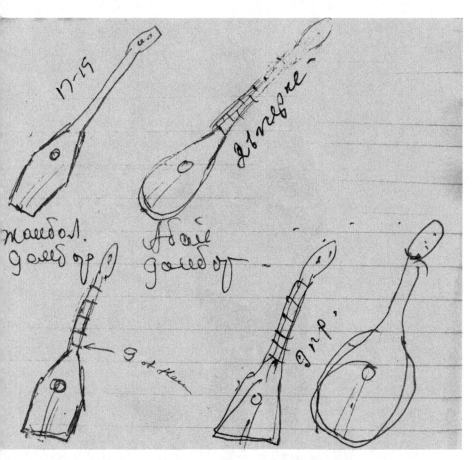

FIGURE 7.1. Drawing by a local cultural official in Khovd sum representing different Mongolian Kazakh dombyra styles, Khovd aimag, 2005. Photo by J. C. Post.

Community members also mentioned the *dombyra* maker Sultanbai, who still lived in Khovd sum but was no longer making instruments.[18] When I met with Sultanbai, a man in his mid-late fifties, he seemed surprised by my interest in his *dombyra*. He said he began making *dombyra* in 1988 when his son showed an interest in playing. After making one instrument, he began to make others for the neighborhood children, altogether completing about ten. Sultanbai called his instruments "not very professional" and referred to himself as an amateur, although other local community members sitting around the room during our discussion all said the *dombyra* he made sounded very good to them. While he no longer had any of his instruments, a community member retrieved one from a nearby home. No longer in playing condition, it was without strings or tuning pegs and had a damaged soundboard. Representing the homemade

FIGURE 7.2. Sultanbai with a *dombyra* he made in the early 1990s, Khovd sum, Khovd aimag, 2005. Photo by J. C. Post.

spade-shaped style, it was boxy with a flat back, and with evidence of nine-ten frets (see Figure 7.2). Sultanbai said he made his *dombyra* using Siberian pine, although sometimes he used Siberian larch for the back. He used fishing line for the strings.

Sultanbai also used the soundboard to display painted images of locally valued resources. The instrument shared with me exhibited an argali (wild mountain sheep) standing on top of a snow-capped mountain, the sun rising behind it. He said local Kazakhs associate the argali with Khovd sum, thus the instrument identifies and embraces the specific Kazakh region in the aimag. Sultanbai, and others in the room, said they are proud to protect this animal that is considered "the rarest and most beautiful, with its long curling horns." Inscriptions to individuals written on the soundboard are common on locally made *dombyra,* and Sultanbai's inscription uses Arabic script (predating Soviet influenced Cyrillic script for Kazakhs).

As I listened to the discussions about the *dombyra* in Khovd sum, viewed Sultanbai's older *dombyra,* and learned from local residents about their knowledge of its history, I saw more clearly how the social life of instruments in the community—and thus music itself—were entangled with the complex Kazakh sociopolitical history in Mongolia and of relationships of Mongolian Kazakhs with Kazakhstan. Identities were expressed in instrument styles and the ornaments, thus images and icons connected them not only to Kazakh identities, but to place as well, even specifying the importance of local ecologies. They were impacted also by the quality of materials available and the influence of the Russian—then Russian-influenced Kazakhstani—theater traditions. The style of *dombyra* that Sultanbai made, represented now by an unplayable instrument, has been all but erased from local use in western Mongolia, although these styles still remain in the memories of makers, musicians, and listeners.

Daniyal

In Bayan-Ölgii, Daniyal's relationships to instruments and materials, production and preservation, and making and growing took place during a long lifetime. His contributions to Mongolian *dombyra* history includes knowledge he brought from Xinjiang, his ability to adjust to new forms and formats for making, and his interest in creating new styles. Entangled with both past and current practices throughout his life, his instruments embody local musical history.

I was introduced to 88-year-old Daniyal in Ölgii city.[19] At first I saw him as a dedicated artist who—despite his age—spent time in his workshop every day making *dombyra* and Kazakh crafts. He told me during our first meeting, though, that he once worked in China as a spy and was trained in medicine, and I learned later that he was also a highly respected poet in Mongolia. The eldest in a family of twelve brothers and sisters, Daniyal was born in 1918 in Altay Prefecture in today's Xinjiang Uyghur Autonomous Region in China. He was engaged in Islamic religious studies with his father between ages five and thirteen and came to Mongolia in 1934 when he was sixteen. He studied medicine in Ulaanbaatar and was a doctor in the military, serving in Japan during the 1930s and 1940s. Daniyal said he learned *dombyra* making from his uncle Kusain on his grandfather's side, when he was fourteen, while still in China.

In our conversations, Daniyal shared his knowledge about the different *dombyra* styles, the woods he used, and techniques for building he had experienced during his lifetime. Since he began making *dombyra* in 1932, so he had engaged with its materials, styles, and sounds, as well as the innovative opportunities the instrument offered him, for over seventy years. His social relationships with instruments and materials, along with the communities he was sharing them with, appeared to be important to him throughout his life.

The instrument Daniyal first learned to make was a *dombyra* with a triangular soundbox, a short neck, and seven frets; he referred to it as the instrument he learned to make from his uncle Kusain and called it a "Kusain *dombyra*." The locally highly respected *dombyra* player Seit Zhumazhan who was a member of the Ölgii theater for forty-three years, also referred to the Kusain *dombyra* in a 2005 interview. He said this type, made by his friend's father who was a *dombyra* maker, was his first *dombyra*. Seit described it as "a simple instrument with a triangular shaped resonator—a style made for friends." (Interview, Ölgii city, June 3, 2005). Describing the materials and construction process, Daniyal said the wood he used for this type of *dombyra* was "not special" and each instrument was assembled quickly using nails. He noted that generally they were not well made and the sound was "not very good." Daniyal linked the triangular shaped *dombyra* to his early life in Xinjiang, but he did not reference any connection to historical instruments of central and eastern Kazakhstan with short necks and—sometimes—triangular soundboxes.

In Mongolia, Daniyal was part of a cooperative for building the standardized *dombyra* that was being promoted during socialist time. He said he was the lead instrument maker and taught many makers in the aimag to make *dombyra*, including several artists I also came to know over the years. This includes Tompei, who was still working in Ölgii in 2018, and Esentai, who made instruments in Sagsai sum until his retirement around 2013.

I was not surprised to see a *dombyra* hanging on the wall in Daniyal's living room. Made with a pear-shaped soundbox carved from a single piece of wood, the soundboard was also one piece, and in addition to a central sound hole it had six symmetrically arranged small holes. The instrument was adorned with colorful flowers and designs painted on both the soundboard and soundbox. The frets and strings were made with a thicker nylon than many *dombyra* I had seen being sold at the local Bayan-Ölgii market in the early 2000s. Daniyal said that he made the instrument in 1988 using Siberian fir and that his son had painted the designs. While we were talking, a neighbor arrived with another *dombyra* that Daniyal had made: it was spade-shaped with a flat back similar in design to those illustrated by the cultural official in Khovd sum but was more stylized than the one made by Sultanbai.

In our discussion, Daniyal stressed the importance of specific local materials, especially woods such as Siberian fir, poplar, and Siberian pine. He spoke about materials and structural styles to produce an ideal *dombyra* sound that he tried to maintain, although over time it became increasingly difficult. For example, he said the soundbox for the *dombyra* is best when made from a single piece of wood (rather than built using ribs), and the soundboard is most resonant when it is constructed from a single piece of wood as well. Yet to make a soundbox with one piece, the wood must be soft enough to carve, so Daniyal prefers Siberian fir, which is "light and strong." He said that while he once used poplar, he didn't have access to this wood because of environmental protection policies. Daniyal said it is also difficult to find pieces of wood that are big enough to carve the large *dombyra* soundboxes. While he has carved an entire *dombyra* (back, neck, headstock) using one piece of wood, he feels it is impractical. From the same piece of wood used for one *dombyra* he can make two if he makes it with separate pieces for the soundbox and neck. Daniyal said it usually takes about three days to finish a *dombyra*. He carves the wood for the soundbox, then dries it near the stove in the winter and outside in the shade during the summer. Working primarily alone, he said he sometimes worked with his son; he taught him not only to make the *dombyra* but also saddles, knives, and other metalwork.[20] As we talked in his small workshop, Daniyal sat on the dirt floor on his knees to work. He kept his hand tools for cutting and carving on the ground nearby within easy reach (see figure 7.3). Carving out a block of wood to make the pear-shaped soundbox using a hook knife was a slow and methodical process.

As we talked, I realized that Daniyal had contributed a diverse selection of instruments to the Bayan-Ölgii community. They ranged from simply built instruments in styles established in the region before the mid-twentieth century, including a *dombyra* with a triangular soundbox that he said he made in 1950 for the local museum and spade-shaped and pear-shaped *dombyras* using carved soundboxes (versus the more common instruments made with ribs) that he made for the Ölgii community. Each was embellished with a decorative pattern on the face to mark it as a *dombyra* made by Daniyal. He also designed a *dombyra* that became known in Bayan-Ölgii as the "Daniyal *dombyra*" that is exhibited at the Ölgii Museum. He admitted, though, that the style did not "catch on." He believes that it is because it was too much like the Kyrgyz *komuz*, a three-stringed long-necked lute with a pear-shaped body played in nearby Kyrgyzstan.

Daniyal, who moved to Kazakhstan soon after my visit and passed away there in 2007, contributed socially to the local musical community as a builder and teacher. He maintained concern for quality in his instruments and continued to grow through engagement with current trends. He exhibited innovation as a

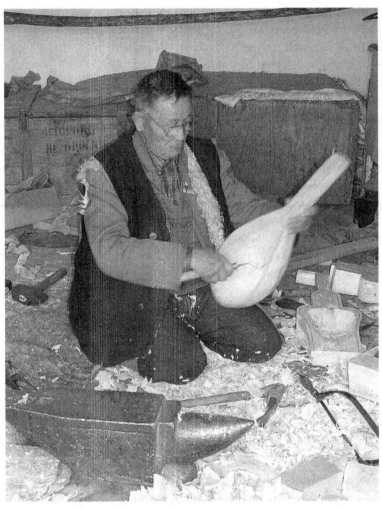

FIGURE 7.3. Daniyal carving a *dombyra* soundbox in his workshop in Ölgii city, 2005. Photo by J. C. Post.

maker and was concerned about conservation of cultural practices as he maintained an ongoing relationship with the local museum, which in turn supported Daniyal's musical, aesthetic, and innovative interests. The Ölgii museum gave him opportunities to share musical history through the *dombyra*, corresponding not only with the local community, but in stories his instruments shared with visitors as well—from the triangular-shaped *dombyra* and Daniyal's own creation, the "Daniyal *dombyra*," to instrument styles established in the socialist period. As a teacher, Daniyal passed his values on to students such as Tompei, and one of Tompei's students is Säken, a maker in Dayan who ultimately forged his own pathway in *dombyra* making.

Säken

Considering engagement with resources as sources for musical sound, Säken, settled in a lake region near the Chinese border called Dayan, offered information on how he has used what he perceived as traditional practice as a foundation for his work in post-socialist Mongolia. His interest in resources for their resonance and reliability gave him strength to continue to pursue his work despite considerable personal challenges. He exhibits knowledge he has gained from materials in his instruments and shared the significance of social connections with wood and the nearby forests that provide the resources he values.

Säken was asleep in a late morning in June 2005 when I arrived at his winter place, a wooden building tucked amid low hills near Dayan Lake, sited and structured to protect occupants from winter and early spring winds and cold temperatures.[21] The low ceiling in the one-room building made it cold and dark, but his relatives made us tea and we waited while 44-year-old Säken got up slowly—leaving briefly to wash—and then returned to sit on the side of his bed, ready to talk about the *dombyra*. Like Sultanbai, Säken appeared to be surprised by my interest in the instrument, yet he gladly showed me a completed *dombyra* made of Siberian spruce that he had made for a resident in the local Dayan community. He then pulled another uncompleted instrument out from under his bed and said he was making this fine *dombyra* for himself. The neck and soundbox were reinforced with hardwood strips, a practice that seemed unusual in the *dombyra* made in Bayan-Ölgii or Khovd because it requires wood that is rare in the aimag and it takes extra time. Säken said that some of his skills came from his experiences working with Tompei; he described the designs he learned from him, but his Dayan instruments were influenced by another source as well. He said his designs, measurements, and tools came from information in a magazine article with instructions for making a *dombyra* published in 1982 in Kazakhstan. The article provided all the information on construction that Säken felt he needed to successfully make instruments on his own. When I asked whether the style of his instruments ever varied from the *dombyra* directions in the Kazakhstani publication, he shook his head.

Säken works alone and sources his wood locally in the Dayan forests, land once managed by the state during socialist times. Some of the older residents who became full-time herders in the 1990s worked in the forest or in the lumber processing "factory," as they called it, including Säken's father who worked for the state from 1968–1988. During that period, Säken said the socialist project was responsible for the "destruction" of nature and his local community that housed, protected, and used the forests never benefited. Wood taken from the forests was distributed to other regions in Mongolia, and some lumber was taken to Russia. The large old growth trees (essential for making quality musical instruments), and a source for added protection for livestock and wildlife, are now gone.[22] The young pine and fir forests now circle the region, but deep in the woods, up close to the Chinese border, old stands of endemic Siberian spruce remain. Säken travels up there on horseback to find fallen trees that he drags back to his home. He looks for logs that have not been invaded by insects as the holes spoil the wood's sound. The logs and tree stumps he collects sit outside—sometimes for several years—until he is ready to use them. Even before he cuts the logs, Säken said he listens to the sound of the wood and then listens carefully also as he makes each *dombyra* part. The spruce he uses "makes a good sound" when he taps it. He described what he identifies as three layers in a log: the most valuable part of the tree is the "third layer" (its core) that is dense and has a good sound, the second layer is usable but not very good, and the outer layer cannot be used to make an instrument: "It has no sound," Säken said.

I returned to Dayan to see Säken the next year, in 2006, when he was in his summer settlement. *Dombyra* parts were piled up in a corner of the ger—Säken said he prepared them during the winter and planned to work on completing the instruments during the summer and autumn. Looking both satisfied and proud, he showed me the completed *dombyra* he made for himself using *shyrshya* (spruce) and *qadaghai* (pine). The fret board was made from the wood from an old Russian chair, and he glued and then lacquered paper-cut designs on the neck and soundboard, including an eagle with wings around the central soundhole. He also added f-holes, he said, "because many fine instruments have them."[23]

Traveling throughout the region and returning each year to see Säken, I learned that Dayan residents rely on his *dombyra*. Some pay for them in Mongolian tögrög, others offer a sheep or arrange for a barter. Many members of the Dayan community are eager to acquire one of his instruments; they value its sound as they play *küi* and accompany their songs. The instrument also commonly hangs on the wall of a winter home or spring-summer yurt in order to display Kazakh heritage. In fact, many people I have met with tied to the Dayan community who want a "Säken *dombyra*" have a hard time acquiring one. While most other small communities outside of Ölgii city lost their *dombyra* makers in the late twentieth century, as makers aged and younger people were less interested in learning a practice with limited economic benefit, Säken has helped to maintain a valued tradition for this community. Once an individual or family receives a *dombyra* from Säken the instrument becomes a status symbol, displaying the owner's relationship to this locally respected maker. Stepping into a yurt or wooden winter home with my Kazakh traveling companions, or sitting for tea when visitors arrive, I can see that the distinctive decorative style that Säken has maintained over the years catches their eyes quickly (see figure 7.4).

FIGURE 7.4. Säken with a newly made *dombyra*, Dayan köl, Bayan Ölgii, 2014. Photo by J. C. Post.

I seemed to arrive each year to visit Säken at a critical time in his life. One year he was in a yurt celebrating his wedding; the next year I arrived just days after the birth of his first child. I found him another year in a newly built wooden three-room home in the Dayan community, having abandoned altogether a mobile way of life as a herder. He showed me half-finished instruments he was storing in the corner of a room in his new home, but he didn't offer information on when he expected to complete them. In fact, Säken said he was too tired to work and talked about giving up making instruments altogether. When I returned in 2011 after an absence of several years, Säken told me he had been in Ulaanbaatar for heart surgery and was still recovering. He seemed in better spirits and was making *dombyra* again, but then in 2013 there was an outbreak of foot-and-mouth disease and Säken's family lost all their livestock. Sometime in the midst of all these events, Säken also sold the fine *dombyra* he had made for himself to visitors from an organization in Kazakhstan who came to the region seeking "cultural products." He said they paid good money for it. With new energy and improved health, Säken seemed to manage his personal struggles by focusing on his instrument making and becoming involved in fine carpentry work as well.

I often thought about that fine *dombyra* Säken began to make before 2005 and finished in 2006—that he had let go to Kazakhstan. I wondered whether he would ever make another such instrument again. The *dombyra* style he produced for his community from the aged spruce he gathered in the forest was a good instrument with fine sound, but it showed little variation and innovation. Säken's life events seemed to make it difficult for him to focus creatively, or to invest in the time needed to produce a unique instrument. The opportunity came when his young daughter showed interest in playing *dombyra*. In 2015, Säken used strips of oak (*emen*) that he said he purchased in Xinjiang to make an instrument that was both visually appealing and structurally stronger than the instruments he had been making. He did this, as he had done previously, using techniques that fine luthiers use to stabilize necks and make soundboxes stronger and aesthetically appealing with hardwood strips rather than making the neck using a single pliable piece of wood. After that, Säken began to experiment with a few new techniques to enhance his *dombyra* both structurally and visually. In 2018 he was still relying on being able to gather spruce in the nearby forests, but his greater mobility also has provided opportunities for him to travel to seek other wood sources as well.

Säken's growth as a maker occurred in the midst of life events that he sometimes struggled to manage. His isolation in a rural lake region populated with village residents and spring, summer, and autumn pastoralists, largely from Ulaankhus and Sagsai sums, means that his instruments remain locally shared. His choices of woods and other materials, the designs he adheres to, the ornamentation of the soundboard that marks his identity as a maker, models the significant role a *dombyra* maker plays in the musical life of a Mongolian Kazakh community.

Medixat

While Daniyal and Säken had direct and indirect relationships to local workshops established during socialism, Medixat developed his skills in a different way. From the beginning he created instruments with an eye for style and an ear for sound and structure. His social experience with the instruments themselves helped him explore possibilities for structural changes, not only to improve their strength and sound, but to improve their cultural value in his community.

I first saw Medixat in 2005 near the entrance to the local Ölgii city market.[24] He was sitting on an old tire holding three *dombyra* he was trying to sell (see figure 7.5). They had pear-shaped soundboxes and soundboards that displayed the Bayan-Ölgii seal. Visiting him at his home later that week, Medixat, age 44 at the time, told me he had been making instruments for about six years. One of twelve children in a herding family from the village of Sogog, north of Ölgii, previously he worked as a carpenter for the government. He learned to make *dombyra* by disassembling instruments that had "good sound" and studying their

FIGURE 7.5. Medixat at the Ölgii city market, 2005. Photo by J. C. Post.

structure. He considered ways he might improve their strength and sound and tested his changes at the market as he developed his skill as a maker. In general, he said, he has streamlined his processes over the years. While Medixat said in 2005 he worked alone, I could see that his production actually involved several members of his family. One of his sons was always on hand to help, especially as he finished each *dombyra*. His young son Haynazar applied the cut paper designs that he lacquered onto the soundboard. Medixat's wife helped to string the instruments once they were dry. Medixat said he used Siberian pine when he was able to get it. In fact, he had two large logs, each fifteen inches in diameter, that he had acquired. He preferred to build instruments beginning with a log (rather than lumber from the market), although most of the time he had to rely on market wood. I could see that Medixat's interest in wood extended also to its physical characteristics; he looked carefully at wood as he cut it, and again as he constructed the ribs for the soundbox, in order to create a visually pleasing instrument. Yet when I asked in 2005 whether he put extra effort into making high-quality *dombyra* (*sapaly dombyra*), he said that he didn't have time—he had two children at university and his primary goal was to earn what he could by making instruments quickly. Medixat's workshop was in a small building next to the family living quarters. He used this for wood processing, but his work expanded into outdoor spaces as well as the family kitchen for some tasks. Selling instruments at the market meant he had to work on instruments at night so he could go to the market during the day to sell them.

As we continued to talk about materials and processes for his instruments in the following years, Medixat admitted that he sometimes looked around his home at his beams and furniture considering the dry wood that he could use for *dombyra* parts. He also expressed frustration about the way he has been forced to acquire wood: standing outside the fenced lumber market to wait for the proprietor to slide boards over the fence; thus he had no opportunity to select his own wood. Yet to offer strong and stable necks that will not warp, as many Ölgii *dombyra* necks that are typically made with soft lumber do, and to make ribs for the soundbox that provide volume and a clear sound, Medixat needed access to dry and resonant wood. Most Ölgii makers build instruments as a form of subsistence living and Medixat has navigated this difficult terrain over time with an interest in making a living, but also in providing both high quality and innovative instruments.

Each year when I visited Medixat I was introduced to changes in his workshop space, instrument designs, and even woods. He continued to expand his workshop, creating a larger, more fully designated space for instrument making. Stepping into his expanded workshop in 2011, Medixat was working with his son Haynazar on completing a *dombyra*. There was the sweet smell of wood in his new mud-clay two-room building. Medixat and Haynazar were focused on wood at every stage of *dombyra* making. As they cut, carved, planed, sanded, and pieced an instrument together, they used hand tools, from a knife to handsaws, a few electric tools, including a bandsaw and an old electric disc sander, and homemade tools, such as wooden clamps. The workshop was quiet, punctuated by brief casual conversations or the sound of a bandsaw when one of them needed to cut one or two pieces of wood.

Medixat's attention throughout the building process remained on quality control. He carefully prepared wood for the soundbox's seven ribs and five pieces for the soundboard, and he also showed particular attention to the wood for the neck. These three elements determine the finished instrument's acoustic and structural quality and stability, as well as its appearance. He knows wood needs to be dry, but with limited time to accomplish this ideal, Medixat uses his woodstove and the sun, when available, to dry parts of the instrument during building.

Medixat and his son prepared the ribs for the *dombyra* as a team; he used a homemade metal form to mark each piece of planed wood for cutting. The wood appeared to be burned on one side from the wood stove. As he marked each piece, he dropped it on the floor and his son, who was sitting nearby, reached down and picked it up. He used a knife to cut the stylized shape along the lines his father drew. Haynazar's movements were accurate and quick, and once he was done his father planed the edges, checking each carefully on a flat surface. His son then took each rib and moved it across a large flat sanding board using broad strokes. This kind of partnership, built over time, engaged the makers with gestures linked also to expectations of the wood and ultimately of the finished instrument.

Medixat's innovations carried him well into the second decade of the twenty-first century. I arrived once to find he had made a double-neck *dombyra* after seeing one on a television program transmitted from Kazakhstan. During that period Medixat began to travel regularly to Kazakhstan to sell instruments, and later he and his sons sold instruments at the markets in Xinjiang. In 2015, Medixat greeted me with a mischievous smile; he wanted to tell me about his latest innovation. Still struggling to find quality wood, he was wandering through the local market and saw tools, such as large axes from China and Russia, with walnut (*zhangghaq*) and oak (*emen*) handles. At the same time, Medixat was receiving more attention for the quality of his instruments and orders were beginning to come in, meaning he did not have to go to the market to sell his instruments as often. He received one order to complete a set of six *dombyras* to give as gifts during an event in Khovd aimag. He and his sons worked as a team to make fourteen ribs for each back using different hard- and softwoods. Each neck was reinforced with strips of oak to strengthen them and he used a strip of walnut for each fretboard. The design on the soundboard featured an eagle's head and wing feathers around the edge; the central sound hole was the bird's eye (see figure 7.6). While the sound of each instrument was not the same as those he made with Mongolian softwood, it was a clear, resonant sound that he had been searching for.

When I first met Medixat in 2005 he was but one of a growing group of men with carpentry skills who were attempting to learn to make *dombyras* as a means to an income during difficult economic times in the aimag. Only a few older makers that were part of the collective system were still working in the early 2000s. The standardized instrument established during the socialist era both helped and challenged makers. The dimensions and other characteristics (such as wood thickness for the soundboard) provided a well-tested format for instruments. Local makers were all challenged, though, by the struggle to obtain wood that sings. I have witnessed many provincial residents as they arrived at the local market from the countryside or city to buy a *dombyra* for a child, a family member, or for a gift. They try them out, listening carefully to each before making a purchase. The increasing mobility between Bayan-Ölgii and China to buy and sell goods, and between Bayan-Ölgii and Kazakhstan for resettlement or to visit relatives, offered new pathways for some makers, such as Medixat,

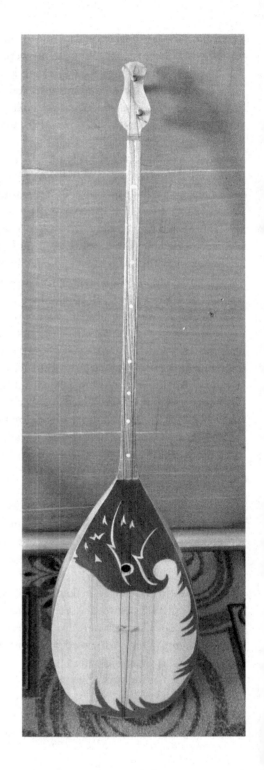

FIGURE 7.6. New style Medixat
dombyra, Ölgii city, 2017. Photo by
J. C. Post.

with interest in growth of their business and access to materials and ideas. Access to new knowledge occurs through technology (such as television) as well, and musicians and instrument makers have been impacted by the changing instruments and sounds displayed in both Chinese and Kazakhstan media.

Conclusion

The social lives of Mongolian Kazakh *dombyra* makers engage them with family members, neighbors, and musicians, and with the materials they use as they plan and construct an instrument. As makers continue an artistic practice learned in their youth, or develop new skills during a career change, *dombyra* makers experience growth that occurs before, during, and after each instrument is made. The instrument also grows and changes in the hands of a musician, when carried in a procession, or displayed on a wall, and the materials change their character as they are used during construction and then age during their lives as a musical instrument. The making and growing process for *dombyra* makers in western Mongolia also entangles them with local issues related to resource availability, sociopolitical changes that affect economic and social health and well-being, as well as personal challenges. The process of learning about the *dombyra* and its local history from Bayan-Ölgii makers also enabled my own growth through correspondence with them and their practices (Ingold 2013).

The entanglement of materials, makers' histories, and local lifeways in western Mongolia has contributed to the development of specific characteristics found in each Mongolian Kazakh *dombyra* made since the early twentieth century. The Mongolian processes and practices contrast with those in Kazakhstan where makers can more readily access hardwood, such as maple or even imported African woods for the soundbox and spruce for the soundboard. Many makers there are trained in workshops and compete for status in yearly contests, promoting quality instruments and particular building styles. The Kazakhstani *dombyra* in Bayan-Ölgii is inaccessible to all but the economically and musically privileged residents. In Mongolia, makers' patterns and practices were built over time in relationship with life experiences in Xinjiang, Mongolia, and Kazakhstan. Locally, the instrument and maker grew in the mountains and steppes of western Mongolia as the Kazakh residents moved seasonally with their livestock in rural lands, settled in small sums in both Khovd and Bayan-Ölgii aimags, and contributed to the cultural life of the small city of Ölgii. While there have been influences from Kazakhstan, makers in Mongolia seldom have access to formal training. For most, the only wood they can use is softwood lumber trucked in from another region in Mongolia. They are also not part of an economic system that allows them time to age wood before beginning the process of building each *dombyra*, making the instruments more vulnerable to environmental changes as well. The Kazakhs in Mongolia live in a country where the Mongol *morin khuur* is a national icon, and there is no national or regional system for promoting the Mongolian *dombyra*. Yet the makers and materials used for the *dombyra* are part of an active system to provide an iconic instrument for a community of Kazakhs eager to continue their local musical practices in western Mongolia.

Notes

1. Unless otherwise noted, all language references in this chapter are Kazakh.

2. See also Roda (2014) for additional information on the social relations of instruments and their materials.

3. See our companion website, www.mongoliansoundworlds.org, for additional information on the musical traditions included in this volume.

4. Most Kazakhs in Mongolia arrived from China in the nineteenth or early twentieth century. A small number of Kazakhs also reached Mongolia by way of the Altai region in Russia. (Soni 2003).

5. In 2015, there were 114,506 Kazakhs in Mongolia, which is 3.9 percent of the population.

6. For information on these genres in Kazakhstan, see Kendirbaeva (1994) and Kunanbaeva (2002).

7. An historical collection of *dombyra*, and other Kazakh instruments, is housed in the Kazakh Museum of Folk Musical Instruments in Almaty, Kazakhstan.

8. The regions are also associated with two contrasting instrumental playing styles of *küi: tökpe* in western Kazakhstan and *shertpe* in the eastern regions. (Kunanbaeva 2002).

9. Information on *dombyra* styles in Kazakhstan are repeated in several publications, including Slobin (1977); Kunanbaeva (2002); Daukeyeva and Nyshanov (2018).

10. Locally made instruments from these makers have not been adopted for use in the Ölgii theater. Instead, the theater supported the import of instruments and instrument makers from Kazakhstan that met and maintained Soviet standards set during the socialist era.

11. Makers report that the wood for ribs should be 2–4 mm thick and for the soundboard 2–3mm thick.

12. Siberian pine (*qaraghai*) (*Pinus sibirica*); Siberian fir (*samyrsyn*) (*Abies sibirica*); Siberian spruce (*shyrsha*) (*Picea obovata*); Siberian larch (*balqadaghai*) (*Larix sibirica*).

13. The subject of aging, drying, or soaking wood, common actions for many luthiers in order to provide stability for the wood, is seldom discussed. Makers in these remote and economically vulnerable communities say they cannot afford to add extra time to their processes.

14. I interviewed *dombyra* makers in Khovd sum in Khovd aimag (2005), and in Altansogts, Sagsai, Tolbo, and Tsengel sums, at Dayan Lake, and in Ölgii city.

15. I met with Sultanbai just once due to my brief stay in Khovd aimag. My in-

terviews with Daniyal occurred only in 2005 because he moved to Kazakhstan in 2006 and passed away in 2007.

16. Khovd aimag population was 88,447 in 2018. In this ethnically diverse province, Kazakhs make up 12.2 percent of the population (2015). Khovd sum, close to the western border of Bayan-Ölgii, with a population of about 3500 residents (2018), is nearly 100 percent Kazakh (MSIS 2019).

17. These different styles are also sometimes referred to as Zhambyl and Abai *dombyra*.

18. Discussions with Sultanbai (b. c. 1955) and members of his community took place in Khovd sum, Khovd aimag, May 2005.

19. Discussion and interviews with D. Daniyal (1918–2007) took place in Ölgii city (May-July 2005).

20. Daniyal also carved other objects of interest especially to tourists, including practical implements used "in the old days" in rural life, he said, such as ladles and large wooden bowls for milk. These were carved with designs on the outside, and sometimes painted. In the past, he also carved the outside of some dombyras in the same way. Daniyal also did some instrument repair work, including repairs to the bowed *qobyz* for the theater.

21. Discussions and interviews with Säken Alhan (1961–2021) took place at several residential sites near Dayan Lake, Bayan-Ölgii, 2005–2018.

22. Säken provided this information and it was confirmed by other long-term residents at Dayan.

23. The technique for cut paper designs may be linked to a Mongolian paper cutting tradition, although *dombyra* makers who use cut paper to embellish their instruments usually link the practice to Japan rather than Mongolia or China (where the tradition is well documented).

24. Discussions and interviews with Medixat Khizirkhan (b. 1961) took place at his home in Ölgii city, Bayan-Ölgii, 2005–2017.

References

Barcus, Holly, and Cynthia Werner. 2010. "The Kazakhs of Western Mongolia: Transnational Migration from 1990–2008." *Asian Ethnicity* 11(2):209–228.

Bates, Elliot. 2012. "The Social Lives of Musical Instruments." *Ethnomusicology* 56(3):363–395.

Daukeyeva, Saida, and Nurlanbek Nyshanov. 2018. "Narrative Instrumental Music." In *The Music of Central Asia*, edited by Theodore Levin, Saida Daukeyeva, and Elmira Köchümkulova, 234–264. Bloomington: Indiana University Press.

Dawe, Kevin. 2003. "Lyres and the Body Politic: Studying Musical Instruments in the Cretan Musical Landscape." *Popular Music and Society* 26(3):263–283.

Diener, Alexander. 2009. *One Homeland or Two? The Nationalization and Transnationalization of Mongolia's Kazakhs*. Stanford, CA: Stanford University Press.

Finke, Peter. 1999. "The Kazaks of Western Mongolia." In *Contemporary Kazaks: Cultural and Social Perspectives*, edited by Ingvar Svanberg, 103–139. New York: St. Martin Press.

———. 2013. "Historical Homelands and Transnational Ties: The Case of the Mongolian Kazaks." *Zeitschrift Für Ethnologie* 138(2):175–193.

Hallam, Elizabeth, and Tim Ingold. 2014. *Making and Growing: Anthropological Studies of Organisms and Artefacts*. Farnham, MD: Ashgate.

Ingold, Tim. 2013. *Making: Anthropology, Archaeology, Art and Architecture*. London: Routledge.

Kendirbaeva, Gulnar. 1994 "Folklore and Folklorism in Kazakhstan." *Asian Folklore Studies* 53:97–123.

Kunanbaeva, Alma. 2002 "Kazakh Music." In *The Garland Encyclopedia of World Music, Volume 6: The Middle East*, edited by Virginia Danielson, Scott Marcus, and Dwight Reynolds, 949–964. New York: Routledge.

Levin, Theodore. 2018. "Music in Central Asia: An Overview." In *The Music of Central Asia*, edited by Theodore Levin, Saida Daukeyeva, and Elmira Köchümkulova, 3–25. Bloomington: Indiana University Press.

Marsh, Peter. 2009. *The Horse-head Fiddle and the Cosmopolitan Reimagination of Tradition in Mongolia*, New York: Routledge.

MSIS (Mongolian Statistical Information Service). 2019. National Statistical Office. Ulaanbaatar. http://1212.mn/.

Post, Jennifer C. 2014. "Performing Transition in Mongolia: Repatriation and Loss in the Music of Kazakh Mobile Pastoralists." *Yearbook for Traditional Music* 46:43–61.

———. 2019. "Climate Change, Mobile Pastoralism and Cultural Heritage in Western Mongolia." In *Cultural Sustainability: Music, Media, Language, Advocacy*, edited by Tim Cooley, 75–86. Urbana: University of Illinois Press.

Qureshi, Regula. 2000. "How Does Music Mean? Embodied Meanings and the Politics of Affect in the Indian Sarangi." *American Ethnologist* 27(4):805–838.

Roda, P. Allen. 2014. "Tabla Tuning on the Workshop Stage: Toward a Materialist Musical Ethnography." *Ethnomusicology Forum* 23(3):360–382.

Slobin, Mark. 1977. *Music of Central Asia and of the Volga-Ural Peoples*. Bloomington: Indiana University, Asian Studies Research Institute.

Soni, Sharad K. 2003. "Kazakhs in Post-Socialist Mongolia." *Himalayan and Central Asian Studies* 7(2):100–115.

Yagi, Fuki. 2018. "The Theater Functioning as Music School: A Case Study of Modified Musical Instruments and The Orchestra of Kazakh Folk Musical Instruments in Bayan-Ölgii, Mongolia." In Japanese. *Sokendai Culture and Science Study* 14:109–126.

———. 2019. "Systematization of Kazakh Music in Mongolia: Activities of Theater and Radio Station during the Soviet Era." *Asian Ethnicity* 20(3):413–424.

PART FOUR

Heritage and Globalization

Everything Has Two Sides

An Interview

ANDREW COLWELL
AND D. TSERENDAVAA

Tserendavaa Dashdorj (b. 1955), a well-traveled *khöömiich* and state-recognized artist, was searching for his herd of sheep and goats by motorcycle with me sitting in the passenger seat, holding onto the rack. We were in the vicinity of his son's summer encampment (*zuslan*) and yet the herd was nowhere to be found. So, he drove us to a nearby hill to take a look around the surrounding steppes. Like many of the hills in the area, this one also had a sacred rock cairn (*ovoo*) at its top. This cairn consisted of a large piece of weathered wood sticking out of a pile of rocks. However, Tserendavaa had not come to make an offering to the local deities this time, which is customary at such places. Instead, he sat down next to the cairn, leaned into it, and scanned the land with his binoculars.

There was a slight breeze, the sky was hazy, and it was cool. There had not been rain in a while and the winter had been dry so the hills were rocky with desiccated, leafless plants branching out between cracks. And it was remarkably quiet, despite being in the wide open. Even the beating of a crow's wings a hundred feet in the air above was clear and sharp.

After no results, Tserendavaa decided to leave the hill and drive us onto the steppes below. He put the bike into neutral to coast downslope and save gas, turning on the motor only when we plateaued and began to lose speed.

Before us were the Jargalant-Altai Mountains, rising above everything else, cutting into the sky. As many locals had said, they emitted a drone (*düngenekh*) whenever a storm was building up on the opposite side. The steppes rose and fell in waves in the distance as we rode into them. Tserendavaa's flock might have been just beyond that nearby hill, or another.

FIGURE (INTERLUDE) 4.1. Tserendavaa searches for his flock, Chandman' sum, 2014. Photo by A. Colwell.

Luckily, it was not long before he spotted them in the distance. We went to them and then entered into a whole spectrum of sounds: stomping hooves, clashing horns of rival males, child-like yelps, puttering farts, a general cacophony to my lay ears. The sheep and goats all looked up and around with anticipation at the arrival of their "master" *(ezen)*.

Tserendavaa told me to get off and help send them along in the direction of his son's summer encampment. As he zig-zagged on the far edges of the herd on motorcycle, I walked behind, waving my hands and screaming "haaa! haaa!" or throwing stones in the path of any animal that attempted to dart off in a different direction.

Once the herd was on its way home, Tserendavaa came back to pick me up and we drove to a nearby outcrop.

"This is a good time to talk," he said, and we sat down on the hard, rocky earth for an interview (May 9, 2014) I had requested earlier.

I wanted to talk about herders' usages of sound to call or communicate with their herds. Tserendavaa was more than obliging and seemed to have a lecture on sound, pastoralism, and *khöömii* already prepared. He was quite used to being interviewed and having foreign researchers stay with him and ended up outlining a range of issues and tensions affecting Mongolian sound worlds in the midst of global change.

"So," he began, "herd animals have their own sounds. In general, any living thing, be it a worm or insect, has its sound. Whether birds, wild animals, or the five livestock—all living creatures have their own given sounds. For example, when herds are sent out to pasture in the morning, their sounds are numerous: hoof sounds; quite fast, fast, quick, quick, rhythmic 'chir, chur.' Like this they quickly tread.

"Around one, three, or four o'clock they return, having eaten, and the herds' sounds are diminished. Full with grass, lying around, they snort. Their hoof sounds are few. For example, 'tur,' they say, grunting and chewing cud, one can hear a 'shir, shir, shir' sound. A herder watching their herd may say to their goats, 'chaa, chaa,' or 'khaiya, khaiya, khakhaaiya, khakhaaiya.' If their herd is moving faster, faster, it is then made to gather and become calm.

"It is as if they know language. The herds seemingly know their master's language and so they gather, eat, and sit. These sonic feelings (*duu aviany medremj*) also lie between herds and people."

He went on until I eventually interrupted him, recalling how his grandson once implored me not to whistle before the wind, lest I stir up an angered storm. So I asked him about the relationship of people, according to pastoral custom:

"One *can* influence the weather with one's sounds. When doing *khöömii* or whistling from their own true character, and the natural world (*baigal'*) is witnessed before one's eyes, the natural world's local deities (*lus savdag*) can provide and realize one's wishes—if they desire, dream, and pray from their true mind-spirit. These are my own thoughts."

The lecture then took a turn toward the origins of Mongolian "national art," which had to do with Tserendavaa's previous discussion of animal sounds.

"Ok, so each herd animal has a different call, for example, when being coaxed (*avakhuulakh*) to accept a rejected offspring. Beginning with a goat . . ."

He began performing some of these calls for me:

"'Cheeg, cheeg, cheeg, cheeg, cheeg, cheeg, cheeg, cheeg, cheeg, cheeg . . .' 'Zuuzuu uu, zuuzuu uu, zuuzuu uu, zuuzuu uu, zuuzuu . . .' Melodizing like this other beautiful folk melodies, such as beautiful long-songs, were made to sound (*duu avia egshiglekh*) as people would melodize (*ayalakh*) in remarkable ways following their own thoughts or feelings (*setgel*) during the activity of calling animals, making all kinds of melodies with all kinds of methods, techniques, rhythms and timing. These things are also connected to national art."

He demonstrated what he meant. For camels, one enunciates in a high, loud voice: "'Tooor l' tooo . . . tor, tor, tor, tor, tor . . .'" This spoken call began transforming into a more defined tone with a slight vibrato: "'Toooo, TOOOR, toooo, khoo, khoo, toooor." The call shifted down a minor third, then back up, where it became "a melody," as was the point of his demonstration.

Such musical shifts from herding call to musical melody, in other words, exemplified an evolutionary shift from "pastoral technique" to "national art," a theory common in Mongolian music research, which was highly influenced by Soviet and European folkloristics of the nineteenth century. Through such calling, shouting, whistling, and "melodizing," Tserendavaa continued, herder children developed (*khögjikh*) their voices and herder peoples developed their signature musical practices, like *khöömii* or long-song (*urtyn duu*). Such practices, correspondingly, could never have evolved among sedentary peoples or in urban locations:

"The majority of Mongolian nomadic voices are able to sing beautiful long-songs loudly and calmly. Their vocal melodies are greatly pristine and good. Among herder peoples such beautiful voices can arise. Why? Because from two to three kilometers they call out to their herds starting from childhood on, screaming and making sounds from afar, and so their voices develop from an early age. This is also a foundation of national art. In contrast, people who live in buildings with two or three rooms don't scream or call to their animals on the streets. Up there, they don't scream loudly. The people of these sedentary places speak softly, have few sounds, and think it is bad not to be so. That you must be pleasant and not sound is a socialist cultured custom (*sotsialist soyoltoi zan uil*). And so, in this way the voices of city youth and children are less developed and worse than country people, as I evaluate from my own research."

In this way, we arrived at a difficult topic. Tserendavaa fell silent, as he had done before when discussing the futures of pastoralism in another interview. I decided not to press him this time. But I was reminded of how the parents of one wealthy Mongolian child I met discouraged him from sounding his voice "in weird ways," as he told me, when he was trying to practice *khöömii* at home after I had shown him some basic exercises.

Like Tserendavaa said, sedentary peoples "speak softly, have few sounds, and think it is bad not to be so."

And yet Mongolia is increasingly becoming urban as rural residents move to city centers. Pastoralism is becoming too difficult with increasingly difficult weather due to climate change. In fact, only one of Tserendavaa's seven children had decided to follow suit and live as a herder, the rest having moved to urban centers to pursue personal livelihoods or professional careers, including two who had become established *khöömiich* in their own right.

Later on, during this same research trip, I returned to Tserendavaa's yurt for another interview about these difficult topics. This time I asked Tserendavaa directly about his own thoughts on the radical social, economic, and cultural changes of the last two decades associated with "development" and "globalization." His response was notably pithy:

"Everything has two sides, one good, one bad," he answered. "Everything in the universe has two paths. Mongolia is walking towards world development. And while walking towards world development, world development is entering Mongolia, opening up all kinds of good and bad paths . . ."

CHAPTER 8

Chandman' and Beyond

Heritage-making of Mongolian Khöömii in Past and Present

JOHANNI CURTET

Khorvoogiin altan taizan deer khöömiin egshig n'
uyangalakhaar
Khökh Mongolygoo shuud orlodog Chandman'
(When the melody of *khöömii* resonates on
the golden stage of the universe Chandman'
becomes Blue Mongol!)
—Extract from *Chandman' nutagtaa örgökh shüleg*
(Poem of offering to Chandman') May 30th 2000,
anonymous (Tsednee 2005:125)

Since the 1990s, *khöömii* has become one of Mongolia's most recognized musical practices performed globally for its distinctive and unusual sound. Its status as a Mongolian cultural heritage product exists alongside cultural markers such as yurts, blue skies, green steppes, Chinggis Khan, and nomadic culture. Yet before the 1950s, few people outside of various small communities in western or northern Mongolia even knew of the vocal practice. It has taken seventy years for this transformation to occur and during this time one particular sum (rural district) called Chandman' in Khovd aimag (province) became renown in Mongolia as "the birth-place of *khöömii*" in light of the significant role of its community members in popularizing, professionalizing, and promoting the vocal practice locally, nationally, and internationally.

In this chapter, I address the growth of *khöömii* in Mongolia from a local to a national tradition and discuss the specific role that one western Mongolian community in Chandman' sum, Khovd aimag, has played in the process. I begin by exploring the musical and performative characteristics of *khöömii* and introduce some of its practitioners, and then illustrate how *khöömii* became the centerpiece of Mongolia's important cultural heritage through the process of institutionalization and international recognition during and after the socialist era. My findings point clearly to the central role that Chandman' and its community played in the growing popularity of *khöömii* in Mongolia and globally.[1]

At the center of my argument are three phases of institutionalization in Mongolia during and after socialism. These forms of institutionalization transformed everyday events and actions into performance, adjusted practices to meet academic standards, and engaged with social processes to help recognize artistic practices as heritage (Parent 2010). During the socialist period, *khöömii* was transformed to meet an aesthetic standard for stage performances, including developing a system of formal transmission process in Mongolian conservatories and universities. In the 2000s, the national implementation of UNESCO's Intangible Cultural Heritage (ICH) further encouraged the Mongolian claim on *khöömii* as an important heritage product.

It was serendipitous for Luvsansharav Dagv (1926–2014), a musical professional and composer in the capital city of Ulaanbaatar, to first meet with a *khöömiich* (*khöömii* performer) from Chandman' in 1954. Ensuing and sustained collaborations between herders, musicians, composers, folklorists, officials, and foreigners were the result of concerted efforts to "develop" a national culture during socialism and then to "preserve" cultural heritage in the democratic era. The inscription of *khöömii* on the Representative List of the ICH of UNESCO in 2010 is only the most recent permutation of an enduring relationship between pastoral, professional, and official actors, and the role of Chandman' in shaping these relationships is significant.

One way of illustrating the importance of Chandman' in the social and institutional history of *khöömii* in Mongolia is revealed through a brief survey of available recordings of Mongolian *khöömii*. For example, the first recordings by Mongolian National Radio in the 1950s and 1960s featured four *khöömiichid* residing in or visiting Ulaanbaatar from Chandman', amounting to just sixteen individual tracks over the span of two decades. But since the 1980s, and in roughly the same amount of time, there have been more than thirty-one recordings issued by over eighteen *khöömiichid* (Curtet 2013). Among these proliferating numbers of practitioners following the 1950s debut of *khöömii* on the stage, a great number of the most influential were, and still are, from Chandman'. Research associates I have worked with since 2004, both within and beyond Chandman', have consistently reinforced this Chandman'-centric *khöömii* narrative in conversations, interviews, and at various cultural events.

Accordingly, there is a well-established historical narrative in Mongolian and Western scholarship that presents these influential *khöömiichid* from Chandman' as the engineers of a national musical aesthetic (Badraa 1983; Pegg 1992). However, a more recent body of academic work mostly from Europe and America (Levin and Süzükei 2006; Curtet 2013; Colwell 2018), and also from Mongolia (Enebish 2009; Sandagjav 2010), has explored the complications, nuances, and gaps in the previous dominant narrative. Previously, academics would point to Chandman' as the root of one aesthetic in *khöömii* development. Later scholars showed how the development of *khöömii* came from other places and people in Mongolia, by revealing the diversity and depth of *khöömii* in Mongolia beyond Chandman' sum.

During my own research, for example, I quickly learned about other communities with significant practitioners or communal histories of practicing *khöömii*, especially in western Mongolia. Various Mongolic and Turkic peoples across the Altai-Sayan Mountain region of Inner Asia practice *khöömii* or interrelated forms of "throat singing." The practices are found in the republics of Altai, Khakassia, Tuva, and Bashkortostan in Russia (Pegg 1992); nationally in Mongolia (Curtet 2013); in northern Xinjiang in China (Mergejikh 1997); and most recently in Inner Mongolia, Buryatia and Kalmykia (Curtet 2013). Within Mongolia, there are similarly Turkic and Mongolic peoples with a wide range of histories, understandings, and practices of *khöömii*. I further illustrate the examples of these diverse *khöömii* practitioners from various locations in Mongolia in a later section.

What Is *Khöömii*?

According to legends gathered by researchers in the field, practitioners in Mongolia developed *khöömii* out of a desire to imitate the sounds of the wind, water, and birdsong (Badraa 1983, 1998; Desjacques 1988, 1992; Pegg 1991, 1992; Kherlen 2010; Curtet 2013). The Mongols have an animistic understanding of the world that perceives natural phenomenon and some inanimate objects as imbued with spirit life. These beliefs are expressed in particular through the arts. As the practice of *khöömii* is related to the daily life and environment of nomadic peoples, it conveys a spiritual relationship with them as well. *Khöömii* expresses a conception of the Mongol world that uses a stratified vertical and hierarchical sense of space. We find this, for example, in vertical deer stones, the Mongolian vertical script *(Mongol bichig)*, and the circular and vertical conceptualization of space in the *ger*. It also becomes a subtle way for practitioners to inhabit, play, and interact with this space (see figure 8.1).

In Mongolian, *khöömii* means "the bottom of the palate" (Tsevel 1966) or "pharynx" (Desjacques 1992; Hangin 1986; Bawden 1997). It is not referred to as a type of "singing" *(duulakh)* but as a way of sounding *(duugarakh)* the vocal apparatus (Curtet 2013; Colwell 2018). Grammatically speaking, one may "do *khöömii*" *(khöömiilökh)*, but one cannot say they "sing *khöömii*" *(khöömii duu-*

Mongol World	*Khöömii* Techniques	*Khöömii* Timbral Composition
sky	High	overtones and resonances
ground	Middle	drone
underground	Deep	double drone

FIGURE 8.1. Interaction between Mongolian conceptualization of the world and *khöömii*, 2020. Diagram by J. Curtet.

lakh). Also, those who do *khöömii* can be referred to as a *khöömiich* (literally, *khöömii*-er) but they cannot be referred to as a *khöömii* "singer" *(duuchin).* This means that terms from the English translations common in academic literature or popular discourse like "throat singing" or "overtone singing" diverge significantly and fundamentally from Mongolian understandings of the vocal practice, an issue that several scholars have discussed (Tongeren 1995; Levin and Süzükei 2006; Curtet 2013) and which Colwell (2018) in particular addresses.

Technically, one person doing *khöömii* intentionally and simultaneously superimposes several layers of sounds with his voice, including two distinct lines, called *suur' öngö* (literally, "basic color," corresponding to the vocal drone) and *isgeree* (literally, "whistling," corresponding to the melodic line of overtones). This set of sounds suggests other superimposed colors *(davkhar öngö)* and echoes *(tsuurai).* It is interesting to note that, while the Mongols do not have a vernacular term for "harmonics," "overtones," or "drones," western descriptive terminology for these practices places an emphasis on these terms. In fact, the Mongolian use of terms such as *suur' öngö* to refer to "drone," and *isgeree* to refer to "overtone," might have emerged due to the desire to translate the Western acoustic terms.

Physiologically speaking, one does *khöömii* by first contracting the vocal cords to produce a richer, denser timbre and second by placing the tongue into particular resonant positions that emphasize the naturally occurring harmonics of the human voice (Trân Quang 1975; Pegg 1992; Desjacques 1992). The various styles and techniques of *khöömii*, accordingly, are variations of this basic use of the vocal apparatus. Depending on this modulation, the pitch of the drone and the pressure on the throat, there are many techniques of *khöömii*, identifiable by their variations of vocal timbre. Mongolians have traditionally referred to these techniques in metaphoric, rather than acoustic or technical, terms that tie the style to broader values or understandings of the natural world. For example, the prominent harmonics of *isgeree khöömii* (literally translated as "whistle *khöömii*") are not "whistles," acoustically speaking, but Mongolians refer to it as such because it resembles a whistling sound. This association ties *isgeree khöömii* to various animistic beliefs about the power of whistling to call up—or even anger—local master-spirits that preside over the natural world. Another important style is *kharkhiraa*, a style most foreigners might describe as "guttural," although the Mongolian term is an onomatopoeia for various natural sound sources including waterfalls *(khürkhree)* and the calls of a certain kind of crane (Desjacques 1992). Once again, there is a wide gap between non-Mongolian and Mongolian descriptions for *khöömii* technique and style.

The connections between technique (*isgeree khöömii* and *kharkhiraa*) with nature through metaphor suggests how important the natural world is to Mongolian understandings of *khöömii*. Mongolian and Tuvan *khöömiichid* often refer to practices of learning from or imitating rivers and other natural sound sources (Desjacques 1988; 1992; Badraa 1998; Pegg 2001; Levin and Süzükei 2006; Curtet 2013). However, many rural practitioners consider the quality of the natural environment to be a direct influence on the talent of musicians and singers and it is not uncommon for practitioners to pray to local master-spirits who preside over a mountain or river and request they receive musical talent (Colwell 2018).

There is a common understanding among pastoralists throughout Mongolia that creativity and artistry emerge from the natural world. For example, anthropologist Laurent Legrain (2009:98) writes that "in Darhad country [in northern Mongolia], all the valleys of the liminal belt of steppes are perceived as the natural cradles of vocal talents." Several communities in Khovd aimag, including Khovd's Chandman' sum, similarly affirm that local geography located in the Altai mountain range is the ultimate source of local musical talent. Its location between two mountains (Jargalant Khairkhan and Bumbat Khairkhan) and three large lakes (Khar-Us Nuur, Khar Nuur, and Dörgön Nuur) is significant for residents in that it helps explain why the sum would have produced so many gifted *khöömiichid* over the years.[2] Many mothers of these talented people with whom I have spoken have often said that any child born in this region will typically have similar facility with this vocal technique.

Two traditional methods of teaching music were highlighted by Carole Pegg. The first, *geriin surguul'* (home school) is where music is passed on by parents or those around them. The second, *nair naadmyn surguul'* (the festival school) is its transmission by renowned artists during their involvement in the context of a domestic celebration or an arts festival (2001:256). Including those contexts, *khöömii* has always been transmitted orally from generation to generation in many ways. I learned from Chandman' herders and *khöömiichid* Darjaa Düger (1933–2016), Margad Gombotseden (1939–2005), and Shagj Myatav (1939–2010) that before the 1950s transmission occurred by imitating each other within the community. There were no specific exercises related to an elaborate pedagogy. Everyone had to find out for themselves by following the instructions of the elders: namely, how to take and manage the breath, how to contract the muscles of the throat and place the tongue in the oral cavity to modulate the overtones, and more important, how to connect with nature, such as in the mimesis of the wind, water, and so on. This process is still going on. With the spread of *khöömii* through the airwaves since the 1950s, some people learned on their own from the radio. This includes Erdenekhüü Ayuurzana (b.1957) from Kharkhorin in central Mongolia, who imitated Zavkhan aimag's *khöömiich* Chimeddorj Gaanjuur (1931–1980). But the vertical teaching between master and apprentice had started by the end of the 1970s with Chandman'-born *khöömiichid* Sundui Dovchin (1938–2003), Sengedorj Nanjid (1948–2020), Davaajav Rentsen (b.1952), Tserendavaa Dashdorj (b.1954), and Ganbold Taravjav (1957–2011).[3] Each teacher developed his own pedagogy and created the first orally transmitted "schools" of *khöömii* in the country.[4]

Who Practices *Khöömii*?

In rural western Mongolia, the connection to nature is important. Through my many journeys in Mongolia, my own learning as a musician with masters Tserendavaa and Odsüren Baatar (b.1949), and my ongoing involvement in the lives of these artists through concert tours I have produced in Europe with my NGO Routes Nomades, I have encountered the inner worlds of many *khöömiichid* and then learned about the spiritual aspects of their tradition. For Sengedorj, to become a good *khöömiich* you have to practice constantly, particularly in a special place rich with sounds of nature. For Tserendavaa, a good *khöömiich* must be strong, honest, intelligent, respectful of others, and, if possible, be a good rider and a good wrestler. *Khöömiichid* agree that the quality of a *khöömii* performance can be observed in the choice of timbre, one's breathing capacity, the power of the voice, the melodic beauty, and finally, the performer's ability to evoke the natural environment (Legrain 2007, 2011). On the other hand, Odsüren maintains another view of the *khöömii* tradition, which I observed in his *khöömii* class during my scholarship at the University of Arts and Culture *(Soyol Urlagiin Ikh Surguul')* from 2006–2007. For Odsüren, the attitude of the Mongolian *khöömiich* during a performance is of particular importance. In performance, singers must be relaxed, especially in the face. In fact, nothing should be tense and the *khöömii* should come from the belly, from within. He also teaches that one should not show feelings on the face and if one

FIGURE 8.2. Herder and *khöömii* master Davaajav Rentsen during the recording of the CD *An Anthology of Mongolian Khöömii*, Chandman', Khovd aimag, 2015. Photo by J. Curtet.

of his pupils has the misfortune of showing a grimace, he risks having his lips pursed or face slapped by the teacher. This teaching method is a persuasive way to prevent students from adopting "bad habits." Odsüren considers such habits to be idiosyncrasies of countryside *khöömiich*, such as having a red face and moving the lips all over the place while performing *khöömii*. Odsüren wanted to change these habits to "develop" *khöömii* in order to distinguish it from rural practices. He believes his method is based on a custom in Mongolia whereby Mongols observe the outward appearance of children so that they can become good wrestlers, or that of horses so that they become good steeds.

While collecting data for my PhD thesis between 2007 and 2013, and later while making field recordings for my CD project *An Anthology of Mongolian Khöömii* (Curtet and Nomindari 2017), I gathered the essentials of this vocal technique in Mongolia from early sound archive to the present day. In the process, I realized how many *khöömii* bearers there are in today's Mongolia. Indeed, there are many more now than in the 1950s. Since that time, the number of practitioners has increased, growing slowly at first, until the 1970s, and then consistently in the twenty-first century. The well-known masters are not always professionals. For example Tserendavaa and Davaajav in Chandman' are mainly herders, and the rest of their time is dedicated to teaching or practicing *khöömii*. Sengedorj worked in all positions in Khovd's drama theater, from sweeper and lighting designer, to actor, singer and *khöömiich*, and then director.

In Ulaangom city, Uvs aimag, the Bayad master Toivgoo Ejee (b.1957) is retired from the local theater now, but he worked his whole career as a professional *khöömiich* with a civil servant status. He taught dozens of children, some of whom became internationally well-known *khöömiichid*, such as Otgonkhüü Orshikh (b.1974) and Lkhamragchaa Lkhagvasüren. In Tes sum, Uvs aimag, the Bayad elder and herder Mangaljav Lkhamsüren (b.1943) taught *khöömii* to his extended family and local children, as well as to his grandson Baska who is now a celebrated *khöömiich*. In Tsengel sum in Bayan-Ölgii aimag, a sole Tuvan teacher named Papizan Badar (1957–2016) taught local children for many years, some of whom have become teachers and established performers in their own right, such as Batsükh Dorj (b.1990). Papizan was an important keeper of Tuvan traditions, and also a multitalented artist and instrument maker. In Zavkhan, aimag musicians who contributed to national *khöömii* history include Chimeddorj Gaanjuur (1931–1980), one of the first *khöömiich* to perform on stage, and Odsüren, who was the first to teach this vocal technique in a university. In Bayankhongor aimag as well, Pürev Byakhar (1949–2009) worked as a professional *khöömiich* at the local theater for thirty years. Other *khöömiichid* of western Mongolia are known only by the local *khöömii* community. They are just herders or work in an office or a shop. They are not teachers, nor do they appear on stage or in competitions.

Traditionally, it was said that women were not permitted to perform *khöömii* because it is believed the practice causes infertility in women (Pegg 1992). Tserendavaa and Odsüren are recognized as the first who were open to teaching women. Tserendavaa started with three women in 1982: Bolormaa Begz (b.1968), Davaasüren Margad (b.1968) and Serjmyadag (b. unknown). He was very proud that the first *emegtei khöömiichid* (female *khöömii* performers) were from Chandman'. Odsüren was Alimaa Gavaa's (b. unknown) early teacher, and his student Ösökhjargal Pürevsüren (b.1973) became the first female *khöömii* performer abroad; she performed as soloist for Khukh Mongol ensemble in Ingolstadt, Germany. Later, Odsüren's *khöömii* class at the University of Arts and Culture in Ulaanbaatar hosted several women, such as Undarmaa Altangerel (b.1986) (see figure 8.3) from Ulaangom, who worked as a soloist in the National Theater and became an independent artist. Another is Zolzayaa Damba from Chandman', who is now working as a soloist at the theater in Khovd. In 2008, Toivgoo taught his first two female students: D. Tseveenchimed, a dancer from his theater company, and D. Bolormaa. While there are timbral differences between women and men's practice due to their gender and vocal range, each one is able to perform the same techniques and styles.

FIGURE 8.3. Undarmaa Altangerel during a recording session for the CD *An Anthology of Mongolian Khöömii*, Ulaangom, Uvs aimag. Summer, 2015. Photo by Sh. Nomindari.

In the past forty years, the *khöömii* training and transmission developed, spread, and grew each decade, increasingly reinforcing it as a national heritage. The following section introduces an outline of how *khöömii* became a national heritage practice, and a description of the major steps of its institutionalization that led it to the contemporary practice of *khöömii* becoming a national tradition.

From Steppe to Stage

How did *khöömii*, transition from a practice performed in pastoral and natural settings where spiritual connections can still be found to become a practice for the professional stage in urban settings? The answers, I suggest, revolve around the transformation of the performance practices during the socialist period, specifically starting in the 1950s followed by the transmission of the practices to academic institutions after socialism in the 1990s. This culminated in the reframing of *khöömii* as Mongolian national heritage. *Khöömii*'s institutionalization, according to Pegg (1992), began during the Soviet period, providing post-socialist heritage-making with a preexisting conceptual, political, and policy foundation.

The general aim of socialist cultural policy in Mongolia was to create a new national culture that resident pastoralists unfamiliar with socialism would self-identify with and espouse in everyday and public behavior, values, and social life through folklorization (Stolpe 2008; Hamayon 1990; Marsh 2009). Musically speaking, realizing this aim meant selecting specific local practices for "cultural development" in order to promote them to a level of performance. Once an art form was professionalized, it could thus be considered "national" according to standards derived from Soviet cultural policy (Curtet 2013). Professionalism, in turn, meant the ability to perform appropriately on the stage in concert settings before a seated audience in a concert hall. But by the 1950s, after socialism had been seeking to create a national culture for almost thirty years (since the revolution in 1924), cultural elites and official folklorists charged with selecting practices for cultural development had yet to encounter *khöömii*, a rare practice even within its few communities in western and northern Mongolia. Other practices had already been adapted to the stage at this time, such as performances on the horsehead fiddle *(morin khuur)*, short-song *(bogino duu)*, and long-song *(urtyn duu)* (Yoon 2011).

This situation changed when the composer D. Luvsansharav, then director of the Musical and Drama Theater of Khovd aimag in Khovd city, happened to hear *khöömii* in 1954 during a rehearsal for the approaching Khovd Ten Days of Art Festival *(Arvan khonog urlagiin naadam)* to be held in the distant capital of Ulaanbaatar (Enebish 2009; Sandagjav 2010; Kherlen 2010; Curtet 2013). In this rehearsal, a young Khalkh[5] student and actor from Chandman' called S. Tsedee (1924–2004), who had learned *khöömii* from the brothers Derem and Chuluun Togooch, approached the composer to demonstrate *isgeree khöömii* (Enebish 2009:157). Thoroughly impressed by Tsedee's *khöömii*, Luvsansharav then decided to incorporate it into the finale of his choral arrangement of "Altai magtaal" (In praise of Altai), whose key motifs he had derived from various regional versions of the praise-song among epic singers.[6] For the composer, the finale with *khöömii* resounded as an appropriate climax to follow the praise-song's final refrain, a nationalistic ode to the majesty of the Altai Mountains but also a political salute to prominent politicians at the time from western Mongolia.[7]

In 1954 Tsedee became the first to perform solo, unaccompanied *khöömii* on stage at the local Khovd theater and then later in Ulaanbaatar. Local authorities on the Central Party Committee greatly appreciated Luvsansharav's arrangement and gave it a certificate of honor (Sandagjav 2010). For this recognition and artistic capacity for the stage, practitioners and scholars would later consider Tsedee to be the first "professional" *khöömiich*. Chimeddorj Gaanjuur from Zavkhan aimag became the first to perform *khöömii* overseas in another arrangement of the Altai praise-song. He learned the vocal practice from Tsedee and then from Sundui Dovchin, a Chandman' native who succeeded Tsedee at the Khovd theater in the 1960s. In academic histories, these individuals became "pioneers" of sorts as the first performers to adapt *khöömii* technique and repertoire for the professional technical and acoustic demands of the stage (Pegg 1992; Enebish 2009; Curtet 2013).

Later, Sundui began exploring aspects of Western classical music, departing from indigenous aesthetic values to the degree that he sought to adapt techniques of *bel canto* for *khöömii* performance. As historian Françoise Aubin writes, by the 1970s this Western vocal technique performed with traditional instruments was already a success in rural areas (1973). Even Badraa Jamts (1926–1993), a staunch advocate for traditional culture, proudly wrote how "having opera singers is one of the important achievements of our socialist musical culture. It is also our pride of development!" (2005 [1977]:151). As ethnomusicologist Alain Desjacques (2009) writes, Sundui first demonstrated how virtuosity in *khöömii* performance could be instantiated by employing vibrato, a hallmark of *bel canto* singing, but never heard in prior recordings of *khöömii*. Notably, Desjacques observed that there seems to have been no equivalent to vibrato in traditional horsehead fiddling or singing, and the technique likely appeared alongside the introduction of radio and television to the country in the 1960s. Sundui studied with the voice pedagogue Dorjdagva Jigzav in Ulaanbaatar, learning during this period the *bel canto* technique (Colwell 2018). The addition of vibrato in Dorjdagva's teaching helped Sundui to stand out from rural folk artists who did not employ vibrato (Desjacques 2009).[8] Vibrato, moreover, was not only an aesthetic move, but a political means of instantiating progress away from the rural past and toward a Western ideal of performance (see Chapter 3 in this volume).

Sundui's example inspired a great number of *khöömiich* from Chandman', such as the previously mentioned Sengedorj Nanjid, Davaajav Rentsen, Tseren-davaa Dashdorj, and Ganbold Taravjav, to similarly pursue professional paths in the 1970s. These musicians would go on to receive recognition, in their own right, and teach their own aesthetic versions of *khöömii*, which they derived in great part from what they would begin calling Sundui's "high" or "fluid" *(shin-gen)* style, marking a general Chandman' aesthetic. Some of these teachers also created novel styles of their own, such as Tserendavaa's "combined" *(khosmoljin) khöömii*, or expanded the existing limited repertoire of *khöömii* by creating solo demonstration pieces, self-accompanied by a fiddle, as T. Ganbold did, and later with a small ensemble of traditional instruments. The arrangements were written in Western style, especially in the harmonization of traditional melodies (Curtet 2013).[9] By the fall of socialism in 1990, these now established masters would become the first to teach and perform overseas, whereas socialist restrictions had previously barred Sundui from teaching foreigners (Desjacques, personal communication).

Such professionalization and innovation, on the other hand, raised concerns about the continuity and meaning of traditional culture as well, especially among a growing set of intellectual elites in the capital city during the 1970s. In particular, the influential composer, politician, and Party member Jantsannorov Natsag (b.1949), along with the music researcher J. Badraa, began advocating for traditional culture in his official capacity as Minister of Culture in the 1980s. They then redirected political orientations toward a more Mongolian than Russian culture, effectively inviting Mongolian composers to assert their identity (Marsh 2009).

Despite the proliferating practitioners and innovations discussed earlier, only one cultural institution in Mongolia, the Khovd Theater, had an officially designated professional position for a *khöömiich*. This continued until the 1970s, when in Ulaanbaatar the National Song and Dance Ensemble officially hired Sundui, resulting in two such positions. Singers, fiddlers, and dancers, among others, had numerous official positions in provincial theaters throughout the country, suggesting how rare *khöömii* remained for decades before its globalization began in the 1990s. While the academic institutionalization of rural practices like the horsehead fiddle (Marsh 2009) and long-song (Yoon 2011) started in the 1940s, practitioners began teaching *khöömii* in universities only in the 1990s when Badraa, once again, sought to introduce the vocal practice into higher education.

Through Badraa's initiative, the National University of Mongolia held a class in 1992, although the goal was to train researchers more than performers (Kherlen 2010). It took over a decade before the first class of professional *khöömiich* would graduate with a diploma, but from the University of Arts and Culture. In both cases, the teaching was entrusted to Odsüren, who remained, until 2019, the sole academic professor of *khöömii* in Mongolia.[10] Unlike *khöömiichid* from the Altai region in western Mongolia, as noted previously, Odsüren developed a pedagogy strongly inspired by Western conservatories and he contributed by developing the shape of its performance and, generally, standardizing *khöömii* at the national level.

Since these first classes, the numbers of his students, many of whom also learned through kinship networks in rural places like Chandman', have proliferated greatly. Accordingly, they tend to espouse a generalized aesthetic and perception of *khöömii* that reflects Odsüren's views. And their professionalism at home for cultural tourism or abroad for concert tours also requires that they emphasize a Mongolian homogeneity, rather than individual idiosyncrasies, familiar pedagogies, or communal or regional styles they may have grown up with.

FIGURE. 8.4. In the *khöömii* classroom of B. Odsüren at the University of Arts and Culture, with Inner Mongolian visiting students, beginners level, 2010. Photo by J. Curtet.

Current Phase: Heritage-making and Community Institutions

During the socialist period, the *khöömii* tradition moved from the mountain steppe to the stage at a time when Mongolia had little interaction with the non-Soviet or capitalist world. More recently, the cultural management of *khöömii* by the UNESCO Intangible Cultural Heritage project set its development on different paths. While the institutional aims of both regimes were equally based upon the western ideologies of stage performance, professionalism, and institutionalized training systems, the transition from socialist cultural management with its aim of building a new and modern national culture, to democratic-era "cultural heritage safeguarding" with the aim of preserving "traditional culture" in its very fluid form, was significant (Tsetsentsolmon 2015). However, Nomindari Shagdarsüren, a specialist in Mongolian intangible cultural heritage, notes how some pre-socialist laws and legal instruments demonstrated an awareness of "heritage" with protections for natural elements (2010:16–19).[11]

More generally, heritagization (in French *patrimonialisation*) can be understood as "the process by which a supposedly traditional social or cultural fact sees its practice voluntarily relaunched in parallel or at the end of an inventory and a safeguard" (Charles-Dominique 2013). On one hand, the concept is meant to embrace and promote difference. But on the other hand, as created by UNESCO, it is Western in origins, meaning, and implementation. The result is a tension between the promotion of Indigenous culture by framing it as cultural heritage and the use of foreign frames and values to do this promotion.

Badraa (1998), for example, navigated this tension when promoting *khöömii* through various Western frames that he also tried to resignify. For instance, in the late 1970s, he advocated that the vocal practice be categorized as a form of "classical art," following a reconsideration of what "classical" itself means (see also Curtet 2013; Colwell 2019). He made this argument in the context of socialist cultural policy, which officially designated various levels of "development" of musical practices, European classical music being the most "developed" and "universal," and traditional Mongolian music being the least in both regards. Badraa, however, argued that "classical" referred to the "most select" practice of any people, regardless of their provenance, which evinces "professionalism" through the formality of its techniques, technical vocabulary, and difficulty (Badraa 1998). In this regard, Mongolia had promoted genres such as *khöömii* and *urtyn duu* (long-song) as "classical" practices, thereby influencing their selection for programming and further development.

Because of such efforts to promote traditional music through foreign frames and forms of institutional management, the novel concept of heritage *(öv)* was not very difficult for Mongolian intellectuals, performers, and officials to latch onto following the democratic revolution of 1990, which resulted in the quick development of various new cultural heritage policies (Jargalsaikhan 2007).[12] These policies reflected the government's desire for "development" modeled on capitalist (no longer Soviet-aligned) countries. As a practice that Badraa and others had already marked as distinct and important during socialism, *khöömii* would soon become a focus of presidential decrees between 2006 and 2014 proclaiming the need to develop the vocal practice (Curtet 2013).[13]

Post-socialist heritage-making creates various other tensions. The *Decree of the President on the Development of the Art of Khöömei* (2006), for example, was purely political and institutional in nature with little communal input from practitioners regarding its conceptualization or implementation. Only the head of the Ulaanbaatar based Mongolian Khöömei Association *(Mongol Khöömein Kholboo)* at the time had any influence on or say about the program. To this degree, such a national program did not reflect key tenets of community participation given in the *Convention for the Safeguarding of the Intangible Cultural Heritage* (UNESCO 2003). Unfortunately, it is quite common generally for states to implement this convention similarly without communal input and guidance (Foster and Gilman 2015). Another tension lies in how UNESCO-oriented heritage-making in Mongolia had framed *khöömii* as an endangered musical tradition in need of safeguarding after successive threats of Sovietization, Westernization, urbanization, industrialization, and extraction-based capitalism. And yet *khöömii* was promoted and popularized precisely during socialism for the sake of cultural development and building a national culture (Nomindari 2012). Many goals of Mongolia's heritage programming for *khöömii* have been achieved over the years. There have been various national and international festivals at which competition winners won medals; the publication of two works entirely devoted to *khöömii* (Kherlen 2010; Sandagjav 2010); the Mongolian Khöömei Association's 2012 release of an album featuring exemplary *khöömiichid* from the 1950s, 1960s, and 1970s (*Altan üyeiin ankhdagchid*); and, perhaps most celebrated, the registration of *khöömii* on the List of the Intangible Cultural Heritage of Humanity by UNESCO in 2010. Yet regarding transmission, institutional academic instruction has become more and more privileged as a means for students to learn the practice, receive diplomas, and emerge with demonstrable professional performance skills that can be featured in conservatories, national ensembles, and tourism-oriented concerts. In short, the emphases on stage performance and institutions has left little tangible support for rural tradition-bearers who teach *khöömii* in traditional, pastoral contexts.

Chandman'

In the following case study on Chandman' sum, Khovd aimag, I explore the institutional realities of the implementation of heritage-making and how it has shaped rural *khöömii* performance, practitioners, and their communities. Some of my research indicates that post-socialist heritage-making was primarily an institutional phenomenon with little community input. However, Chandman' local residents, in response to its development in the twentieth century, have created their own institutions to reframe *khöömii* as local cultural heritage. This observation leads us to Chandman' sum to see how one rural community with a tradition of *khöömii* performance has responded to heritage-making in the democratic era. Locally organized programs and events reveal how the community's leaders and teachers have relied upon local forms of institutionalization to promote a narrative that Chandman' *is* "the birth-place of *khöömii*" in light of how its native-born *khöömiichid* have consistently been featured in the history of *khöömii*'s cultural development during and after socialism. The best example of these efforts is the construction of a local "Khöömii Palace" in 2009–2010 in the center of the sum using provincial and national funding (see figure 8.5).

The palace is just across from the local elementary and high school, which is named after D. Sundui, the local and national *khöömii* hero. The school also has a classroom that the director, Sundui's little brother Myagmarjav Dovchin,

FIGURE 8.5. The "Stone" of *Khöömii*, Facing Jargalant Khairkhan (also known as Jargalant Altai), Chandman', Khovd aimag, 2010. Photo by J. Curtet.

dedicated to *khöömii* by decorating its walls with photos and documents detailing the lives of famous local *khöömiichid* and various important feats they accomplished, such as Tsedee's first performance on the stage. While local teachers have traditionally taught in their homes or when out herding, Tserendavaa and Davaajav have adjusted their practices by teaching at this palace and at the school. It is not uncommon to hear a mother saying that at the school, any child can have the gift of *khöömii*.

FIGURE 8.6. N. Sengedorj's *khöömii* students learning epic singing (with *tovshuur* accompaniment) in Duut's school, Khovd aimag, 2010. Photo by J. Curtet.

Local leaders and organizers have also "registered" *khöömii* as cultural heritage in other ways. For example, when I began studying with Tserendavaa he took me to a stone by a waterfall high up in the nearby Jargalant Khairkhan (see figure 8.5), which has the following inscription on it:

A melody unequalled in the world / *Delkhiid khosgüi egshiglen*
Khöömii originates in these waters / *Khöömii ene usnaas ekhleltei*

Whether or not one can verify these origins, the stone bears witness to a broader communal effort to maintain *khöömii*'s national and international prominence through programming, architecture, and monuments. The notion of ICH was built initially upon the notion of "tangible heritage," and this example shows how it is important for people to refer to something tangible when they need to express the intangible.

This heritage-making in Mongolia, as mentioned earlier, consists primarily of institutional policy, programming, and implementation with little community input, Chandman' locals have done their own heritage-making through local institutions and creative acts as well. In both cases, heritage-making also reflects local or governmental projects to promote perceptions that *khöömii* originates in Mongolia or, more specifically, in Chandman'.

FIGURE 8.7. Papizan Badar and Batsükh Dorj during the field work of *An Anthology of Mongolian Khöömii* project, Tsengel sum, Bayan-Ölgii aimag, 2015. Photo by J. Curtet.

Chandman' sum has vested political and economic interests in maintaining its position as "the homeland of *khöömii*." For example, local teachers have been invited to neighboring sums to teach the vocal practice to local students, providing an additional source of income. While Chandman' demographics are primarily Khalkh, neighboring sums where these teachers travel are populated by ethnic groups, including Zakhchin and Altai Uriankhai. This is particularly notable because these ethnic groups used to have prominent *khöömiich* of their own, according to fieldwork and archive material (Curtet 2013). But when I asked Altai Uriankhai students of Sengendorj (see figure 8.6), a renowned *khöömiich* and teacher from Chandman', in Duut sum about their reasons for learning *khöömii*, they gave the following responses:[14]

"*Khöömii* is one of our national arts." Ankhbayar Nanzaddorj (b.1994)

"*Khöömii* is a national art recognized by UNESCO in the name of Mongolia." Baljinnyam Bataa (b.1998)

"*Khöömii* comes from our Mongolia, it's Mongolian national music." Amarbold Enkhsaikhan (b.1997)

These statements suggest that these students are motivated to learn the vocal practice because of national sentiment, in contrast to local sentiment derived from local *khöömii* practices and heritage in Duut sum specifically.

Conclusion

Khöömii in Mongolia today emerged in the 1950s with the first steps toward professionalization, followed by the considerable contribution of Sundui's vibrato in the local and national *khöömii* aesthetic, then the creation of new pedagogies spread broadly, and finally the use of tangible elements to express a claim to ownership. Chandman' played a role at every stage of the heritage-making process of *khöömii*, as it was acknowledged as national heritage then international ICH. While looking at the definition of the vocal technique and presenting those who are its bearers, I have highlighted the diversity of its practice, so that we can understand the heritagization as a multifaceted process that started in Chandman' but spread then in many other directions.

With these perspectives in mind, It might be worthwhile asking: what does heritage-making mean from the inside and outside? The *Convention for the Safeguarding of the Intangible Cultural Heritage* (UNESCO 2003), aims to protect the existing traditions and, as Khaznadar (2009) says, to maintain traditions over time. In fact, the transmission process is at the heart of the heritage-making project of intangible cultures, which is shown in Article 14 of the Convention (UNESCO 2003). Noriko Aikawa-Faure (2011), one of the founders of the Convention, explained that their document calls for the respect of authenticity in the transmission processes. The UNESCO heritage issue is a political project in which people make choices that are necessarily oriented and influenced by international foreign policy. As Luc Charles-Dominique explains (2013:84), "at the level of a community, a region or a state, heritage policies are part and parcel of identity strategies." *Khöömii*, of course, is a tradition shared by peoples divided by colonial borders, including Tuva, Altai, and Khakassia (Russia), western and northern Mongolia, and Xinjiang and Inner Mongolia (China). It makes sense that governmental heritage-making focused on *khöömii* has resulted in regional tensions, following China's inscription of *khöömii* as a UNESCO ICH in 2009. To this degree, heritage-making has created novel forms of cultural conflict for national governments (Nomindari and Curtet 2015; Curtet 2021; Colwell 2018). At stake in these debates are the cultural and economic capital that registration engenders in the form of medals, recognition, and tourism opportunities.

The stakes of heritage-making are also international in economic scope. For example, Inner Mongolian music students especially in Hohhot (China) are increasingly studying traditional Mongolian music in the pursuit of professional careers in the world music industry or in ethnic minority ensembles. Without any local teachers of *khöömii*, these students have been learning from teachers coming from Mongolia since the 1990s, but more recently from Tuvan teachers as well. As Tsenrendavaa's son and *khöömiich* Tsogtgerel told me in 2013, their lessons now constitute a significant source of income as some of them now travel annually to Inner Mongolia to teach. The impacts of institutionally driven heritage-making have most likely expanded the economic opportunities for teachers, in this sense.

If some ethnic groups turn to the Khalkh to learn, the fact that the practices of Tsengel Tuvans were mentioned in the Mongolian dossier presented to UNESCO (2010) opened doors for them in their recognition in Mongolia. But aside from the case of Papizan and his protege Batsükh (see figure 8.7), who performed at the Grand Folk Arts Festival in Ulaanbaatar in 2011, it seems that few of the unestablished *khöömiichid* have benefited from their inclusion or recognition in heritage programming.

Nowadays, becoming a *khöömiich* can give rise to national and sometimes international recognition. The one who learns better than the others is no longer seen as a herder capable of *khöömiilökh*, but directly as a *khöömiich*, usually qualified as a professional. The Mongolian language makes the distinction between a "professional *khöömii* performer" *(mergejliin khöömiich)* and a "popular talent" *(ardyn av'yaastan)*. The latter category is equivalent to the status of amateur. Quite often in my field, as I trace the links from teacher to student, I have noticed that the *ardyn av'yaastan* have once been the role models for practicing professionals today. The teaching of Mongolian oral music in institutions and the fixing of repertoires by writing (recording or arrangements and compositions) have only widened the gap between the generations.

For *khöömii*, this differentiation came to its peak with the successive opening of *khöömii* classes at the university in Ulaanbaatar. Due to the kinds of distinctions between professional and amateur brought about by the university training system that has produced a young generation who are focused toward technicality and virtuosity, *khöömiichid* herders point to their inability to read music theory as a reasoning for not considering themselves to be good *khöömiichid*. The link between school and professionalization of the form as performance is important in their mind. However, these rural *khöömiichid* know much more about *khöömii* that is not transmitted in the city. The embodiment of the natural spaces that they carry within them certainly has greater force in their performances than knowing how to perform *khöömii* renditions of *O sole mio* by Eduardo Di Capua, or an extract from *Carmen* by Georges Bizet.

For the young generation, there are many models. Some prefer to turn to the model of the lyrical prowess of a Pavarotti, which many audiences enjoy. Others look for new influences such as the trendy ethno-rock that started with the band Altan Urag and has become internationally recognized with the recent world phenomenon The Hu (see Chapters 5 and 10 in this volume). Legrain suggests that domestic artists' primary aesthetic criteria is often linked to feelings of nostalgia for the native country (2011:86,458). Here, the significance of *khöömii* is not the same as one moves from the countryside to the city, although the latter now tends to set the tone and pace across the country, leaving the nomadic heritage itself and its relationships to nature as the responsibility of local practitioners and heritage institutions in places such as Chandman'.

Notes

1. See our companion website, www.mongoliansoundworlds.org, for additional information on the musical traditions included in this volume.

2. This would be a typical tendency of Mongolian musicians to make their birthplace the cradle of their musical or artistic specialty. In the Uriankhai sums of Duut and Mönkhkhairkhan, for example, the interpreters of epic *tuul'* and *tsuur* flute also emerged from these mountainous areas of the Altai.

3. Ganbold is the uncle of Egschiglen ensemble's *khöömiich* Amartüvshin Baasandorj.

4. For more information about the diversity of teaching *khöömii* in Mongolia, see Curtet 2013.

5. The majority ethnic group in Mongolia.

6. To listen to this recording, see Curtet and Nomindari (2017), *An Anthology of Mongolian Khöömii*, CD-1 track 15.

7. This is a direct quote from Luvsansharav recorded on April 9, 2011 at his home in Ulaanbaatar. See the complete score in Curtet (2013:460–467).

8. Listen to Sundui accompanied by a *morin khuur* fiddle in Curtet and Nomindari (2017), *op.cit.*, CD-1 track 17.

9. Listen to T. Ganbold accompanied by *yatga* and *yochin* zithers in Curtet and Nomindari (2017), *op.cit.*, CD-1 track 22.

10. Before this period Odsüren also taught as a guest at universities in Inner Mongolia (China) and Buryatia (Russia).

11. Chinggis Khaan's *Ikh zasag* (Great Power, thirteenth century, date unknown) and *Khalkh juram khuul'* (1709, Law "Khalkh Rule"); or the protection of the tangible heritage under the Soviet period, such as *Sudar Bichgiin khüreelengiin dürem* (Regulation of the Institute of Letters, 1921), *Ardyn Zasgiin Gazryn 32 dugaar togtool-Ekh orny tüükhend kholbogdokh dursgalt züilsiig khamgaalakh tukhai düren* (Ordinance No. 32 of Government of the People-Regulations on the Protection of the Historical Remains of the Fatherland, 1942), *BNMAU-yn soyolyn dursgalt züiliig khamgaalakh khuul'* (Law of the Mongolian People's Republic on the Protection of Cultural Remains, 1970).

12. *Mongol ulsyn ündsen khuul'* (Constitution of Mongolia, 1992) ; *Mongol ulsyn töröös barimtlakh soyolyn bodlogo* (State Strategy on Culture, 1996); *Soyolyn tukhai khuul'* (Loi sur la Culture, 1996); *Soyolyn öviig khamgaalakh tukhai khuul'* (Law

on the Protection of Cultural Heritage, 2001); *Soyolyn biet bus öviig khamgaalakh tukhai UNESCO-giin 2003 ony Konventsid negden orokh tukhai khuul'* (Ratification of the 2003 UNESCO Convention for the Safeguarding of the Intangible Cultural Heritage, 2005).

13. *Mongol ulsyn yerönkhiilögchiin Mongol khöömiin urlagiig khögjüülekh tukhai zarlig* (Decree of the President on the development of the art of khöömii, 2006); *Mongol Khöömii ündesnii khötölbör* (National program Mongol Khöömii, 2008–2014). which includes the project of nomination of *khöömii* to UNESCO's Representative List of Intangible Cultural Heritage.

14. Testimonies recorded at Duut on September 14, 2010.

Bibliography

Aikawa-Faure, Noriko. 2011. Roundtable "Transmettre, oui, mais comment?" *8e Journée du Patrimoine Culturel Immatériel*, March 30, 2011. Paris: Maison des cultures du monde.

Altan üeiin ankhdagchid (The first pioneers). 2012. 1 CD. Ulaanbaatar: National Academic Ensemble of Music and Dance /Mongol Khöömein Kholboo.

Aubin, Françoise. 1973. "Fêtes et commémorations en République Populaire de Mongolie: apport à l'étude de la propagande éducative en pays socialiste." *Revue française de science politique*, 23e année 1:33–58.

Badraa, Jamts. 1998. *Mongol ardyn khögjim* [Mongolian folk music]. Ulaanbaatar.

———. 2005. *Ardyn bilig ukhaany onis* [Folklore: intellectual matters]. Ulaanbaatar: Bembi San.

Badraa, Jamts, and Khishigt Demid. 1983. *Mongol khöömei*, 21' documentary, Ulaanbaatar: Mongol televiziin telekino üildveriin büteel.

Bawden, Charles, R. 1997. *Mongolian-English Dictionary*. London: Kegan Paul International.

Charles-Dominique, Luc. 2013. "La patrimonialisation des formes musicales et artistiques: anthropologie d'une notion problématique." *Association Canadienne d'Ethnologie et de Folklore* 35(1):75–101.

Colwell, Andrew. 2018. "Sounding Original: Nature, Indigeneity, and Globalization in Mongolia (and Southern Germany)." PhD diss., Wesleyan University.

———. 2019. "The Return of the Far-Off Past: Voicing Authenticity in Late Socialist Mongolia." *Journal of Folklore Research* 56(1):37–69.

Curtet, Johanni. 2013. *La transmission du höömij, un art du timbre vocal: ethnomusicologie et histoire du chant diphonique mongol*. PhD diss., University of Rennes 2.

———. 2021. "Khöömii, the World Lists, and the Question of Representation." *Asian Music* 52(2): 108–138.

Curtet, Johanni, and Nomindari Shagdarsüren . 2017. *An Anthology of Mongolian Khöömii*. 2 CDs, booklet (46pp.) and 12 online videos. Paris: Routes Nomades/Buda Musique.

Desjacques, Alain. 1988. "Une considération phonétique sur quelques techniques vocales diphoniques mongoles." *Bulletin du Centre d'Études de Musique Orientale* 31:46–54.

———. 1992. *Chants de l'Altaï mongol*. PhD diss., University of Paris IV-Sorbonne.

———. 2009. *Rhapsodie en sol mongol*. Lille: Le Rifle.

Enebish, Jambal. 2009. "Khöömeilekh urlag" [The art of performing khöömii]. *Khögjmiin urlag sudlal* [Studies on the art of music] 22:155–160.

Foster, Michael Dylan, and Emily Gilman. 2015. *UNESCO on the Ground: Local Perspectives on Intangible Cultural Heritage.* Bloomington: Indiana University Press.

Hamayon, Roberte. 1990. *La chasse à l'âme: esquisse d'une théorie du chamanisme sibérien.* Nanterre: Université Paris-X, Société d'ethnologie.

Hangin, Gombojab, and John R. Krueger. 1986. *A Modern Mongolian-English Dictionary.* Indiana University Uralic and Altaic series, 150. Bloomington: Indiana University, Research Institute for Inner Asian Studies.

Jargalsaikhan, Tsamb. 2007. *Soël urlag shine nökhtsöld-V. Soël, urlagiin ajiltnuudad zoriulsan gariin avlaga* (The New Terms of Art and Culture Vol.5. Handbook for the Art and Culture Sector Employees). Ulaanbaatar: Ministry of Education, Culture and Science.

Khaznadar, Chérif. 2009. "Les dangers qui guettent la convention de 2003. *Internationale de l'Imaginaire.*" *Le patrimoine culturel immatériel à la lumière de l'extrême-orient,* 24:101–109.

Kherlen, Lkhasüren. 2010. *Mongol khöömein utga kholbogdol.* Ulaanbaatar: National University of Mongolia.

Legrain, Laurent. 2007. "Chants longs, rivières et mémoire, in *journée d'étude 'Perceptions esthétiques en contexte mongol.'*" Paris: 3e congrès du Réseau Asie.

———. 2009. "Façonner des musiques et des territoires: l'expérience d'écoute des Darkhad de Mongolie septentrionale." In *Comment la musique vient aux territoires,* edited by Yves Raibaud, 85–103. Pessac: MSHA/Ades-CNRS.

———. 2011. S'attacher à transmettre et transmettre un attachement: Les Darhad, leur répertoire et le continuum sonore en Mongolie contemporaine. PhD diss., Université Libre de Bruxelles, Ecole Pratique des Hautes Etudes.

Levin, Theodore, and Valentina Süzükei. 2006. *Where Rivers and Mountains Sing: Sound, Music and Nomadism in Tuva and Beyond.* Bloomington: Indiana University Press.

Marsh, Peter. 2009. *The Horse-head Fiddle and the Cosmopolitan Reimagination of Tradition in Mongolia.* New York: Routledge.

Mergejikh, Fülongag. 1997. *"Khooloin tsooryn nooz"* [The secret of khooloin tsoor]. In *Mongol dagu khögjim-un sudulul,* 92–97. Studies on Mongolian Music. Urumci: Sinžijang-un arad-un heblel-un horiya.

Mongol ulsyn yerönkhiilögchiin Mongol khöömiin urlagiig khögjüülekh tukhai zarlig [Decree of the President on the development of the art of khöömei]. 2006. Ulaanbaatar.

Nomindari, Shagdarsüren. 2010. *Mongol uls dakh Soyolyn biet bus öviin khadgalalt, khamgaalaltyn ulamjlal, shinechleliin asuudald* [Questions on safeguarding intangible cultural heritage in Mongolia: tradition and modernization]. Masters thesis, Ghengis Khan University, Ulaanbaatar.

Nomindari, Shagdarsüren. 2012. "Safeguarding Intangible Cultural Heritage in Mongolia: Needs and Challenges." In *Asian Cooperation Program on Conservation Science, The 1st ACPCS Workshop, Establishing a Platform for Building a Regional Capacity,* 70-80. Daejon: National Research Institute of Cultural Heritage.

Nomindari, Shagdarsüren, and Johanni Curtet. 2015. "Les transformations d'un patrimoine immatériel mongol: de pratiques locales du *khöömii* à l'objet d'une patrimonialisation." In *Le Patrimoine Culturel Immatériel. Regards croisés de France et d'Allemagne*, 74–87. Les Cahiers du CFPCI, 3. Vitré: CFPCI.

Parent, Marie-Christine. 2010. "La patrimonialisation et l'appropriation des traditions musicales: quelques exemples brésiliens." *Les Cahiers de la Société québécoise de recherche en musique* 11(1–2):137–147.

Pegg, Carole. 1991. "'The Revival of Ethnic and Cultural Identity in West Mongolia: The Altai Uriangkhai *Tsuur*, the Tuvan *Shuur* and the Kazak *Sybyzgy*." *Journal of the Anglo-Mongolian Society* XIII (1–2):71–84.

———. 1992. "Mongolian Conceptualizations of Overtone Singing." *British Journal of Ethnomusicology* 1:31-53.

———. 2001. *Mongolian Music, Dance, and Oral Narrative: Performing Diverse Identities*. Seattle: University of Washington Press.

Sandagjav, Erdene-Ochir. 2010. *Mongol khöömei* [Mongolian khöömei]. Ulaanbaatar: Soyombo.

Stolpe, Ines. 2008. "Display and Performance in Mongolian Cultural Campaigns." In *Conflict and Social Order in Tibet and Inner Asia*, edited by T. Huber and F. Pirie, 59–84. Leiden: Brill.

Tongeren, Mark, van. 1995. "A Tuvan Perspective on Throat Singing." In *Oideion: The Performing Arts World-wide*, edited by Wim van Zanten and Marjolijn van Roon, 293–312. Leiden: Centre of Non-Western Studies.

Trân, Quang, Hai. 1975. "Technique de la voix chantée mongole: Xöömij." *Bulletin du Centre d'études de musique orientale* 14–15:32–36.

Tsednee, Sanjjav, dir. 2005. *Khovd aimagiin Chandman' sumyn 80 jiliin oid*. Chandman': Mayor of Chandman'.

Tsetsentsolmon, Baatarnarany. 2015. "Music in Cultural Construction: Nationalisation, Popularisation and Commercialisation of Mongolian Music." *Inner Asia* 17:118–140.

Tsevel, Yadamjav. 1966. *Mongol khelnii tovch tailbar tol'* [Explanatory dictionary of Mongolian Language]. Ulaanbaatar: Ulsyn khevleliin khereg erkhlekh khoroo.

UNESCO. 2003. *Convention for the Safeguarding of the Intangible Cultural Heritage*. Paris: UNESCO. https://ich.unesco.org/en/convention.

———. 2010. *Mongolian Traditional Art of Khöömei*. UNESCO, https://ich.unesco.org/en/RL/mongolian-traditional-art-of-khoomei-00396.

Yoon, Sunmin. 2011. "Chasing the Singers: The Transformation of Long-song (Urtyn Duu) in Post-socialist Mongolia." PhD diss., University of Maryland, College Park.

CHAPTER 9

Mongolian Music, Globalization, and Nomadism

ANDREW COLWELL

This chapter addresses the historical and contemporary relationships of Mongolian musical performers to globalization, a process and discourse that has figured deeply into Mongolian sound worlds as well as ethnomusicological research. In Mongolia, scholars, policy makers, and performers refer to globalization as *dayaarshil*, or sometimes *globalagchlal*. Both terms are direct translations of a notion that probably entered the Mongolian language in the 1990s, after the fall of socialism in 1992, when the country transitioned from authoritarian socialism to free-market democracy. As foreign companies began doing business in Mongolia, musicians and genres began circulating openly into and out of Mongolia as well, resulting in the formation of new rock, pop, or hip-hop scenes, expatriate bands catering to foreign listeners, and cultural tourism focused on nomadic culture. It was around this same time that ethnomusicologists began seeking novel ways of comprehending the burgeoning global picture in response to similar drastic social, cultural, economic, and political changes occurring around the world. These attempts generally fell into two categories, as Martin Stokes (2004) surveyed: sweeping theories of the prevailing capitalist world system (Erlmann 1999; Jameson 1991) and cautious depictions of the emerging transformations (Slobin 1993; Appadurai 1996). Yet both categories emphasized the hegemony of capitalism, worldwide economic interdependency, the commodification of difference in all its forms, rapid cultural change especially in the form of migration and circulation, and the resulting threats to traditional, "folk," or Indigenous culture throughout the world.

Nevertheless, after two decades of transition and scholarship, globalization has revealed itself to be a complicated subject of which no single perspective can take full account, even as global changes continue to shape Mongolian life, music, and scholarship. For such reasons, following the work of scholars such as Anna Tsing (2005), James Clifford (2013:6) conceives of globalization as "a name for the evolving world of connections we know, but can't adequately represent" in contrast to invoking an immanent "foreign," "neoliberal," and "capitalist world system." My conversation with Tserendavaa (see Interlude 4 in this volume) would suggest that such caution to the worldly connections of Mongolian musical performers, whether professional musicians, urban youth, or talented herders, is appropriate. As ethnomusicologist Bob White (2012:4) recommends, scholars of music should "focus on what globalization does or, more precisely, what people do with globalization, rather than fretting over theories or definitions." And so, this chapter provides perspective on the evolving world of connections—and worldly connections—of Mongolian musicians. It asks how these connections developed in the recent or far off past, what they mean in the entangled global present, and what they suggest about the burgeoning futures of Mongolian music in the midst of global change.

Such worldly connections, most notably, have raised questions over what Theodore Levin refers to as "the future of the past" (2016:ix), a widespread concern among cultural producers throughout Inner Asia over the integrity and meaning of cultural heritage in the midst of commercialism, social change, political exigency, and environmental degradation germane to globalization. Mongolian responses to these questions appear to be strategic and evolving, whether in southern Germany or among the Altai Mountains of western Mongolia. While taking advantage of *dayaarshil*'s various promises or benefits, many performers also seek the maintenance of salient values like *yazguur*, a postcolonial notion that fuses the socialistic onus to sound "original, distinct from others" with veneration for "place of origin, birth" (Colwell 2019). Returning to Tserendavaa's reference to the "good" and "bad" paths of "world development" in the interlude, economic opportunity is among the "good" paths. And among the "bad" is the feared demise of *yazguur* as younger performers increasingly learn practices of pastoral origin, like *khöömii* (throat-singing), in urban places. In the opinion of many elder performers and scholars, they thereby forego the sounds and sentiments of *baigal'* (nature, existence) and the pastoral aesthetic it engenders.

Whatever *dayaarshil* entails, this chapter emphasizes that it is a pivotal and evolving moment of drastic change that Mongolians have engaged during a number of innovative, creative, and customary projects and movements since even before the rise of the Mongolian term for globalization, as I discuss in the following section. Following this discussion of what globalization itself means in Mongolia, I discuss how Mongolian musicians have created worldly connections for Mongolian music during and after socialism, when participating in government cultural delegations during socialism, or when forming independent bands with the transition to democracy. *Khöömii* (throat-singing, also overtone singing) features prominently among these delegations and bands as a central means of re-creating and representing Mongolness to the Mongolian nation as much as the international world. As the editors of one world music textbook write, "It is 'overtone singing' that has brought Mongolian music to world attention" (Miller and Shahriari 2012:214). Of course, one could seek to understand globalization in Mongolia from many other sonic or musical perspectives. But these circulations of Mongol musicians, in particular, vividly reminds us to avoid simple oppositions between the global and the local, modernity and tradition, foreignness and Mongolness, innovative change and traditional loss when trying to understand the global futures of Mongolian music.[1]

Globalization and Globalism

Globalization is not only a process, but also a discourse. As a process, it is typically associated with capitalist production and economic interdependency, and their corresponding social or political effects. But as an idea, it has also been leveraged to promote neoliberal or Euro-American interests at home and beyond. For these reasons, some scholars take care to distinguish "globalization," the *process* entangling disparate peoples and places through mutual and capitalistic economic dependency, from "globalism," the *discourse* of promoting capitalism to serve neoliberal or Eurocentric agendas.[2] In this light, it can certainly be said that *globalism* took root in Mongolia alongside the drastic changes of transitioning to a free-market democracy in the early 1990s. But in the case of *globalization*, there are important socialist and pre-socialist precedents that have long shaped not only the societies and economy of Mongolia, but also the culture and music of Mongol peoples. Most importantly, these precedents challenge perceptions that Mongolian musical culture arose from an untouched, purely nomadic, and insular traditional society that is now suddenly facing the external, foreign threats of globalization.

To begin with, world-systems scholars, in fact, debate when and where globalization first started taking place. André Frank and Barry Gills (1993), for example, note that trade across long distances and capital accumulation (both typified hallmarks of globalization) have existed for at least 5,000 years while Janet Abu-Lughod (1989) stresses its advent in Eurasian societies before the age of European hegemony starting around 1500 C.E. Christopher Beckwith, meanwhile, considers the role of Inner Asian and especially Mongol empires in shaping trade and capital accumulation well before 1500 C.E. (2009). A host of other scholars have also sought to rethink, or rather finally acknowledge, the central role of Mongol peoples in engendering globalization itself (Weatherford

2004). The resulting connections and changes of this historical globalization and empire still resonate today in the shared sounds, sentiments, and musical practices of Eurasia's historically sedentary and nomadic peoples. Lutes, fiddles, and oral traditions like epic singing, which were reframed in the twentieth century as national icons by Soviet socialist governments or as unique examples of cultural heritage by international organizations like UNESCO, demonstrate these long-standing regional interconnections in their construction, aesthetic values, and associated meanings.[3]

Globalism, on the other hand, is more circumspect in its account of worldly interconnection. Globalist narratives typically suggest that globalization began with the advent of European capitalism, industrialization, and democracy in the eighteenth and nineteenth centuries. Western Europeans, accordingly, then exported these modes of production and governance to "the rest of the world," resulting in a global increase in living standards and food production that alternative modes of production (such as socialism, agrarianism, hunter-gathering, or pastoralism) cannot achieve.[4] The fall of the Soviet Union, in particular, led many scholars to portray globalization as an inevitable, and even "natural," historical force with European origins that would eventually sweep up the rest of humanity (Fukuyama 1992). The ensuing adoption of free market economy and democracy throughout most of the world seemed, for many, to evidence a corresponding argument that "opening up" to the capitalist world necessitates leaving behind pastoralism in order "to catch up" in terms of "development." The most renowned exponent of this view is former Mongolian president Enkhbayar Nyambar (2005–2009). As he is famously quoted when discussing his perspective on the question of national development, "It is not my desire to destroy the original Mongolian identity but in order to survive we have to stop being nomads." (Murphy 2001:30). Many similar narratives of opposition between modernity and tradition, capitalism and pastoralism, the future and the past, continue to discuss globalization as an inevitable outcome, as the one and only way in which modern societies around the world can organize their economies (Campi 2006).

However, there is no inherent opposition between economic, social, cultural, or political systems like pastoralism and capitalism. As anthropologists Caroline Humphrey and David Sneath stress, pastoralism "is compatible with many different social and economic systems, including technologically advanced and market-oriented ones" (1999:3). Instead, it is adherents of ideologies like globalism or modernism that promote perceptions that pastoralism has no future in "the modern world." As with the desire to distinguish globalization from globalism, some scholars respond to this problem by distinguishing pastoral *lifeways* from the *discourse* of stereotyping pastoralists by reserving the term "nomadism." *Nomadism*, in their usage, refers to the Inner Asian variant of Orientalism that portrays pastoral peoples as "wanderers," "barbarians," or "peaceful wild-people" (Said 1978; Sneath 2007; Orhon 2011). *Pastoralism* refers to the lifeway of herders who practice transhumance and are highly mobile. I have found it very useful to take up this distinction when writing about Mongolian music, although important to note is that many scholars also use these two words interchangeably when referring to either the discourse or the lifeway. In the performance of Mongolian traditional music, a similar dynamic between the discourse of nomadism and pastoral lifeways plays out. Many musicians must address a tension between urban economic livelihoods centered around representing a nomadic Mongolia and the original aesthetic of *yazguur* that privileges pastoral relations with *baigal'*.

In any case, it is globalism—not socio-economic reality or culture itself—that presumes globalization to be an all or nothing at all conflict between one way of life and another. More recent scholarship, accordingly, has sought to complicate the Eurocentric simplicity of globalism by lending due attention to the role of non-European peoples in coproducing globalization. It also draws more attention to the severe ecological and climactic impacts of global capitalism that are undermining living standards (especially of lower income, non-European peoples) and to the loss of traditional knowledge, practices, and lifeways as societies or peoples integrate, often by force, with the global economy.[5] Accordingly, Mongolian music reveals a long and complicated range of worldly connections both on the steppe and on the stage.

Globalization, in this light, is a conflicted process that is entangling disparate worldviews and social worlds, engendering debates and discussions about the future and meaning of what makes music "Mongol." On one hand, global integration promises access to foreign world music markets for professionally trained musicians and, for rural herders more often without professional backgrounds, a degree of access to cultural tourists interested in pastoralism. On the other, such access is concomitant with larger social transformations, such as mining, urbanization, and government economic policy that contribute to the undermining of pastoralism as a viable lifeway across Mongolia. Today, many bands professionally trained in the performance of traditional or national music incorporate novel genres (such as heavy metal or alternative rock) and instruments (such as the guitar or djembe) while some rural herders pursue their own stake in the cultural tourism market as entrepreneurs by networking with tourists directly or through tourism companies. On television or in the yurt, scholars, elders, musicians, and publics continue to debate what "Mongol music" should or could sound like if it is to reflect pastoralism, history, and traditional values alongside Mongolia's long history of engendering and pursuing worldly connection.

Soviet Internationalism and "Cultural Development"

Both domestic and foreign listeners tend to regard traditional music as among the most nomadic, ancient, and original of Mongolian expressions. For example, on April 30, 2015, many Mongolians were excited to learn that the band Khusugtun had qualified for the final stage of *Asia's Got Talent*. Many supporters had been spreading the news and had concerted their efforts to get the vote out in favor of Khusugtun. While the band's first performance in episode two had been a success for the judges, it was the fans alone who could vote them into the top nine. The effort worked and was widely reported and commented upon in Mongolian newspapers, television, and social media. As one commenter stated just days before the finale in the comments to a news article in the UB Post, "You are almost a world band."[6] As for the members, they seemed to be fulfilling their raison d'etre. As they describe themselves on their website,

> We are a group of Mongolian folk musicians with the objective of bringing Traditional Mongolian music to the world. We are inspired by our nomadic ancestry and by our historic civilization. In addition to the traditional instruments of our group, we also incorporate the breath taking throat singing of our forefathers. We hope you can feel the passion and pride in our music as strongly as we do. We are KHUSUGTUN . . . conveyors of the Mongolian nomadic culture.[7]

After hearing the band perform "a traditional Mongolian musical piece, initially starting with bird chirps and a few instruments," one Mongolian journalist wrote (B.Tungalog 2015), the celebrity judges then gave highly positive remarks and the band eventually secured second place, a remarkable feat.

There is indeed compelling evidence to suggest that various Turkic and Mongolic peoples of Inner Asia have long practiced instrumental or vocal practices like those that Khusugtun presents for millennia, possibly in relation to animistic and pastoral customs and lifeways. At the same time, a significant amount of archival evidence, oral testimonies, and scholarship show how traditional Mongolian musicians continuously transform these practices in relationship to contemporary lifeways, economics, and politics. For example, when socialist cultural policy began implementing musical educational programs to professionalize Mongolian musicians in the 1950s, *khöömiich* (throat-singers) began experimenting with novel formats, aesthetics, and settings in order to reflect a socialist professional aesthetic, radically transforming the techniques and meanings of the vocal practice in the process. These socialist-era transformations then became foundations for the performance of traditional musics and dance forms on the stage, lasting into the democratic-era and influencing performers like Khusugtun to this day.[8] It was no different in the case of many other practices, such as the horse fiddle (*morin khuur*), which gained its f-holes through the collaborations of Soviet and Mongolian luthiers (Marsh 2009). These performative transformations stemmed in no insignificant part from the creative drive of talented musicians, who were genuinely interested in the unfamiliar possibilities of professional stage performance. But the authoritarian Mongolian People's Republic (MPR), a satellite state to the Soviet Union, and its socialist policies of "cultural development," national distinction, and international recognition, first set these transformations into motion (Pegg 2001; Marsh 2009).

During the 1950s, in particular, the Soviet Union sought to forge international relationships after decades of isolationism under Stalin's leadership in a bid to compete with the United States for allies in the so-called Third World and to promote its own version of modernity. As Tobias Rupprecht (2015:3) writes, "Internationalism was not only an empty political catchphrase, but an ideal that many soviet scholars, intellectuals, cultural figures, political decision makers and, through the consumption of internationalist cultural products, ordinary citizens actually subscribed to." Following historians Tom Ginsburg (1999) and echoing Chatterjee (1989), ethnomusicologist Peter Marsh (2009:99) discusses how Mongolian elites "cultivated close relationships with their Soviet counterparts as a calculated political strategy, like those among other colonized peoples in history, i.e., learning to use the tools of power colonialists held in order to claim a degree of control over themselves." Accomplishing this goal required, in part, the international promotion of socialism as a viable, inclusive, and alternative world order to the emerging democratic capitalism of western Europe and the United States. And one way to do so was by organizing large, televised cultural festivals with Soviet-aligned nations, like Mongolia (a satellite state) or Cuba (a fellow socialist nation).

In this vein, the MPR regularly included select professional musicians in cultural delegations that traveled overseas annually to promote national culture at the World Youth Festivals, national competitions, or other cultural events. This international effort started in the 1950s, in tow with the Soviet Union's policy of internationalism, and was accompanied by a domestic effort to identify and professionally train rural talents at newly built district, provincial, and national musical institutions. Following the lead of the Soviet Composer's Union and official Soviet folklorists sent to document and "develop" Mongolian folk music (Smirnov 1975), Mongolian composers and musicians, both amateur and professional, were then tasked with creating a "national culture" to announce the young Mongolian socialist nation on not just any "stage" (*taiz*), but "the *world* stage" (*tavtsan*), a notion for which Khalkh Mongolian reserves a distinct term. They did so by adapting traditional practices or genres to the acoustic and aesthetic demands of the stage, long before the commercial adjustments of post-socialist musicians to cultural tourism and concert touring.[9]

The performative results were radically transformative, especially in the case of *khöömii*. For example, the music scholar Jamts Badraa (1998:47), who played a direct role in cultural policy at the time, writes in retrospect of how the vocal practice was not yet "developed" before the 1950s. For him, this meant that *khöömiich* did not yet perform recognized folk song melodies, which for government cultural policy of the time especially instantiated "national culture," echoing an emphasis placed on promoting folk music throughout the Soviet Union (Levin 1996; Olson 2004). Instead, interviews, archival recordings, and scholarship suggest that Mongol *khöömiich* performed a small set of "tunes," such as "The Melody of the River Eev," or mimetic improvisations in informal settings, such as when herding alone or in communal gatherings. As Curtet details in this volume (see Chapter 8), this situation changed in the 1950s with the first performances of *khöömii* on stage, the first through-composed arrangements that included *khöömii* performance, and the creative explorations of Chimeddorj Gaanjuur, who first learned how to perform folk song melodies with *khöömii*. It was through these first encounters, seminal concerts, and aesthetic transformations that *khöömii* first registered under socialism's cultural radar as "national culture" for Mongolian intellectuals, elites, music researchers, and publics in the capital and beyond.

As is well detailed in the literature and interviews, Chimeddorj was first to introduce *khöömii* to "the world" when participating in cultural delegation tours to Europe and East Asia, including the Fifth World Youth Festival in Warsaw, Poland, in 1955. Of the 134 Mongolian participants (Krzywicki 2009:305), just one was a khöömiich, the rest being singers, dancers, athletes, intellectuals, and politicians. Rare black and white footage of this seminal performance reveals one of the first times that Mongol *khöömii* "opened up to the world," this time in the auditorium of the Palace of Culture and Science. Members of cultural delegations from other countries sit in the myriad rows, which extend upward into the indoor distances of the auditorium. We then cut to a close-up of the folk choir, a popular Soviet-era musical genre (Smith 1997; Olson 2004), this time with the composer Damdinsüren Bileg conducting. The camera pans from left to right to highlight the upright qualities of the singers as stand-ins for the Mongolian people, women in front and men in the back. After several minutes of an upbeat, march-like performance, the conductor eventually seems to nod at a member of the choir, and the other singers fade into a low hum. A metallic whistle sounds at a fifth above the choral arrangement's tonic, and then flutters down and resolves. The camera cuts to the folk choir again, except now a man is standing out in front. It is Chimeddorj. His hands are behind his back. His lips are pursed and motionless, despite emitting a wide range of pitches along with a drone. He repeats the same phrase as the choral voices continue to hum. We cut once more to the lofty ceiling and farthest seating of the auditorium. The camera seems to suggest that the sound is "up there," too, reaching the international world. But then the scene cuts abruptly to the end of the choral performance. The choir bows in unison twice as the audience roars with applause.

The state-honored singer, Zangad, who performed at this festival, preserved and kindly shared the program for this concert. While the Polish-language program does not mention *khöömii* at all, it does provide insight into the significance of the first worldly connection of Mongolian khöömii under socialism. The following brief description and lyrics are given for "Pochwala Altaju" (Altai Praise-song):

"ALTAI PRAISE-SONG"
An old Mongolian song about the mighty Altai Mountains of the MPR

From their eternally snow-capped peaks
The meadowy and forested slopes
Beautiful and generous
Ever mighty
Flowing Altai
Famous Altai
Abundant Altai[10]

The language of the program's introduction is explicit and didactic: "The youth," who are "democratic," we are told, are already invested in "a global fight," as are "all people of good will," for a "better future, for peace, and friendship." We are told that the festival itself is a "review of the power of the youth of the whole world." The program continues by indicating how the festival's performers, each representing their "nationality," in its specifically Soviet sense (see Hirsch 2005), demonstrate this "good will" and worldly engagement via the presentation of their respective musical performances. But it is important to recall the state-honored horse fiddler Batchuluun Tsend here, who said in an interview with the linguist Saruul-Erdene Myagmar, "If you didn't sing like Norovbanzad [the famed long song singer] you didn't go overseas."[11] Under the gaze of the international world, only select talents could stand in for the nation by reflecting the aesthetic ideology of socialism.

The aim of cultural delegations was not only to demonstrate cultural distinction to "the world," but also, conversely, to "the nation," producing a feedback loop between foreign and domestic perceptions, aesthetics, and values, as was the case with Tuvan *khöömii* (Beahrs 2014). One channel of this feedback loop consisted of published reports on the achievements of cultural delegations in official journals like *Soyol* (*Culture*). One particularly exemplary report comes from Lkhavsüren (1973:44), the head of a cultural delegation to the 1973 World Youth Festival in partition-era Berlin. He noted how . . .

> [a]t the great festival, we successfully included our art, receiving praise from the government for the development of our national art—proof of our ongoing attention and consideration—while our artists demonstrated the energy they are putting into their creative efforts.

Socialism, as the numbers in Lkhavsüren's report evidence, was highly invested in quantifying "cultural development" by giving numbers of participants, medals, feats, estimated audience size, or collaborations with radios or orchestras. Over seventy "talents" participated, many of them achieving a "professional level" of performance to receive nineteen medals altogether, including gold for the delegation's sole khöömiich. Sengedorj Nanjid (1948–2020), originally a herder-cum-construction-worker from Chandman' sum (district) who could sound khöömii very well, was one such example of "professional uplift." Two years after he participated in the 1973 World Youth Festival in Berlin, he became the resident *khöömiich* at Khovd aimag (province)'s Music and Drama Theater, in addition to working there as an actor. In our interview, he regarded "cultural development" positively while noting conflicts between socialist ideology and Indigenous aesthetics elsewhere. As he stated,

> We prepared for two months. We did so much preparation. And so, before going abroad they taught classes on how to posture your body correctly. One had to be cultured when arriving at those countries, one had to posture their body and go in a cultured way. The government supervised as much as possible. I fondly remember those times. From getting off at the station to the food, we received the healthiest and highest quality treatment because these were officially connected things. (Interview, September 26, 2013)

Whether a well-known genre like long-song, or a then-rare vocal practice like khöömii, everyone was taken very seriously as a representative in delegations since "culture," in a particularly socialist sense (Stolpe 2008; Tsetsentsolmon 2014) was considered a sanctified mode of address between nations within the Soviet sphere of influence (Rouland 2004; Rupprecht 2015).

Originality, Cultural Sovereignty, and Nomadism

Beyond the Soviet sphere of influence, however, listeners understood Mongolian traditional music in somewhat different terms, as became evident as the Mongolian government began pursuing diplomatic relationships with nonsocialist nations. Japan was among the most significant of these new worldly connections, eventually becoming the largest development assistance provider to Mongolia (Narangoa 2009:373). For example, the Japan Foundation sponsored a cultural exchange project in 1978 to promote "communication and exchange between Asian countries in the field of *traditional* performing arts" (Emmert and Minegishi 1980:vi; italics added), centering around the theme of that year: the voice. The Mongolian delegation included Norovbanzad, the famed long-song singer, and Sundui, another Chandman' native whose style would eventually become hailed as an aesthetic ideal among later generations of khöömiich. Involved researchers and musicians alike focused on "points of comparison" arising from "voice production, text, melody relationships, techniques, textual content, revealing a people's way of thinking and feeling" (ibid.). But important to note here is how the authors of the report resulting from this cultural exchange emphasized the locality, tradition, and nomadic origins of *khöömii*, while contemporary Mongolian accounts of overseas performances typically inspired perceptions that khöömii was of "international quality," "developed," and even an exemplar of "world classical music." Numerous biographical descriptions of Sundui, for example, valorize his performances in the 1970s of "world classical works," more specifically the thematic melodies of European masterpieces (Myagmarjav 2015:36), a topic that Curtet details in this volume (see Chapter 8).

These contrasting interpretations of khöömii had important political dimensions, especially as intellectual elites in Mongolia began challenging Soviet Eurocentricism (Marsh 2009:100–120) in the 1980s by legitimizing traditional expressive culture as a worldly pinnacle of its own, as I detail elsewhere (Colwell 2018, 2019). The key figures behind this movement were the famous composer Natsag Jantsannorov and the music scholar Jamts Badraa, but a wide range of performers, music researchers, and officials participated in this effort to increase Mongolian cultural sovereignty. Jantsannorov and Badraa centered their efforts around the legitimation of a novel cultural category called *yazguur* to add to the prevailing categories of "folk," "national," and "classical." Badraa first proposed the notion in the late 1970s when referring to what he called *ardyn yazguur urlag*, which he translated himself into English as "authentic folk art," following European and Soviet folkloristics (2005:56).[12] But it is likely that he also associated *yazguur* with the Russian term *samobytnost'*, meaning "originality," a politically salient concept at the time that he references elsewhere for similar purposes (Badraa 1981 [1978]). Mongolian dictionaries (Tsevel 1966; Bawden 1997) reinforce this suggestion by defining *yazguur* as a reference to "origins" and being "original" depending on its use as a noun or adjective. Badraa's aim was to specify expressive practices that originated in a far-off, pre-socialist, and thus more originally Mongol past, with *khöömii* and long-song serving as his key exemplars. In this light, the accordion could be considered a "folk" practice, but not an "original" one, due to its introduction by the Soviets. For

FIGURE 9.1. Tserendavaa (far left) performs as part of a cultural delegation in 1988 that would eventually go to New York City. Photo courtesy of D. Tserendavaa.

these reasons I translate the term as "originality" in order to reflect these other meanings, which exceed those of "authenticity." In any case, soon after Badraa proposed the idea of *yazguur*, Jantsannorov (1996:156) personally warned the current general secretary, Tsedenbal Yumjaa, on numerous occasions of the possible demise of "original art," eventually securing approval and funding for a national art inspection of rural talents in the early 1980s. *Yazguur* then became an official concern of cultural policy with the issuing of a government resolution toward this inspection's completion (Jantsannorov 1989:19), culminating in the organization of two highly influential cultural festivals in 1983 and 1988 that focused on exemplars of Mongolian originality.

But affiliates of this cultural movement remained concerned with the international world. *Yazguur* performances, in fact, became a means of projecting another Mongolia to foreign audiences, one that was more nomadic than socialist, in a growing official effort to de-associate the satellite state from the Soviet Union and bridge ties with "the West." For example, in 1987 a cultural delegation—headed by Badraa and including Tserendavaa, one of his chief *khöömii* collaborators—performed in New York City at the Asia Society to mark the occasion of establishing official diplomatic ties with the United States (see figure 9.1). A journalist who witnessed the New York concert wrote how the delegation "provided a cogent and charming sampling of traditional Mongolian movement, song and music-making . . . that made one forget one's surroundings," especially the long songs which "evoked dreams of exotic temples and ancient rites" (Sommers, 1987). As for Tserendavaa, his performance of khöömii "sounded just like a synthesizer." After the concert, as Tserendavaa recalled in an interview (May 9, 2014), another incredulous journalist then approached him with a strange request. This journalist believed that Tserendavaa might have a metallic apparatus of some sort lodged in his throat, producing the unfamiliar and seemingly nonhuman sound of *khöömii*. In response, he asked Tserendavaa to eat a banana, an apple, drink some water, and only then perform. Tserendavaa kindly obliged and wowed the journalist even more. For these journalists, Mongolia was terra incognito just as *yazguur* practices like *khöömii* and long-song appeared to them as "mysteries" in need of explanation, recurring to a well-studied Orientalist, and nomadist, trope. But whereas Euro-American audiences tended to focus on the traditionalism, naturalness, and nomadism of these performances, the Mongolian performers also considered themselves to be demonstrating the worldly legitimacy of *yazguur* and Mongolness itself in their pursuit of cultural sovereignty from the Soviet Union. It is also important to note here that the official emphasis on *yazguur* did not translate into a shift in economic policy to promote pastoral lifeways, even after the fall of the Soviet Union, when radical changes associated with globalization would suddenly sweep through a country heading chaotically toward free market democracy.

Egschiglen: A Post-socialist Beginning

The transition to a free market democracy dramatically altered the conditions under which musicians could secure livelihoods. As Marsh reviews (2009:121–123), students began protesting for democratic change in January of 1990, echoing protest movements throughout the Soviet Bloc. A few months later, the Politburo, the principal policy-making committee of the communist party, decided behind closed doors that it would resign. The news soon went public, along with an announcement for democratic elections that same year. To complicate matters, the Soviet Union also dissolved, resulting in the instant cessation of significant economic aid to Mongolia. With socialism's fall in 1992, state-support for the arts and culture in Mongolia vanished overnight. The tögrög, Mongolia's currency, became worthless. Even food became scarce. Musicians had to seek out new livelihoods as cultural institutions closed their doors, leaving their members to their own devices.

But at the same time, the transition engendered novel cultural, economic, and political possibilities, which actors immediately capitalized upon out of existential necessity as much as creative interest. Most significantly, perhaps, the distribution of private passports to citizenry for the first time provided a hitherto unknown option: independent travel overseas. Professional musicians began organizing and managing their own tours, no longer as part of cultural delegations or officially sanctified ensembles like the People's Folk Song and Dance Ensemble (*Ardyn duu büjigiin ulsyn chuulga*) (PFSDE) but as bands and groups of their own making. No longer was it only officially selected exemplars who could tour overseas, as socialist policy once dictated, but any musician with the right blend of connections, talent, and resilience could go. In several highly influential cases, solo artists and bands even emigrated to central or western Europe, especially Germany due its being a hub for world music. Perhaps the most influential of these path-breakers was the band Egschiglen, whose name means "melodious sound." They would set an aesthetic standard for stage performances of Mongolian music for later generations, including Khusugtun over twenty years later. Although Egschiglen's membership has changed over the years, three core members continue to perform regularly after twenty-plus years of expatriate life in Germany. None of the initial members performed khöömii, although that would soon change once they began adjusting to the European world music economy and its growing demand for the vocal practice in the wake of successful Tuvan bands like Huun-Huur-Tu, which began touring internationally in the early 1990s.

Egschiglen was founded in 1991 when its four initial members graduated from the Music and Dance Middle School, now the Music and Dance College. However, they were not yet a band, but rather a quartet of three horse fiddlers—Tümenbayar Migdorj (b.1969), Khayagsaikhan Luvsansharav (b.1971), Tömörsaikhan Janlav (b.1972)—and bass fiddler (*ikh khuurch*) Ganpürev Dagdan (b.1971). The quartet was a socialist import that reserved itself for the performance of music modeled upon European classical music. Egschiglen, however, was founded on the cusp of socialism's fall, so its members were immediately challenged to procure livelihoods without institutional support. At the same time, Euro-American popular music was already making inroads into Mongolian life with the weakening of socialist control in the 1980s. (One socialist-era journal article from 1988 even briefly introduced the heavy metal band Iron Maiden.) Egschiglen altered their repertoire and aesthetic accordingly. Their early repertoire, for example, consisted of the once officially approved works of Mozart and Mongolian classical composers, like Jantsannarov, alongside once banned compositions and composers like the Inner Mongolian horse fiddler Chi Bulag and the Beatles.

But another influence, as the quartet's first horse fiddler Tömörsaikhan explained in our interview (January 11, 2016), was their trip to Tuva in 1991, where they performed with the renowned *khöömiizhi*[13] Gennadi Tumat (1964–1996). This concert featured many other renowned *khöömiizhi* and their groups, including Huun-Huur-Tu (then called Kungurtuk), the highly influential band whose performance style would become an aesthetic model for later Tuvan bands (Levin and Suzukei 2006; Beahrs 2014:75–83). Following the Tuvan tour, Egschiglen remained a quartet. But the experience did convince them that they needed a stronger vocal element in their group. In 1995, they eventually enlisted the now-renowned *khöömiich* Khosbayar "Hosoo" Dangaa (b.1971), who is better known as Hosoo, as he transliterates his own name, and thus expanded their quartet into a band. However, Egschiglen did not emulate the Tuvan band's aesthetic, whose initial releases evinced what Beahrs describes as an "experimental, ambient" and "neotraditional groove" aesthetics. He is referring to Huun-Huur-Tu's engagement with various Euro-American pop and rock qualities to present "old songs and tunes" and evoke the "ancientness" of Tuvan music and *khöömii* while consciously foregoing the Soviet-sanctified aesthetics of prior ensembles (Beahrs 2004:77–84). Egschiglen, by contrast, continued to perform socialist-sanctified classics, relying upon their professional conservatory training, while developing their own approach to *yazguur* performance by incorporating *khöömii*, among other visual and acoustic changes.

In 1993, they had their first opportunity to tour Europe and perform at a range of folk music festivals, thanks to the support and facilitation of an expatriate Mongolian connection residing in Italy. The tour was a pivotal learning experience for Egschiglen, which helped them succeed quickly when they moved to Germany a few years later. As Tömörsaikhan said of the 1993 tour, "Our eyes and ears were opened." It was the same for the audiences. As he elaborated, listening to a Mongolian horse fiddle quartet perform European classical music and the Beatles alongside praise-songs like "Altai Praise-song" came as a big surprise for European audiences for whom Mongolia was wholly unfamiliar. It was the combination of familiar and unfamiliar elements that explained the band's success, Tömörsaikhan surmised. The band adapted quickly, especially by learning from the other bands they encountered during the 1993 tour, and they soon hired an amateur agent called Rudi Wagner to help bring them back the following year in 1994.

Wagner has since continued to operate as a "culture broker" for Mongolian bands in Germany by both managing the logistics of touring for musicians and interpreting Mongolian music for European listeners during pre-concert talks.

As anthropologist Robert Paine writes, the cultural broker is "one who, while purveying values that are not his own, is also purposively making changes of emphasis and/or content" (1971:21). In our interview, Wagner did not elaborate on how he represented Egschiglen in the early 1990s, but he did discuss how he represents Khukh Mongol, a band that was founded by former members of Egschiglen in the late 1990s:

I always tell the people that I will take them on a journey to Mongolia. We will begin with the Altai Mountains and I say what the Altai look like, what livestock there is, and try and associate them [with the music], the region and the mountains, or the desert and the lakes. And the horses. . . . That is really what the people should imagine with their eyes, they are now in the desert or the mountains and hear them. The people must now go there for a little bit. To just make a program, and play a few songs, without any background, is certainly not helpful. If you present it like this, then one experiences it differently and it sticks more. (January 10, 2016)

Egschiglen's record label Albakultur follows this focus on nature and nomadism in its online description for the band's first album release, titled *Traditional Mongolian Song* (*Traditionelle mongolische Lieder*):

On the one hand Mongolian sounds seem *strange* and *mysterious* to *Western* ears. On the other hand the music sounds familiar, expressing *basic human feelings* such as love, longing, sorrow and thankfulness. This album is a collection of *pure traditional* musics from Mongolia presented in *fine-tuned* arrangements. With their virtuosity Egschiglen musically transmit the *harmony* of *their culture* and show an impressive *variety* and *delicacy* of expression.[14] (italics added)

But despite this strategy tailored to European nomadist perceptions of Inner Asian pastoralists, bands like Khukh Mongol and Egschiglen are invested in performing *yazguur* in order to promote and legitimate Mongolian culture on a worldly scale as much as to succeed in the world music economy.

The pieces on the album, accordingly, reflect a diversity of genres that do not easily fit into the Euro-American notions of traditionalism and nomadism in that many of them are socialist-era compositions by Mongolian classical composers (e.g., "On the Shore of Flower Lake" by C.Sükhbaatar and "Serenade" by Mend-Amar Jambal) based upon European classical harmony and composition. Others are novel reinterpretations of traditional genres, like the praise-song (*magtaal*), that were thoroughly reworked to suit the aesthetics of the concert stage ("Dunjingarav praise-song" and "Altai praise-song") despite their roots in pastoral epic ritual and customs. Such cultural brokerage and adaption are key practices for many musicians who are invested in representing themselves to novel audiences, especially in Europe and North America, requiring them to "reproduce and transform tradition in dialogue with the people, places, and ideas they encounter" (Ruskin 2011:86; Klein 2007), reflecting the productive and destructive "frictions" of globalization (Tsing 2005).

These frictions had ramification not only for expatriate musicians in Germany but also among musicians in Mongolia who were similarly invested in performing and representing *yazguur* in the post-socialist era. After the successful release of Egschiglen's second album, *Gobi*, in 1997, for example, Hosoo, along with bassist Ganpürev, left to start a briefly extant band together. They, in turn, parted ways to establish more enduring bands of their own, like the latter's Boerte (founded in 2000) and the former's TransMongolia (founded in 2005), which Hosoo founded after establishing himself as a solo artist. Before them, Erdenebold Dashtseren, a flautist who briefly joined Egschiglen for their early overseas tours, did the same when establishing Khukh Mongol. The memberships of these expatriate offshoots would change more regularly than Egschiglen's over the following years, creating a transnational circuit of Mongolian musicians. After seeking success primarily in Germany, as their predecessors had, these circulating musicians then tended to move back to Mongolia, where they formed other bands of their own that would then travel overseas, in turn, by relying upon their expatriate knowledge of the world music economy.

Many of these "third generation" offshoots are now themselves aesthetic and economic models of performance for younger musicians graduating from the music programs at Ulaanbaatar's colleges and universities. The leaders of Domog (founded in 2006) and Khusugtun (also founded in 2006), for example, both had brief stints as members of Khukh Mongol, and the members of Sedaa (founded in 2010) got their start in Hosoo's band TransMongolia. After two decades of transnational circulations and offshoots, devising a comprehensive list of all these members would require some in-depth genealogical research. Other bands took cues from Egschiglen by experimenting with the band format's instrumentation and genres to explore aesthetics such as "folk rock," in the case of Altan Urag in the 2000s, or more recently "folk metal" in the case of the Hu (see Chapter 10 in this volume).

The expatriate experiences also helped many musicians to do business in the cultural tourism industry that arose after the fall of socialism. Today, *khöömii* is a critical element of any of the myriad culture shows in Ulaanbaatar that tailor to foreigners by performing only during the summer tourist season. But anyone can easily hire a *khöömiich* or a band to perform privately at their hotel or yurt camp thanks to formal and informal verbal contracts between tourism organizations and musicians. Individual entrepreneurs have also sought to leverage cultural tourism on their own terms, and in the case of Hosoo, the aim is not only to do business but also to expose foreigners to a more *yazguur* Mongolia. He became particularly adept at leveraging cultural tourism to complement his economic life in Germany, even obtaining a degree in business management from a German university. In the early 2000s, he began leading his own cultural tours to Mongolia, personally escorting his guests to his hometown of Chandman' sum (rural district) in Khovd aimag where he conducted plein air *khöömii* workshops that focused on understanding the vocal practice, and pastoral music more generally, in its original context. Later tours, however, have ceased to travel to Chandman' sum for logistical and budgeting purposes. Participants have tended to be Germanic amateur musicians or vocalists who learned about the tour when attending Hosoo's concerts or workshops in Central Europe.

Conclusion

Expatriate concert touring and domestic cultural tourism have engendered ongoing debates over the meaning of *yazguur* and Mongolian identity in what some intellectuals refer to as "the age of the free market." Mongolian music researcher Kherlen Lkhavsüren (2010), for example, is among those who hail the post-socialist promotion and popularization of Mongol *khöömii* while addressing the challenges of globalization. The critical issue for her is how Mongolians are "to combine" globalization and "original folk art" (ibid:5). Hosoo himself addressed this same tension in our interview when problematizing the transmission of khöömii in non-pastoral, and thus non-original, settings where *yazguur* aesthetic values are foregone in the absence of nature (September 9, 2013). The music scholar Jambal Enebish makes a similar point in an article on the problems of preserving the cultural heritage of Mongolian "people of the felt tent" (*tuurgatan*), a pan-nomadic term for Inner Asian peoples who reside in yurts, regardless of their Turkic or Mongolic ethnicity. As he writes,

> It is impossible to consider the artistic thinking of Mongolian people who were raised in pastoral lifeways, along with the real meaning and significance of their creative means, apart from the nature that birthed them, their geographic surroundings, the seasons, daily living with herds, custom, and free labor. (2012:71)

He goes on to argue for a focus on the "artistic thought" of pastoral culture bearers alongside a more direct consideration in cultural heritage preservation of *baigal'* due its role as a moral authority and aesthetic model in pastoral expressive culture.

Significant efforts to promote and preserve cultural heritage have sought to address such widespread concerns in the last two decades. However, the democratic government remains focused on promoting mining, sedentarization, higher education, and tourism—all factors that are radically challenging or effecting pastoral communities throughout Mongolia. Musical actors throughout Central Asia remain concerned with "the future of the past," as Levin puts it, and "how traditional forms of music-making are being adapted, appropriated, transformed, and revitalized by a variety of contemporary actors and stakeholders in the domain of arts and culture" (2016:ix). While some argue that Mongol *khöömii* has successfully been "preserved" and "developed" into a "worldly classical art," others lament that the "original quality" of *khöömii* is either on the brink of "destruction" (*ustgal*) or has already been destroyed despite record numbers of professionally trained *khöömiich* at Ulaanbaatar's conservatories. These laments accompany discussions about globalization wherein cultural heritage requires "preservation" at the risk of its loss as society "develops" further and further away from the past, the source of Mongolian origins and originality. On one hand, socialist-era "cultural development" reveals how aesthetics, notions, and practices now considered to be *yazguur* arose out of a creative dialogue with foreign aesthetics, formats, and performance settings. On the other hand, the increasing unfamiliarity of younger performers of Mongolian music with pastoralism and its environmental musical aesthetics would seem to suggest that Mongolia is indeed at a hitherto unencountered crossroads, even despite its long history of worldly interconnection. Whatever globalization and "world development" entail, to return to Tserendavaa's words, it is critical to understand how these processes continue to open up paths that are both "good" and "bad," productive and destructive, original and interconnected in a globalizing Mongolia.

Notes

1. See our companion website, www.mongoliansoundworlds.org, for additional information on the musical traditions included in this volume.

2. See Fairclough (2006) and Turino (2003) for cogent discussions of these terms and the relationship between the processes of globalization and neoliberal discourses that self-associate with them. Marin (2008), Sneath (2002), and Stolpe (2006) provide various perspectives from Mongolian studies on the subject of globalization and globalism in Mongolia.

3. See Levin (1996), Levin and Suzukei (2006), Levin and During (2002), and Levin, Daukeyeva, and Küchümkulova (2016), among many others, for perspectives on these regional interconnections.

4. See Turino (2003) for an overview of examples of globalism in the scholarly literature on globalization, including in ethnomusicology.

5. See Apffel-Marglin and Marglin 2011[1990];et al. ; Humphrey and Sneath (1999); Buyandelger (2008); and Schwartz, ed. (2006), among many others, for a range of alternative perspectives onto the impacts of globalization and development in Mongolia and beyond.

6. See http://ubpost.mongolnews.mn/?p=14397. Accessed May 25, 2017.

7. See: http://www.khusugtun-group.com/#about. Accessed May 25, 2017.

8. See Levin and Suzukei (2006); Enebish (2012); Curtet (2013); Beahrs (2014); Colwell (2018).

9. See Pegg (2001) and Marsh (2009) for a range of musical perspectives on socialist "cultural development" in Mongolia and Central Asia.

10. All translations from the Polish by Agnieszka Rec.

11. See http://saruul.niitlelch.mn/content/8319.shtml. Accessed June 2, 2017.

12. The exact date of this article is not made clear but circumstantial evidence suggests that it was published in the late 1970s.

13. The Tuvan spelling for *khöömiich*, although the term also implies the performer to be a master.

14. See http://www.albakultur.de/egschiglencds.html. Accessed May 27, 2017.

Bibliography

Abu-Lughod, Janet. 1989. *Before European Hegemony: The World System A.D. 1250–1350*. New York: Oxford University Press.

Apffel-Marglin, Frédérique, and Stephan Marglin. 2011[1990]. *Dominating Knowledge: Development, Culture, and Resistance*. Oxford: Oxford University Press.

Apffel-Marglin, Frederique, Sanjay Kumar, and Arvind Mishra. 2010. *Interrogating Development: Insights from the Margins*. New York: Oxford University Press.

Appadurai, Arjun. 1996. *Modernity at Large: Cultural Dimensions of Globalization*. Minneapolis: The University of Minnesota Press.

Badraa, Jamts. 1998. *Mongolian Folk Music* [Mongol ardyn khögjim]. Ulaanbaatar: T&U Printing Company.

———. 1981 [1978]. "'Høømi' i 'urtyn duu'-specificheskie javlenija mongol'skoj tradicionnoj klassicheskoj muzyki"] ['Xöömei' and 'long song': Specific phenomena of Mongolian traditional classical music]. In *Professonal'naja mukyka: ustnoj tradicii narodov blizhnego, srednego vostoka i sovremennost'* [Professional music: Oral traditions of the Near and Middle East, and modernity], edited by Yu.V. Keldysh, F. M. Karamatov & D. A.Rashidova, 116–119. Tashkent: The Gafura Gujama Press for Literature and Art.

———. 2005[1977]. *"Ardyn uran büteeliin sudlakh arga zuin acuudald"* The problem of a methodology for studying folk creative works]. In *Ardyn bilig ukhaany on's* [Folklore: Intellectual matters], 47–57. Ulaanbaatar: Bembi San Printing.

Batchuluun, Tsend. 2009. Quartet of Morin Khuur. Ulaanbaatar: ADMON.

Bawden, Charles. 1997. *Mongolian-English Dictionary*. New York: Kegan Paul International.

Beahrs, Robert. 2014. "Post-Soviet Tuvan Throat-Singing (Xöömei) and the Circulation of Nomadic Sensibility." *PhD diss.*, University of California, Berkeley.

Beckwith, Christopher I. 2009. *Empires of the Silkroad: A History of Central Eurasia from the Bronze Age to the Present*. Princeton: Princeton University Press.

Buyandelger, Manduhai. 2008. "Post-Post-Transition Theories: Walking on Multiple Paths." *Annual Review of Anthropology* 37:235–50.

Campi, Alicia. August, 2005. "Globalization's Impact on Mongolian Identity Issues." Paper given at The 800th Anniversary Conference. Ulaanbaatar, Mongolia.

Clifford, James. 2013. *Returns*. Cambridge: Harvard University Press.

Colwell, Andrew. 2018. "Sounding Original: Nature, Indigeneity, and Globalization in Mongolia (and Southern Germany)." PhD diss., Wesleyan University.

———. 2019. "The Return of the Far-Off Past: Voicing Authenticity in Late Socialist Mongolia." *Journal of Folklore Research* 56(1):37–69.

Curtet, Johanni. 2013. "La transmission du *höömij*, un art du timbre vocal: ethnomusicologie et histoire du chant diphonique mongol." PhD diss., Université Rennes 2.

Emmert, Richard and Yuki Minegishi. 1980. *Musical Voices of Asia: Report of Asian Traditional Performing Arts*. Tokyo: Heibonsha.

Enebish, Jambal. 2012. "Mongol tuurgatny biyet bus soyolyn öviig khadgalakh, khamgaalakh asuudal" [The problem of preserving and protecting the Intangible Cultural Heritage of Mongolian felt-tent dwellers]. In *Mongolyn khögjim cydlalyn deej bichig* [The best of Mongolian music research], edited by author, 70–77. Ulaanbaatar: The Ministry of Education, Culture, and Science.

Erlmann, Veit. 1999. *Music, Modernity and the Global Imagination*. New York: Oxford University Press.

Fairclough, Norman. 2006. *Language and Globalization*. New York: Routledge.

Frank, André Gunder, and Barry Gills. 1993. *The World System: Five Hundred Years or Five Thousand?* New York: Routledge.

Fukuyama, Francis. 1992. *The End of History and the Last Man*. New York: The Free Press.

Hirsch, Francine. 2005. *Empire of Nations: Ethnographic Knowledge and the Making of the Soviet Union*. Ithaca: Cornell University Press.

Humphrey, Carolyn, and David Sneath. 1999. *The End of Nomadism?: Society, State and the Environment in Inner Asia*. Durham: Duke University Press.

Jameson, Fredric. 1991. *Postmodernism, or the Cultural Logic of Late Capitalism*. Durham: Duke University Press.

Jantsannorov, Natsag, ed. 1989. "Introduction." In *Mongolyn khögjim sudlal* [Mongolian Music Research], edited by author, 5–23. Ulaanbaatar: National Publishing Place.

———, ed. 1996. *Mongol khögjim'n arvankhoyor khörög: sonatyn allegro* [Twelve Mongolian musical portaits: Sonata allegro]. Ulaanbaatar: N.P.

Kherlen, Lkhavsüren. 2010. *Mongol khöömii utga kholbogdol* [The Significance of Mongol Khöömii]. Ulaanbaatar: National University of Mongolia Press.

Klein, Debra L. 2007. *Yorùbá Bàtá Goes Global: Artists, Culture Brokers, and Fans*. Chicago: The University of Chicago Press.

Krzywicki, Andrzej. 2009. *Poststalinowski karnawał radości: V Światowy Festiwal Młodzieży i Studentów o Pokój i Przyjaźń—Warszawa 1955 r* [The V World Festival of Youth and Students for Peace and Friendship—Warsaw 1955]. Warsaw: Wydawnictwo TRIO.

Levin, Theodore. 1996. *The Hundred Thousand Fools of God: Musical Travels in Central Asia (and Queens, New York)*. Bloomington: Indiana University Press.

Levin, Theodore, and Jean During. 2002. *The Silk Road: A Musical Caravan*. CD. Washington D.C.: Smithsonian Folkways Recordings.

Levin, Theodore, with Valentina Suzukei. 2006. *Where Rivers and Mountains Sing: Sound, Music, and Nomadism in Tuva and Beyond*. Bloomington: Indiana University Press.

Levin, Theodore, Said Daukeyeva, Elmire Küchümkulova. 2016. *The Music of Central Asia*. Bloomington: Indiana University Press.

Lkhavsüren, D. 1973. "Manai toglolt airgiin tavd" [The 'top five' of our concert]." *Soyol* [Culture] 4:44–45.

Marin, Andrei. 2008. "Between Cash Cows and Golden Calves: Adaptions of Mongolian Pastoralism in the 'Age of the Market.'" *Nomadic Peoples* (12(2):75–101.

Marsh, Peter K. 2009. *The Horse-Head Fiddle and the Cosmopolitan Re-imagination of Tradition of Mongolia.* New York: Routledge.

Miller, Terry E., and Andrew Shahriari, eds. 2012. *World Music: A Global Journey.* 3rd ed. New York: Routledge.

Murphy, David. 2001. "No Room for Nomads." *Far Eastern Economic Review* 164(21):30–32.

Myagmarjav, Dorchin. 2015. *Aya egshigiin ikh manlai* [The finest of melodic tones]. Ulaanbaatar: Selenge Press XXK.

Narangoa, Li. 2009. "Mongolia and Preventive Diplomacy: Haunted by History and Becoming Cosmopolitan." *Asian Survey* 49(2):358–379.

Olson, Laura J. 2004. *Performing Russia: Folk Revival and Russian Identity.* New York: Routledge.

Orhon, Myadar. 2011. "Imaginary Nomads: Deconstructing the Representation of Mongolia as a Land of Nomads." *Inner Asia* 13(2):335–362.

Paine, Robert. 1971. *Patrons and Brokers in the East Arctic.* St. John's: Memorial University of Newfoundland.

Pegg, Carole. 2001. *Mongolian Music, Dance, & Oral Narrative: Performing Diverse Identities.* Seattle: The University of Washington Press.

Rouland, Michael. 2004. "A Nation on Stage: Music and the 1936 Festival of Kazak Arts," in *Soviet Music and Society under Lenin and Stalin: The Baton and Sickle*, edited by Neil Edmunds, 181–209. Abingdon: Routledge Curzon.

Rupprecht, Tobias. 2015. *Soviet Internationalism after Stalin: Interaction and Exchange between the USSR and Latin America during the Cold War.* Cambridge: Cambridge University Press.

Ruskin, Jesse. 2011. "Talking Drums in Los Angeles: Brokering Culture in an American Metropolis." *Black Music Research Journal* 31(1):85–103.

Said, Edward W. 1978. Orientalism. London: Routledge and Kegan Paul.

Schwarz, Henry, ed. 2006. *Mongolian Culture and Society in the Age of Globalization.* Bellingham: Western Washington University, East Asian Studies Press.

Slobin, Mark. 1993. *Subcultural Sounds: Micromusics of the West.* Hanover: University Press of New England.

Smirnov, Boris G. 1975. *Muzika narodnoi mongolii* [Mongolian folk music]. Moscow: Muzika.

Smith, Susannah Lockwood. 1997. "Soviet Arts Policy, Folk Music, and National Identity: The Platnitskii State Russian Folk Choir, 1927–1945." PhD diss., University of Minnesota.

Sneath, David. 2002. "Mongolia in the 'Age of the Market': Pastoral Land-use and the Development Discourse." In *Markets and Moralities: Ethnographies of Postsocialism*, edited by Ruth Mandel, and Caroline Humphrey, 191–210. Oxford: Berg.

———. 2007. *Headless State: Aristocratic Orders, Kinship Society, and Misrepresentations of Nomadic Inner Asia.* New York: Columbia University Press.

Sommers, Pamela. 1987. "The Marvels of Mongolia." *The Washington Post*, October 12.

Stokes, Martin. 2004. "Music and the Global Order." *Review of Anthropology* 33:47–72.

Stolpe, Ines. 2006. *Educational Import: Local Encounters with Global Forces in Mongolia.* Gordonsville, VA: Palgrave Macmillan.

———. 2008. "Display and Performance in Mongolian Cultural Campaigns." In *Conflict and Social Order in Tibet and Inner Asia*, edited by T. Huber and F. Pirie, 59–84. Leiden, The Netherlands: Brill.

Tsetsentsolmon, Baatarnaran. 2014. "The 'Gong Beat' against the 'Uncultured': Contested Notions of Culture and Civilization in Mongolia." *Asian Ethnicity* 15(4):422–438.

Tsevel, Yadamjaviin. 1966. *Mongol khelnii tovch tailbar tol'* [Abbreviated Mongolian language explanatory dictionary]. Ulaanbaatar: Ulsyn khevleliin khereg erkhlekh khoroo.

Tsing, Anna. 2005. *Friction.* Princeton, NJ: Princeton University Press.

Tungalog, B. 2015. "Khusugtun Makes Top 9 of Asia's Got Talent." *The UB Post*, May 3. http://ubpost.mongolnews.mn/?p=14397.

Turino, Thomas. 2003. "Are We Global Yet? Globalist Discourse, Cultural Formations and the Study of Zimbabwean Popular Music." *British Journal of Ethnomusicology* 12(2):51–79.

Weatherford, Jack. 2004. *Genghis Khan and the Making of the Modern World.* New York: Penguin Random House.

White, Bob, ed. 2012. *Music and Globalization: Critical Encounters.* Bloomington: Indiana University.

CHAPTER 10

"We Were Born with Global Ambition"

Continuity, Innovation, and a New Chapter in the Development of Mongolian Popular Music

PETER K. MARSH

In relative terms, the success of the Mongolian "heavy metal" band The Hu has been quite sudden. The group released the first music videos for its songs "Yuve yu" and "Wolf Totem" (Video Examples 1 and 2) in late 2018. Both videos feature the musicians sporting hand-tooled black leather jackets, heavy buckles, and traditional boots performing in stunning locations of the Mongolian countryside. The group's instrumentation and musical style draw from Western rock and Mongolian folk music traditions. Posted on YouTube.com, these two videos caught the attention of Western audiences and quickly "went viral." By June 2019, they had been viewed twelve million and nineteen million times, respectively.[1] By fall of that year, the band had signed a recording contract with New York–based Eleven Seven Music, home to such established heavy metal groups as Mötley Crüe, Five Finger Death Punch, and Papa Roach, and released their debut album, *The Gereg*, which quickly topped Billboard magazine's Top New Artist chart and reached near the top of its Indie Label chart. It also ranked in the top five of U.K.'s Rock & Metal Album chart and Album Downloads list (Farber 2019). By the end of 2019, The Hu was in the midst of a world concert tour that included sold-out shows in clubs and headlining performances at major rock music festivals in Europe, North America, and Australia.

The degree of penetration into the Western popular music mainstream that The Hu achieved in less than a year is extraordinary. No other Mongolian musical artist or group has managed to achieve this level of international recognition or attention, even after years of trying. Some have done well, such as the Mongolian folk ensembles Khusugtun and the Altai Band.[2] The Mongolian "folk rock" group Altan Urag (Golden Urag) achieved popular attention in the West for its work on the soundtracks to the movie *Mongol: The Rise of Genghis Khan* (2007) and Netflix's *Marco Polo* (2014–2016) (Cengel 2019). Although many Mongolian rock and pop artists have toured in North America and Europe since the 1990s, their audiences have often been limited primarily to members of the Mongolian diaspora.

Perhaps the closest parallel to The Hu has been the Mongolian heavy metal group Tengger Cavalry (see Interlude 2 in this volume). The group's leader was from Inner Mongolia, China, but formed the group in Beijing before later relocating it to New York City. As can be seen in the YouTube video for its song "Lone Wolf" (released in May 2019; see Video Example 3), the band features a similar mixture of Western and Mongolian instruments and the lead singer, Nature Ganganbaigal, alternates between the use of *khöömii* and a more conventional rock vocal style. Between 2010 and 2019, Tengger Cavalry released a number of studio albums (the last released on the Austrian label Napalm Records); undertook concert tours through the U.S., Europe, and China; provided music for two video games;[3] and even performed a concert at Carnegie Hall in New York City.[4] Yet, even with such accomplishments, Tengger Cavalry did not achieve the level of success that The Hu had attained by the end of 2019.

This chapter explores the possible reasons why The Hu was able to achieve a level of international recognition and success that earlier generations of Mongolian artists and bands were not able to do. An examination of the imagery and music of these first two songs reveals clear continuities between The Hu and developments in the history of Mongolian popular music over the previous nearly five decades. The lyrical references of the group's songs also locate them in a contemporary Mongolian context. Yet, The Hu has also brought to their game important innovations in the areas of sound, imagery, and dissemination that has set them apart from previous Mongolian artists and has helped it to connect with the transnational metal community. What The Hu has accomplished points to how Mongolian artists are getting better at reading and reacting to shifts in the global popular music landscape and suggests major changes may be taking place in the dynamics that shape and control the global flows of popular music and culture that may benefit small nations like Mongolia.[5]

Pass the Popcorn: Mongolian Youth and Cultural Loss in "Yuve yuve yu"

A close examination of The Hu's first music video, "Yuve yuve yu" (Video Example 1), released in September 2018, reveals music and messages that may be new to many non-Mongolian audiences but will be familiar to many Mongolian ones. Interestingly, the video begins with a 40-second prelude before the song begins. In quick succession, we see individual members of the band in various urban locations, presumably in Mongolia's capital, Ulaanbaatar. We first see the lead singer, "Gala" (Galbadrakh Tsendbaatar), sitting at a table in a coffeeshop playing a video game on his smartphone. Next, we see another member sitting on a couch in front of his television playing a video game (simulated European football). We see a third member sitting in front of his television, munching popcorn while watching a movie (in English), while a fourth is shown sleeping on this stomach in bed, the alarm clock showing it is almost noon. At first, non-Mongolian viewers may be struck by just how normal this scene is. Viewers can easily imagine young people in urban areas around the world doing the same kinds of activities, suggesting that The Hu wants its audience to understand that, despite its geographic distance from the West, they and their viewers share a common cosmopolitan youth culture. At the same time, the prelude does not portray these characters very sympathetically: each appears isolated, alone, and devoted only to his respective screens, as if each was sleeping—or sleepwalking—through life. But then the characters are jolted out of their stupor by the unexplained and mysterious appearance of the Mongolian countryside. It appears first to a character who opens a door in his apartment and then to the others on their phones as texted images. The next scene switches from the dark and cramped interiors of city apartments to a beautiful, light-filled vista of a lake in the countryside. A band member enters the frame, admires the view, takes a deep breath, and then picks up his instrument and begins to play, marking the start of the song. From this point, the video features constantly shifting images of band members sitting or standing in various stunning locations in the Mongolian countryside. Though physically distanced from each other, they are clearly playing together, communing both with each other and the surrounding landscape, which, clearly, is meant to be another character in this video.

The Hu doubtlessly meant their viewers to note the contrast between the characters portrayed in the prelude and those performing the song. Those in the prelude appear slouched over their phones or TV sets or shuffling, sleepily, through their apartments. But in the song, they appear standing or sitting erect and confidently, feet planted squarely on the earth, making strong, forceful movements with their arms and legs, their heads bouncing to the beat of the music. The contrast is made starker by the visual power of each performer's location, e.g. at the edge of a steep cliff, on a mountain summit, or upon the sands of a vast desert. The band seems to suggest that while they partake in urban cosmopolitan youth culture, their true identity as young people is most powerfully expressed when they put on their Mongolian clothing, pick up their

Mongolian instruments, and set foot in the Mongolian countryside to play their own Mongolian music.

This sense of power connected with the homeland is further emphasized through musical and vocal styles. The band's instrumentation mixes Mongolian folk instruments (*tovshuur* or two-stringed lute, *morin khuur* or horsehead fiddle, and the *tömör khuur* or jaw harp) and Western rock instruments (electric guitar and bass, electric keyboard, and drum set), with the timbral balance tilting in favor of the Mongolian instruments. All four core members of the band sing together in unison, an octave apart, each using one of the forms of *khöömii*, creating a block of vocal sound with a timbral "edge" or "roughness" that easily projects through the instrumental texture. The song verses are sung in a style that resembles that of a traditional folk singer reciting a legend or epic song and accompanying himself on a string instrument.

The song's lyrics are also directed at a domestic audience. They are sung in the Mongolian language and stated in the form of a complaint to the people of their nation:

> You [Mongolians] have been born in the ancestor's destiny, and yet you've been sleeping deeply and cannot be wakened; . . . You take our Great Mongol ancestors' names in vain; . . . Yet, you would not honor our oath and destiny; . . . Why is it so difficult to cherish the ancestor's inherited land? . . . Why is the priceless edification of our elders turning to ashes?

The singers allege that Mongolians today are quick to boast to others about Chinggis Khan and the Great Mongol Empire of the thirteenth century, but slow to honor the responsibilities that this "honor" or "destiny" grants them. They are quick to turn their backs on their ancestral lands, wisdom, and customs that are their cultural inheritance. The allegation that Mongolians are sleeping, or sleepwalking, through their lives is an allusion to the characters in the video's prelude who seem similarly "lost" in their urban cosmopolitan bubbles.

This fear, that Mongolians are "sleeping" or "forgetting" their past, is a cultural trope with deep roots in contemporary Mongolia. Filmmaker Benj Binks records the Mongolian epic singer B. Bayarmagnai expressing it for his 2012 documentary *Mongolian Bling*:

> Now it's the generation of youth. All those old folk songs that our past epic singers used to sing have been lost to the Heavens along with the elders. The youth don't understand our traditions. Mongolian traditional folk singing is part of our identity. Today, there are so many things to see and watch due to mass media, such as many TV channels and the internet. Half of Mongolia's population lives in Ulaanbaatar. The more they settle down in the city, the more they lose their nomadic traditions. Urbanization is a great thing, but we should not forget our customs (Binks 2012).

Bayarmagnai is pointing to the paradox at the heart of the processes of westernization and urbanization, which were introduced into Mongolia in the decades following the People's Revolution of 1921. While they benefited the nation and people, such as by improving healthcare, education, and communications, they also had negative consequences, such as the slow, but steady, ebbing away of common knowledge about the nation's cultural heritage. The process of opening our society to Western culture is a double-edged sword, Bayarmagnai seems to say: that our youth today can share in a cosmopolitan youth culture is a good thing, but at what cost?

It is ironic that a similar question led to the creation of the first popular music ensemble in Mongolia nearly five decades earlier.

"Sound the Bells": Youth Transgressions in the Socialist Period

The "mass media" in Mongolia in the late 1960s and early 1970s consisted primarily of radio, television, and cinema along with the dissemination of LP records and was controlled and managed by the ruling Mongolian People's Revolutionary Party (MPRP). A political satellite of the U.S.S.R., the Mongolian People's Republic closely aligned its cultural policies with those of its Soviet "brother" nations. And thus, what Mongolians experienced through these various media forms was carefully curated to promote the Party's political and cultural aims. Music one might hear on the state radio would include recordings of modernized folk music and song, classical music by both Mongolian and Western composers, *zokhiolyn duu* (modern songs about countryside life that were composed by urban composers in folk song styles), and songs from Mongolian movies.

In the same period in the U.S. and U.K., music was undergoing a revolution in content, style, and expressive power. Rock and pop music were a significant part of the musical mainstream in these nations and they were quickly being disseminated to other parts of the West and the world. The Community Party of the Soviet Union (CPSP) considered this music to be a threat to their ideological control over young people, portraying it as "one of the cleverest ideological diversions yet invented by capitalist imperialists" (Sarkitov 1987:93). The CPSP denounced and actively suppressed its consumption and practice, and the MPRP followed in step.

Young people in Mongolia, on the other hand, found the Western music they heard as intoxicating, and like their counterparts in other socialist nations of the period, they found ways to get their hands on it. In her documentary *Live from UB*, Lauren Knapp records the Mongolian visual artist Altanzaya comparing this trickle of access to Western popular music to the act of peering through a small hole in a wall into an entirely different and tantalizing world (Knapp 2015).[6] Knapp also records the Mongolian parliamentarian Oyungerel saying that when she was a teenager in the late 1960s and 1970s, she and her friends had reliable, if sporadic, access to "unofficial" music, namely, LPs of Western pop music by the Beatles, Jimi Hendrix, ABBA, Smokey Robinson, and others (ibid.). She and others of her age in Ulaanbaatar typically spoke Russian, had access to radios and turntables, and generally had more wealth and freedom to explore alternative identities than their rural counterparts. It was these youths, some of whom were children of Party officials, who were at the center of this illicit trade in Western pop cultural products (Marsh 2010).

This access to Western music transformed the musical ideas and expectations of young people in Mongolia. They began to compose and perform their own songs on themes of everyday life, often critical of societal problems and the workings of the government. Young people performed these songs in their homes or on the steps of their apartment complexes for themselves and their friends, away from the eyes and ears of party officials. Officials knew what was going on, however, and in the early 1970s the Party sanctioned the creation of several state-funded *estrad* (the Russian word for "staged") music ensembles that integrated the musical styles and instruments of Western popular music with contemporary Mongolian folk music. The goal was to create a form of popular music that, while resembling the Western styles and forms, would be identifiably Mongolian and would uphold the party's broader ideological goals: cultural progress and uplift.

Soyol Erdene (Cultural Jewel) was formed in 1971 and became the first of these state-controlled popular music ensembles. The core of the group, consisting of standard rock band instrumentation (i.e., electric guitar and bass, electric keyboard, and drum set), was at times expanded with Mongolian traditional instruments. For instance, the song "Tsenkher zalaa" (Sky-blue crest, Video Example 4), from the early 1970s, prominently features the sound of the Mongolian *yatga* (a Mongolian zither), including a solo by the instrument later in the song. The Party managed all aspects of the musicians' professional lives, from where they performed to how they styled their hair (Marsh 2010). Their songs were about love but also farm tractors and the electrification of the countryside, and all were composed by urban, professional composers with the aim of propagandizing the Party's efforts at "building socialism."

By the late 1980s, however, rising social concerns were pushing popular musicians to test the limits imposed upon them by the Party. Young people were increasingly supportive of calls for the government to distance itself from the Soviet Union. A movement for greater independence was brewing in Ulaanbaatar that would lead to widespread popular protests and the eventual collapse of the MPRP. Party officials were becoming less able, or perhaps less willing, to enforce the strict cultural policies of previous decades, and young musicians were some of the first to publicly challenge them. In 1988, the then-lead singer of Soyol Erdene, D. Jargalsaikhan, recorded his song "Chinggis Khan," which praised the spirit of the thirteenth-century military leader and founder of the Mongolian nation and asked him to forgive the Mongolian people for forgetting about him. A song on this subject was still, even then, considered politically taboo, and yet, despite this open challenge to Party authority, Jargalsaikhan was not arrested or persecuted. Knapp records the singer as saying that the Party's decision not to prosecute him for this song was an indication of just how far the attitudes toward dissent were changing in this period (Knapp 2015).

A year later, the pop-duo Khonkh (Bell) helped to crystalize growing popular sentiment against the Party with its song "Khonkhny duu" (Sound of the bell). Its lyrics called upon the Mongolian people to "awake" to the dawning of a new day, a veiled sentiment that many Mongolians understood as a jab at single-party rule:

> The sound of the bells,
> Let us awake, awake.
> The sound of the bells,
> Let us awake (Kristof 1990)

The melody of the song became an anthem sung by protestors in street demonstrations and rallies, many of which took place outside government buildings between 1989 and 1990. Jargalsaikhan describes the song as "the anthem of democracy" that contributed to the fall of socialist rule in 1990 (Knapp 2015).

Such songs resonated with a widespread sense of unease about a national leadership that many felt to be more focused on maintaining a "brotherly friendship" with the Soviet Union than in understanding and responding to the everyday needs of its citizens. Mongolian popular music artists and groups, responding to a fear that their nation was "forgetting" its past or "sleeping" when it needed to be awake, demonstrated an increasing unwillingness to passively glorify state ideology. Such independence demonstrated the emerging maturity and authority of popular music in Mongolia, which it would maintain without pause into the post-socialist era.

From Madonna to Nirvana: Mongolian Pop Music's Embrace of the West

Around the time of the so-called democratic revolution of 1990, popular music was rife with political ideas and criticism. D. Jargalsaikhan recalls this as the time "when politics was in the air we breathed" (Marsh 2010:347). But youth interest in politics faded fast following the rapid introduction of market economic reforms and the successful completion of the nation's first multiparty election. The severe economic downturn that accompanied the sudden end to generous Soviet subsidies, coupled with doses of economic shock therapy advocated by the World Bank, contributed to the turn away from overt political messages in popular music. Mongolians suddenly faced not only the disappearance of many social services they had come to rely upon, but also a steep decline in their standards of living. For many, even finding enough food to eat was difficult. Mongols had finally won the right to freely travel and speak their minds, but few had the resources to do so.

Despite the difficult economic situation, however, Mongolian popular culture expanded dramatically in the first half of the 1990s, fueled in large part by the growth of the communications and broadcast sectors of the economy. Privately owned media and broadcasting companies, including satellite and cable TV service providers, began operations in Ulaanbaatar by the mid-1990s, introducing such popular channels as MTV, MTV-Asia, and Star-TV and bringing real competition to the still state-run Mongolian Television & Radio. This, along with the opening of Internet cafes, allowed Mongolian young people direct access to the transnational flows of popular culture for the first time. In the same period, the availability of relatively inexpensive electronic recording and production equipment gave them the means to record, mix, and master their own audio and video recordings at levels of quality and control that were unavailable to earlier generations of artists.

Mongolian popular music became increasingly diverse throughout this period as artists began to experiment with new Western musical genres, including R&B, boy- and girl-bands, jazz, different styles of rock music—such as hard rock, heavy metal, and alternative rock—and rap and hip-hop music. Some of the most famous performers of this period included the balladeers D. Jargalsaikhan, B. Sarantuya, and T. Ariunaa, and the bands Hurd ("heavy metal"), Haranga, and Niciton (both "hard rock").

The popular music artists I met in the late-1990s made it clear that their audiences and fans did not want to hear imitations of Western pop music but rather Mongolian versions of it (Marsh 2010). Still, that Mongolian artists and fans were paying close attention to their Western pop idols is evidenced in their discourse. The singer T. Ariunaa was dubbed by her fans the "Madonna of Mongolia." Members of the boyband Camerton, one of the most popular and influential groups of the late 1990s and early 2000s, described to me how they fashioned their music and stage presence after the American boy-band Boys II Men. They explained how they would watch their music videos and imitate their a cappella, R&B vocal harmonies and musical textures as well as the ways in which they moved and interacted with their audiences while on stage. One member told me that he even sought out the same style of glasses worn by a member of the group (group interview, Ulaanbaatar, February 1999).

The alternative rock band Nisvanis was, as the name suggests, deeply influenced by the music of the American "grunge" rock group Nirvana and tried to channel its transgressive sentiments. Music producer Natsagdorj described to Knapp how Nisvanis's music changed "people's perceptions—showing them that they could think differently. You don't have to live by society's rules. You can live your way, following your own belief," adding that this band "opened the gates for musicians to come" (Knapp 2015).

While many Mongolian pop artists and bands seemed to be channeling Western pop idols, some continued to experiment with the synthesis of Western pop and Mongolian folk musical elements, as Soyol Erdene had done decades earlier. Hurd's song "Bakharahal" (Pride) includes a horsehead fiddle player performing alongside other members of the heavy metal group in something of a forerunner of The Hu. Even the members of Camerton described to me how the lyrical nature of their songs as well as their focus on topics of romantic love draw deeply from the Mongolian song traditions (group interview, Ulaanbaatar, February 1999). But it was the "techno-rap" group Har Sarnai (Black Rose) that most forcefully and vocally continued this trend, incorporating into their songs and stage shows *khöömii*, long-songs (*urtyn duu*), folk dances, and rapping on passages from famous Mongolian poetry.[7] The group's lead singer "Amraa" (Sukhbaatar Amarmandakh) told Knapp that Mongolian young people needed to be reminded about their nation's past:

> During the purges of the 1930s, it was forbidden to talk about our history or even mention the names of our great kings: Chinggis Khaan and Batmunkh Dayan Khaan. At one point we had accepted the Cyrillic script and left our traditional Mongolian script behind. Being forbidden from knowing our history for about 100 years, caused the Mongolians to forget their traditions and history. So, we wanted to revive Mongolian heritage and started producing songs praising our country (ibid.).

We see, once again, the trope of "forgetting" in Amraa's words. But it is also interesting how the group's inclusion of folk cultural elements in their music and public performances was not merely about adding interesting sonic or visual displays. Amraa's stance is that of an activist: Har Sarnai will use these references of the past to not just remind Mongolians of their history and cultural heritage but to "revive" it. Such a bold agenda for popular music was not very popular in the 1990s. But this would change with the new millennia.

"We Can't Eat Money": Mongolian Pop Music's Embrace of the Past

A series of major events throughout the first two decades of the twenty-first century led to rising popular distrust of the government and criticism of its policies, particularly those related to the development of the huge Oyu Tolgoi mine complex run by the multinational mining corporation Rio Tinto in the southern Gov' Desert. While contributing a significant level of income to the state government after it started operations in 2010, it also became for many a symbol of broader societal problems, such as governmental corruption, environmental degradation, and endemic economic inequalities that divide urban and rural sectors of society (Gillet 2012; Langfitt 2012; Theunissen 2014). A downturn in the nation's economy after 2012 only deepened public anger, much of it directed at the contracts the government had made with Rio Tino and other foreign-owned mining conglomerates—deals that many deemed to be overly generous to these foreign corporations.

The fear that foreign entities were exploiting the nation's mineral wealth stoked nationalist sentiments, which quickly found expression in popular culture. Hip-hop was already a mature art form in Mongolia at that time. Having emerged in Ulaanbaatar in the late 1990s, it quickly became a medium for youths to critique contemporary Mongolian society. The most popular hip-hop groups of this period, Dain ba Enkh (War and Peace), Lumino, IceTop, and Digital, often took aim at ineffectual or corrupt government institutions, lampooning them through sharp visual and musical satire. They also rapped about the problems of domestic violence, alcoholism, or being young, poor, and powerless in a society of enormous inequalities (Marsh 2010).

"Gennie" (Gennie Bolor), who represents the next generation of hip-hop artists, is one of the first female rappers to appear on the scene. Called by her friends the "Queen of Mongolian hip-hop," she has broadened the perspectives of hip-hop's societal gaze since she started singing in the early 2000s (Binks 2012).[8] Gennie was one of many in Mongolia, including artists, politicians, and environmentalists, who raised concerns about the environmental and social costs of mining in the nation's countryside. She equated the foreign mining corporations and Mongolians getting rich from their connections to them as "muggers" plundering the nation's natural wealth:

> While the drunken Mongolia stumbles in madness and insanity,
> Everything is taken from us, robbed and exploited by piracy,
> The land is excavated and made a desert,
> While the poor live for the day, these muggers get rich (ibid.).

In the music video for their 2013 song "Minii nutgiig nadad uldee" (Leave my homeland to me, Video Example 5), the rappers Gee and Jonon imagine a near-future homeland decimated by mining. The Mongolian countryside is depicted as a barren landscape of sand and scrub. The once bountiful natural environment has disappeared and, with it, the culture and customs that had for centuries sustained the people who had lived within it. Gee, Jonon, and a small, ragged band of survivors stagger through this landscape, finding buried in the sand bits and pieces of the life they—and by extension, their nation—once had. The singers' message is stark:

> We are forgetting our ancestors.
> The real treasure doesn't exist underground,
> It exists in our intelligence, our blood, and our land.
> We trade the gold for money, but we can't eat money.

In referencing tropes of land, blood, and the ancestors, these songs move beyond mere social criticism to sentiments of nationalist outrage. Some organizations have fed off of such sentiments, including neo-Nazi groups that have threatened violence against foreigners, particularly those perceived as being ethnically Chinese (Barria 2013, Henderson 2016). While few Mongolians openly support such extreme views, Khaltmaa Battulga was elected in the 2016 presidential election. His populist messages amplified fears of threats to the nation's sovereignty posed by foreign corporations and he called for changes at the highest levels of the nation's government (Campbell and Edwards 2019; Edwards 2016).

In contrast to the outrage and pessimism of the hip-hop artists, R&B singer D. Bold saw the opportunity in 2010 to promote a different vision of Mongolia's future. One of the founding members of the 1990s boyband Camerton, Bold described his new project, Mongol Pop, as a "new trend in Mongolian pop music," one that "combines the old traditional instruments with modern pop music, making a new style that does not lose the beauty of the traditions of my nation" (D. Bold interview by Lauren Knapp, April 12, 2012). He introduced the new style in two solo albums from this period, *Mongol Pop* (2010) and *Mongol Pop 2* (2013).

The song "Kheeriin salkhtai ayalguu" (Melody of the windy steppe, Video Example 6), from the first of these albums, provides a good example of this so-called new style. Like many songs in both Mongolian and R&B traditions, "Kheeriin salkhtai ayalguu" is about love; but in this case the object of the singer's attention is not a person, but the horsehead fiddle or *morin khuur*, a folk musical instrument with deep roots in Mongolian culture (see Chapter 5 in this volume). For many Mongolians, the instrument has become a cultural icon whose image and sound embodies Mongolia's ancient cultural heritage (Marsh 2009:133). The video associates the instrument with Chinggis Khan, the

Mongol Empire, and a host of other cultural elements: a man carving wood to make the horsehead fiddle, a young woman in traditional dress performing a folk dance, and a child undergoing his first haircutting ceremony. At one point, an intergenerational group of Mongolians are shown gathered for a traditional *nair* (an informal social gathering) where they drink milk tea, flirt, and listen to fiddle music. At another point in the video, young buff Mongolian herders chase after and lasso wild horses. And throughout the video, paralleling the refrain, "My horsehead fiddle, whose sound is the highest worship," people are shown raising horsehead fiddles into the air, strings upward, in a sign of respect. For Mongolian viewers, such lyrical and visual references point to cultural elements rooted in the Mongolian deep past, the period preceding the People's Revolution of 1921 (Humphrey 1992:375). But Bold also includes images of well-known contemporary folk fiddlers and ensembles, including the State Horsehead Fiddle Ensemble. The cover photograph of the *Mongol Pop 2* album shows a similar mixture of old and new, featuring Bold in suit and tie presiding over a "party" with other young Mongolian millennials, some dressed in Western clothing and others in traditional clothing (some even from the pre-Revolutionary period).

Bold's vision of the future appears quite different from those of the rappers Gennie, Gee, and Jonon. In contrast to the dystopian vision portraying Mongolians walking mindlessly (that is, sleepwalking) into a period of cultural forgetting and destruction, Bold's vision appears more utopian, one in which Mongolians live a cosmopolitan lifestyle that embraces and honors both the best of the global and the local. For him, it seems, a synthesis of the traditional and the modern, the past and present, is the only way to move forward. That such views parallel the Mongolian government's policies of cultural preservation and promotion could explain, in part, why it awarded Bold the prestigious *Töriin shagnalt* (State Award) in 2014, the highest award presented to Mongolian citizens by the government.[9] The contrasting approaches to these issues may also be related to a difference in perspective between those of the cultural elite, to which Bold belongs, and those of the lower or middle classes, to which Gee and Gennie belonged when they wrote their songs.

"Nobody Understands It but Everyone Feels It": The Hu Plots Global Conquest

The Hu came together as a band in 2016 within this cultural milieu, and by the time it released its first video two years later, there was little to point to in the band's makeup, instrumentation, appearance, or lyrics that was radically different from what had come before. The band's mixture of Mongolian and Western rock styles and instruments was hardly new; Mongolian popular music has been syncretic since its origins in the 1970s. The band's costumes, body movement (including the "head banging") and use of nature imagery in its videos are also all variations on what other Mongolian artists and bands had done for decades. And, lyrical references to Mongolians sleeping, forgetting, or mindlessly wandering through life were well established tropes long before The Hu used them, as was the practice of using popular music to critique social behavior and advocate for "remembering" or "honoring" their nation's past and its "oath" to its ancestors.

And yet, within weeks of their release, The Hu's first two videos were viewed and shared by millions of people around the world, and within months the band began to receive offers to record and tour in the West. While there are many factors that account for this rapid and extraordinary success, the two innovations that stand out are the transcultural nature of the band's music and imagery and the means by which the band has promoted them. The four core members of The Hu and its producer, Dashka (B. Dashdondag), all keen observers of global metal, fashioned a sonic and visual syncretism that mixed key elements of this global musical tradition with their own folk cultural heritage and then took advantage of the transnational nature of the global metal community, of which social media platforms play a key role, to get this music into the ears and before the eyes of as many people as possible. More than any other Mongolian artist or band, The Hu has fashioned a syncretic product that was designed from the start to "go viral."

In *Metal Rules the Globe* (2011), Jeremy Wallach, Harris Berger, and Paul Greene list a set of core musical qualities that characterize the metal genre and provides "a musical center of gravity to the growing and diversifying global scene." These qualities include: "the distinctive timbre of the heavily distorted electric guitar;[10] either soaring or raspy and unpitched vocals (including shouting, shrieking, and growling); prominent use of a Western drum set, often with a heavy emphasis on double-bass drums; and energetic and prominent guitar figuration, in the form of the virtuosic melodic expression of classic heavy metal guitar solos or the fast-paced riffs of thrash metal" (Wallach et al. 2011:11). The Hu's form of metal provides an interesting take on this list. While the band uses an electric guitar and bass, the lead roles are played by two horsehead fiddles and a *tovshuur*, and in many of the group's songs, the mixing of the electric guitar, bass, and amplified folk instruments produces a musical timbre that sounds akin to the "distorted" guitar sound referred to by Wallach et al. The solos, played by electric guitar in most other metal bands, are performed by one or both horsehead fiddles. In addition to a Western drum set, the band uses what it calls "Mongolian drums," basically a set of large drums of various sizes that emphasize lower frequency beats and rhythms.[11] The group's vocals are typically sung in one or more forms of *khöömii*, individually or in various groupings, which gives them a raspy and often guttural timbre that sounds, again, akin to those often heard in other forms of metal music.

The core members of the band (Gala and Enkush on horsehead fiddle, Jaya on vocals, and Temka on *tovshuur*) constitute a folk or folk-rock music ensemble of the sort that would be familiar to their domestic audiences, whether or not the group is playing by themselves or with the other members of their extended group.[12] But many non-Mongolian listeners report hearing this syncretism as a subgenre of metal. Through their reaction videos, metal influencers were some of the first to promote the music of The Hu and many of their responses have focused on the band's unique music sound. Metalhead Reacts, for instance, describes the sound of "Yuve yuve yu" as "very interesting. It's got a very tribal feel about it. . . . It's the way they've merged the classic native style of the Mongolian music with the rock elements, and it really works very well."[13] He goes on to say, "It's just so much fun, such an enjoyable piece of music . . . It made me happy! . . . And it's something I've never even thought of before. You hear of Viking metal and all these sorts of metal, like Pirate metal, for example, but I've never even considered Mongolian rock. It's one of those things that's never crossed my mind, yet it seems so obvious, really." Gaming Patrol says, "I loved the aspects of the traditional. I liked the bit of modern rock, the modern heavy metal."[14] Bowser's Reaction Pit compared the music of this song to that of Rammstein, the German heavy metal group: "It's a different kind of Rammstein, but it reminds me a lot about it!"[15] The Nobodies, a father and son pair, asked if The Hu's music was really heavy metal but then answered the question themselves: "It's such a weird form of metal. I've never heard a song like this," and then ended their video saying, "That had to be the weirdest-slash-most unique metal song I think I have ever listened to. I'm so lost at what was happening, but it was so freakin' good!"[16]

Rock critics have also described the group's style as a genre of heavy metal rock music and not a "metal-like" folk music. Neil McCormick of *The Telegraph* called The Hu "the biggest Mongolian throat singing heavy metal band in the world. To be fair, it's a niche genre" (McCormick 2020). Roison O'Connor of the *Independent* writes, "The HU may be pegged as a metal band—you can certainly hear traces of Metallica and Rammstein—but there's a level of technical skill their classical training . . . provides that feels relatively unmatched in modern popular music" (O'Connor 2020). British journalist Robin Askew gets at the transcultural aspect of the music in her review:

> [Heavy] metal is a universal language, inspiring and exciting musicians around the world. Rather than simply aping the likes of Iron Maiden and Judas Priest, the best of them bring their own culture and instrumentation to the form. The classically trained members of The Hu are no exception (Askew 2020).

Non-Mongolian audiences also appear to experience the band's music in ways similar to other more mainstream forms of metal. Numerous videos posted on YouTube.com show live performances of the band in various locales in the U.S. and Europe, from nightclubs to festival stages, with audiences packed together by the hundreds or thousands (these concerts preceded the global pandemic of 2020–2021). Many in these audiences visibly respond to the musical sound by head-banging and raising their hands in the air to either clap or show the Dio sign (the index finger and the little finger are upright and the thumb is clasped against the two middle fingers)[17] to communicate their appreciation to the band. While we cannot say for sure without formal surveys what these audience members were experiencing, we can deduct from their behavior that many of them were feeling intense pleasure or "flow" from the music. They may have been experiencing what Wallach et al. call "affective overdrive," a kind of sonic and affective saturation generated by the "sheer volume and rich timbres of metal fill[ing] the audible sound spectrum," which is a key constituent of the global metal tradition (Wallach et al. 2011:13).

Such powerful sonic experiences are often associated with equally powerful ideas and stories. Wallach et al. found that "[d]espite significant differences across national and regional metal scenes, . . . all metalheads, regardless of their preferred subgenre or subgenres, view metal as the opposite of light entertainment. To them, it is a form of serious music that endorses a particular set of values" (ibid. 2011:8). The Hu's songs deal with "serious" themes, such as the need to remember and connect with one's ancestors ("Yuve yuve yu"), that strength can be found within one's community ("Wolf Totem" and "The Great Chinggis Khan"), and that greed can lead to personal and communal destruction ("Sad But True").

What is particularly interesting, however, is that The Hu only sing its songs in the Mongolian language, meaning that most of the group's non-Mongolian audience do not understand its lyrics. And yet, many in the English-speaking audiences outside of Mongolia report that the language is not an issue for them. Some even likened the sound of the Mongolian language (with its sharp consonances, heavy accents, and guttural sounds) as being like "another instrument"[18] and as deepening their affective experience with the music. The metal influencer Galacticriminal says in his response video to "Yuve yuve yu" that "doing [the song] in their style but also doing it in their own language just gave it this different edge and feel and tone . . . [and added] to the eerie nature of this thing . . . that, man, gives me chills each and every single time"[19] Many of his viewers express agreement with him in their comments: "Nazaire Dragonash" writes: "Mongolian throat singing was MADE for metal. Lol! these guys rock it"; "Larry Paul" writes: "You don't need to understand what they are saying for it to sound great!" Similar responses are posted in the comments of other of The Hu's videos. "Eric Mink" writes: "Nobody understands it but everyone feels it."[20] "Neko Bat" writes: "I don't have to understand the words. I feel it in my soul. It speaks to me on a deep level as if I should know somehow."[21]

In fact, the range of responses in English posted in YouTube.com alone points to just how broad an audience the band is reaching. Many responders appear to be metalheads, relating the sound of the band to other Western and Asian metal bands, but others admit to being moved by particular aspects of the music. The masculine and warrior-like character of the music and visuals evokes in some responders a sense of the primitive. "RoadLord2000" writes: "I love the fusion of rock rhythms with traditional instruments, these guys put forth a killer primordial, atavistic sound. Honestly, Klingons made real, warrior/poets right here on Earth."[22] "Just Kylie" writes: "This animalistic, primal, masculine kind of stuff really gets into my soul as a human woman. It's why I love metal-type music so much. We don't see much masculinity in society today, especially in modern music, so seeing it 'worshipped' in a pure form within alternative musics still, and appreciated by people, is so refreshing."[23] "Cj W" was one of many viewers looking in from outside the metal community who wrote of being surprised by the power and attractiveness of the group's music: "I'm a 58yr old Grandma. Thought my headbanging days were over. NOPE! Teaching my grandkids with The HU!!!"[24] Other responders explain how they related to the environmental and spiritual messages in The Hu's music. "Eric Davis" writes:

> Yuve Yuve Yu is a song about cultural identity and heritage, questioning why so much has been lost, and yearning to recover the wisdom of the elders. . . . I feel that is a common thread and common yearning and desire among many people . . . to rediscover their cultural roots and heritage, and identity. Many of us are not alone in having that feeling. It's there for a reason. I believe that is why this song makes us a bit happy. We are not alone in looking for old and powerful truth, and honorable wisdom.[25]

And "Beanee B." connects The Hu's mission to his own Brazilian culture and family:

> I think that living in modern times, we forget how powerful nature, art and belief is a thread that combines us to our ancestors. It is foolish to think we have 'outsmarted' our past with modern technology because our past is forever linked to us. We should cherish it. This [music] is so beautiful and reminds me of my Brazilian culture and how our family links the importance of our ancestry into our present. It reminds me to never forget and honor those who came before us. They laid the path we follow.[26]

Such wide-ranging and culturally specific responses to The Hu's music points to the band's ability to create musical experiences that speak to people of diverse backgrounds and interests.

That the music of The Hu could even reach such a broad and diverse community is also related to important innovations in how the band disseminated its music. Earlier generations of Mongolian popular artists and bands first built their reputations by giving concerts, selling recordings, and touring. Later generations added Facebook accounts, websites, and videos on television and YouTube. While all these strategies helped many performers establish their careers domestically and to some extent internationally (particularly in diaspora communities around the globe), Mongolian popular music never really caught on or took off outside of its home country. Mongolian artists have long had to contend with a global system of popular music dissemination that was decidedly stacked against them and other "small" nations. The transnational flows of popular music have long been viewed as moving from a center to the periphery, dominant cultures to marginal ones, or "developed countries—particularly the United States—to the rest of the world" (Garofalo 1993:17). Even with the rise of new centers of musical production in Asia, the music of the 'peripheries' like Mongolia was still broadly controlled by powerful corporations that maintained the ability to define and label what is heard in the musical mainstream.

But the rise of social media and accompanying global financial platforms in the past decade has dramatically shifted these dynamics. Korean popular music or K-pop used highly produced and near-cinematic quality music videos and a convergence of international marketing and promotions connected with international sales and streaming platforms, which helped them to disseminate their music beyond their national borders and into markets in the West in the late 2000s and 2010s (Puri 2019). That the first video to reach one billion views on YouTube.com was Psy's "Gangnam Style" (2012), a video sung almost entirely in the Korean language, demonstrates the new opportunities these technological and financial advancements give to global popular artists.

Perhaps following in line with their Korean neighbors, The Hu choose to introduce itself via two highly produced and high-quality music videos that were disseminated via YouTube and other forms of social media. Doing this allowed the group to bypass the hegemonic mediators of traditional media corporations that had so limited the music of earlier generations of Mongolian popular artists. The Hu also leveraged the transnational character of the global metal community. Wallace et al. argues that metal has "constituted itself as a set of communities of fans, bands, and mediators" on a global scale that is not defined by national borders nor shared languages (2011:46).[27] Metal influencers like "Metalhead Reacts" were some of the first to widely spread the group's songs within the metal community in late 2018. But comments on their videos also suggest that fans were discovering and sharing the videos with others on their own as well.[28]

That the band had hoped for this kind of viral spread of its music throughout this community is suggested in comments members made to journalist Zigor Aldama of the *Post Magazine*. Horsehead fiddler Enkush told him, "'We were confident in word-of-mouth and it has worked a miracle. Our success has been organic. There has been no promoting or using management tools to increase visits. People are just telling friends they have to hear our songs'" (Aldama 2019). The band has continued to expand its presence within the metal community through media interviews and its "discover The Hu"-type videos, which allow fans behind-the-scenes views into the lives of the band's members. Lead singer Jaya added, "'We kind of expected this reaction, because we thought our music would fit better with foreign audiences. We were born with global ambition'" (ibid.).

While The Hu's initial success has been extraordinary, it is still small relative to the enormous success Korean popular music groups, such as BTS, have achieved in the same period.[29] But that small Asian nations could reach this degree of mainstream recognition and success points to how far the dynamics of global popular music have shifted in the preceding decade, particularly with the rise of international sales and streaming platforms. Fatima Bhutto (2019:19) sees another reason for the wide acceptance of Korean pop music and culture, pointing to what she describes as "a vast cultural movement emerging from the Global South" that is increasingly creating and consuming pop culture not specifically Western but "global in its range and allure":

> Carefully packaging not-always-secular modernity with traditional values in urbanized settings, they have created a new global pop culture that can be easily consumed, especially by the many millions coming late to the modern world and still negotiating its overwhelming challenges.

Bhutto argues that this new global pop culture represents "new arbiters of mass culture arising from the East" that threatens the continued dominance of Western forms of popular culture. The degree to which The Hu's music and imagery diverges from its Western models, particularly in its openness to traditional spirituality, embrace of the national, and critique of Western forms of modernity, suggests that it too may be added to Bhutto's list of cultural forms.

The Hu has shown itself to be especially good at reading and reacting to shifts in the global popular music landscape. It has fashioned high-quality sounds and images that are compelling to non-Mongolian audiences around the world, packaged them in formats well suited to the small screens of computers and mobile devices, and focused on cultivating a place within the transnational metal community. The band's success has already brought renewed attention to other Mongolian heavy metal groups, including those of Inner Mongolian origin, such as Tengger Cavalry, Hanggai, and Nine Treasures, and even Tuvan folk-metal groups, such as Yat-Kha and Hartyga. It may be too early to measure the scope of The Hu's rapid and extraordinary success on Mongolian popular music as a whole. But it is possible that the band's unique tweaking of past practices and innovative embrace of new ones will serve as a model for other artists seeking to bring Mongolian music to global audiences.

Notes

1. By September 2021, these figures had reached 82 million and 58 million views, respectively.

2. Both folk music groups have actively toured outside of Mongolia. Khusugtun appeared at the BBC Proms music festival in 2011 and Asia's Got Talent in 2015 (the YouTube recordings of each have garnered over 4.8 million views and 3.4 million views, respectively, as of September 2021). The Altai Band's YouTube video "The Altai Band from Mongolia" had 2.3 million views as of January 2021.

3. "Civilization VI: Mongolia Theme, Morin Khuur and throat singing by Nature," YouTube video, uploaded by Tengger Cavalry Official, 16:36, February 7, 2018, https:// www.youtube.com/watch?v=ZqkrBkITgDo; "Doom Video Game Composer Assembles Metal Vocalists for 'Doom Eternal' Soundtrack," *Ghost Cult Magazine*, March 16, 2019, https://www.ghostcultmag.com/doom-video-game-composer-assembles -metal-vocalists-for-doom-eternal-soundtrack.

4. Carnegie Hall, "Presented by Tengger Calvary: Mongolian Nomadic Folk Music Concert," Concert Announcement, September 20, 2018, https://www.carnegiehall .org/calendar/2018/09/20/mongolian-nomadic-folk-music-concert-0800pm.

5. See our companion website, www.mongoliansoundworlds.org, for additional information on the musical traditions included in this volume.

6. In the post-socialist period, Altanzaya installed a monument in central Ulaanbaatar in honor of the Beatles that incorporated this concept of a peephole.

7. Har Sarnai's song "Minii nutag" (My homeland) is based on the words of a famous poem of the same name by the twentieth-century Mongolian poet Dashdorjiin Natsagdorj.

8. In one scene in *Mongolian Bling*, Gennie begins a rap she wrote about the status of women in Mongolia: "I'm one of the women who are the majority among our few people, / In this society of chaos, everybody says they have equal rights, / To be honest, there is very little truth in that" (Binks 2012).

9. As the youngest recipient of this award, the decision to select him for it was controversial among many in Mongolia, given that it typically goes to individuals at the end of their careers who have made important lifetime contributions to Mongolian society and culture.

10. In 1993, Robert Walser characterized the heavily distorted guitar sound as "the most important aural sign of heavy metal" (1993:41). Wallach et al. further this point by describing this sound as "a central and defining feature of heavy metal, and a musical performance that lacks this timbre probably would not be considered part of the metal scene" (Wallach, Berger, and Greene 2011:11).

11. One of the drummers for the group stated in an interview how he played on "custom-made drums based on the size and sound of many Mongolian drums" (The Hu, "The HU—Covid-19 Relief Effort Fundraising Concert," YouTube video, 1:16:14, posted by The HU, June 28, 2020, https://www.youtube.com/watch?v=ik5qhnqIZy8.). But it should be noted, however, that drums are not typically used in Mongolian folk music.

12. YouTube videos are available that feature the four core members performing acoustic versions of their songs.

13. "Metalhead, "Metalhead Reacts to 'Yuve Yuve Yu' by The Hu," YouTube video, 14:13, posted by MetalHead Reacts, November 26, 2018, https://www.youtube.com/watch?v=5TjYOcWy5cc.

14. "The Hu Yuve, Yuve, Yu Reaction." YouTube video, 9:45, posted by Patrol Gaming, August 5, 2019, https://www.youtube.com/watch?v=vGWnG2lmO74.

15. "The HU, Yuve, Yuve, Yu—Reaction." YouTube video, 8:41, posted by Bowzer's Reaction Pit, January 2, 2019, https://www.youtube.com/watch?v=gWX75BvhD3E.

16. "THESE GUYS NEVER DISAPPOINT!!!: Yuve, Yuve, Yu (The Hu) (reaction)." YouTube video, 12:09, posted by The Nobodies Reacts, May 21, 2019, https://www.youtube.com/watch?v=EnTMSb6ZhdY.

17. BBC World Service, "Dio's Two-finger Gesture—What Does it Mean," News Magazine, May 18, 2010, http://news.bbc.co.uk/2/hi/8687002.stm.

18. "Metalhead Reacts to 'Yuve Yuve Yu' by The Hu," YouTube video, 14:12, posted by MetalHead Reacts, November 26, 2018, https://www.youtube.com/watch?v=5TjYOcWy5cc.

19. "The HU—Sad But True (Metallica Cover) Reaction / Review," YouTube video, 11:14, posted by Galacticriminal, December 9, 2019, https://www.youtube.com/watch?v=rsiRtbFUisk.

20. The Hu, "Yuve Yuve Yu (Official Music Video)," YouTube video, 5:52, posted by The HU, September 27, 2018, https://www.youtube.com/watch?v=v4xZUroBEfE.

21. "The HU—Wolf Totem feat. Jacoby Shaddix of Papa Roach (Official Music Video)," YouTube video, 5:14, posted by The HU, December 13, 2019, https://www.youtube.com/watch?v=sv29DzgiXZA.

22. "The HU—Covid-19 Relief Effort Fundraising Concert," YouTube video, 1:16:14, posted by The HU, June 28, 2020, https://www.youtube.com/watch?v=ik5qhnqIZy8.

23. "Vocal Coach reacts—The HU-Wolf Totem," YouTube video, 10:11, posted by Rebecca Vocal Athlete, February 25, 2020, https://www.youtube.com/watch?v=JdYptfDPIjo.

24. "The HU—Covid-19 Relief Effort Fundraising Concert," YouTube video, 1:16:14, posted by The HU, June 28, 2020, https://www.youtube.com/watch?v=ik5qhnqIZy8.

25. "Metalhead Reacts to 'Yuve Yuve Yu' by The Hu," YouTube video, 14:13, posted by MetalHead Reacts, November 26, 2018, https://www.youtube.com/watch?v=5TjYOcWy5cc.

26. "The Hu—Shireg Shireg (Acoustic Performance)," YouTube video, 5:47, posted by Better Noise Music, July 1, 2020, https://www.youtube.com/watch?v=8O7mJwuSyVA.

27. Weinstein (2011:46) suggests, "Metal is transcultural, not cross-cultural. In other words, metal is not a music tied to a particular culture, which people in other cultures happen to enjoy as outsiders; rather, metal is the music of a group of people that transcends other preexisting cultural and national boundaries."

28. Metalhead Reacts' video of "Yuve Yuve Yu," for instance, was posted in late November 2018, about two months after The Hu released the video, and it includes many fan comments describing how they were made aware of the video by the You-Tube "suggestion" algorithm or by others in their online community ("Metalhead Reacts to 'Yuve Yuve Yu' by The Hu," YouTube video, 14:13, posted by MetalHead Reacts, November 26, 2018, https://www.youtube.com/watch?v=5TjYOcWy5cc.).

29. BTS, which *Time Magazine* named the 2020 "Entertainer of the Year," typically has hundreds of millions of views of its songs on YouTube.com.

Video Examples

Video 1: The Hu, Yuve Yuve Yu (Official Music Video). https://www.youtube.com/watch?v= v4xZUroBEfE.

Video 2: The Hu, Wolf Totem (Official Music Video). https://www.youtube.com/watch?v= jM8dCGIm6yc.

Video 3: Tengger Cavalry—Lone Wolf (Official Video). https://www.youtube.com/watch?v= 7rL7-WfzdLI.

Video 4: Soyol Erdene, Tsenkher zalaa. https://www.youtube.com/watch?v=z6m EemDp9qo.

Video 5: Gee and Jonon, Minii nutgiig nadad uldee. https://www.youtube.com/watch?v= Xr25ljRX-lY.

Video 6: D. Bold, Kheeriin salhitai ayalguu. https://www.youtube.com/watch?v= Q61d4B7GCqM.

Bibliography

Aldama, Zigor. 2019. "The Hu: Mongolian Folk Rockers Ready to Conquer the World with Throat Singing and Traditional Instruments." *Post Magazine. South China Morning Post*, June 1. https://www.scmp.com/magazines/post-magazine/long-reads/article/3012549/hu-mongolian-folk-rockers-ready-conquer-world.

Askew, Robin. 2020. "Review The Hu, O2 Academy," *Bristol24/7*, February 11. https://www.bristol247.com/culture/music/review-the-hu-o2-academy.

Barria, Carlos. 2013. "Mongolia Neo-Nazis Announce a Change of Tack—Pollution Control." *Reuters*, July 2. https://www.reuters.com/article/us-mongolia-rightwing/mongolia-neo-nazis-announce-a-change-of-tack-pollution-control-idUSBRE96108 N20130702.

Bhutto, Fatima. 2019. *New Kings of the World: Dispatches from Bollywood, Dizi, and K-Pop*. New York: Columbia Global Reports.

Binks, Benj. 2012. *Mongolian Bling*. DCP, DVD. King Island, TAS, Australia: Flying Fish Films.

Campbell, Matthew, and Terrence Edwards. 2019. "Mongolia's President Is a Genghis Khan-Idolizing Trump of the Steppe." *Bloomberg Businessweek*, September 25.

Cengel, Katya. 2019. "How A Mongolian Heavy Metal Band Got Millions of YouTube Views." *National Public Radio*, January 5. https://www.npr.org/sections/goatsandsoda/2019/01/05/680528912/how-a-mongolian-heavy-metal-band-got-millions-of-youtube-views.

Edwards, Terrence. 2016. "Mongolian Opposition Wins Landslide, Voters Fed Up with Hard Times." *Reuters*, June 29. https://www.reuters.com/article/us-mongolia-election/mongolian-opposition-wins-landslide-voters-fed-up-with-hard-times-idUSKCN0ZF0PE.

Farber, Jim. 2019. "Steppe Change: How Mongolian Rock Band the Hu Conquered the World." *The Guardian*, October 22. https://www.theguardian.com/music/2019/oct/22/its-something-new-how-mongolian-rock-band-the-hu-went-viral.

Garofalo, Reebee, 1993. "Whose World, What Beat: The Transnational Music Industry, Identity, and Cultural Imperialism." *The World of Music* 35(2):16–32.

Gillet, Kit. 2012. "Though Not Yet Open, a Huge Mine Is Transforming Mongolia's Landscape." *New York Times*, September 13. https://www.nytimes.com/2012/09/14/world/asia/oyu-tolgoi-mine-in-khanbogd-is-transforming-mongolia.html.

Henderson, Tony. 2016. "Mongolia Election Win Puts Poverty on the Breadline." *Pressenza*, January 7. https://www.pressenza.com/2016/07/mongolia-election-win-puts-poverty-breadline.

Humphrey, Caroline. 1992. "The Moral Authority of the Past in Post-Socialist Mongolia." *Religion, State and Society* 20(3–4):375–389.

Knapp, Lauren. 2015. *Live from UB*. DVD. Documentary Education Resources.

Kristof, Nicholas. 1990. "A Mongolian Rock Group Fosters Democracy." *New York Times*, March 26, C11:1.

Langfitt, Frank. 2012. "Mineral-Rich Mongolia Rapidly Becoming 'Mine-golia.'" *National Public Radio*, May 21. https://www.npr.org/2012/05/21/152683549/mineral-rich-mongolia-rapidly-becoming-minegolia.

Marsh, Peter K. 2009. *The Horse-Head Fiddle and the Cosmopolitan Reimagination of Tradition in Mongolia*. New York: Routledge.

———. 2010. "Our Generation Is Opening Its Eyes: Hip-Hop and Youth Identity in Contemporary Mongolia." *Central Asian Survey* 29(3):345–358.

McCormick, Neil. 2020. "The Hu, Electric Ballroom, Review: A Galloping Triumph of a Show from these Mongolian Heavy-metal Warriors." *Telegraph*, February 12. https://www.telegraph.co.uk/theatre/what-to-see/hu-review-electric-ballroom-galloping-triumph-show-mongoliain.

O'Connor, Roisin. 2020. "The HU Review, Electric Ballroom London: Mongolian Metal Band Are like Nothing You've Seen Before." *Independent*, February 13. https://www.independent.co.uk/arts-entertainment/music/reviews/the-hu-review-mongolian-metal-band-the-gereg-album-tour-dates-a9332846.html.

Puri, Kavita. 2019. "How Did K-Pop Conquer the World?" *The Inquiry*, May 15. https://www.bbc.co.uk/programmes/w3csytfy.

Sarkitov, Nikolay-Dautovich. 1987. "Ot 'khard-roka' k 'khevi-metallu': Effektoglupleniya" ("Hard-rock" to "heavy-metal": The stupefaction effect). *Sotsiologicheskie Issledovaniya* 14(4):93–94.

Theunissen, Tirza. 2014. "Poverty, Inequality, and the Negative Effects of Mongolia's Economic Downturn." *In Asia*, June 14. https://asiafoundation.org/2014/06/25/poverty-inequality-and-the-negative-effects-of-mongolias-economic-downturn.

Wallach, Jeremy, Harris M. Berger, and Paul D. Greene. 2011. "Affective Overdrive, Scene Dynamics, and Identity in the Global Metal Scene." In *Metal Rules the Globe: Heavy Metal around the World*, 3–33. Durham: Duke University Press.

Walser, Robert. 1993. *Running with the Devil: Power, Gender, and Madness in Heavy Metal Music*. Middletown, Conn.: Wesleyan University Press.

Weinstein, Deena. 2011. "The Globalization of Metal." In *Metal Rules the Globe: Heavy Metal around the World, edited by Jeremy Wallach*, Harris M. Berger, and Paul D. Greene, 34–59. Durham: Duke University Press.

Glossary

All entries below are Mongolian-language terms unless otherwise noted.

aimag: Province (named league or *chuulgan* in Inner Mongolia).
aizam urtyn duu: Extended long-song.
aqyn: Kazakh poet-singer.
Ar Mongol: Northern Mongolia (Mongolia).
auyl: Kazakh residential community.
baigal': Nature, existence.
banner (khoshuu): Regional subdivisions in Inner Mongolia that were put into place during the Qing Dynasty.
besreg urtyn duu: An abbreviated long-song that is less demanding in terms of musical technique.
bie/biyelgee: A form of traditional dance.
bogino duu: Short-song.
bönjignökh: A soft trill in long-song.
chimeglel: Ornaments.
choor: Skin-faced, two-string spike fiddle from eastern Inner Mongolia.
dayaarshil: Globalization.
dombyra: Two-string Kazakh plucked lute.
domog: Legend or folktale.
dörvön chikhtei khuur: Four-string spike fiddle.
doshpuluur: Three-string Tuvan plucked lute.
duuchin/duuch: Singer.
gazryn ezed: Spirit beings who are considered masters of the land.
ger: Portable, round felt tent (yurt).
igil: Skin-faced ladle fiddle from Tuva.
ikh khuur: Bass fiddle.
ikil: Skin-faced ladle fiddle from western Mongolia.

isgeree khöömii: Mongolian whistle-style *khöömii*.

jiriin urtyn duu: Medium-length long-song (lit. common song). Exchangeable with terms such as *suman urtyn duu, tügeemel urtyn duu*.

kargyraa: Tuvan chest-style *khöömii*.

khadag: Ceremonial silk scarf presented to elders and honored guests as a sign of respect. Also tied to a tree or post near an ovoo and on the neck of a stringed instrument.

khalyq äni: Kazakh folk song.

khamtlag: Ensemble or band (*zuhe* in Chinese).

kharkhiraa: Mongolian chest-style *khöömii*.

khar'ltsaa duu: A repartee song.

khöömii: Throat singing (also spelled *khöömei* [*xöömei*] mainly in Tuva).

khöömiich: Performer of Mongolian throat singing (*khöömeizih* in Tuvan).

khuur: Fiddle (generic) or two-string spike fiddle (specific).

khuurch: Fiddler.

küi: Kazakh narrative instrumental genre.

limbe: Side-blown flute.

magtaal: Praise song.

morin khuur: Two-string horsehead fiddle.

naadam: The annual national festival in Mongolia held in July featuring horse racing, wrestling, and archery.

nair: Celebration, feast.

Nei Menggu: Inner Mongolia in Chinese.

nugulaa: Short ornament or appoggiatura in long-song.

nutag: Homeland.

Övör Mongol: Southern Mongolia (Inner Mongolia).

ovoo: Rock cairn.

qara öleng: Kazakh lyrical song, often with improvised text.

shakhaa: Technique of vocal tension or pressed phonation used to produce dense timbres in *khöömii*.

shurankhai: Falsetto used in long-song.

sihu: Chinese term for the Mongolian four-string spike fiddle (*dörvön chikhtei khuur* in Mongolian).

sum: Smallest level of land-based division in Mongolia and Inner Mongolia.

sybyzghy: Kazakh end-blown flute.

tabighat: Kazakh term for nature.

tatlaga: Genre of fiddle music often used to accompany dance in western Mongolia, uses double-stops and ostinati to imitate the sound of a horse's gait.

terme: Kazakh vocal composition shared in social gatherings; texts record historical and geographic information.

tögrög: Mongolian currency.

toi: Kazakh celebration.

tolghau: Kazakh vocal composition, often with reflective and philosophical lyrics.

tovshuur: Two-string plucked lute.

tsagaan sar: Lunar new year celebration (lit. white month).

tsam: Ritual masked dance performed as part of Mongolian and Tibetan Buddhist ceremonies.

tsokhilt/tsokhilgo: A strong laryngeal trill in long-song; also a technique to express percussive movement (strumming/tonguing) in instrumental music.

tsuur: End-blown flute made of wood or reed (known as *modyn tsuur* in Inner Mongolia).

tughan zher: Kazakh term for homeland.

tuul': Historical or heroic epic.

tuul'ch: Performer of epic songs.

ulaanmöchir: Traveling performing arts troupes in Inner Mongolia (lit. red branch).

ülger: Tale.

ündesten: Nationality.

urtyn duu: Long-song.

Wai Menggu: Outer Mongolia in Chinese.

xiaoshu minzu: Minority nationality in Chinese.

yastan: Sub-ethnic group (lit. bone group).

yatga: Zither with movable bridges.

yazguur: Origin.

yerööl: Prayer.

yochin: Hammered dulcimer.

yuanshengtai: Term in Chinese associated with artistic and cultural forms that maintain connections to their roots or source (lit. original ecology).

zhaylau: Kazakh summer encampment.

zhyrau: Kazakh epic singer.

zokhiolyn duu: Composed song mostly in the country-folk style.

Contributors

BAYARSAIKHAN BADAMSÜREN is a luthier and musician in Ulaanbaatar, Mongolia. He has been making the *morin khuur* (horsehead fiddle) for over twenty years and has also studied violin-making in the UK.

OTGONBAYAR CHULUUNBAATAR studied Mongolian Studies and Linguistics at the National University of Mongolia in Ulaanbaatar. She works as a contracted researcher at the Mongolian Academy of Sciences. Her research focuses on the music, heritage, and language of the Mongolian peoples. Currently, she is investigating song lyrics and musical instruments from the everyday culture of the Oirad people in western Mongolia. Since her youth, she has been both a singer of and an expert in Mongolian music.

ANDREW COLWELL is an applied ethnomusicologist with a focus on indigeneity, heritage-making, and globalization. He currently serves as Project Director and Staff Ethnomusicologist at the Center for Traditional Music and Dance in New York City. As a practicing *khöömiich* and multi-instrumentalist, he has given numerous workshops and performances and has collaborated with artists that include the ethno-rock band Altan Urag, English pianist Steve Tromans, and others.

JOHANNI CURTET is a musician, ethnomusicologist, producer, and *khöömii* teacher. His research focuses on traditional Mongolian music, transmission, history, and intangible cultural heritage. He teaches ethnomusicology at the University of Rennes 2, and has given guest lectures in Switzerland, the US, and Mongolia. He is also an Artistic Director of Routes Nomades, an organization with which he has arranged tours for Mongolian musicians since 2006. In 2010, he participated in writing the proposal to nominate *khöömii* for inscription on the UNESCO Representative List of the Intangible Cultural Heritage of Humanity. He has also produced films and recordings of *khöömii*.

TSERENDAVAA DASHDORJ is a celebrated khöömii singer from Chandman' in Khovd aimag, Mongolia. He has performed widely, not only in Mongolia but also in other Asian regions and in Europe.

CHARLOTTE D'EVELYN is a faculty member in the Department of Music at Skidmore College in Saratoga Springs, NY. She focuses her research on music, ethnic identity, musical borderlands, and heritage politics in Inner Mongolia, China. Aside from her academic work, she considers herself a lifelong student of the Chinese erhu, Mongolian morin khuur, Irish fiddle, and classical viola.

TAMIR HARGANA is a Chicago-based musician and award-winning performer of Mongolian and Tuvan music. He grew up in Inner Mongolia and received an MA in World Music Performance from Northern Illinois University in 2017.

PETER K. MARSH focuses his scholarly work on issues related to musical tradition and modernity in Mongolia, with particular emphasis on two-string folk fiddles and popular music. He is an ethnomusicologist and music historian with broad interdisciplinary training and experience as a teacher, scholar, and administrator. He is also a specialist in the area of Asian music and culture. A Professor in the Department of Music at California State University, East Bay, Peter served as Founding Resident Director of the American Center for Mongolian Studies, an academic-oriented nongovernment organization based in Ulaanbaatar, Mongolia.

K. OKTYABR spent his childhood and young adulthood in Deluun sum in Bayan-Ölgii province in Mongolia as a herder and poet-musician. He moved from the countryside to Ölgii city in 2008.

REBEKAH PLUECKHAHN is a McArthur Research Fellow in Anthropology at the School of Social and Political Sciences at the University of Melbourne. Her research discusses emerging urban politics and ethics of ownership in Ulaanbaatar, Mongolia, as well as explorations of sociality and performance. Prior to joining the University of Melbourne in 2019, Rebekah worked as a postdoctoral Research Associate for four years at University College London—Anthropology (UCL).

JENNIFER C. POST engages in scholarly research on Central and Inner Asian music and musical instruments and their production. Her studies in Mongolia with Kazakh pastoralists living in the Altai Mountain region address music in relation to homeland and place, new mobilities, well-being, and environmental change. Recent work also explores sound and music as expressive forms that are sources for sustaining traditional ecological knowledge in social, cultural, and ecological systems in Mongolia and other locations. She teaches ethnomusicology at the University of Arizona.

SUNMIN YOON'S research focuses on the Mongolian oral traditions and music-making involved in a broad range of folk song traditions, particularly *urtyn duu* (long-song). Her work covers rural/urban dialogues, sensory/ecological connections to local oral performance practices, and the ideological dimension of music during the socialist and post-socialist eras. She is currently teaching at the School of Music and the Department of Languages, Literatures & Cultures at University of Delaware.

Index

doshpuluur (Tuvan plucked lute), 57, 71, 150
Dugarjav, M., 8
Dukha ethnic group, 23, 31
Dundgov' aimag, 33

ecological environments, 29, 95, 107, 175, 179; health and well-being, 22, 29, 41; impact, changes and challenges, 27, 28, 34, 41, 172, 175, 231; knowledge, 30, 40, 43; markers, 88, 162; ecological support, 21
economic system, 24, 173, 191, 230; benefits (of mining), 24, 184; changes, 24, 173, 227, 257; dependency/interdependency, 227, 229, 231; growth, 140, 221; market economy, 24, 165, 170; opportunities, 27, 28, 155, 165, 175, 222, 228, 239; policy, 231, 239; power, 27, 258; problems, 36, 135, 189, 257; success, 28, 34; support, 21, 239
Egschiglen ensemble, 13, 239–244
Eljigen (Eljigin) Khalkh ethnic group, 98–99, 100, 102, 104, 108n3
Empson, Rebecca, 115–116
Enebish, J., 136, 147, 244
Enkhbalsan, T. (*tovshuur* maker), 156, *158*, 161, 166n8
Enkhbat, A., 8
Enkhbayar, Se., 6
epic singing (*tuul'*), 2, 13, 90, 103; epic custodians (*tuul'ch*), 121, 122, 138; gendered musical practice and, 112, 149; men's inherited right to perform, 115, 120; praise-song, 212; preservation of, 164, 167n13; *tovshuur* and, 155, 156, 162, 164, *219*; women's musical knowledge and, 113, 121–122, 157, 160
Erdenet, city of (Mongolia), 24, 96
Erdenet copper mine, 24
erhu (Chinese two-string fiddle), 61, 144
estrad (Russian: "staged") music ensembles, 255
ethnic diversity, 91, 108, 86, 87–88, 104
"ethno-punk," 135, 152
ethno-rock, 222–223
Eurocentrism, 229, 237
Evenki (Ewenke) ethnic group, 26, 76, 80n3

Fijn, Natasha, 28, 31
film music (*kinoni khögjim*), 6
Fine Arts School [*Uran saikhany surguul'*] (Ulaanbaatar), 141
folklorization, socialist, 212
folk music, 3, 65, 254; National Academic State Ensemble and, 9; revival of, 68, 70; Soviet emphasis on promoting, 234

forests, 23, 34, 37, 43, 186; coniferous, 26; destruction of old-growth forests, 184
Frank, André, 229

"Galloping horses" [Mandarin: *Wanma Benteng*] (Chi Bulag), 146–147
Ganbold, M., 101
Ganbold, T., 208, 213, 223n3
Gandan Monastery, 10
Ganganbaigal, Nature, 59, 251
Gee (rapper), 260, 261
gender, 28, 37, 111, 115–117. *See also* men; women
"Gennie" (Gennie Bolor), 259, 261, 268n8
ger (yurt) camps, 5, 21, 27–28, 117; Chinese tourism in Inner Mongolia and, 66; conception of space in, 205; as cultural marker of Mongolia, 203; fiddles and gendered structure of, 147–148; fiddles seized by communist soldiers from, 136; as interspecies social/sonic spaces, 37; Kazakh, 37–38, 173; musical instruments in, 163, 166n5, 184; as pan-nomadic symbol, 244
geriin surguul' (home school), 207
Germany, Mongolian music in, 240
Gills, Barry, 229
gingoo song, 4
Ginsburg, Tom, 233
global economy, 231, 240, 242, 243
globalization (*dayaarshil*), 13, 165, 201, 239, 242; complicated nature of, 227–229; globalism compared with, 229–231; Mongol peoples' role in engendering, 229; "original folk art" combined with, 244–245; as process and discourse, 229
goats, 18, 36, 147; herders' vocalizations to, 31, 198; skin used for instruments, 166n4
Gobi (Egschiglen album), 242
"Gooj Nanaa" song, 4
Gov' (Gobi) Desert, 259, 24, 25, 63, 144
Gov'-Altai aimag (Mongolia), 100, 103, 109n3
Grasslands. *See* steppes
Great Lakes Depression, 23
Great Leap Forward, 66
Greene, Paul, 262

Hailar, city of (Inner Mongolia), 55, 60, 70
Han Chinese, 11, 63, 65, 78; dominance in cities of Inner Mongolia, 27; instrument makers, 145; touristic fascination with minority "other," 66–67, 71

Jangar epic, 160, 161
Jangar Khan, 75
janggarch (singer-storytellers of Janggar), 75
Jantsannorov, N., 3, 214, 237, 238
Japan, Imperial, 135, 139
Japan, postwar, 236–237
Jargalsaikhan, D., 257, 256
Javkhlan, S., 87–88, 108
jazz, 257, 58
Jigmed *khuurch*, 140
Jirem league [Tongliao Municipality] (Inner Mongolia), 64, 73, 74
Jonon (rapper), 260, 261
Ju'uda league [Chifeng Municipality] (Inner Mongolia), 73, 74

Kalmykia, Republic of (Russia), 155, 156, 205
Kalmyks, 1, 88
Kam people (China), 69
Kaplonski, Christopher, 91
kargyraa (Tuvan chest style of throat-singing), 74, 76, 57, 59, 71
Kazakh language, 17, 20n1, 36, 179
Kazakh music: on CDs/VCDs, 39, 44n12; pastoralism and nature in, 39–43
Kazakhs, Mongolian, 1, 2, 12, 23, 88; in Bayan Ölgii aimag, 12, 34, 36, 172–173; as eagle hunters, 170; *ger* tents of, 27, 37; herders, 17; in Khovd aimag, 172–173; as percentage of Mongolian population, 192n5; spiritual beliefs of, 30; summer settlements at Dala köl, 35
Kazakhstan, 13, 34, 43, 172, 181; *dombyra* in, 174, 183, 189, 191, 192n7; Mongolian Kazakhs and, 172, 173; post-Soviet, 39, 42; *qara öleng* in, 41
Khakassia, Republic of (Russia), 205, 221
Khalkh ethnic group, 1, 24, 27, 155, 222; local knowledge of, 105; long-songs, 9; as "Mongol of Mongols," 91; Oirads as Other to, 89–92; "Soviet modernism" and, 88, 91; *züün ayalguu* (east-melody) and, 86
khalyq äni (Kazakh folk song), 39
Khamag Mongol [*Every Mongol*] (Javkhlan, 2016), 87–88, 108
Khangai Mountains, 23
Khangai region (Mongolia), 28, 96, 98, 99, 105
"Khan uulyn oroi" [The peak of Khan uul] (Zakhchin song), 103
khar'ltsaa duu (repartee songs), 98
Khaznadar, Chérif, 221
"Kheeriin salkhtai ayalguu" [Melody of the windy steppe] (Mongol Pop song), 260

Khentii aimag (Mongolia), 3, 5
Khentii Mountains, 23
Kherlen, Lkhavsüren, 244
Kherlengiin bar'ya (Sharav), 5
"Kherlengiin bar'ya" [The banks of the Kherlen river] (long-song), 5
Kherlen River, 5
khiil khuur (box fiddle), 64, 139, 144, 148
Khogjilt, 144
khögjimchin (musicians), 113, 118–119
kholoin tsuur ("throat flute"), 76
Khongorzol, G., 5
Khonkh [Bell] (pop-duo), 256
"Khonkhny duu" [Sound of the Bell] (Khonkh song), 256
khöömii ("throat singing"), 2, 4, 34, 38, 90, 151, 197; amateur and professional performers, 222; Anda Union and, 71, 75, 80; *bel canto* technique adapted to, 213; *davkhar öngö* (superimposed colors), 206; definition and description of, 205–208; early international presence of, 237; *ez-engileer* (Tuvan style), 57, 74; global popularity of, 203, 204; in heavy metal bands, 251; heritage-making and, 215–217, 224n13; The Hu and, 251, 262; institutionalization of, 204, 211–214, 217–221; *isgeree* (whistle-style, overtone), 56, 58, 71, 206, 207, 212; *kharkhiraa* ("guttural" style), 207; *khöö-mei* (Tuvan style), 71, 79, 215; *khosmoljin* ("combined") style, 213; learned in urban places, 228; musical techniques of, 13; natural sounds referenced by, 31, 199, 205, 207; "original quality" of, 244–245; pastoralism and, 198–199; politics of heritage and, 80, 211; popular music and, 258; practice techniques and training, 208–211; recordings of, 204, 209; *shakhaa* (constricted throat technique), 71, 74, 77; *shingen* ("high" or "fluid") style, 213; socialist-era transformations of, 232; stone inscription near Jargalant Khairkhan, 218, 219; *suur' öngö* ("basic color"; vocal drone), 206; *sygyt* (Tuvan style), 71; *tsuurai* (echoes), 206; Tuvan, 31, 235, 240–241; women's participation in, 149, 210, 211
"Khoor nutgiin erkh" [The power of two homelands] (Altai Uriankhai song), 117–118
Khorchin region (Inner Mongolia), 63, 64, 74, 79, 144
Khoshuud ethnic group, 155
Khotgoid ethnic group, 96, 99, 104, 108n3
Khoton ethnic group, 101, 100, 103, 104, 108n3

Oirads (western Mongols), 1, 13, 63, 75, 79, 108; *baruun ayalguu* (west-melody) and, 86; *ikil* fiddle of, 32; local knowledge of, 105; Othered vis-à-vis Khalkh identity, 89–92, 107; regions and tribes of, 155; *tovshuur* as iconic instrument of Oirad epics, 155–156, 165–166, 167n14; *yastan* groups, 114

Oktyabr, 12, *18*; song about the steppe, 17–20

Old Town School of Folk Music (Chicago), 59

Ölgii city, 36, 39, 43, 44n12; *dombyra* culture in, 170, 174, 176, 180–182, 186, *187*, 188, *189*, 192n10; Music and Drama Theater, 42

"Önchiin tsagaan botgo" [Orphaned white camel] (folk song), 4, 6

"Öndör khökhii" [High and dark] (song), 102–103

"On the Shore of Flower Lake" (Sükhbaatar), 242

Ööld ethnic group, 23, 103, 155. *See also* Oirads

opera (*duur'*), 3, 6, 213; legacy of Mongolia's first opera, 6–9; as Soviet-developed musical phenomenon, 11; Western opera, 8

oral tradition, 108, 207–208, 230

Ordos region (Inner Mongolia), 64, 77, 79

orientalism, 107, 231, 239

Orientalism (Said, 1978), 86

originality, folk practice and, 237–238, 244–245

Orochen [Oronchon] ethnic group (Inner Mongolia), 26, 76, 80n3

Otai (Khorchin prince), 136, 138

Othering, in *urtyn duu* tradition, 86, 107

ovoo (sacred cairns), 30, 197

Övörkhangai aimag (Mongolia), 98

Oyu Tolgoi mine, 24, 259

Paganini, Niccolò, 146

Paine, Robert, 241

Papizan, B., 210, 220, 222

pastoralism, nomadic, 2, 4, 11, 186, 245; capitalist relation to, 230; dislocation from, 64; embedded history of, 21; in Inner Mongolia, 26, 63; Marxist view of, 135–136; as memory or imagined history, 24; Mongolian identity and, 26; in Mongolian Kazakh music, 39–43; music and instruments associated with, 34; as nation-building tool, 29; relationship with nature and, 29; seasonal sound and music of, 5; sound worlds and, 30; stereotyped discourse about, 231–232; *tsatslyn khalbaga* (wooden milk spoon), 161; uncertain future of, 200

Pearce, Tim, 72

Pegasus [formerly Zeebad] (Bayarsaikhan's workshop), 130, *130–132*

Pegg, Carole, 32, 91, 101, 105, 121, 166n4; on fiddle playing by women, 148–149; on Mongol traditions maintained by men, 147; on music teaching methods, 207; on political persecution in socialist period, 137

People's Folk Song and Dance Ensemble [PFSDE] (*Ardyn duu büjigiin ulsyn chuulga*), 240

petroglyphs, 34, 44n10

piano, 4, 142

pitch, 98, 141, 153n2, 206

plant life, 23, 30

Plueckhahn, Rebekah, 12–13

popular music, urban, 2, 7, 14; global flows of, 251; *khöömii* (throat singing) and, 31; Khotgoid singing arranged as, 96; Mongolian pop music's embrace of past tradition, 259–261; Mongolian pop music's embrace of the West, 256–258; musicians of Bayan-Ölgii and, 42–43; syncretic nature of Mongolian pop music, 261; *tovshuur* and, 165; Western/Anglo-American, 240, 254, 255, 257

Post, Jennifer, 12, 13

praise-song. See *magtaal*

professionalism, musical, 215, 67–68, 105–106, 145, 212

qara öleng (Kazakh song form), 39, 41, 42

Qiang people (China), 69

Qing (Manchu) Dynasty, 53, 63, 73, 144; administrative units of Mongolia under, 89, 109n4; Mongol—Chinese conflict at end of, 139; Oirads defeated by (1757–1759), 156; Sangrup's performances in Peking, 138; *tovshuur* (*tuobushu'er*) and, 166n3

Qinghai region (China), 155

qobyz (two-string Kazakh bowed instrument), 42, 193n20

Rae, James Deshaw, 88

railway networks, 24

Rees, Helen, 69

reindeer, 31

Reichl, Karl, 121

revolutionary songs, 9

Routes Nomades, 208

Rupprecht, Tobias, 233

rural–urban relationship, 12, 21, 24, 44; sound worlds and, 30, 34; urbanization plans and, 27; *urtyn duu* and, 32, 33

Russian Federation, 88, 108n3, 109n4; Altai

107; Sükhbaatar Square, 6, 7, 10; summer travelers in, 11
Ulaanchab, city of, 27
ulaanmöchir (arts troupe in Inner Mongolia), 53–55, 60n2, 65
ülger (tale), 4, 64
Undarmaa, A., 210, *211*
ündesten (root, nation), 88, 91, 109n6
UNESCO "Representative List of the ICH of Humanity," 68–69, 204, 215, 216, 217, 224n13
United States: diplomatic ties with Mongolia established (1988), 238; Mongolian music in, 58, 60, 80, 150, 152
urbanization, 26, 200, 217, 231; forgetting of customs and, 253; in Inner Mongolia, 64
Urgen (Anda Union member), 74, 77
Uriankhai ethnic group, 27, 34, 41, 108n3; Turkic origin of, 113; *urtyn duu* singers, 103, 104. See also Altai Uriankhai ethnic group
Urtnasan, G. (Urtaa), 151–152, *151*
urtyn duu (long-song), 2, 5, 6, 98, 108; adapted to concert stage, 212; at Altai Uriankhai weddings, 116; *baruun ayalguu* (right side, west-melody), 85, 86, 92, 104, 105; as "classical" art, 216; Darkhad, 97; ethnicity and, 12; in Inner Mongolia, 54–55; *jiriin [sumun]* (medium-length) *urtyn duu*, 93, 94, 102, 106; Khalkh, 9; Khovd aimag as origin place of, 101; nomadic way of life and, 199; opera and, 9; Othering and, 86, 107; pastoral traditions and, 32, 34; popular music and, 258; regional and ethnic styles, 64, 85–87, 95; as shared practice of Mongolia and Inner Mongolia, 61; socialist notion of culture and, 236; Soviet researchers and, 92–93; spiritual dimension of, 33; transformed with decline in pastoralism, 73–74; *züün ayalguu* (left side, east-melody), 85, 86, 92, 104, 105. See also *aizam*; *besreg*
urtyn duu (long-song) techniques: *bönjignökh* (soft trill), 94, 100, 104; *chimeglel* (improvisatory ornaments), 93, 94, 104; *gulsakh* (small intervallic downward slides), 102, 103; *khadgalakh* (small intervallic upward slides), 102; *nugalaa* (short appoggiatura), 94, 100, 104; *örgölgt* (some upward emphasis), 102, 103; *shurankhai* (falsetto), 93–94, 99, 104, 107; *tseejnii tsokhilt* (chest voice/ breathing), 99; *tsokhilt [tsokhilgo]* (laryngeal trill), 93–94, 99, 104, 107
Uvs aimag (Mongolia), 89, 109n3; Bayad and Khoton singers in, 99–100, 104; Eljigen (Eljigin) Khalkh singers in, 98–99, 104;

khöömii in, 210; landscape of, 105, *106*; Oirads of, 155
Uyghurs, 69
Üzemchin ethnic group, 63, 86, 90

violin, 144, 146
violoncello, 141, 142, 144, 149
Vladimirtsov, B. Ya., 92–93, 156, 162–163

Wagner, Rudi, 241
Wallach, Jeremy, 262, 264, 266
Walser, Robert, 268n10
water, sounds of, 31, 37, 205
waterfalls (*khürkhree*), sounds of, 207
Weina, Oyuna, 33
well-being, 22, 29, 43
Westernization, 68, 217
whistling, 199, 200
White, Bob, 228
wildlife, 18, 23, 30, 34, 43; destruction of old-growth forests and, 184; health of, 37; represented on *dombyra* soundboards, 170, 178; represented on *tovshuur* headstocks, 161, 166n8, 167n9; sounds of, 37
Wind Horse (Anda Union album, 2011), 70, 72
winds, sound of, 31, 37, 138, 205
wolves, 18, 28, 31, 40
women, 28, 37; fiddle playing by, 148–149, *150*, 153n3; fluidity of women's roles, 115–117; gendered musicality and, 112; gendered structure of *ger* and, 148; Kazakh women milking yaks, 38, *38*; *khöömii* and, 210, *211*; mothers/motherhood, 116, 120, 123; musical knowledge and, 117–118, 120–123, 157, 160; musicians and "good singers," 118–120; *qara öleng* sung by, 42; as *tovshuur* players, 157, *160*; veneration of musical exemplars, 112–113, 123n2; vocalizations of, 30
World Youth Festivals, 233, 234, 236

Xinjiang Uyghur Autonomous Region (China), 1, 13, 89, 114; Altay Prefecture, 75, 179; Bortala Prefecture, 75; *dombyra* in, 174, 189; Kazakh music CDs/VCDs in, 44n12; *khöömii* (throat singing) in, 205; *khöömii* in, 221; Mongolian Kazakh links to, 172, 179, 189, 192n4; Mongol singers' "commute" to, 2; Oirads in, 63, 75, 155; Uigaryn Mongols of, 101
xiqin (Chinese Song Dynasty fiddle), 144

yaks, 18, 36, *38*
Yan'an Talks on Literature and Art (Mao), 65

yastan (sub-ethnic group, "bone group"), 63, 80, 91, 109n6, 114
yatga (zither), 149, 255
Yat-Kha (Tuvan folk-metal group), 71, 268
Yatskoviskai, Kh., 92–93
yazguur (roots, origin), 5, 13, 152, 231; *ardyn yazguur urlag* ("authentic folk art"), 237; dialogue with foreign influences and, 245; Egschiglen ensemble and, 241, 242; foreigners' exposure to, 243; originality and, 238; as post-colonial notion, 228
Yin Mountains (Inner Mongolia), 25
Yo (master fiddle teacher), 151
Yoon, Sunmin, 12, 33
youth culture, cosmopolitan, 252
yuanshengtai ("original ecology") movement (Inner Mongolia), 69, 70, 152

Zakhchin ethnic group, 23, 89, 100, 108n3, 155; historical military role of, 103; *khöömii* and, 220; singers in Khovd aimag, 103–104; *tovshuur* and, *158, 163*, 167n11. *See also* Oirads
"Zambuu tiviin naran" [The sun over the world] (folk song), 4
Zangad, 235
Zasagt Khan (aimag under Qing rule), 89, *90*
Zavkhan aimag, 208, 210, 212–213
"Zes guai" [Mr. Zes] (song), 99
zhaylau (Kazakh summer encampment), 38, 40, 41
zhyrau (Kazakh epic-singer), 39
zokhiolyn duu (composed songs in folk style), 2, 6, 254
Zungarian Empire, 164
"Zunyn delger sar" [In high summer] (feast song), 102
Züüngar State (1636–1755), 89

The University of Illinois Press
is a founding member of the
Association of University Presses.

———————————————————

University of Illinois Press
1325 South Oak Street
Champaign, IL 61820-6903
www.press.uillinois.edu